The Problem of the Essential Indexical and Other Essays
Expanded Edition

The Problem of the Essential Indexical and Other Essays
Expanded Edition

John Perry

CSLI
PUBLICATIONS
Center for the Study of
Language and Information
Stanford, California

Library of Congress Cataloging-in-Publication Data

Perry, John, 1943–
    The problem of the essential indexical : and other essays / John Perry.-- Exp. ed.
        p. cm.
    Includes bibliographical references and index.
    ISBN 1-57586-269-7 (pbk. : alk. paper) -- ISBN 1-57586-246-8 (cloth : alk. paper)
    1. Meaning (Philosophy) 2. Belief and doubt. I. Title.

B105.M4 P47 2000
121'.68--dc21
                                                                                00-029236

∞ The acid-free paper used in this book meets the minimum requirements of the
American National Standard for Information Sciences—Permanence of Paper for
Printed Library Materials, ANSI Z39.48-1984.

Please visit our web site at
http://cslipublications.stanford.edu/
for comments on this and other titles, as well as for changes
and corrections by the author and publisher.

To Frenchie

Contents

Preface to the Expanded Edition

I am very thankful to Dikran Karagueuzian, Director of Publications at CSLI, for the suggestion to re-issue *The Problem of the Essential Indexical* in paperback, and to add seven essays completed since 1992.

These seven essays continue the themes of the first fourteen in various ways. Essays 15, and 16 explore what I consider mistaken paths in semantics. Essay 15 examines Davidson's argument for taking sentences to be the basic units of meaning; Essay 16 re-explores an argument Church, Davidson, Quine, and others have used to convince philosophers that sentences should have truth values as their basic semantics values—an argument Barwise and I dubbed "the slingshot" in (Barwise and Perry, 1981). If one goes down both of these mistaken paths, one arrives at the odd view that the fundamental fact about meaning is the distribution of truth values across sentences. Many members of my generation of analytic philosophers were imbued with these principles and this conclusion in graduate school. The discovery that the resulting semantics can provide no very plausible account of conditionals, belief, knowledge, intention, possibility, causation, information, or indeed much of anything, with the possible exception of "and" and "or," has led influential members of this cohort to various sorts of despair; some see the end of analytical philosophy, some see the end of philosophy altogether. A more optimistic course is to try to evade the arguments that would leave analytical philosophy so impotent. My analysis of the slingshot, although recognizably derived from (Barwise and Perry, 1981), also benefitted from working with Ken Olson while he wrote his Stanford dissertation, the basis of his excellent monograph (Olson, 1987).

Jerry Fodor has long been a hero to those of us with a more positive conception of what analytical philosophy can offer. He wages the good fight against holism and despair. David Israel and I argued in Essay 14 that a good theory of information, based on some of the ideas from (Barwise and Perry, 1999), could provide his insights an improved defense. In the *The Elm and the Expert* Fodor draws the conclusion that an informational theory of content forces him to retreat from the pretty picture he had developed about the relation between psychological explanations and computational implementations. In Essay 17

I argue that this is not so, and try to explain in a general way a picture of information that will allow one to fit everything together.

The last four essays, 18–21, return to issues of the indexicality, "I" and the self, with which the very first essays in the book are concerned. In Essay 6 I began to explore the relations between a theory of information based on constraints between types of situations, and issues of indexicality and the self. This exploration, continued in Essays 9–11 and Essay 13, is developed further here. Two key ideas are the distinction between reflexivity and indexicality, and the concept of an information game.

I argue that our philosophical conception of content has been modeled on one special kind of truth conditions, the fully *incremental* truth conditions of an utterance, mental event, or other content bearing situation. One explanation for the focus on this kind of content is provided in Essay 21, in terms of the "detach and recognize" information game. The fully incremental truth conditions are the truth conditions *given* the facts of reference, the facts that connect the utterance or mental state with the objects and properties in the world it is about. The information is detached from the particular features of the perception or utterance that carried it. This kind of information is what we typically are interested in remembering, communicating, uploading, downloading, looking up in Encyclopedias, and so forth. Equally important, and for the purposes of analysis often more important, are various kinds of less incremental truth conditions, including reflexive truth conditions. Reflexive truth conditions do not take the connections between the utterance or mental state and the rest of the world as given, and so include conditions on the utterance or mental state *itself*. We rely on such reflexive content in our everyday interpretation of contentful events, and it is of great theoretical importance. Indexicality is reflexivity harnessed by meaning, but while indexicality is a rather special linguistic phenomenon, reflexivity is of the essence of the use of content to classify meaningful events, and has its roots in the structure of information and action (See Essays 13 and 14, (Israel and Perry, 1990), (Israel and Perry, 1991), and (Israel, Perry and Tutiya)).

I thank Lauri Kanerva who went over the penultimate version catching many errors and infelicities.

Work on the series of essay in this volume began in 1976, as a digression. I was working on a book on personal identity. I decided I couldn't continue on that work until I knew what it was to have a thought about oneself. My best answer to date is given in Essay 19. Whatever the ultimate merits of that account, I feel I have made some progress on this problem over the past twenty-four years.

John Perry
February, 2000

Preface to the First Edition

This volume contains fourteen essays that deal with problems of meaning and belief. Most consider the phenomenon of "self-locating belief." This is the sort of belief that one naturally expresses with a sentence containing an indexical or a demonstrative: "I am spilling the sugar," or "That is Hoover Tower." In the early essays, I argue that an account of these sorts of beliefs requires us to distinguish what is believed from how it is believed, and the rest of the essays discuss various aspects and implications of that distinction and issues closely related to it.

Some of the essays attracted a fair amount of attention on their first appearance; others, to use Hume's phrase, fell still-born from the press. Reprinting the former may be a convenience to those who find them cited and wish to read them; reprinting the latter may give them another shot at notoriety. I believe the various problems these essays discuss remain interesting, and that these papers each manage to say something clear enough to be worth studying. I hope they point towards part of the truth; if not, they are at least a careful statement of sincerely believed error. They are not offered as a comprehensive treatise, but as self-contained essays that deal with a family of closely related problems and exhibit a certain consistency in approach and doctrine.

The consistency may not be too apparent, however; the terminology is surely not consistent, and the point of view developed considerably over the fifteen-year period in which they were written. Early on, I avoided the term "proposition"; in the later papers, I use it freely. Stalnaker thinks something is missing from the account given in Essay 2. I think I make progress in finding it in Essay 6 and put my hands on it in Essay 11. More and more structure is attributed to beliefs as the papers proceed. Not much is said beyond talking about states in the early papers; the need for enduring structured beliefs with relations of internal identity is seen in Essay 4; by Essay 12, these structures play a key role in a theory of belief reports. Self-locating thoughts about objects break up into indexical thoughts and thoughts concerning objects in Essay

10; the distinction would have been helpful in the earlier papers. By the later papers, the two-tiered system inspired by Kaplan's content/character distinction is interpreted in terms of the concept of more and less incremental truth conditions.

I believe the developments and changes are not only consistent with the original view, but follow naturally from it. I wish I could go a step further and say that they simply make clearer what I had in mind all along. But the evidence is against that. I remember a spirited dinner with Hugh Mellor, in which I tried to explain to him what was wrong with his Reichenbachian take on Kaplan's character/content distinction. Somehow by the end of dinner I seemed to have adopted most of his views. But it seemed I had not given up anything essential in mine. I guess he helped me to see what I should have had in mind all along. I remember Joseph Almog telling me that what was important about Essay 4 was the recognition that beliefs and their components were particulars, and that this permitted the possibility not just of two beliefs with the same content, but two beliefs with the same character. I did not quite see the big deal. Mark Crimmins saw this point independently; by the time he explained it to me a few years later I had "learning readiness." So perhaps it was not quite something I fully believed all along. Howard Wettstein and I used to argue endlessly whether some version of Kaplan's character/content distinction solved Frege's problems of cognitive significance. It certainly took me a very long time to come up with the account of Essay 11, if it is what I had in mind all along. And it was not until working on this volume that I saw the connection between that theory and the concept Stalnaker develops in his criticism of Essay 2. Perhaps I should say that the developments and additions in later essays give a clearer view of one thing I might have had in mind and I now think should have had in mind all along.

I made some changes in the papers. For the most part, these are limited to repairs of typographical errors and clear lapses in grammatical judgment. In Essay 4, the terminology and notation have been changed to conform more closely to later essays. I have added a few footnotes (marked by brackets) and added Afterwords to a number of the essays, in which I discuss some of the criticisms that have appeared of the ideas in them.

I want to add a couple of acknowledgments to those in the individual papers. Essays 3–8 were written during the period I worked intensively with Jon Barwise on the development of situation semantics and our book *Situations and Attitudes*. Essays 9–14 were written during the period in which David Israel and I have been working on a theory of information, and Israel, Syun Tutiya, and I have been working on a theory of action. Ken Olson and I have been working for a long time on some ideas about intentionality. I have never written anything with John Etchemendy, but have helped myself to many of his ideas in the years he has been a student and a colleague at Stanford. Essay

12 was written with Mark Crimmins, and Essay 14 with David Israel. I thank Crimmins and Israel for their ideas and the fun of working with them, and for their permission to reprint our joint efforts. Olson, Etchemendy, and Crimmins are three of a number of very talented graduate students whom we have had the good fortune to have at Stanford. What understanding I have of the issues discussed in these essays owes a great deal to these students.

The manuscript for this book was put together with the assistance of Ingrid Deiwiks, who then converted that manuscript to a camera-ready version using the fine facilities of CSLI. I thank Deiwiks very much for her help in this project.

Frenchie Perry was extraordinarily supportive of the efforts that went into these papers over the fifteen-year period in which they were written. I am happy to have this book to dedicate to her, although she deserves much better.

John Perry
June 1992

Acknowledgments

"Frege on Demonstratives" was first published in *The Philosophical Review* 86, no. 4 (1977): 474–97. Copyright 1977 Cornell University. Reprinted by permission of the publisher.

"The Problem of the Essential Indexical" was first published in *Noûs* 13 (1979): 3–21. Reprinted courtesy of Basil Blackwell Ltd.

"Belief and Acceptance" was first published in *Midwest Studies in Philosophy* 5 (1980): 533–42. Reprinted courtesy of University of Minnesota Press.

"A Problem About Continued Belief" was first published in *Pacific Philosophical Quarterly* 61 (1980): 317–32. Reprinted courtesy of Basil Blackwell Ltd.

"Castañeda on *He* and *I*" appeared in *Agent, Language, and the Structure of the World: Essays Presented to Hector-Neri Castañeda with his Replies*, ed. James E. Tomberlin, 15–41. Indianapolis: Hackett Publishing Company, 1983. Reprinted by permission of Ridgeview Publishing Company.

"Perception, Action, and the Structure of Believing" was first published in *Philosophical Grounds of Rationality. Intentions, Categories, Ends*, ed. Richard E. Grandy and Richard Warner, 333–61. Oxford: Clarendon Press, 1986. Reprinted courtesy of Oxford University Press.

"From Worlds to Situations" was first published in *Journal of Philosophical Logic* 15 (1986): 83–107. Also Report No. CSLI–87–73. Copyright 1986 by D. Reidel Publishing Company. Reprinted by permission of Kluwer Academic Publishers.

"Possible Worlds and Subject Matter" appeared in *Possible Worlds in Humanities, Arts and Sciences: Proceedings of Nobel Symposium* 65 (August 1986), ed. Sture Allén, 124–38. Berlin/New York: Walter de Gruyter, 1989. Reprinted courtesy of Walter de Gruyter & Co.

"Circumstantial Attitudes and Benevolent Cognition" was first published in *Language, Mind and Logic*, ed. J. Butterfield, 123–34. Cambridge: Cambridge University Press, 1986. Also Report No. CSLI–86–53. Reprinted courtesy of Cambridge University Press.

"Thought Without Representation" was first published in *Supplementary Proceedings of the Aristotelian Society* 60 (1986): 137–52. Reprinted courtesy of The Aristotelian Society.

"Cognitive Significance and New Theories of Reference" was first published in *Noûs* 22 (1988): 1–18. Also Report No. CSLI–88–109. Reprinted courtesy of Basil Blackwell Ltd.

"The Prince and the Phone Booth: Reporting Puzzling Beliefs" (with Mark Crimmins) was first published in *Journal of Philosophy* LXXXVI, no. 12 (1989): 685–711. An earlier version appeared as Report No. CSLI–88–128. Reprinted courtesy of *The Journal of Philosophy*.

"Individuals in Informational and Intentional Content" first appeared in *Information, Semantics and Epistemology*, ed. Enrique Villanueva, 172–89. Cambridge: Basil Blackwell, 1990. Reprinted courtesy of Basil Blackwell Ltd.

"Fodor and Psychological Explanations" (with David Israel) first appeared in *Meaning in Mind*, ed. Barry Loewer and Georges Rey, 165–80. Oxford: Basil Blackwell, 1991. An earlier version was published as Report No. CSLI–91–146. Reprinted courtesy of Basil Blackwell Ltd.

"Davidson's Sentences and Wittgenstein's Builders" was the 1994 Presidential Address to the Pacific Division of the American Philosophical Association; it first appeared in the *APA Proceedings*, 1994. Reprinted courtesy of the American Philosophical Association.

"Evading the Slingshot" first appeared in *Philosophy and Cognitive Science: Categories, Consciousness, and Reasoning* , Proceedings of the Second International Colloquium on Cognitive Science, edited by Andy Clark, Jesus Ezquerro, and Jesus M. Larrazabal. Reprinted courtesy of Kluwer Publishing.

"Broadening the Mind" first appeared in *Philosophy and Phenomenological Research* LVIII, no. 1, March, 1998, 223–231. Reprinted courtesy of *Philosophy and Phenomenological Research*.

"Myself and *I*" first appeared in Marcelo Stamm, editor, *Philosophie in Synthetisher Absicht* (A festschrift for Dieter Heinrich), Stuttgart: Klett-Cotta, pp. 83–103. Reprinted courtesy of Klett-Cotta.

"Reflexivity, Indexicality and Names" first appeared in *Direct Reference, Indexicality and Proposition Attitudes* edited by Wolfgang Künne, Martin Anduschus, and Albert Newen. Stanford, CA: CSLI-Cambridge University Press, 1997. Reprinted courtesy of CSLI-Cambridge University Press.

"Rip Van Winkle and Other Characters" first appeared in *The European Review of Analytical Philosophy* Volume 2: *Cognitive Dynamics*, 13–39. Reprinted courtesy of the *European Review of Analytical Philosophy*.

1

Frege on Demonstratives

In "The Thought," Frege briefly discusses sentences containing such demonstratives as "today," "here" and "yesterday," and then turns to certain questions that he says are raised by the occurrence of "I" in sentences (1918/1967, 24–26). He is led to say that, when one thinks about oneself, one grasps thoughts that others cannot grasp, that cannot be communicated. Nothing could be more out of the spirit of Frege's account of sense and thought than an incommunicable, private thought. Demonstratives seem to have posed a severe difficulty for Frege's philosophy of language, to which his doctrine of incommunicable senses was a reaction.

In the first part of the paper, I explain the problem demonstratives pose for Frege and explore three ways he might have dealt with it. I argue that none of these ways provides Frege with a solution to his problem consistent with his philosophy of language. The first two are plausible as solutions, but contradict his identification of the sense expressed by a sentence with a thought. The third preserves the identification, but is implausible. In the second part, I suggest that Frege was led to his doctrine of incommunicable senses as a result of some appreciation of the difficulties his account of demonstratives faces, for these come quickly to the surface when we think about "I." I argue that incommunicable senses will not help. I end by trying to identify the central problem with Frege's approach, and sketching an alternative.

I

Before explaining the problem posed by demonstratives, certain points about Frege's philosophy of language need to be made.

In "On Sense and Reference," Frege introduces the notion of sense, in terms of the cognitive value of sentences (1892/1960). He then goes on to make two key identifications. First, he identifies the sense of a sentence with the thought it expresses. Then, he identifies the thought expressed by a sentence, and so the sense it has, with the indirect reference of the sentence in the scope of a cognitive verb.

The phrases "the sense of a sentence," "the thought expressed by a sentence," and "the indirect reference of a sentence," are not mere synonyms. They have different senses, though, if Frege's account is correct, they have the same reference. In particular, each is associated, as Frege introduces it, with a separate criterion of difference.

Sense

In the beginning of "On Sense and Reference," Frege introduces the notion of sense as a way of accounting for the difference in cognitive value of the senses of "$a = a$" and "$b = b$," even when both are true, and so made up of coreferential expressions (1892/1960, 56–58). So a criterion of difference for sense is,

> If S and S' have differing cognitive value, then S and S' have different senses.

Dummett's explanation of sense will help us to convert this to something more helpful. He emphasizes that sense is linked to understanding and truth. The sense of an expression is "what we know when we understand it," and what we know when we understand it is something like an ideal procedure for determining its reference (1973, 293, 589ff). In the case of a sentence whose reference is truth-value, the sense is what we know when, roughly, we know what would have to be done—whether or not this is humanly possible—to determine whether or not it is true.

What Frege seems to have in mind at the beginning of "On Sense and Reference," then, is a situation in which some person A who understands both "$a = a$" and "$a = b$" accepts the first while rejecting, or being unsure about, the second. The assumption seems to be that if A associated just the same ideal procedures with both sentences, he would accept the second if he accepted the first. So he must not associate the same ideal procedures with both sentences, and so, since he understands them, their senses differ. So we have:

> If A understands S and S', and accepts S as true while not accepting S', then S and S' have different senses.

This criterion of difference allows that sentences might have different senses, though provably or necessarily equivalent. A complex true mathematical equation might be provably equivalent to "$2+3 = 5$," and yet a perfectly competent speaker might accept the latter and reject the former, having made an error in calculation. To know an ideal procedure for determining reference is not necessarily to have carried it out, or even to be able to.

Thought

"Thought" is not just a term introduced by Frege as another way of saying, "sense of a sentence." The notion derived from Frege's untangling of the jumbled notion of a judgment, into act, thought, and truth-value. The thought is, first and foremost, "that for which the question of truth arises" (1918/1967, 20–22). This is clearly intended to be a criterion of difference for thoughts:

If S is true and S' is not, S and S' express different thoughts.

Indirect Reference

Consider a report of a belief, "Copernicus believed that the planetary orbits are circles." On Frege's analysis, this is relational. "Believed that" stands for a relation that is asserted to hold between Copernicus and whatever it is that "the planetary orbits are circles" refers to as it occurs in this sentence. Standing alone, "the planetary orbits are circles" would refer to the False, but here it clearly does not have that ordinary reference. If it did, the substitution of any false sentence at all should preserve truth of the whole report (1892/1960, 66–67). The notion of the indirect reference of "the planetary orbits are circles," is just whatever it is, that this sentence has a reference here. (The phrase is first used in connection with indirect discourse (1892/1960, 59).) Now if "aRb" is true, and "aRc" is not, b is not c. So we have a clear criterion of difference:

If "A believes S" is true, and "A believes S'" is not, then S and S' do not have the same indirect reference.

So we have three separable criteria of difference. But Frege, as noted, identifies the sense of S as the thought expressed by S, and the indirect reference of S. So we are led to a further principle:

S and S' have different senses, if and only if they express different thoughts, and if and only if they have different indirect references.

Sense Completers

Frege takes the structure of language as a suggestive guide to the structure of senses and objects. Just as he views the sentence,

two plus two equals four

as the result of combining the complete

two

with the incomplete

( ) plus two equals four,

so he sees the sense of "two plus two equals four" as determined by the sense of "two" and the sense of "( ) plus two equals four." The sense of the latter is incomplete; the sense of the former completes it, to yield the complete sense of "two plus two equals four."

"( ) plus two equals four" could also be made into a sentence by writing "something" in the blank; similarly the sense of "( ) plus two equals four" can be completed with the sense of "something." The sense of "something," however, unlike the sense of "two," is itself also incomplete. Where "two" refers to an object, "something" refers to a concept. Two appropriately related incomplete senses can combine to form a complete sense; two complete senses cannot combine at all (1923/1968, 538).

Thus the class of *sense completers* for a given incomplete sense is hybrid, containing both complete and incomplete senses. But the term will be useful in what follows.

Sense Had and Sense Expressed

The structure of language is not always a sure guide to the structure of senses. Not everything we count as a sentence has a complete sense. Consider (1),

(1) Russia and Canada quarreled when Nemtsanov defected.

"Russia and Canada quarreled," as it occurs as a clause in (1), does not have a complete sense (1892/1960, 71; 1918/1967, 37). It refers to a concept of times and thus must have an incomplete sense. "When Nemtsanov defected" refers to a time; the sentence is true if the time referred to falls under the concept referred to. Thus the sense of "when Nemtsanov defected" is a sense completer for the sense of "Russia and Canada quarreled."

So the sense of the sentence "Russia and Canada quarreled" is not a thought. Not any sentence, but only a sentence "complete in every respect," expresses a thought (1918/1967, 37).

Now "Russia and Canada quarreled" could be used, without a dependent clause, to express a thought. If it appeared alone, we might take it to express, *on that occasion*, the sense of

> At some time or other Russia and Canada quarreled.

In another setting, for example, after the question, "What happened when Nemtsanov defected?" the sentence would express the sense of (1). So we must, even before considering demonstratives, distinguish between the sense a sentence *has* on each occasion of use and the senses it *expresses* on various occasions of use. For an "eternal" sentence, one that really is "complete in every respect," the two will be the same; for a sentence like "Russia and Canada quarreled," the sense *had* is incomplete; the sense *expressed* on a given occasion will be the result of completing that sense, with some sense completer available from the context of utterance. It is clearly only the sense expressed on such occasions that Frege wants to identify with a thought.

The Problem Posed by Demonstratives

We are now in a position to see why demonstratives pose a problem for Frege. I begin by quoting the passage in which Frege discussed demonstratives in general.

> Often ... the mere wording, which can be grasped by writing or the grammophone, does not suffice for the expression of the thought .... If a time indication is needed by the present tense [as opposed to cases in which it is used to express timelessness, as in the statement of mathematical laws] one must know when the sentence was uttered to apprehend the thought correctly. There-fore, the time of utterance is part of the expression of the thought. If someone wants to say the same today as he expressed yesterday using the word "today," he must replace this word with "yester-day." Although the thought is the same its verbal expression must be different so that the sense, which would otherwise be affected by the differing times of utterance, is readjusted. The case is the same with words like "here" and "there." In all such cases the mere wording, as it is given in writing, is not the complete expression of the thought, but the knowledge of certain accompanying con-ditions of utterance, which are used as a means of expressing the thought, are needed for its correct apprehension. The pointing of fingers, hand movements, glances may belong here too. The same utterance containing the word "I" will express different thoughts in the mouths of different men, of which some may be true, others false (1918/1967, 24).

Consider (2),

(2) Russia and Canada quarreled today.

The sentence "Russia and Canada quarreled" has in (2), as in (1), only an incomplete sense. So presumably "today" in (2) must somehow do what "when Nemtsanov defected" does in (1) and supply us with a completing sense. But it does not seem to do this at all.

If I uttered (2) on August 1, I expressed something true, on August 2, some-thing false. If "today" had the same sense on August 1 as on August 2, then (2) in its entirety must have had the same sense on both occasions. If so, the sense of (2) must be incomplete, for if it were complete, its truth-value could not change.

So, if "today" provides a completing sense on both days, its sense must change just at midnight. But what we know when we understand how to use "today" does not seem to change from day to day.

When we understand a word like "today," what we seem to know is a rule taking us from an occasion of utterance to a certain object. "Today" takes us to the very day of utterance, "yesterday" to the day before the day of utterance, "I" to the speaker, and so forth. I shall call this the *role* of the demonstrative. I take a context to be a set of features of an actual utterance, certainly including time, place, and speaker, but probably also more. Just what a context must include is a difficult question, to be answered only after detailed study of various demonstratives. The object a demonstrative takes us to in a given context, I shall call its value in that context or on that occasion of use. Clearly, we must grant "today" a role, the same on both occasions of use. And we must, as clearly, give it different values on the two occasions.

Any reasonable account has to recognize that demonstratives have roles. The role of a demonstrative does not seem reducible to other notions available from Frege's philosophy. Senses do not carry us from context to references, but directly to references, the same on each occasion of use. One might suppose that "yesterday" could be thought to have just the sense of "the day before." But,

(3) Russia and Canada quarreled the day before

does not have the same sense as (4).

(4) Russia and Canada quarreled yesterday.

If I ask on August 5, "Did Russia and Canada quarrel August 2?" (3) would imply that they quarreled on August 1, (4) that they quarreled on August 4. If (3) were uttered when no day had already been mentioned, it would not express anything complete, but simply give rise to the question, "before what?" An utterance of (4) would still be fully in order.

Frege recognizes that demonstratives have roles, or at least that the context of utterance is crucial when dealing with demonstratives. He does not talk about the sense of "today" or "I" so he also seems to have recognized that the role of a demonstrative is not just a sense, as he has explained senses.

But Frege clearly thinks that, given knowledge of the accompanying conditions of utterance, we can get from an utterance of a sentence like (2) or (4) to a thought. He must have thought, then, that the demonstrative provides us not simply with an object—its value on the occasion of utterance—but with a *completing sense*. This is puzzling. Neither the unchanging role of "today," nor its changing value, provides us with a completing sense. A day is not a sense, but a reference corresponding to indefinitely many senses (1892/1960, 71). There is no route back from reference to sense. So how do we get from the incomplete sense of "Russia and Canada quarreled," the demonstrative "today," and the context, to a thought? This is the problem demonstratives pose for Frege.

I shall first describe two options Frege might have taken, which would have excused him from the necessity of finding a completing sense. I shall argue that Frege did not take these options, and could not, given his identification of a sense expressed and thought.

Senses as Roles?

Let $S(d)$ be a sentence containing a demonstrative d. Without the demonstrative, we have something, $S(\ )$, that has an incomplete sense, and so refers to a concept. This may actually still be a sentence, as when we remove "today" from (2), or it may look more like it should, as when we remove the "I" from "I am wounded."

The following scheme gives us a rule for getting from a particular context to a truth-value for any such sentence $S(d)$.

> $S(d)$ is true when uttered in context c, if and only if the value of d in c falls under the concept referred to by $S(\ )$.[1]

Such a rule is the *role of $S(d)$*. It is just an extension of the notion of the role of a demonstrative. Roles take us from contexts to objects. In the case of a sentence, the object is a truth-value.

Thus (4) is true as uttered on August 2, if and only if August 1 is a day that falls under the concept referred to by "Russia and Canada quarreled." "I am ill" as uttered by Lauben is true if and only if Lauben falls under the concept referred to by "( ) is ill."

The role of a sentence containing a demonstrative is clearly analogous in many ways to the sense of a sentence not containing a demonstrative. The role is a procedure for determining truth-value, just as the sense is. The difference is that the role is a procedure that starts from a context.

This analogy suggests an option, which Frege might have taken. He might have identified the sense expressed by a sentence containing a demonstrative with its role. This would amount to a generalization of the notion of sense. On this view, an incomplete sense like that of "Russia and Canada quarreled," could be completed in two ways. A sense completer, such as the sense of "when Nemtsanov defected," gives us a complete sense of the old sort. A demonstrative, like "today," yields a sense of the new sort, a role. No complete sense of the old sort is involved at all in the utterance of a sentence containing a demonstrative, so no completing sense need be found.

But this cannot have been Frege's view. For it is clear that he thinks a thought has been expressed in the utterance of a sentence containing a demon-

---

[1] Here and elsewhere I assume, for the sake of simplicity of exposition, that we are considering sentences containing no more than one demonstrative. Given the notion of a sequence of objects, there would be no difficulties in extending various suggestions and options for the general case. In some of the examples I use, additional demonstratives are really needed. "Lauben is wounded," for example, still needs a time indication.

strative. The role of the sentence cannot be identified with the thought, for a sentence could express the same role on different occasions while having different truth-values. So by the criteria of difference for thoughts, roles are not thoughts. By the identification of the sense expressed by a sentence and the thought expressed, roles are not the senses expressed by a sentence.

Thoughts as Information?

We can put the problem this way. (2), as uttered on August 1, with the role of "today" fully mastered, seems to yield just this information:

(i) an incomplete sense, that of "Russia and Canada quarreled";

(ii) an object, the day August 1, 1976.

(i) and (ii) do not uniquely determine a thought, but only an equivalence class of thoughts. Belonging to this equivalence class will be just those thoughts obtainable by completing the sense of "Russia and Canada quarreled" with a sense completer that determines, as reference, August 1, 1976. I shall call thoughts related in this manner *informationally equivalent*.[2]

The second option I shall discuss is introducing a new notion of a thought, corresponding to such a class of informationally equivalent thoughts. Since the information in (i) and (ii) is sufficient to identify such a class, without identifying any one of its members, this would explain how we can get from (i) and (ii) to a thought, without needing a completing sense.

On this view, an utterance of $S(d)$ in context c, and $S'(d')$ in context c', will express the same thought if the (incomplete) senses of $S(\ )$ and $S'(\ )$ are the same, and if the value of d and c is the same as the value of d' and c'. Thus (2), uttered on August 1, and (4), uttered on August 2, would express the same thought. Dummett interprets Frege in this way (1973, 384). Frege's remark,

> If someone wants to say the same today as he expressed yesterday using the word "today," he must replace this with "yesterday." Although the thought is the same its verbal expression must be different (1918/1967, 24).

But this cannot have been Frege's view. This criterion actually introduces a new kind of thought, corresponding to informationally equivalent classes of thoughts of the old kind. The thought expressed by Lauben when he says "I am wounded" to Leo Peter, cannot be identified with the thought expressed by any nondemonstrative completion of the same incomplete sense in which the singular term refers to Lauben, such as

The man born on the thirteenth of September, 1875, in N.N. is wounded.

---

[2]This notion is taken from Burks (1949, 685). In this pioneering and illuminating work on demonstratives, Burks emphasizes the ineliminability of demonstratives.

The only doctor who lives in the house next door to Rudolf Lingens is wounded.

These express different thoughts, so the thought Lauben expresses with "I am wounded" cannot be identified with *the* thought they both express; there just is not any such thought. There is no more reason to identify it with the one than with the other, or with any other such thought. Nor can thoughts of this new type be identified with classes of thoughts of the old, for in different possible circumstances the pair, Dr. Lauben and the incomplete sense of "( ) am ill," would correspond to different sets of Fregean thoughts. If Lauben had moved, the two Fregean thoughts in question would not be informationally equivalent. We have here a radically new kind of thought, of which Frege would not have approved, even if he had seen its necessity. We have in effect made the value of the demonstrative a part of the thought. But Frege insists that only senses can be parts of senses.

Dummett remarks,

> It is, of course, quite unnecessary to suppose that a thought expressible by the utterance on a particular occasion of a sentence containing a token reflexive expression can also be expressed by some "eternal" sentence containing no such expressions (1973, 384).

But it is not only unnecessary, but impossible, on this account, that the thought should be expressed by an eternal sentence. It is not the right kind of thought for an eternal sentence to express.

Second, and closely related, this notion of a thought would violate the criteria of difference.

Suppose I am viewing the harbor from downtown Oakland; the bow and stern of the aircraft carrier *Enterprise* are visible, though its middle is obscured by a large building. The name "*Enterprise*" is clearly visible on the bow, so when I tell a visitor, "This is the *Enterprise*," pointing towards the bow, this is readily accepted. When I say, pointing to the stern clearly several city blocks from the bow, "That is the *Enterprise*," however, she refuses to believe me. By the criterion of difference, a different sense was expressed the first time than the second. On the present suggested criterion of identity for thoughts, the same thought was expressed; the incomplete sense was the same in both cases, and the value of the demonstratives was the *Enterprise* in both cases. To adopt this notion of a thought, Frege would have to give up the identification of sense expressed and thought expressed.

This is, of course, simply a variation on Frege's own Morning Star example. Suppose I point to Venus in the morning, and again in the evening, saying, "That is the Morning Star." My listener may accept what I say the first time, and continue to think I was right, while rejecting what I say the second time.

Here the *same* sentence has a different cognitive value at different times—for my listener has not changed her mind. The sentence does not have different cognitive values because the words have undergone a change of meaning, but because the sentence alone does not express a complete sense. Some supplementation is needed; here the gestures toward Venus provide it. But just what supplementation do they provide? If the supplementation was merely taken to be Venus, itself—which is what the present proposal amounts to—then the sense of the sentence would have been supplemented in the same way on both occasions. But then we would have the same sense expressed in both occasions, in violation of the criterion of difference for senses.

Frege does not explicitly mention the demonstratives "this" and "that." So it is worth pointing out that examples can be constructed using demonstratives he does mention. For example, I might accept what you say at 11:50 P.M. when you utter "Russia and Canada quarreled today," but disbelieve you at 12:15 A.M. when you utter "Russia and Canada quarreled yesterday," having lost track of time.

Of course, Frege may have meant to introduce such a new notion of a thought at this point. That he does not explain it, counts against this interpretation. And what he goes on to say, in the next paragraphs, seems to make it totally implausible. There he discusses proper names, and arrives at a point where he has all the materials for this notion of a thought in his hand, so to speak, and yet passes up the opportunity to mold them into the new notion. He describes a situation in which two men express different thoughts with the sentence "Gustav Lauben has been wounded," one knowing him as the unique man born a certain day, the other as the unique doctor living in a certain house. He recognizes that these different thoughts are systematically equivalent:

> The different thoughts which thus result from the same sentence correspond in their truth-value, of course; that is to say, if one is true then all are true, and if one is false then all are false (1918/1967, 25).

But he insists,

> Nevertheless their distinctness must be recognized (1918/1967, 25).

His reason here is clearly a complex example he has just constructed, in which sentences expressing such informationally equivalent thoughts have different cognitive value:

> It is possible that Herbert Garner takes the sense of the sentence "Dr. Lauben has been wounded" to be true, while, misled by false information, taking the sense of "Gustav Lauben has been wounded" to be false. Under the assumptions given these thoughts are therefore different (1918/1967, 25).

If demonstratives had driven Frege, three paragraphs before this, to the introduction of a class of thoughts, corresponding to a class of informationally equivalent thoughts of the old sort, I think he would have employed it, or at least mentioned it, here.

Senses, considered to be roles, cannot be thoughts. Thoughts, considered as information, cannot be senses. If Frege is to keep his identification of sense expressed by a sentence, with thought expressed by a sentence, he must find, somewhere, a completing sense.

Demonstratives as Providing a Completing Sense

How can we extract from a demonstrative an appropriate completing sense? Such a sense, it seems, would have to be intimately related to the sense of a unique description of the value of the demonstrative in the context of utterance. But where does such a description come from? "Today" seems to get us only to a day. And a day does not provide a particular description of itself.

In the case of proper names, Frege supposes that different persons attach different senses to the same proper name. To find the sense a person identifies with a given proper name, we presumably look to his beliefs. If he associates the sense of description D with Gustav Lauben, he should believe,

Gustav Lauben is D.

Perhaps, with demonstratives too, Frege supposes that speakers and listeners, in grasping the thought, provide the demonstrative with an appropriate sense. To understand a demonstrative, is to be able to supply a sense for it on each occasion, which determines as reference the value the demonstrative has on that occasion.[3] This is, I think, as near as we are likely to come to what Frege has in mind.

There is a problem here, with no analog in the case of proper names. One can attach the same sense to a proper name, once and for all. But, since the demonstrative takes a different value on different occasions, different senses must be supplied. So the demonstrative could not be regarded as an abbreviation, or something like an abbreviation, for some appropriate description.[4]

But still, can we not say that for each person the sense of the demonstrative "today" for that person on a given day is just the sense of one of the descrip-

---

[3] This interpretation was suggested to me by Dagfinn Føllesdal.

[4] [This is too cautious, in a way that has misled some commentators. The significant point is not that the demonstrative could not be regarded as an abbreviation for a description. It is rather that the sense of a demonstrative cannot be one that determines its reference independently of context. It does not matter whether these senses are identified by definite descriptions, or expressions of some other type, or cannot be identified linguistically at all. I admit that I was assuming that senses of names and indexical terms would be similar to those of descriptions. However, even if this traditional view is wrong, the problem that demonstratives pose for Frege do not disappear, as Gareth Evans suggested in "Understanding Demonstratives" (1990). I discuss Evans' account in the Afterword.]

tions D (or some combination of all the descriptions) such that on that day he believes,

> Today is D.

One objection to this is that we seem to be explaining the sense of sentences containing demonstratives in terms of beliefs whose natural expressions contain demonstratives. But there are three more serious problems.

The first problem might be called the *irrelevancy of belief.*[5] The sense I associate with my use of a demonstrative does not determine the thought expressed by a sentence containing that demonstrative.

Suppose I believe that today is the fourteenth of October, 1976. From that it does not follow that, when I utter,

> Today is sunny and bright,

I express the thought,

> The fourteenth of October is sunny and bright.

For suppose today is really the fifteenth, cloudy and dull. Then what I have said is wrong, whatever the weather was like on the fourteenth.

The second problem we might call the *nonnecessity of belief.* I can express a thought with "Today is sunny and bright"—that is, say something for which the question of truth arises—whether or not I associate any correct sense at all with "today." I may have no idea at all what day it is, and not be able, without recourse to "today" or other demonstratives, to say anything about today at all, that does not describe dozens of other days equally well.

Both of these problems are illustrated by Rip Van Winkle. When he awakes on October 20, 1823, and says with conviction,

> Today is October 20, 1803,

the fact that he is sure he is right does not make him right, as it would if the thought expressed were determined by the sense he associated with "today." And, what is really the same point from a different angle, he does not fail to be wrong, as would be the case if "today" had to be associated with a completing sense that determined the value of "today" as reference, before the question of truth arose for sentences in which it occurs.

To state my third objection, the *nonsufficiency of belief*, I shall shift to an example using the demonstrative "I." I do so because the objection is clearest with respect to this demonstrative, and because some awareness of this prob-

---

[5]In the three problems that follow, and the balance of the paper, I am much in debt to a series of very illuminating papers by Hector-Neri Castañeda. The fullest statement of his view is in Castañeda 1967. See also Castañeda 1966, 1968. All the examples of what I later call "self-locating knowledge" are adaptations from Castañeda, and the difficulties they raise for Frege's account are related to points Castañeda has made.

lem might help explain how consideration of "I" led Frege to incommunicable senses.

Let us imagine David Hume, alone in his study, on a particular afternoon in 1775, thinking to himself, "I wrote the *Treatise*." Can anyone *else* apprehend the thought he apprehended by thinking this? First note that what he thinks is true. So no one could apprehend the same thought, unless they apprehended a true thought. Now suppose Heimson is a bit crazy and thinks himself to be David Hume. Alone in his study, he says to himself, "I wrote the *Treatise*." However much his inner life may, at that moment, resemble Hume's on that afternoon in 1775, the fact remains: Hume was right, Heimson is wrong. Heimson cannot think the very thought to himself that Hume thought to himself, by using the very same sentence.

Now suppose Frege's general account of demonstratives is right. Then it seems that, by using the very same sense that Hume supplied for "I," Heimson should be able to think the same thought, without using "I," that Hume did using "I." He will just have to find a true sentence, which expresses the very thought Hume was thinking, when he thought to himself "I wrote the *Treatise*." But there just does not seem to be such a thought.

Suppose Heimson thinks to himself, "The author of the *Inquiries* wrote the *Treatise*." This is true, for the sense used to complete the sense of "( ) wrote the *Treatise*" determines Hume, not Heimson, as reference. But it seems clear that Hume could acknowledge "I wrote the *Treatise*" as true, while rejecting, "The author of the *Inquiries* wrote the *Treatise*." He might have forgotten that he wrote the *Inquiries*; perhaps Hume had episodes of forgetfulness in 1775. But then the thought Heimson thinks, and the one Hume apprehended, are not the same after all, by the identification of thoughts with senses, and the criterion of difference for senses.

One might suppose that, while there is no particular sentence of this sort that must have had, for Hume, the same cognitive value as "I wrote the *Treatise*," there must be some such sentence or other that would have had the same cognitive value for him.

But I see no reason to suppose this is so. For now we have reached just the point where the first objection takes hold. There is no reason to believe we are on each occasion each equipped with some nondemonstrative equivalent of the demonstratives we use and understand. This goes for "I" as well as "today." After all, as I am imagining Heimson, he does not have any correct demonstrative-free description of himself at hand. Every correct demonstrative-free description he is willing to apply to himself refers to Hume instead. I'm not at all sure that I have one for myself. To keep the identification between thought and sense intact, Frege must provide us with a completing sense. But then his account of demonstratives becomes implausible.

II

Frege follows his general discussion of demonstratives by saying that "I" gives rise to certain questions. He then makes the point, with the examples concerning Dr. Lauben discussed above, that various persons might associate various senses with the same proper name, if the person were presented to them in various ways. This discussion seems intended to prepare the way for the startling claim about thoughts about ourselves,

> Now everyone is presented to himself in a particular and primitive way, in which he is presented to no one else. So, when Dr. Lauben thinks that he has been wounded, he will probably take as a basis this primitive way in which he is presented to himself. And only Dr. Lauben himself can grasp thoughts determined in this way. But now he may want to communicate with others. He cannot communicate a thought which he alone can grasp. Therefore, if he now says "I have been wounded," he must use the "I" in a sense which can be grasped by others, perhaps in the sense of "he is speaking to you at this moment," by doing which he makes the associated conditions of his utterance serve for the expression of his thought (1918/1967, 25–26).

Frege's doctrine appears to be this. When I use "I" to communicate, it works like other demonstratives, and perhaps could even be replaced by some phrase that included only other demonstratives. The sense would be completed in whatever way is appropriate for sentences containing these demonstratives. When I use "I" to think about myself, however, it has an incommunicable sense.

This is not quite right, for Frege would not have thought it necessary, in order to think about oneself, to use language at all. It is at this point that Frege makes his famous remark, about how the battle with language makes his task difficult, in that he can only give his readers the thought he wants them to examine dressed up in linguistic form.

Nevertheless, it seems clear that Frege thinks there are senses, for each of us, that determine us as reference, which are incommunicable, and which would be the natural sense to associate with "I" if it did happen to be used, not merely to communicate with others, but think about oneself.

I suggest this doctrine about "I" is a reaction to the problems just mentioned, the third in particular. I am not at all certain that this is so. Philosophers have come to hold somewhat similar views about the self, beliefs about oneself, and "I," without thinking as rigorously as Frege did about these matters. Perhaps Frege had adopted some such view independently of his thinking about demonstratives, and simply wished to show he could accommodate it. It seems to me more likely, however, that Frege was led to this view by his own philosophical work, in particular, by some realization of the problems I have discussed for his general account, as they apply particularly to "I." All three problems turned on the failure to find a suitable description for the value of the demonstrative, whose sense would complete the sense of the sentence in just the right way. If the sense we are looking for is private and incommunicable, it is no wonder the search was in vain.

But the appeal to private and incommunicable senses cannot, I think, be a satisfactory resolution of the problem.

In the first place, I see no reason to believe that "everyone is presented to himself in a particular and primitive way." Or at least, no reason to accept this, with such a reading that it leads to incommunicable senses.

Suppose M is the private and incommunicable sense, which is to serve as the sense of "I" when I think about myself. M cannot be a complex sense, resulting from the compounding of simpler, generally accessible senses. For it seems clear that it is sufficient, to grasp the result of such compounding, that one grasp the senses compounded. So M will have to be, as Frege says, primitive.

A sense corresponds to an aspect or mode of presentation (1892/1960, 57, 58). There are, I hope, ways in which I am presented to myself that I am presented to no one else, and aspects of me that I am aware of, that no one else is aware of. But this is not sufficient for Frege's purposes.

Suppose that only I am aware of the scratchiness of a certain fountain pen. Still, "thing that is scratchy" does not uniquely pick out this pen; this pen may not be the only one that falls under the concept this phrase stands for, though perhaps the only one of which I am aware. Similarly, just because there is some aspect, such that only I am aware that I have it, and M is the sense corresponding to that aspect, it does not follow that M determines as reference a concept that only I fall under, or that *the M* (by which I mean the result of combining the sense of "the" with M) is a sense that determines just me as reference and can appropriately be associated with my utterances of "I."

What is needed is a primitive aspect of me, which is not simply one that only I am aware of myself as having, but that I alone have. While there are doubtless complex aspects that only I have, and primitive aspects that only I am aware of myself as having, I see no reason to believe there are primitive aspects that only I have. Even if there were, if they were incommunicable, I should have no way of knowing there were, since I hardly ask others if they happened to have *mine*. So I should not know that *the M* determined me as reference. But I do know that I am thinking about me, when I use the word "I" in thinking to myself.

My second point in opposition to incommunicable senses is that the third objection does not merely apply to "I," but to at least one other demonstrative, "now." However one may feel about one's private and unique aspects, Frege's doctrine must appear less plausible when it is seen that it must be extended to other demonstratives.

Suppose the department meeting is scheduled for noon, September 15, 1976. Then only at that time could we say something true with (5).

(5) The meeting starts now.

Now consider any of the informationally equivalent thoughts we might have had the day before, for example, (6).

(6) The meeting starts at noon, September 15, 1976.

It seems that one could accept this the day before, and continue to accept it right through the meeting, without ever accepting (5), and even rejecting it firmly precisely at noon, simply by completely losing track of time. So (5) and (6) express different senses, and so different thoughts. And it seems this would be true, no matter what nondemonstrative informational equivalent we came up with instead of (6). So with "now," as with "I," it is not sufficient to grasp the thought expressed with a demonstrative, to grasp an informational equivalent with a complete sense. Frege will have to have, for each time, a primitive and particular way in which it is presented to us at that time, which gives rise to thoughts accessible only at that time, and expressible, at it, with "now." This strikes me as very implausible. An appeal to incommunicable senses will not serve to patch up Frege's treatment.

I will conclude by sketching an alternative treatment of these problems. I try to show just how these recent examples motivate a break between sense and thought, and how, once that break is made, senses can be treated as roles, thoughts as information, and the other examples we have discussed handled.

III

Consider some of the things Hume might have thought to himself,

> I am David Hume.
> This is Edinburgh.
> It is now 1775.

We would say of Hume, when he thought such things, that he knew *who* he was, *where* he was, and *when* it was. I shall call these self-locating beliefs. The objections, posed in the last section to Frege's account of demonstratives, may be put in the following way: Having a self-locating belief does not consist in believing a Fregean thought.

We can see that having such beliefs *could* not consist *wholly* in believing Fregean thoughts. Consider Frege's timeless realm of generally accessible thoughts. If Hume's knowing he was Hume consisted in his believing certain true thoughts in this realm, then it would seem that anyone else could know that *he* was Hume, just by believing those same thoughts. But only Hume can know, or even truly believe, that he is Hume. Analogous remarks apply to his knowing where he was, and when it was.

Either there are some thoughts only Hume can apprehend, and his believing he is Hume consists in believing those thoughts, or self-locating knowledge does not consist wholly in believing some true subset of the Fregean thoughts. Frege chose the first option; let us see what happens when we choose the second.

We accept that there is no thought only Hume can apprehend. Yet only he can know he is Hume. It must not just be the thought that he thinks, but the way that he thinks it, that sets him apart from the rest of us. Only Hume can think a true thought, by saying to himself,

> I am Hume.

Self-locating knowledge then requires not just the grasping of certain thoughts, but the grasping of them via the senses of certain sentences containing demonstratives.

To firmly embed in our minds the importance that thinking a thought via one sense rather than another can have, let us consider another example. An amnesiac, Rudolf Lingens, is lost in the Stanford library. He reads a number of things in the library, including a biography of himself, and a detailed account of the library in which he is lost. He believes any Fregean thought you think might help him. He still will not know who he is and where he is, and no matter how much knowledge he piles up, until that moment when he is ready to say,

> *This* place is aisle five, floor six, of Main Library, Stanford.
> *I* am Rudolf Lingens.

If self-locating knowledge consists not merely in believing certain thoughts, but believing them by apprehending certain senses, then senses cannot be thoughts. Otherwise it would make no sense to say that Hume and Heimson can apprehend all the same thoughts, but Hume can do so by apprehending different senses.

Let us then see how things begin to resolve themselves when this identification is given up. Let us speak of *entertaining* a sense and apprehending a thought. So different thoughts may be apprehended, in different contexts, by entertaining the same sense (without supposing that it is an incomplete sense, somehow supplemented by a sense completer in the context), and the same thought, by entertaining different senses.

By breaking the connection between senses and thoughts, we give up any reason not to take the options closed to Frege. We can take the sense of a sentence containing a demonstrative to be a role, rather than a Fregean complete sense, and thoughts to be the new sort, individuated by object and incomplete sense, rather than Fregean thoughts. Though senses considered as roles, and thoughts considered as information, cannot be identified, each does its job in a way that meshes with the other. To have a thought we need an object and an incomplete sense. The demonstrative in context gives us the one, the rest of the sentence the other. The role of the entire sentence will lead us to Truth by leading us to a true thought, that is just in case the object falls under the concept determined as reference by the incomplete sense.[6]

Let us see how some of the examples we have discussed are handled.

We must suppose that both Hume and Heimson can entertain the same senses and think the same thoughts. The difference between them is that they do not apprehend the same thoughts when they entertain the same senses. When Heimson entertains the sense of "I am the author of the *Treatise*" he apprehends the thought consisting of Heimson and the sense of "( ) is the author of the *Treatise*." This thought is false. When Hume entertains the same sense, he apprehends the thought consisting of Hume and the sense of "( ) is the author of the *Treatise*," which is true. Hume is right, Heimson is crazy. Similarly, only at noon can someone think the thought consisting of noon and the sense of "The meeting starts at ( )" by entertaining the sense of "the meeting starts now."

Why should we have a special category of self-locating knowledge? Why should we care how someone apprehends a thought, so long as he does? I can only sketch the barest suggestion of an answer here. We use senses to individuate psychological states, in explaining and predicting action. It is the sense entertained and not the thought apprehended that is tied to human action. When you and I entertain the sense of "A bear is about to attack me," we behave similarly. We both roll up in a ball and try to be as still as possible. Different

---

[6]The notions of the role of a sentence and of a thought as information are similar to the concepts of *character* and *content* in Kaplan 1979. This is no accident, as my approach to these matters was formed, basically, as a result of trying to extract from this work of Kaplan's, and Kaplan himself, answers to questions posed by Castañeda's work. One should not assume that Kaplan would agree with my criticisms of Frege, my treatment of self-locating knowledge, or the philosophical motivation I develop for distinguishing between sense and thought. [At the time this essay was written, "On the Logic of Demonstratives" had not been published, but a mimeographed version had been circulated; I had seen this and talked to Kaplan about it. While I thought the distinction between character and content provided the key to answering the problems posed by Castañeda's work, I preferred to use role and information (from Burks, see note 2) for a couple of reasons. Kaplan's concepts are developed within the framework of possible-worlds semantics, so that the characters of terms are functions from contexts to *individual concepts* (rather than functions from contexts to individuals), and contents are intensions. Individual concepts seems to obscure the points on which I was focusing in this essay, and I was not sure how to fit intensions into the alternative treatment I developed in part III. "On the Logic of Demonstratives" was subsequently published (1979), and the technical part was included as an appendix to Kaplan's monograph *Demonstratives* (1989). In *Demonstratives*, Kaplan discusses the import of his treatment of demonstratives and the character/content distinction for the sorts of problems I discuss in this essay.]

thoughts apprehended, same sense entertained, same behavior. When you and I both apprehend the thought that I am about to be attacked by a bear, we behave differently. I roll up in a ball, you run to get help. Same thought apprehended, different sense entertained, different behavior. Again, when you believe that the meeting begins on a given day at noon by entertaining, the day before, the sense of "the meeting begins tomorrow at noon," you are idle. Apprehending the same thought the next day, by entertaining the sense of "the meeting begins now," you jump up from your chair and run down the hall.

What of the indirect reference? Is the indirect reference of a sentence containing a demonstrative in the scope of such a cognitive verb the sense or the thought?

It seems, a priori, that the "believes that" construction (to pick a particular verb) could work either way. That is,

A believes S

might be designed to tell us the sense A entertains, or the thought A apprehends. The first seems a little more efficient. If we know the sense entertained, we can compute the thought apprehended, given the believer's context.

Nevertheless, it is surely the thought apprehended that is the indirect reference of a sentence containing a demonstrative in the scope of "believes." Consider (7), (8), and (9),

(7) I believe that Russia and Canada quarreled today.

(8) Mary believed that Russia and Canada quarreled today.

(9) Mary believed that Russia and Canada quarreled yesterday.

Suppose Mary utters (7) on August 1, and I want to report the next day on what she believed. If I want to report the sense entertained, I should use (8). But now I would simply manage to say something false, that Mary believed that Russia and Canada quarreled on August 2. Clearly, I would use (9) to report her beliefs. But (9) does not exhibit the sense Mary entertained. It does get at the thought she apprehended. To get from the sentence embedded in (9) to the thought Mary apprehended, we take the value of the demonstrative in the context of the belief reporter, not in the context of the believer.

It has been suggested that we try to use the sense entertained by the believer in reporting his belief whenever possible. What we have just said does not conflict with this. The point is simply that the function of thought identification dominates the function of sense identification, and when we use demonstratives there is almost always a conflict.

There will be no conflict when one is dealing with eternal sentences, or when one is reporting one's own current beliefs. The need for distinguishing sense from thought will not be forced to our attention, so long as we concentrate on such cases.

Let us now consider the Morning Star example.

Mary says, "I believe that is the Morning Star" in the morning while pointing at Venus, and "I believe that is not the Morning Star" at night while pointing at Venus. It seems that Mary, though believing falsely, has not changed her mind and does not believe a contradiction.

As long as we think of thoughts as senses, it will seem that anyone who understands the relevant sentences, will not believe both a thought and its negation. So long as we think of senses as thoughts, we shall think that anyone who accepts a sense at one time, and its negation at another, must have changed her mind. The correct principle is simply that no thoughtful person will accept a sense and its negation in the same context, since by understanding the language she should realize that she would thereby believe both a thought and its negation.

We should take "believing a contradiction," in the sense in which thoughtful people do not do it, to mean accepting senses of the forms S and not-S, relative to the same context of utterance. Mary does not do this; she accepts S in the morning, not-S in the evening. Has she then changed her mind? This must mean coming to disbelieve a thought once believed. We should not take it to mean coming to reject a sense once accepted. I can reject, "Today is sunny and bright" today, though I accepted it yesterday, without changing my mind about anything. So Mary has not changed her mind, either.

What she does do is believe a thought and its negation. (Here we take the negation of a thought consisting of a certain object and incomplete sense, to be the thought consisting of the same object, and the negation of the incomplete sense.) I am inclined to think that only the habit of identifying sense and thought makes this seem implausible.

I have tried to suggest how, using the concepts of sense, thought, and indirect reference in a way compatible with the way Frege introduced them, but incompatible with his identifications, sentences containing demonstratives can be handled. I do not mean to imply that Frege could have simply made these alterations, while leaving the rest of his system intact. The idea of individuating thoughts by objects, or sequences of objects, would be particularly out of place in his system. The identification of thought with complete sense was not impulsive, but the result of pressure from many directions. I do not claim to have traced the problems that come to surface with demonstratives back to their ultimate origins in Frege's system.

IV

I have argued that Frege's identification of senses of sentences with thoughts leads to grave problems when sentences containing demonstratives are considered. The utterance of such a sentence in a context seems to yield only an incomplete sense and an object, not a complete sense of the sort a Fregean thought is supposed to be. He probably supposed that context supplies not just an object, but somehow a completing sense. There seems no place for such a sense to be found, save in the mind of the person who apprehends the thought expressed by the sentence. But to understand such a sentence, it is neither necessary nor sufficient to have grasped, and associated with the value of the demonstrative, any such sense. Frege's appeal to incommunicable senses in the case of "I," is probably an implausible attempt to deal with these problems. What is needed is to give up the identification of sense expressed with thought expressed. This would allow us to see the sense as a procedure for determining reference from a context, and the thought as identified by the incomplete sense and the value of the demonstrative. The identification of the thought, with the indirect reference of the sentence in the scope of a cognitive verb, need not be given up.[7]

Afterword

In 1975–76, I had a sabbatical leave from Stanford University. I tried to write a book on personal identity—a book that is still not finished. I spent almost all of the year on the problem of self-knowledge. The result was a long draft of a chapter, "On Self-Knowledge," which I read at colloquia at Stanford and UCLA. This chapter was basically an early version of Essay 2 but it began with a quick treatment of Frege. The paper got a lukewarm reaction, and Julius Moravcsik suggested I break it into two, one of which focused on Frege more adequately, the other on the contemporary distinction between *de dicto* and *de re* belief.

In claiming that demonstratives and indexicals pose a problem for Frege's theory of sense and reference, I did not mean to reject Frege's insight that when we think about an object or refer to one, some "mode of presentation" is involved. I denied only that such modes of presentation are involved in the propositions believed or expressed, which is where Frege's theory locates them. This location, and the rest of Frege's theory, impose certain conditions on modes of presentation, which I denied that they had to meet. That is not to deny Frege's insight, but a specific theory he used to explain and accommodate it. In a sense, most of the essays in this book are attempts to find the right place, or places, to put modes of presentation, once we also grant the insights of Kaplan, Kripke, Donnellan, and others that they are not part of the propositions expressed by statements involving indexicals, demonstratives, and names.

I take a mode of presentation to be a uniquely satisfiable condition. There

[7]Discussions of these issues with Robert Adams, Michael Bratman, Tyler Burge, Keith Donnellan, Dagfinn Føllesdal, Alvin Goldman, Holly Goldman, David Kaplan, and Julius Moravcsik were enormously helpful. This paper was written while I was a Guggenheim Fellow, and on sabbatical leave from Stanford University. I thank both institutions for their support.

may be many tall, bearded philosophers, but there could only be one tall*est* bearded philosopher. Being the tallest bearded philosopher is a uniquely satisfiable condition. No more than one object can meet the condition—although it is possible that less than one does so. Definite descriptions often convert nonuniquely satisfiable modes of presentation to uniquely satisfiable ones. For example, "The tall, bearded philosopher" expresses the condition of being the unique tall, bearded philosopher, a condition that is not in fact met, since there are a number of them.

We need to distinguish between absolute and relative modes of presentation. The latter are conditions that identify an object only relative to some other factor—another object, or a time or a place, for example. Absolute modes are not relative in this way. (To say that a mode of presentation identifies a given object absolutely is not to say that it does so necessarily. "The tallest bearded American philosopher in 1991" identifies an individual absolutely, but not necessarily. Suppose Dan Dennett meets this condition. He does not just meet it relative to some time or place at which the description is used, but absolutely. But he does not meet it necessarily. In some other "possible world," otherwise pretty much the same as ours, Jon Barwise, David Nivison, or David Lewis might be taller than Dennett.)

A phrase like "the tallest philosopher in this room now" supplies only a relative mode of presentation. It identifies a person only relative to a certain room and a certain time. The modes of presentation that we naturally associate with the meanings of indexicals and demonstratives are relative, not absolute. Consider the word "tomorrow." This term denotes a day only given a day; it denotes relatively, not absolutely. What I call "roles" correspond to such relative modes of presentation. They are rules for determining reference by its relation to an element of the context of utterance. What language associates with the indexical word is such a relative mode of presentation.

The problem I found with Frege's theory of sense and reference was basically that (i) relative modes of presentation are somehow involved in important types of beliefs—beliefs about oneself, the present moment, the objects one is perceiving, and the like; (ii) these relative modes of presentation do not seem to require supplementation by completing senses to understand either the cognitive state of the believer or the conditions of truth and falsity of the belief. It is hard to account for this on Frege's theory. Frege's theory requires a single entity, the thought, to be the object of belief, that for which truth arises, and the sense of the sentence. Leaving the relative modes of presentation unsupplemented works fine for the last task, but not the first two. Supplementing them with object rather than senses works fine for the first two, but not the last.

A number of writers have thought that my criticisms of Frege are incorrect. Gareth Evans' (1990) paper "Understanding Demonstratives" is probably the most influential. In this essay, Evans proposed a somewhat different way of patching up Frege's theory, which he seemed to think was what Frege himself actually had in mind. He spelled out his proposal in the last section of his paper. (He used the example "Today is F" but I am going to change it to "Tomorrow is F," to make it easier to say how I think his proposal falls short. I replace his relation R_2 in (13) and (14) below with R_{tom}.)

Suppose we combine the relative mode associated with "tomorrow" with a specific day. Call this a "particular mode of presentation." This hybrid entity, part individual, part condition, will determine a day to serve as the reference of use of "tomorrow" on a given day. Could not Frege supplement his theory with such particular modes of presentation? Then the thought expressed by, say, "Tomorrow is F," said on a certain day d, could be taken to consist of or be determined by the particular mode of presentation provided by d and "tomorrow," together with the sense of "is F." Evans uses set theory to identify this thought, giving us two formulations (I use his numbering):

(13) $\langle \lambda x(R_{tom}(x, d)),$ *Sense of* "(ξ) *is F*"$\rangle$

(14) $\langle d, \lambda x \lambda y(R_{tom}(x, y)),$ *Sense of* "(ξ) *is F*"$\rangle$

The relational mode of presentation provided by "tomorrow" combined with a particular day d seems to provide the relational property of being the day after d. The lambda notation in (13) gives us just such a property. (Evans' R_{tom} is not quite the relation of being the day after, but a relation that implies it—see his discussion of the relation corresponding to "I" in the previous section of his paper.) Different relational properties would be provided on different days. The day d itself, rather than any mode of presentation of it, seems crucial to individuating these properties, and so too the thoughts determined by them together with the sense of "is F"; this is quite explicit in (14). Thus if I say "Tomorrow is F" on July 3, this theory provides us with a particular mode of presentation of July 4, but buried inside of that mode of presentation is the day July 3, rather than a mode of presentation of it.

If objects, rather than modes of presentation of them, figure in Evans' thoughts, then they represent the same *sort* of departure from Frege's theory as do the "thoughts as information" that I proposed. (If not, the proposal remains completely obscure.) There is no reason for me to reject Evans' suggestion as being a more radical departure from Frege than my own. It is a departure, for Frege disavowed such hybrids. After all, as long as we have such objects in our thoughts, it will be possible to have different cognitive fixes on the same thought, as a result of thinking of that object in different ways. This runs contrary to Frege's argument for introducing senses, of which thoughts are a species, in the first place. Evans may have hit on an amendment that will solve Frege's problems better than the ones I suggested, but it is surely an amendment.

Evans' suggestion does not keep all of Frege's theory intact, however. His theory does keep the modes of presentation in the thoughts, and so represents less of a departure from Frege on that score than my proposal. The problem is with indirect discourse and propositional attitude reports. On Frege's approach, the thought expressed by the embedded sentence in a belief report should be the thought believed. But this will not be the case on the proposed modification. Suppose you say on d, "Tomorrow is July 4," and the next day, d', I say, "You said that today is July 4." The sentence you used, and the sentence embedded in my report, do not express the same thought on Evans' proposal. The thought corresponding to my embedded sentence will incorporate a particular mode of presentation of d' provided by d' and "today" (roughly the property of being identical with d'), while the thought you expressed would incorporate a mode of presentation of d' provided by d and "tomorrow." Hence the reference of my sentence, as embedded, will not be the thought expressed by your remark.

One might claim that the property of being identical with d' and that of being the day after d are the same property, assuming d' is the day after d, and so the relative modes of presentation can be the same, and so the thoughts can be the same. (I must admit that, in spite of Evans' efforts in this essay to broaden one's sense of what Frege was about, this still seems like a very unFregean move.) To the extent this is plausible, however, it is because of special features about time that provide a disanalogy between temporal indexicals and other families of indexicals. If d' is the day after d, that is, I suppose, something necessary. But it is not necessary that people address whom they address. If Betty says to Max, "You are foolish," and Max says "Betty said I am foolish," he has spoken correctly. But it seems that the particular modes of presentation associated by Evans' approach with Betty's use of "you" and Max's use of "I" will not be the same. And it does not seem at all plausible that the properties of being addressed by Betty, and being identical with Max, are the same.

On my proposal for modifying Frege's account to handle indexicals, the "thought as information" expressed by your sentence on d, will be just that expressed by the embedded sentence in my report of what you said, when this is considered on its own. Following Frege's theory, what is expressed by the embedded sentence considered on its own becomes the reference of that sentence as embedded. Similar remarks apply to the example of Max and Betty. So, on this score, I can claim that my modification is closer to Frege's original theory. The relative modes of presentation will appear in what I called the role of the sentence, but not in the proposition expressed, the "thought-as-information."

A bit later in his essay, Evans notes that the notion of "entertaining the role of 'I' " falls rather short of saying what it is to have an I-thought. I agree with this. My ambition was to make a distinction between two kinds of similarity in belief. This is a preliminary to understanding self-knowledge, not a theory of it.

The way I look at it, there are two different but systematically related ways in which believers can be similar. Consider the belief George Bush expresses with "I live in Kennebunkport." There are two groups of people that have similar beliefs: those who believe that Bush lives in Kennebunkport and those who believe that they live in Kennebunkport. Both sets contain virtually everyone who lives in Kennebunkport, but for different reasons. This is true of the first set because Bush and facts about him are very well known, especially, one assumes, to his neighbors in Kennebunkport. It is true of the second because most people know where they live. The first set contains lots of people who live outside of Kennebunkport, while the second probably contains relatively few, all of whom are confused. The different dimensions of doxastic similarity determine different sets that project onto other similarities in different ways and for different reasons.

The two entities with which I wanted to replace Frege's single notion of thought correspond to these two dimensions. I said a case or occasion of believing involves believing a thought (as information) by apprehending a sense (as role) in a certain context. It is important to distinguish a particular case or occasion of belief, from what is believed on that occasion. What Evans' (14) really seems to be supplying us with are some factors involved in a case of belief. In my terminology, the first element d is a bit of the context, the second element is a relation corresponding to the role of "tomorrow," and the third element is the sense of the predicate. We can think of this bundle as a bundle of factors that are involved in a case of belief, and determine both what is believed and how it is believed. So conceived, there is not yet any significant difference between this and my point of view, but there is also no candidate identified for Frege's thought—that which is believed. On the other hand, if we think of this bundle of factors as that which is believed we have identified a candidate for Frege's thought, which is quite different from the one I proposed. But this conception is not plausible. Such a bundle simply does not fit any of the three functions that Frege envisaged for thoughts.

This is not to say that the object Evans identifies in (13) and (14) is of no theoretical interest. I think it corresponds to the information one gets from an utterance when one knows certain basic facts about the utterance and lacks others. This is best brought out with a different example. Suppose that in 1988 two reporters knew that Bush had said "You will be the next vice president" to someone, but did not know to whom. One reporter heard Bush say it (but could not see to whom he was talking), the other learned about it less directly. These reporters would know that Bush's utterance is true if the person to whom he was talking becomes the next vice president. This is not what Bush said; he said that Quayle would be the next vice president. The reporters do not know enough about the context to know what Bush said; to figure this out, they would need to determine to whom Bush was talking. A proposition of the sort Evans associated with the utterance corresponds to the information these reporters have. The fact that Bush, rather than a mode of presentation of him, is a constituent of the proposition reflects that fact that we are getting at what the reporters, who have different modes of presentation of Bush, have in common. In terms of the account of cognitive significance given below in Essays 11 and 13, I would say that what Evans has identified are the incremental truth conditions of an utterance given partial knowledge of the context. In certain cases, the line between this proposition and the proposition expressed is pretty thin. This is the case when the relative mode of presentation is basically identity (as with "I," "now," and "today") and when facts about the relationship require no special knowledge, as with "tomorrow" or "yesterday."

Evans has some interesting and insightful ideas in this essay about what it is to continue to think about the same thing in the same way while one is changing contexts—as, for example, when one is tracking an object. It is hard for me to grasp how these ideas contribute to his defense of Frege, but they do seem an important contribution to the phenomenology of belief and reference. I think the two-tiered theory, particularly as it had been developed in Essay 4 would have actually provided a very good framework for Evans to explore these issues.

2

The Problem of the Essential Indexical

I once followed a trail of sugar on a supermarket floor, pushing my cart down the aisle on one side of a tall counter and back the aisle on the other, seeking the shopper with the torn sack to tell him he was making a mess. With each trip around the counter, the trail became thicker. But I seemed unable to catch up. Finally it dawned on me. I was the shopper I was trying to catch.

I believed at the outset that the shopper with a torn sack was making a mess. And I was right. But I did not believe that I was making a mess. That seems to be something I came to believe. And when I came to believe that, I stopped following the trail around the counter and rearranged the torn sack in my cart. My change in beliefs seems to explain my change in behavior. My aim in this paper is to make a key point about the characterization of this change, and of beliefs in general.

At first, characterizing the change seems easy. My beliefs changed, didn't they, in that I came to have a new one, namely, *that I am making a mess*. But things are not so simple.

The reason they are not is the importance of the word "I" in my expression of what I came to believe. When we replace it with other designations of me, we no longer have an explanation of my behavior and so, it seems, no longer an attribution of the same belief. It seems to be an *essential* indexical. But without such a replacement, all we have to identify the belief is the sentence "I am making a mess." But that sentence by itself does not seem to identify the crucial belief, for if someone else had said it, they would have expressed a different belief, a false one.

I argue that the essential indexical poses a problem for various otherwise plausible accounts of belief. I first argue that it is a problem for the view that belief is a relation between subjects and propositions conceived as bearers of truth and falsity. The problem is not solved merely by replacing or supplementing this with a notion of *de re* belief. Nor is it solved by moving to a notion of a proposition that, rather than true or false absolutely is only true or false at an index or in a context (at a time, for a speaker, say). Its solution requires us to make a sharp distinction between objects of belief and belief states, and to realize that the connection between them is not so intimate as might have been supposed.[8]

Locating Beliefs

I want to introduce two more examples. In the first, a professor, who desires to attend the department meeting on time and believes correctly that it begins at noon, sits motionless in his office at that time. Suddenly, he begins to move. What explains his action? A change in belief. He believed all along that the department meeting starts at noon; he came to believe, as he would have put it, that it starts *now*.

The author of the book *Hiker's Guide to the Desolation Wilderness* stands in the wilderness beside Gilmore Lake, looking at the Mt. Tallac trail as it leaves the lake and climbs the mountain. He desires to leave the wilderness. He believes that the best way out from Gilmore Lake is to follow the Mt. Tallac trail up the mountain to Cathedral Peaks trail, on to the Floating Island trail, emerging at Spring Creek Tract Road. But he does not move. He is lost. He is not sure whether he is standing beside Gilmore Lake, looking at Mt. Tallac, or beside Clyde Lake looking at Jack's Peak, or beside Eagle Lake looking at one of the Maggie peaks. Then he begins to move along the Mt. Tallac trail. If asked, he would have explained the crucial change in his beliefs this way: "I came to believe that *this* is the Mt. Tallac trail and *that* is Gilmore Lake."

In these three cases, the subjects in explaining their actions would use indexicals to characterize certain beliefs they came to have. These indexicals are essential, in that replacement of them by other terms destroys the force of the explanation, or at least requires certain assumptions to be made to preserve it.

Suppose I had said, in the manner of de Gaulle, "I came to believe that John Perry is making a mess." I would no longer have explained why I stopped and looked in my own cart. To explain that, I would have to add, "and I believe that I am John Perry," bringing in the indexical again. After all, suppose I had really given my explanation in the manner of de Gaulle, and said "I came to believe that de Gaulle is making a mess." That would not have explained my stopping at all. But it really would have explained it every bit as much as "I

---

[8]In thinking about the problem of the essential indexical, I have been greatly helped by the writings of Hector-Neri Castañeda on indexicality and related topics. Castañeda 1966, 1967, and 1968 focused attention on these problems, and made many of the points made here. More recently, his view on these matters have been developed as a part of his comprehensive system of generalized phenomenalism. See particularly Castañeda 1977 and 1977a. Having benefited so much from Castañeda's collection of "protophilosophical data," I regret that differences of approach and limitations of competence and space have prevented me from incorporating a discussion of his theory into this essay. I hope to make good this omission at some future time. [See below, Essay 5.]

came to believe John Perry is making a mess." For if I added "and I believe that I am de Gaulle," the explanations would be on par. The only reason "I came to believe John Perry is making a mess" seems to explain my action is our natural assumption that I did believe I was John Perry and did not believe I was de Gaulle. So replacing the indexical "I" with another term designating the same person really does, as claimed, destroy the explanation.

Similarly, our professor, as he sets off down the hall, might say "I believe the meeting starts at noon." In accepting the former as an explanation, we would be assuming he believes it is *now* noon. If he believed it was now 5 P.M., he would not have explained his departure by citing his belief that the meeting starts at noon, unless he was a member of a department with very long meetings. After all, he believed that the meeting started at noon all along, so that belief can hardly explain a change in his behavior. Basically similar remarks apply to the lost author.

I shall use the term "locating beliefs" to refer to one's beliefs about where one is, when it is, and who one is. Such beliefs seem essentially indexical. Imagine two lost campers who trust the same guidebook but disagree about where they are. If we were to try to characterize the beliefs of these campers without the use of indexicals, it would seem impossible to bring out this disagreement. If, for example, we characterized their beliefs by the set of "eternal sentences," drawn from the guidebook they would mark "true," there is no reason to suppose that the sets would differ. They could mark all of the same sentences "true," and still disagree in their locating beliefs. It seems that there has to be some indexical element in the characterization of their beliefs to bring out this disagreement. But as we shall see, there is no room for this indexical element in the traditional way of looking at belief, and even when its necessity is recognized, it is not easy to see how to fit it in.

The Doctrine of Propositions

I shall first consider how the problem appears to a traditional way of thinking of belief. The doctrines I describe were held by Frege, but I shall put them in a way that does not incorporate his terminology or the details of his view. This traditional way, which I call the "doctrine of propositions," has three main tenets. The first is that belief is a relation between a subject and an object, the latter being denoted, in a canonical belief report, by a that-clause. So "Carter believes that Atlanta is the capital of Georgia" reports that a certain relation, *believing*, obtains between Carter and a certain object—at least in a suitably wide sense of the object—*that Atlanta is the capital of Georgia*. These objects are called *propositions*.

The second and the third tenets concern such objects. The second is that they have a truth-value in an absolute sense, as opposed to merely being true for a person or at a time. The third has to do with how we individuate them. It is necessary, for *that S* and *that S'* to be the same, that they have the same truth-value. But it is not sufficient, for *that the sea is salty* and *that milk is white* are not the same proposition. It is necessary that they have the same truth condition, in the sense that they attribute to the same objects the same relation. But this also is not sufficient, for *that Atlanta is the capital of Georgia* and *that Atlanta is the capital of the largest state east of the Mississippi* are not the same proposition. Carter, it seems, might believe the first but not the second. Propositions must not only have the same truth-value and concern the same objects and relations, but also involve the same concepts. For Frege, this meant that if *that S = that S'*, S and S' must have the same sense. Others might eschew senses in favor of properties and relations, others take concepts to be just words, so that sameness of propositions is just sameness of sentences. What these approaches have in common is the insistence that propositions must be individuated in a more "fine-grained" way than is provided by truth-value or the notion of truth conditions employed above.

The Problem

It is clear that the essential indexical is a problem for the doctrine of propositions. What answer can it give to the question, "What did I come to believe when I straightened up the sugar?" The sentence "I am making a mess" does not identify a proposition. For this sentence is not true or false absolutely, but only as said by one person or another; had another shopper said it when I did, he would have been wrong. So the sentence by which I identify what I came to believe does not identify, by itself, a proposition. There is a *missing conceptual ingredient*: a sense for which I am the reference, or a complex of properties I alone have, or a singular term that refers to no one but me. To identify the proposition I came to believe, the advocate of the doctrine of propositions must identify this missing conceptual ingredient.

An advocate of the doctrine of propositions, his attention drawn to indexicals, might take this attitude towards them: they are communicative shortcuts. Just before I straightened up the sack I must have come to believe some propositions with the structure α *is making a mess*, where α is some concept that I alone "fit" (to pick a phrase neutral among the different notions of a concept). When I say "I believe I am making a mess," my hearers know that I believe some such proposition of this form; which one in particular is not important for the purposes at hand.

If this is correct, we should be able to identify the proposition I came to believe, even if doing so is not necessary for ordinary communicative purposes. But then the doctrine of propositions is in trouble, for any candidate will fall prey to the problems mentioned above. If *that* α *is making a mess* is what I came to believe, then "I came to believe that A is making a mess," where A expressed α, should be an even better explanation than the original, where I used "I" as a communicative shortcut. But, as we saw, any such explanation will be defective, working only on the assumption that I believed that I was α.

To this it might be replied that though there may be no replacement for "I" that generally preserves explanatory force, all that needs to be claimed is that there is such a replacement on each occasion. The picture is this. On each occasion that I use "I," there is some concept I have in mind that fits me uniquely, and which is the missing conceptual ingredient in the proposition that remains incompletely identified when I characterize my beliefs. The concept I use to think of myself is not necessarily the same each time I do so, and of course I must use a different one than others do, since it must fit me and not them. Because there is no general way of replacing the "I" with a term that gets at the missing ingredient, the challenge to do so in response to a particular example is temporarily embarrassing. But the doctrine of propositions does not require a general answer.

This strategy does not work for two reasons. First, even if I was thinking of myself as, say, the only bearded philosopher in a Safeway store west of the Mississippi, the fact that I came to believe that the only such philosopher was making a mess explains my action only on the assumption that I believed that I was the only such philosopher, which brings in the indexical again. Second, in order to provide me with an appropriate proposition as the object of belief, the missing conceptual ingredient will have to fit me. Suppose I was thinking of myself in the way described, but that I was not bearded and was not in a Safeway store—I had forgotten that I had shaved and gone to the A&P instead. Then the proposition supplied by this strategy would be false, while what I came to believe, *that I was making a mess*, was true.

This strategy assumes that whenever I have a belief I would characterize by using a sentence with an indexical d,

> I believe that ... d ...

that there is some conceptual ingredient c, such that it is also true that,

> I believe that d is c

and that, on this second point, I am right. But there is no reason to believe this would always be so. Each time I say "I believe it is *now* time to rake the leaves," I need not have some concept that uniquely fits the time at which I speak.

From the point of view of the doctrine of propositions, belief reports such as "I believe that I am making a mess" are deficient, for there is a missing conceptual ingredient. From the point of view of locating beliefs, there is something lacking in the propositions offered by the doctrine, a missing indexical ingredient.

The problem of the essential indexical reveals that something is badly wrong with the traditional doctrine of propositions. But the traditional doctrine has its competitors anyway, in response to philosophical pressures from other directions. Perhaps attention to these alternative or supplementary models of belief will provide a solution to our problem.

De Re Belief

One development in the philosophy of belief seems quite promising in this respect. It involves qualifying the third tenet of the doctrine of propositions, to allow a sort of proposition individuated by an object or sequence of objects, and a part of a proposition of the earlier sort. The motivation for this qualification or supplementation comes from a type of belief report, which gives rise to the same problem, that of the missing conceptual ingredient, as does the problem of the essential indexical.

The third tenet of the doctrine of propositions is motivated by the failure of substitutivity of coreferential terms within the that-clause following "believes." But there seems to be a sort of belief report, or a way of understanding some belief reports, that allows such substitution, and such successful substitution becomes a problem for a theory designed to explain its failure. For suppose Patrick believes that, as he would put it, the dean is wise. Patrick does not know Frank, much less know that he lives next to the dean, and yet I might in certain circumstances say "Patrick believes Frank's neighbor is wise." Or I might say "There is someone whom Patrick believes to be wise," and later on identify that someone as "Frank's neighbor." The legitimacy of this cannot be understood on the unqualified doctrine of propositions; I seem to have gone from one proposition, *that the dean of the school is wise*, to another, *that Frank's neighbor is wise*; but the fact that Patrick believes the first seems to be no reason he should believe the second. And the quantification into the belief report seems to make no sense at all on the doctrine of propositions, for the report does not relate Patrick to an individual known variously as "the dean" and "Frank's neighbor," but only with a concept expressed by the first of these terms.

The problem here is just that of a missing conceptual ingredient. It looked in the original report as if Patrick was being said to stand in the relation of a belief to a certain proposition, a part of which was a conceptual ingredient expressed by the words of "the dean." But if I am permitted to exchange those words for others, "Frank's neighbor," which are not conceptually equivalent, then apparently the initial part of the proposition he was credited with belief in was not the conceptual ingredient identified by "the dean" after all. So what proposition was it Patrick was originally credited with belief in? And "There is someone such that Patrick believes that he is wise" seems to credit Patrick with belief in a proposition, without telling us which one. For after the "believes" we have only "he is wise," where the "he" does not give us an appropriate conceptual ingredient, but functions as a variable ranging over individuals.

We do seem in some circumstances to allow such substitutivity, and make ready sense of quantification into belief reports. So the doctrine of propositions must be qualified. We can look upon this sort of belief as involving a relation to a new sort of proposition, consisting of an object or sequence of objects and a conceptual ingredient, a part of a proposition of the original kind, or what we might call an "open proposition." This sort of belief and this kind of proposition we call "*de re*," the sort of belief and the sort of proposition that fits the original doctrine, "*de dicto*." Taken this way, we analyze "Patrick believes that the dean of the school is wise," as reporting a relation between Patrick and a proposition consisting of a certain person variously describable as "the dean" and "Frank's neighbor" and something, *that x is wise*, which would yield a proposition with the addition of an appropriate conceptual ingredient. Since the dean himself, and not just a concept expressed by the words "the dean" is involved, substitution holds and quantification makes sense.

Here, as in the case of the essential indexical, we were faced with a missing conceptual ingredient. Perhaps, then, this modification of the third tenet will solve the earlier problem as well. But it will not. Even if we suppose—as I think we should—that when I said "I believe that I am making a mess" I was reporting a *de re* belief, our problem will remain.

One problem emerges when we look at accounts that have been offered of the conditions under which a person has a *de re* belief. The most influential treatments of *de re* belief have tried to explain it in terms of *de dicto* belief or something like it. Some terminological regimentation is helpful here. Let us couch reports of *de re* belief in terms "X believes of a that he is so and so," reserving the simpler "X believes that a is so and so" for *de dicto* belief. The simplest account of *de re* belief in terms of *de dicto* belief is this:

X believes of y that he is so and so

just in case

there is a concept α such that α fits y and X believes that α is so and so.

Now it is clear that if this is our analysis of *de re* belief, the problem of the essential indexical is still with us. For we are faced with the same problem we had before. I can believe that I am making a mess, even if there is no concept α such that I alone fit α and I believe that α is making a mess. Since I do not have any *de dicto* belief of the sort, on this account I do not have a *de re* belief of the right sort either. So, even allowing *de re* belief, we still do not have an account of the belief I acquired.

Now this simple account of *de re* belief has not won many adherents, because it is commonly held that *de re* belief is a more interesting notion than it allows. This proposal trivializes it. Suppose Nixon is the next President. Since I believe that the next President will be the next President, I would on this proposal believe of Nixon that he is the next President, even though I am thoroughly convinced that Nixon will not be the next President.[9]

To get a more interesting or useful notion of *de re* belief, philosophers have suggested that there are limitations on the conceptual ingredient involved in the *de dicto* belief that yields the *de re* belief. Kaplan, for example, requires not only that there be some α such that I believe that α will be the next President and that α denotes Nixon, for me to believe of Nixon that he will be the next President, but also that α be a *vivid name of Nixon for me* (1969, 225ff). Hintikka requires that α denote the same individual in every possible world compatible with what I believe (1967, 40ff). Each of these philosophers explains these notions in such a way that in the circumstances imagined, I would not believe of Nixon that he is the next President.

However well these proposals deal with other phenomena connected with *de re* belief, they cannot help with the problem of the essential indexical. They tighten the requirements laid down by the original proposal, but those were apparently already too restrictive. If in order to believe that I am making a mess I need not have any conceptual ingredient α that fits me, *a fortiori* I am not required to have one that is a vivid name of myself for me, or one that picks out the same individual in every possible world compatible with what I believe.

Perhaps this simply shows that the approach of explaining *de re* belief in terms of *de dicto* belief in incorrect. I think it does show that. But even so, the problem remains. Suppose we do not insist on an account of *de re* belief in terms of *de dicto* belief, but merely suppose that whenever we ascribe a belief, and cannot find a suitable complete proposition to serve as the object because of a missing conceptual ingredient, we are dealing with *de re* belief. Then we will ascribe a *de re* belief to me in the supermarket, I believed *of* John Perry that he was making a mess. But it will not be my having such a *de re* belief that explains my action.

Suppose there were mirrors at either end of the counter so that as I pushed my cart down the aisle in pursuit I saw myself in the mirror. I take what I see to be the reflection of the messy shopper going up the aisle on the other side, not realizing that what I am really seeing is a reflection of a reflection of myself. I point and say, truly, "I believe that he is making a mess." In trying to find a suitable proposition for me to believe, we would be faced with the same sorts of problems we had with my earlier report, in which I used "I" instead of "he."

---

[9]For the classic discussion of these problems, see Quine 1966.

We would not be able to eliminate an indexical element in the term referring to me. So here we have *de re* belief; I believe of John Perry that he is making a mess. But then that I believe of John Perry that he is making a mess does not explain my stopping; in the imagined circumstances I would accelerate, as would the shopper I was trying to catch. But then, even granting that when I say "I believe that I am making a mess" I attribute to myself a certain *de re* belief, the belief of John Perry that he is making a mess, our problem remains.

If we look at it with the notion of a locating belief in mind, the failure of the introduction of *de re* belief to solve our problems is not surprising. *De re* propositions remain nonindexical. Propositions individuated in part by objects remain as insensitive to what is essential in locating beliefs as those individuated wholly by concepts. Saying that I believed of John Perry that he was making a mess leaves out the crucial change, that I came to think of the messy shopper not merely as the shopper with the torn sack, or the man in the mirror, but as *me*.

Relativized Propositions

It seems that to deal with essential indexicality we must somehow incorporate the indexical element into what is believed, the object of belief. If we do so, we come up against the second tenet of the doctrine of propositions, that such objects are true or false absolutely. But the tools for abandoning this tenet have been provided in recent treatments of the semantics of modality, tense, and indexicality. So this seems a promising direction.

In possible-worlds semantics for necessity and possibility we have the notion of truth at a world. In a way this does not involve a new notion of a proposition and in a way it does. When Frege insisted that his "thoughts" were true or false absolutely, he did not mean that they had the same truth-value in all possible worlds. Had he used a possible-worlds framework, he would have had their truth-values vary from world to world, and simply insisted on a determinate truth-value in each world and in particular in the actual world. In a way, then, taking propositions to be functions from possible worlds to truth-values is just a way of looking at the old notion of a proposition.

Still, this way of looking at it invites generalization that takes us away from the old notion. From a technical point of view, the essential idea is that a proposition is, or is represented by, a function from an index to a truth-value; when we get away from modality, this same technical idea may be useful, though something other than possible worlds are taken as indices. To deal with temporal operators, we can use the notion of truth at a time. Here the indices will be times, and our propositions will be functions from times to truth-values. For example, *that Elizabeth is Queen of England* is a proposition true in 1960 but not in 1940. Hence "At some time or other Elizabeth is Queen of England" is true, simpliciter.[10]

Now consider "I am making a mess." Rather than thinking of this as partially identifying an absolutely true proposition, with the "I" showing the place of the missing conceptual ingredient, why not think of it as completely identifying a new-fangled proposition, that is true or false only *at a person*? More precisely, it is one that is true or false at a time and a person, since though true when I said it, it has since occasionally been false.

If we ignore possibility and necessity, it seems that regarding propositions as functions to truth-values from indices that are pairs of persons and times will do the trick, and that so doing will allow us to exploit relations between elements within the indices to formulate rules that bring out differences between indexicals. "I am tired now" is true at the pair consisting of the person a and the time t if and only if a is tired at t, while "You will be tired" is true at the same index if and only if the addressee of a at t is tired at some time later than t.

Does this way of looking at the matter solve the problem of the essential indexical? I say "I believe that I am making a mess." On our amended doctrine of propositions, this ascribes a relation between me and *that I am making a mess*, which is a function from indices to truth-values. The belief report seems to completely specify the relativized proposition involved; there is no missing conceptual ingredient. So the problem must be solved.

But it is not. I believed that certain proposition, *that I am making a mess* was true—true for me. So belief that this proposition was true for me then does not differentiate me from some other shopper, who believes *that I am making a mess* was true for John Perry. So this belief cannot be what explains my stopping and searching my cart for the torn sack. Once we have adopted these new-fangled propositions, which are only true at times for persons, we have to admit also that we believe them as true for persons at times, and not absolutely. And then our problem returns.

Clearly an important distinction must be made. All believing is done by persons at times, or so we may suppose. But the time of belief and the person doing the believing cannot be generally identified with the person and time relative to which the propositions believed is held true. You now believe that *that I am making a mess* was true for me, then, but you certainly do not believe it is true for you now, unless you are reading this in a supermarket. Let us call *you* and *now* the context of belief, and *me* and *then* the context of evaluation. The context of belief may be the same as the context of evaluation, but need not be.

Now the mere fact that I believed that proposition *that I am making a mess* to be true for someone at some time did not explain my stopping the cart. You

---

[10]See Montague 1974 (especially "Pragmatics") and Scott 1970.

believe so now, and doubtless have no more desire to mess up supermarkets than I did. But you are not bending over to straighten up a sack of sugar.

The fact that I believed this proposition true for Perry at the time he was in the supermarket does not explain my behavior either. For so did the other shopper. And you also now believe this proposition was true for Perry at the time he was in the supermarket.

The important difference seems to be that for me the context of belief was just the context of evaluation, but for the other shopper it was not and for you it is not. But this does not do the trick either.

Consider our tardy professor. He is doing research on indexicals, and has written on the board "My meeting starts now." He believes that the proposition expressed by this sentence is true at noon for him. He has believed so for hours, and at noon the context of belief comes to be the context of evaluation. These facts give us no reason to expect him to move.

Or suppose I think to myself that the person making the mess should say so. Turning my attention to the proposition, I certainly believe *that I am making a mess* is true for the person who ought to be saying it (or the person in the mirror, or the person at the end of the trail of sugar) at that time. The context of evaluation is just the context of belief. But there is no reason to suppose I would stop my cart.

One supposes that in these cases the problem is that the context of belief is not believed to be the context of evaluation. But formulating the required belief will simply bring up the problem of the essential indexical again. Clearly and correctly we want the tardy professor, when he finally sees he must be off to the meeting, to be ready to say "I believe that the time at which it is true *that the meeting starts now* is now." On the present proposal, we analyze the belief he thereby ascribes to himself as belief in the proposition *that the time at which it is true that the meeting starts now is now*. But he certainly can believe at noon that this whole proposition is true at noon, without being ready to say "It is starting now" and leave. We do not yet have a solution to the problem of the essential indexical.

Limited Accessibility

One may take all that has been said so far as an argument for the existence of a special class of propositions, propositions of limited accessibility. For what have we really shown? All attempts to find a formula of the form "A is making a mess," with which any of us at any time could express what I believed, have failed. But one might argue that we can hardly suppose that there was not anything that I believed; surely I believed just that proposition which I expressed, on that occasion, with the words "I am making a mess." That we cannot find a sentence that always expresses this proposition when said by anyone does not show that it does not exist. Rather it should lead us to the conclusion that there is a class of propositions that can only be expressed in special circumstances. In particular, only I could express the proposition I expressed when I said "I am making a mess." Others can see, perhaps by analogy with their own case, that there is a proposition that I express, but it is in a sense inaccessible to them.

Similarly, at noon on the day of the meeting, we could all express the proposition the tardy professor expressed with the words "The meeting starts now." But once that time has passed, the proposition becomes inaccessible. We can still identify it as the proposition that was expressed by those words at that time. But we cannot express it with those words any longer, for with each passing moment they express a different proposition. And we can find no other words to express it.

The advocate of such a stock of propositions of limited accessibility may not need to bring in special propositions accessible only at certain places. For it is plausible to suppose that other indexicals can be eliminated in favor of "I" and "now." Perhaps "That is Gilmore Lake" just comes to "What I see now in front of me is Gilmore Lake." But elimination of either "I" or "now" in favor of the other seems impossible.

Such a theory of propositions of limited accessibility seems acceptable, even attractive, to some philosophers.[11] Its acceptability or attractiveness will depend on other parts of one's metaphysics; if one finds plausible reasons elsewhere for believing in a universe that has, in addition to our common world, myriads of private perspectives, the idea of propositions of limited accessibility will fit right in.[12] I have no knockdown argument against such propositions, or the metaphysical schemes that find room for them. But I believe only in a common actual world. And I do not think the phenomenon of essential indexicality forces me to abandon this view.

The Obvious Solution?

Let us return to the device of the true/false exam. Suppose the lost author had been given such an exam before and after he figured out where he was. Would we expect any differences in his answers? Not so long as the statements contained no indexicals. "Mt. Tallac is higher than either of the Maggie Peaks" would have been marked the same way before and after, the same way he would have marked it at home in Berkeley. His mark on that sentence would tell us nothing about where he thought he was. But if the exam were to contain such sentences as "That is Gilmore Lake in front of me," we would expect a dramatic change, from "False" or "Unsure" to "True."

Imagine such an exam given to various lost campers in different parts of the

---

[11] Frege seems to accept something like it, as necessary for dealing with "I" (1918/1967).

[12] See Castañeda 1977a, especially section II.

Wilderness. We could classify the campers by their answers, and such a classification would be valuable for prediction and explanation. Of all the campers who marked "This is Gilmore Lake" with "True," we would say they believed that they were at Gilmore Lake. And we should expect them to act accordingly; if they possessed the standard guidebook and wished to leave the Wilderness, we might expect what is, given one way of looking at it, the same behavior: taking the path up the mountain above the shallow end of the lake before them.

Now consider all the good-hearted people who have ever been in a supermarket, noticed sugar on the floor, and been ready to say "I am making a mess." They all have something important in common, something that leads us to expect their next action to be that of looking into their grocery carts in search of the torn sack. Or consider all the responsible professors who have ever uttered "The department meeting is starting now." They too have something important in common; they are in a state that will lead those just down the hall to go to the meeting, those across campus to curse and feel guilty, those on leave to smile.

What the members within these various groups have in common is not what they believe. There is no *de dicto* proposition that all the campers or shoppers or professors believe. And there is no person whom all the shoppers believe to be making a mess, no lake all the campers believe to be Gilmore Lake, and no time at which all the professors believe their meetings to be starting.

We are clearly classifying the shoppers, campers and professors into groups corresponding to what we have been calling "relativized propositions"—abstract objects corresponding to sentences containing indexicals. But what members of each group have in common, which makes the groups significant, is not belief that a certain relativized proposition is true. Such belief, as we saw, is belief that such a proposition is true at some context of evaluation. Now all of the shoppers believe that *that I am making a mess* is true at some context of evaluation or other, but so does everyone else who has ever given it a moment's thought. And similar remarks apply to the campers and the professors.

If believing the same relativized proposition is not what the members of each of the groups have in common with one another, why is it being used as a principle of classification? I propose we look at things in this way. The shoppers, for example, are all in a certain belief state, a state that, given normal desires and other belief states they can be expected to be in, will lead each of them to examine his cart. But although they are all in the same belief state (not the same *total* belief state, of course), they do not all have the same belief (believe the same thing, have the relation of belief to the same object).

We use sentences with indexicals or relativized propositions to individuate belief states, for the purposes of classifying believers in ways useful for explanation and prediction. That is, belief states individuated in this way enter into our commonsense theory about human behavior and more sophisticated theories emerging from it. We expect all good-hearted people in the state that leads them to say "I am making a mess" to examine their grocery carts, no matter what belief they have in virtue of being in that state. That we individuate belief states in this way doubtless has something to do with the fact that one criterion for being in the states we postulate—at least for articulate, sincere adults—is being disposed to utter the indexical sentence in question. A good philosophy of mind should explain this in detail; my aim is merely to get clear about what it is that needs explaining.

The proposal, then, is that there is not an identity, or even an isomorphic correspondence, but only a systematic relationship between the belief states one is in and what one thereby believes. The opposite assumption, that belief states should be classified by propositions believed, seems to be built right into traditional philosophies of belief. Given this assumption, whenever we have believers in the same belief state, we must expect to find a proposition they all believe, and differences in belief state lead us to expect a difference in proposition believed. The bulk of this paper consisted in following such leads to nowhere (or to propositions of limited accessibility).

Consider a believer whose belief states are characterized by a structure of sentences with indexicals or relativized propositions (those marked "true" in a very comprehensive exam, if we are dealing with an articulate, sincere adult). This structure, together with the context of belief—the time and identity of the speaker—will yield a structure of *de re* propositions. The sequence of objects will consist of the values that the indexicals take in the context. The open propositions will be those yielded by the relativized proposition when shorn of its indexical elements. These are what the person believes, in virtue of being in the states he is in, when and where he is in them.[13]

This latter structure is important, and classifications of believers by *what* they believe are appropriate for many purposes. For example, usually, when a believer moves from context to context, his belief states adjust to preserve beliefs held. As time passes, I go from the state corresponding to "The meeting will begin" to the one corresponding to "The meeting is beginning" and finally to "The meeting has begun." All along I believe of noon that it is when the meeting begins. But I believe it in different ways. And to these different ways of believing the same thing, different actions are appropriate: preparation, movement, apology. Of course, if the change of context is not noted, the adjustment of belief states will not occur, and a wholesale change from believing truly to believing falsely may occur. This is what happened to Rip Van Winkle. He awakes in the same belief states he fell asleep in twenty years ear-

---

[13]This two-tiered structure of belief states and propositions was suggested by David Kaplan's system of characters and contents (1979). While Kaplan's motivations for the distinction were basically semantical, it seems to me that the present considerations also supply an epistemological motivation for it. (See also Kaplan 1989.)

lier, unadjusted to the dramatic change in context, and so with a whole new set of beliefs, such as that he is a young man, mostly false.

We have here a metaphysically benign form of limited accessibility. Anyone at any time can have access to any proposition. But not in any way. Anyone can believe of John Perry that he is making a mess. And anyone can be in the belief state classified by the sentence "I am making a mess." But only I can have that belief by being in that state.

There is room in this scheme for *de dicto* propositions, for the characterization of one's belief states may include sentences without any indexical element. If there are any, they could appear on the exam. For this part of the structure, the hypothesis of perfect correspondence would be correct.

A more radical proposal would do away with objects of belief entirely. We would think of belief as a system of relations of various degrees between persons and other objects. Rather than saying I believed in the *de re* proposition consisting of me and the open proposition, *x is making a mess*, we would say that I stand in the relation, believing to be making a mess, to myself. There are many ways to stand in this relation to myself, that is, a variety of belief states I might be in. And these would be classified by sentences with indexicals. On this view, *de dicto* belief, already demoted from its central place in the philosophy of belief, might be seen as merely an illusion, engendered by the implicit nature of much indexicality.

To say that belief states must be distinguished from objects of belief, cannot be individuated in terms of them, and are what is crucial for the explanation of action, is not to give a full-fledged account of belief, or even a sketchy one. Similarly, to say that we must distinguish the object seen from the state of the seeing subject, and that the latter is crucial for the explanation of action guided by vision, is not to offer a full-fledged account of vision. But just as the arguments from illusion and perceptual relativity teach us that no philosophy of perception can be plausible that is not cognizant of this last distinction, the problem of the essential indexical should teach us that no philosophy of belief can be plausible that does not take account of the first.[14]

[14] Versions of this paper were read at philosophy department colloquia at UCLA, Claremont Graduate School, and Stanford University, to the Washington State University at Bellingham Philosophy Conference, and to the Meeting of Alberta Philosophy Departments. I am indebted to philosophers participating in these colloquia for many helpful criticisms and comments. I owe a special debt to Michael Bratman and Dagfinn Føllesdal for detailed comments on the penultimate version. Most of the ideas in this paper were developed while I held a fellowship from the Guggenheim Foundation and was on sabbatical leave from Stanford University, and I thank both for their support.

Afterword

Essay 2 was the second paper that emerged from the chapter "On Self Knowledge" after I followed Moravcsik's suggestion to split it into two. It was given at a number of colloquia and delivered at the Central Division meetings of the American Philosophical Association in Salt Lake City in 1979, and published in *Noûs*. One should note that the positive theory advanced here is not exactly the same as that in Essay 1. In that paper I was trying to construct a conservative modification of Frege's view to take care of the problems I saw indexicals and demonstratives posing for it, while in this paper I was putting forward my own view. The modification of the Fregean view is, I think, fairly described as involving direct and indirect objects of thought. (See Lewis 1979.) Frege's view falls within the classical intentionalist tradition, which sees beliefs as fundamentally characterized by their objects. My own view is that belief involves being in a state with a certain causal role in a set of wider circumstances. One can classify these beliefs in a variety of ways, relying more or less on the state and the circumstance. Characterizing them by the proposition believed is one way; characterizing them by the sentence accepted is another. These characterizations project onto different sets of similarities, and are useful for different purposes. David Lewis argued that his way of dealing with these cases had an advantage over the one I described in Essay 1 in that he has only one object of belief, properties, while I had two (1979). I do not think this criticism applies to the view in Essay 2. In fact, I think my own way of looking at things is more congenial to Lewis' physicalism than his own, although of course his view fits beautifully with his brand of possible-worlds semantics. I say a bit more about Lewis' account in footnote 3 of Essay 6 and the last section of Essay 9.

Robert Stalnaker argues that my account leaves out "the informational content" that is crucial in the case of essential indexicals (1981). His candidate for this role is what he calls the diagonal proposition. Consider the case where I say "I am standing." Call the token I use t. Suppose, for the sake of argument, that tokens are not necessarily tied to their producers—that the very token that one person in fact produces, could have been produced by others. Now consider the set of possible worlds in which t is true. Be careful. Do not consider the set of possible worlds in which *what I say* is true. That is just the set of worlds in which I am standing. In many of these worlds, t will never have been produced. Consider instead the possible worlds in which t is produced by the various people that we have agreed could have produced it. In some of those, the producer will be standing. The set of those worlds is the proposition we want. Call this proposition P.

We might say that P is more tightly tied by the meaning of t to the utterance of t than is the proposition expressed. We can determine the proposition expressed only given information about who is the speaker, but this information is not necessary to determine the diagonal proposition. For this reason, it is natural to think that *P is* an important part of the story. Jaakko Hintikka also recognizes the importance of these diagonal propositions in his theory of demonstrative identification.

I think this proposition is an important part of the story. It gets at the information that someone who hears the utterance, recognizes the type, and understands the meaning will get from the utterance, independently of whether they know the relevant contextual factors. Suppose, for example, I hear a cry, "I am standing" coming from the next room. I do not know who is saying it. But, at least if I regard the utterance as providing information, I do know that *whoever* uttered the token I hear is standing. Stalnaker's diagonal proposition is roughly what I call "the proposition created" in Essay 11 and the "nonincremental truth conditions" in Essay 13. These essays develop an account of the epistemology of utterances that gives this proposition a central role.

So I agree with Stalnaker that something was missing in Essay 2, although I want to insist on a number of points.

The first point is that it is a bit misleading to call the diagonal proposition, important as it is, *the* informational content. It is not the content, in the sense of what is said. It is not the information that one usually intends to convey. It is not the belief that one is attempting to express.

We might then ask, what is it? The answer, from the "classificatory" view of propositional attitudes that is emerging in Essay 2, is that there are many propositions that arise from the meaning of a sentence uttered or accepted that can be used to classify the belief for various purposes. On the classical picture of "intentionality," a propositional attitude consists in a relation to a proposition, what is believed (desired, etc.). That proposition is essential to the attitude. On the classificatory picture, the proposition believed (desired, etc.) is determined in part by external factors that are not essential to the attitude in question. It is one way of classifying belief that is useful for many purposes. The diagonal proposition is another way of classifying the belief that involves quantifying over certain contextual factors rather than fixing them. Stalnaker has found an important proposition that we need in the epistemology of language, one I later call "the cognitive significance of the utterance," but he has not found *the* content. The diagonal proposition simply is not the content, if we use "content" in Kaplan's sense, as what is said. It is not *the* content, if we use "content" to mean a proposition that gets at information that might be conveyed, for there are many contents in this sense.

The idea that to be relevant to classifying a belief, a proposition must be part of what is believed is what is called the "fallacy of misplaced information" in Essay 6 and in Barwise and Perry 1983.

The final point is that I believe the diagonal proposition is best conceived of in the old-fashioned way, the way Reichenbach originally thought about it, as the "token-reflexive proposition." That is, it is a singular proposition about tokens. This is the way diagonal propositions come into the later essays mentioned above, with the important difference that the key proposition is actually an *utterance*-reflexive proposition, rather than a *token*-reflexive one. These propositions, like all singular propositions, can be believed in more than one way, because a single token or utterance can be presented in more than one way. If the reader thinks about tape-recordings, echos, written tokens, and the like, she will be able to think of many examples of this.

3

Belief and Acceptance

When asked what I believe, I typically respond with a sentence, or a sentence embedded in a that-clause: that the Giants will lose; that life is short; that philosophy is noble. I would use the same sentences to describe the world to others, and in my own thinking about it. I shall say that I *accept* them.[15]

I think acceptance is not belief and not analyzable in terms of belief; rather, it is an important component of belief. It is the contribution the subject's mind makes to belief. One has a belief *by* accepting a sentence. Which belief one thereby has also depends on who the believer is and when the believing takes place—factors that need have no representation in the mind. What one thereby believes is not a sentence, nor a sentence meaning, nor one of Frege's thoughts—an abstract object with a sentence-like structure. It is rather, as Russell thought, a complex of objects and properties—objects and properties that are part of the world, not part of the mind (except in rare instances).

In saying that acceptance is the contribution the subject's mind makes to belief, I mean this. When we believe, we do so by being in belief states. These states have typical effects, which we use to classify them. In particular, we classify them by the sentences a competent speaker of the language in question would be apt to think or utter in certain circumstances when in that state. To accept a sentence S is to be in a belief state that would distinguish such speakers who would think and utter S from those who would not. Thus my conception allows an animal or a preverbal child to be meaningfully said to accept a sentence.

How sentences designed to describe a public world can have this secondary role of describing minds is an interesting question, but one I shall not pursue

---

[15] A handy word to use for our attitude toward sentences, "accepts" has been given various technical meanings by various authors. I apologize for appropriating it but ask that the reader avoid reading more into it than I have put, except insofar as is required by ordinary standards of sympathetic understanding.

here.[16] In this paper I merely want to argue that acceptance is not belief, and not reducible to it.

I think confusing acceptance with belief has wreaked havoc in the philosophy of belief, in the philosophy of mind, and in metaphysics generally. It requires that we see what is believed, and so what is true and false, on the model of what is accepted; belief is thus treated as a relation to a sentence or sentence-like entity. When we come across an ineluctably ordinary belief—a belief that some object has some property—we invent a special name for it ("*de re* belief") and wonder how it is possible. The conflation of acceptance and belief creates the sort of tension in which metaphysics is inevitable. We want *what is believed* to classify belief states for purposes of explaining thought and action—the proper role of what is accepted—while at the same time being objectively true or false, the common objects of belief for different persons at different times. This requires that the subject's mind conceptualize its own perspective on the world, a condition that cannot be satisfied; at this point we stop just short of an inarticulate groan and begin to talk of "intuition."

My focus shall be on context-dependent sentences.[17] The acceptance of context-dependent sentences is a matter of some importance. That I accept "This paper is due today" explains, together with certain facts about my work habits, my frantic activity. Section I argues that such sentences are not *what is believed*, and I suspect most will agree with that conclusion. But there remains the possibility that acceptance of context-dependent sentences will be viewed as a by-product combining two things: (i) one's understanding of words like "I" and "now," (ii) beliefs in Fregean thoughts or context-independent sentences, which capture what it is to locate oneself as a certain person at a certain time and place in the world.

In sections II through VI, I try to show that this picture is topsy-turvy by showing that no analysis of acceptance of context-dependent sentences is possible in terms of such *de dicto* beliefs. My goal is negative and limited: acceptance will not be given an iron-clad definition; my positive views will be ill-explained and largely undefended; *de dicto* belief will not be totally banished. My hope is merely to establish that acceptance is an important phenomenon, involved in the structure of belief, and involved not as a by-product but as a central component.

---

[16]This question is addressed in Barwise and Perry 1981a.

[17]I would define context-dependent sentences as those that when accepted by different people or at different times result in different beliefs. Thus if you and I both accept "I wrote this paper," we believe different things. This definition prejudges the issue in section I, however. So until section II we may rely on the definition that context-dependent sentences are those that may be true as uttered by one person at one time, but false as uttered at another time or by another person. A context-dependent term is one that stands for different things as used by different people or at different times.

I

Frege says, "If someone wants to say the same today as he expressed yesterday using the word 'today', he must replace this with 'yesterday' " (1918/1967). I think he is making a correct point about one familiar sense of "say." If I uttered to M. B. tomorrow the same sentence I produced today, viz., "This paper is due today," he could legitimately complain: "That's not what you said yesterday. Yesterday you said that it was due then." And if I say to him tomorrow, "This paper was due yesterday," it would be quite appropriate for him to agree: "That's what you said yesterday." In the first instance, I would have produced the same sentence on successive days yet said different things; in the second instance, I would have produced different sentences but said the same thing. Thus it seems clear that, in this common sense of "say," what is said is not the sentence produced. I produce a sentence, and my producing the sentence is crucial to my saying something: it is just what I do *in order to* say something. But the sentence itself is not *what* I say.

The problem is not that we are dealing with lifeless sentences instead of their vital meanings. The meanings, like the sentences, were the same in the first instance and different in the second. "This paper is due today" will have the same meaning tomorrow as it has today, and "This paper was due yesterday" will never come to mean the same as "This paper is due today," barring a radical change in the language.

Now if belief involves, at least paradigmatically and for reasonably articulate adults, saying or being disposed to say sentences to oneself and to others, it would not be surprising if the same points carried over. And they do. If tomorrow I am disposed to say to myself and others "This paper is due today," I will believe something different from what I now believe; I will have changed my mind. And if I do not change my mind, I will be disposed to say to myself and others, "This paper was due yesterday." Acceptance of the same sentence today and tomorrow indicates that I believed different things; acceptance of different sentences is required to believe the same thing. So it seems that what is believed is not a sentence (nor the meaning of a sentence).

Now in these last remarks, in speaking of what I say to myself and others, I have been using "say" in a sense that contrasts with that used in the quote from Frege. In this sense it seems that what is said *is* a sentence. There clearly is a sense in which, had I uttered "This paper is due today" on the successive days, I would have said the same thing. Now one might think that this is a more "strict" or "literal" sense of "say," from which the sense discussed before has developed as a strictly unnecessary but practically useful way of grouping sentences that are, for certain purposes, only irrelevantly different. And one might further suppose that any of the verbs denoting activities in which the production of sentences or the disposition to produce sentences is a crucial part would admit of a similar strict or literal sense.

But this would be a mistake. For a particularly clear case, consider promising. My brother first drew my attention to these issues by making a promise to me with these words: "I will give you a dollar tomorrow." The next day, when I asked for my dollar, he laughed and said, "I promised to give you a dollar tomorrow, and I will." This kept up for several days until I got what I thought was the point: that tomorrow never comes. I am now sure that the point my brother was after was the difference between the sentence used in promising and what is promised. For, of course, when he said "I promised to give you a dollar tomorrow," he was not right, as he well knew. To make that promise, he would have had to say, originally "I will give you a dollar the day after tomorrow." So what is promised, like what is said, cannot be identified with the sentence used in promising. The point is that unlike "say," "promise" has no sense in which what is promised is a sentence. Certainly a writer might promise to write a sentence, or rewrite one, but then writing or rewriting the sentence is promised, not the sentence itself.

In this particular, believing is like promising and not like saying. I can discover no sense in which what is believed is a sentence. We can believe a sentence to be true, but that does not make the sentence *what is believed*, any more than the fact that we can believe an automobile to be rusty means that automobiles are sometimes *what is believed*.

In constructing reports of beliefs, we use that-clauses containing sentences. When people report their current beliefs, they will put in the that-clause just the sentences they accept. Thus I now report that I believe that this paper is due today using the very sentence I accept: "This paper is due today." This fact suggests the view that this sentence, or something intimately connected to it, perhaps its meaning, is what is believed. If, in thinking about belief, we concentrate on the beliefs we have now, this suggestion will seem compelling.

But the facts of first-person, present-tense reports of beliefs are quite special. In reporting beliefs of others, or our own past beliefs, we will not generally be able to produce a singular term denoting what is or was believed by prefacing the sentence accepted with "that." You now accept, let us suppose, "I did not write this article." If I report "You believe that I did not write this article," I get it wrong. By accepting "I did not write this article," you believe that you did not write this article, not that I did not. Yesterday I accepted "Nothing is due today." I cannot now report the belief I had by saying "I believed that nothing is due today." It is not my purpose in this paper to say much of anything about the nature of what is believed. But I hope a convincing case has been made for the negative claim that what is believed is not in general the sentence accepted.

II

These arguments show that acceptance and belief must be distinguished where context-dependent sentences are involved. One might still try to dismiss acceptance as an important notion in the philosophy of belief by maintaining (i) that for context-independent sentences, acceptance may be identified with belief; (ii) that acceptance of context-dependent sentences may be analyzed in terms of belief in context-independent sentences and certain other notions, such as *understanding* and *meaning*.

I shall not argue against (i) here, though I think it is wrong; I concentrate on (ii).

Now a natural suggestion for carrying out the analysis called for in (ii) is that acceptance of a context-dependent sentence is no more than the belief that the sentence is true by one who understands what the sentence means. If I accept a sentence, and have the concepts of a sentence and of truth, it is natural to suppose that I believe it to be true. Nevertheless, accepting a sentence and believing it to be true are quite different things.

Acceptance is a relation a person has to a sentence at a time. The person is the person who accepts, the time is the time that he does the accepting. Believing to be true is a more complex relation. Someone has to do the believing, and he must do it at some time. But that is not enough. A person and a time have to come in again. For most sentences are not simply true or false, but true or false *as uttered by some person at some time*.

Consider "I am the President." The sentence as such has no truth-value, and no one who understands it would suppose that it does. It would be true if said by Carter now, false if said by him ten years ago, or by Jerry Brown now. To believe it *simpliciter* makes no sense. Thus acceptance is a three-place relation, while believing-true is a five-place relation.

This shows that acceptance and believing-true are different things, but not that they are very different. There might be an analysis of acceptance in terms of believing-true in which the extra argument places are absorbed by appropriate terms.

The simplest possible move would be this:

(A) At t, X accepts "S"

    iff

    For some τ and some α, at t X believes that "S" is true for α at τ.[18]

---

[18]The letter S is a schematic letter in such displayed formulas, while used in the main text as a metalinguistic variable. τ and α are variables ranging over *terms*, which may be thought of either as expressions or as concepts or senses, depending on what sort of thing is taken to be *what is believed*. They are supposed to function appropriately after "believes that." Thus, if we suppose Fregean thoughts are believed, "X believes that 'S' is true for α at τ" means that X believes the thought composed of the sense of " 'S' is true for," α, the sense of "at," and τ. "Designates" will be used later for the relation between terms and what they stand for, and so will share the ambiguity of "term."

This is, of course, not plausible. I believe that "I am President" is true for Carter on July 4, 1979, but I do not accept "I am the President."

The problem, it seems, is that "Carter" and "July 4, 1979" do not designate the right person and time. Suppose we add, then, that α must designate X and τ must designate t:

(B) At t, X accepts "S"
    iff
    There are α and τ such that:(i) At t, X believes that "S" is true for α at τ; (ii) α designates X and τ designates t.

The idea is that acceptance of a sentence—that is, being ready to use it to describe the world and to characterize one's own beliefs—is just the state one is in whenever one believes that sentence to be true for oneself at that moment. One might, of course, believe this of certain sentences that one does not understand and so is hardly prepared to use. So I shall assume that the believer understands the meaning of S.

However, (B) does not work. Let S be "My meeting starts now." If I know on July 4, 1979, that my meeting is scheduled for noon, July 4, 1979, then I may well believe right at noon on that day:

"My meeting starts now" is true for J. P. at noon,
July 4, 1979.

And yet I might not accept "my meeting begins now" right at that moment, having lost track of time (or, less probably, having lost track of who I am).

III

The problem is clearly that for any context-independent α and τ, my thinking that "my meeting begins now" is true for α at τ does not guarantee that I think the sentence true for *me now*—as I would have put it at the time. It is natural, then, to try to work the "me" and the "now" into the right side of the biconditional:

(C) At t, X accepts "S"
    iff
    There are α at τ such that:
    (i)   At t, X believes that "'S' is true for me, now" is true for α at τ.
    (ii) α designates X and τ designates t.

But this condition fails, for the same reason as (B). From the fact that I believe at noon, July 4, 1979, that the sentence

"'My meeting starts now' is true for me, now"

is true for J. P. at noon on July 4, 1979, it simply does not follow that I then accept "My meeting starts now."

IV

Rather than engage in further futile semantic ascent, we might try an epistemic condition.

(D) At t, X accepts "S"
    iff
    There are α and τ such that:
    (i)   At t, X believes that "S" is true for α and τ.
    (ii) α designates X and τ designates t.
    (iii) At t, X believes that *he* is α and it is *then* τ.

I think, on an ordinary reading of (D), it is true—at least if values for X are restricted to those who understand the locution "true for ... at ...." (D) is true because we ordinarily would take the emphasized "he" and "then" in (iii) to be what Hector-Neri Castañeda calls quasi-indicators (1967). Used as a quasi-indicator, "he" performs two functions. First, like a pronoun, it picks up the reference to X. But it also tells us how the believer thinks of X. "He" tells us X thinks of X as *himself*. He thinks of himself in the way that we think of ourselves when we use the word "I." Similarly, "then" tells us that at t, X thought of t as "now."

(D) does not succeed in analyzing acceptance in terms of believing-true, however, for the belief predicate in (iii) is not "believes-true." "Smith believes that *he* is Smith" does not mean that Smith believes that "he is Smith" is true, or believes that it is true for Smith, as reapplications of the arguments and examples used above will show.

I think that when we use quasi-indicators we combine a remark about what Smith believes with a remark, or a hint, about *how* he believes it. In the case of "he," the second bit of information is roughly that he believes what he believes *in virtue of* accepting a sentence with "I" in it. That is, "Smith believes that *he* is α" tells us that Smith believes Smith to be α in virtue of accepting "I am α." More precisely, it tells us that he accepts it in virtue of being in a certain belief state, which in English-speaking adults typically results in the utterance, in appropriate circumstances, of "I am α."

If this is correct, (D) does not succeed as an analysis of acceptance in terms of belief, for the biconditional is true only because of an implicit remark about acceptance on the right-hand side. But another type of account of quasi-indication is possible and must be considered.

V

The second possible explanation of the quasi-indicators "he" and "then" supposes that they go proxy for context-independent terms. "Smith believes that *he* is Smith" tells us that Smith believes that α is Smith, where α is a term that plays a very special role in Smith's thinking, though not in anyone else's. α plays the same role in Smith's thinking that "I" plays in the thinking of English-speakers, so that if Smith believes that α is so-and-so, and speaks English, he will accept "I am so-and-so." On this conception, "I" can play this role in the thinking of each of us *because* it is linked in our thinking to *some* such context-independent term.

Similarly, "At t, Smith believed it was then time to leave" tells us that at t, Smith believed that it was time to leave at τ, where τ is a term that at t, but not at other times, played a very special role in Smith's thinking. τ played the very same role in Smith's thinking, at t, that "now" plays in the thinking of English-speakers at all times. And it is supposed that "now" plays this role, at any given time, by being linked in our thinking to some such context-independent term.

It is clear that α will have to designate Smith, unless he is wrong about who he is, and so each of us will have to have our own special term. This, in the view being considered, explains the usefulness of the quasi-indicator. Often it will be clear to us that a person is thinking of himself with his "special term," though we do not know what term it is.

It seems clear that for many of us, our own proper name will come close to being such a special term for ourselves. Actually, most of us are aware, through hearing of namesakes or through studying Tyler Burge's theory of proper names, that few of us have names that are unique to us. But each of us probably went through a period of time when we were not aware of this. During that time, our proper name played the same role that α is supposed to play for Smith. Indeed, although I have met namesakes *and* studied Burge, this biconditional is probably almost true:

I accept "I am so-and-so" iff I believe that John Perry is so-and-so.

Of course, the special role that "John Perry" and "I" play in my thinking goes far beyond their interchangeability. When I accept "I am to be slugged," I feel terror, for example. (See Essay 2.)

The relation between "I" and my proper name appears to me to be this. "I" has this peculiar role in the thinking of everyone who understands it. Its having this role is tied to its meaning—not the special meaning it has for each of us, but the common meaning it has for all of us. "John Perry," on the other hand, does not have this special role in my thinking in virtue of what it means. It means the same for all of us as it does for me, but plays the special role in question only in my thinking. It has this special role in my thinking because I was taught, when young, to come when I heard the words (roughly) "John Perry better get over here," to say "John Perry is hungry" when hungry, and so forth. *In a sense* "John Perry" has this special role in my thinking because it stands for me, for if it did not stand for me, my parents would not have trained me in this way. But it is the training that is crucial. They could have trained me, perhaps as a patriotic joke, to respond to and use "Dwight David Eisenhower" in this way, and then that name would have played this special role in my thinking. Yet this would not have made "Dwight David Eisenhower" stand for me, even when I used it. (To see this, imagine my parents had taught me wrongly that the state we lived in was California. "California" would then have played a special role in my thought and action; I would have worried about earthquakes more than I did when I heard that California had many of them. This would not mean that "California" stood for Nebraska but that I was wrong about where I was.)

I suspect that my own name acquired a special role in my thinking before I learned that "I" always stood for the person using it, and accepted "I am John Perry." Now, on the other hand, I, like most adults, use "I" rather than my own name to think about myself. It is conveniently short, and we have learned to use it when speaking to others. And at least for philosophers, "I" has a certain epistemic advantage over their own name, since it is easier to imagine one's parents playing a cruel joke about one's name than to imagine being systematically misled by one's whole community about the meaning of "I."

The importance of "I," then, is simply that, thanks to its context dependence, we can all be trained so that it plays the same role in our thinking, while being right about who we are. We could probably get along without "I," or some other context-dependent way of referring to ourselves. On the other hand, our proper names seem dispensable in favor of "I," too.

Now let us return to the account of quasi-indication under consideration. When I say "Smith believes that *he* is so-and-so," it is supposed that I am saying that there is some context-independent term α that plays a special role in his thinking, and that he believes α is so-and-so. Although there may be such context-independent terms for some people some of the time, there is no reason to suppose that there must be such terms for all of us all of the time. Even if I forget my name, or have such a fit of skepticism that I am not sure I have a name, I can still believe things of myself by using the word "I" in my thinking.

But I have admitted that there is nothing inevitable about the word "I." There could be a person who only thought of himself with his name. Is not the account put forward in the last section disproved by this possibility?

I think it is not. The importance of the word "I" is not that everyone who has beliefs about himself must use it, or an indexical like it, to think of himself. Rather, it is that because its role in thinking is tied to its meaning, it can be used to *characterize* that cognitive role in a general way. To *accept* "I am so-and-so," a person need not understand the word "I," but only be in a state that, were he to understand "I," would lead him to use "I am so-and-so."

Suppose a one-and-a-half-year-old, with no mastery of "I," says "Joey wants Post Toasties." We say "he says *he* wants Post-Toasties," where the "he" is a quasi-indicator. We mean he is in a state that would lead him, if he had mastery of "I," to say "I want Post-Toasties."

As far as I can see, it is unnecessary, for such quasi-indexical attribution, that the child have any term for himself at all. I explain a visually disoriented child's ducking when objects are tossed well to one side of him saying, "He sees them as coming toward him." The "him" is a quasi-indicator. He would, if he were an adult, say "They are coming at me." But he is not thinking of himself with a name or under a description or with an indexical. He is simply perceiving things in a certain way that leads naturally to the ducking behavior. We can use the first-person "pronoun" to help describe such ways of perceiving and thinking, not because it is universally present but because, in virtue of its context-dependence, it is universally suitable.

The account of quasi-indication under consideration in this section seems even less plausible when extended to "then," for there do not seem to be the special terms available to make it work. There is not enough *time* to train people to use context-independent terms for times in a special way in their thinking, for they would need a new term for each time. Perhaps I could teach my child to say "Joey wants to eat on September 20 at 5 P.M." if at 5 P.M. on September 20 he wants to eat. But I shall have to teach him something else to use an hour or a day later. What a lot of effort! Much simpler to give him a formula he can produce whenever he is hungry: "I want to eat now!" The meaning of "now" ensures he will have said exactly what he wanted to say. When we want verbal behavior to replace natural behavior, context-independence is our only hope.

VI

I have argued against three proposals for analyzing acceptance of a context-dependent sentence in terms of belief, understanding, and meaning. Let me now give a general argument.

Suppose there were a context-independent sentence S such that (i) I now accept "I am hungry now" if and only if I believe that S and (ii) this is so simply in virtue of my understanding of S. It seems that S will have to consist of context-independent terms that designate me and the present time, and some two-place predicate—for example, "_____ is hungry at ..." or " 'I am hungry now' is true for _____ at ...." Let α and τ be the terms and H be the predicate, so S is $H(\alpha,\tau)$.

The problem is that if my belief that S leads me to accept "I am hungry now," at t, simply in virtue of understanding its meaning, why should it not also lead me to accept it later, at t + ten minutes? None of the meanings would have changed; S would still be true, since it is context-independent, even if I had had a ham sandwich at t + five minutes. And you might well believe that S too, since it is as true for you as for me, being context-independent. But if my belief that S and my understanding of S suffice to explain my acceptance, then if you understand it and believe that S, you should also accept "I am hungry now," even though you are stuffed. My acceptance of "I am hungry now" cannot be completely explained by my belief that S and my understanding of the meanings of "I," "now," α, and τ, for otherwise these other acceptances, which did not occur, would have.

The additional facts needed in the explanation, the facts that separate me at t from me at t + ten minutes, and me from you, are these: I accepted "it is now τ" at t, but not later, and I accept "I am α," and you do not. Acceptance plays an irreducible role in belief.[19]

Afterword

Essay 3 is an attempt to clarify the difference between accepting a sentence, in my sense, and believing that a particular sentence is true. I also discuss the relation between the meaning of the word "I" and its ability to express thoughts about ourselves; contrary to what some assume from the title of Essay 2, I do not think that having a first-person pronoun in one's vocabulary is necessary to having such thoughts. Given that it was written with the intention to clarify, the paper has not been particularly successful, but the basic argument still seems correct to me. Let me do a bit more clarifying.

I am not thinking of the concept of acceptance as an *analysis* of the mental states involved in belief. In particular, I am not saying that a belief state consists in a relation to an internal sentence of mentalese that translates the accepted sentence. The concept of acceptance is neutral on this issue. It simply provides a method of classification. People who believe the same thing are doxastically similar in one way. People who accept the same thing are doxastically similar in a different way. People who accept the same thing are similar in a way that depends less on circumstances outside the believer. The notion of acceptance is still a very rough and ready way of getting at belief states. But, for certain purposes, it is a better way of classifying believers than by what they believe.

My use of the term "state" has confused some readers. Philosophers use this term in a variety of ways. I think it almost always connotes the properties a thing has at a time in virtue of a subset of its properties, roughly those that would survive if its internal configuration stayed intact but its relations to things other than its own parts were changed. But one can mean by "the state of x at t" either a more or less concrete particular event involving x, or some complex universal that x at t exemplifies, possibly in common with other objects at other times. And, in this second sense, the state might be partial, or it might comprise all of the relevant properties. I meant belief states to be universal and

---

[19] Jon Barwise, Michael Bratman, and John Etchemendy gave me detailed and helpful comments on (several) penultimate drafts of this essay.

partial. Suppose, that is, that Rip Van Winkle and his neighbor Harold who has just awakened him both say "Yesterday was a fine day." I want to say that there is a belief state they are both in. Since they are both in it, it is a universal. And since they are doxastically dissimilar in many ways, it is partial.

One way in which Rip and Harold differ is beliefs about their context—that is, beliefs about the objects that are involved in the interpretations of indexicals and demonstratives they might use. Rip, we may suppose, believes that it is June 20, 1770, while Harold knows that it is June 20, 1790. These differing beliefs about the context will lead them to different behavior in certain circumstances. If we could persuade them to take a trivial true/false test, Rip would check "Today is June 20, 1790" false, while Harold would check it true. Their total belief states are not the same, but they still have something in common.

To determine what someone said, we consider the meaning of the sentence they used and the facts of the context in which they said it. To explain *why* they said what they did, we would need to consider the meaning of their sentence and their beliefs about their context. This is what will determine what they think they are saying. Consider a version of an example from David Kaplan. He is giving a lecture in a familiar seminar room; he gestures behind him where he believes there to be a picture of Rudolph Carnap, and says "That man is the greatest philosopher of the twentieth century." We will assume, for the sake of the example, that he believes that Carnap is the greatest philosopher of the twentieth century, that he wants to convey to the audience that he believes this and thinks saying it is the way to do that, that he thinks that "that man" refers, in a context, to that man who is most salient in the context, and that because of his gesture and the picture, he believes Carnap is the man most salient in the context. All of that explains why he speaks as he does. But if the picture has been changed without Kaplan's noticing it to one of Dan Quayle, he will not have *said* that Carnap was the greatest philosopher of the twentieth century, but merely tried to; he will have said something he did not intend to say.

This suggests that things do work in just the way I say they do not work in the paper. In the example, Kaplan has beliefs about his context and beliefs about English and beliefs about the history of philosophy. These beliefs explain his acceptance of "That man is the greatest philosopher of the twentieth century." But what I deny in the paper is that belief, conceived as a relation to context-independent sentences or Fregean thoughts, explained acceptance. When we press on this example, we will see that it does not count against that claim. Kaplan's beliefs about his context, for example, have to be what I call self-locating beliefs. He is not motivated to speak as he does merely because he believes that David Kaplan is in a position to express the proposition that Carnap is the greatest, but because he believes this in a certain way. He believes it by being in such states as the one I characterize as accepting "The picture behind me is of Rudolph Carnap."

4

A Problem About Continued Belief

I believe we have and probably need the notion of "continuing to believe the same thing." Suppose, for example, that Julius points to a man at a party, saying "That fellow near the bar is a dean." I believe him, saying the same sentence to myself. Later on, Julius is near the bar, the man is next to me, and I say "So you are a dean." A week later I see him in the quad and think to myself, "He is a dean." I think I came to believe something when Julius spoke, and continued to believe it until the end of the story.

Another example. My father told me "Santa Claus has a white beard." I continued to believe this for a couple of years, until I gave up believing in Santa Claus altogether.

In this paper, I first offer an analysis of continued belief in terms of an account of belief that distinguishes sharply between acceptance of a text and belief in a proposition. This account readily suggests two analyses of continued belief, neither of which seems quite right. Nevertheless, it seems to me that the account is supported on balance by its ability to distinguish between various possible concepts of continued belief, and so to finally suggest a less obvious but more adequate analysis. I then consider a problem, that of internal identity, that seems to arise with the suggested account. This problem leads to a theoretical notion, that of a file, which results from the adaptation of some ideas of Keith Donnellan's.

Texts

Suppose an articulate, sincere adult, eager to please, is asked to describe his beliefs. The result, we may suppose, is a set of true sentences of the form "I believe that S." The set of sentences S contained in these avowals are the *belief texts* from that subject at that time.[20] They seem to tell us something important about the believer. For example, if one of them were "I will be killed if I do not

---

[20]I borrow the term "text" from Michael Pendlebury (1982). He got the term from Gustav Bergman.

leave the room immediately," we might reasonably expect the subject to try to leave the room. Now we can assign even obstinate inarticulate adults sets of belief texts, in virtue of the sentences of the form "I believe that S" that would be true, if they were clever enough to think of them and cooperative enough to produce them. Perhaps if we include in the set of possible texts sentences or groups of symbols not in ordinary languages, consisting, say, of pictures, we might extend the notion to include children and even less articulate believers. At any rate, whatever problems are involved in the notion of a text, it seems to me to be one that is implicitly used in virtually all attempts to philosophize about belief, and so it is of some value to get it out in the open and think about it, as I try to do in this paper. (See also Essay 3.)

What is Believed

I think that belief, like perception, is a relation we have to things not in our heads, partly in virtue of what goes on in our heads. If, as I shall put it, I *accept* the text "My wife has brown hair," then I am related to two things that are not inside my head, my wife and the property of having brown hair. Corresponding to these two things are a number of objects. For certain purposes, I think we need to distinguish:

1. the situation that makes it the case that she has brown hair;

2. the fact that she has brown hair;

3. the state of affairs that she does have brown hair, and the state of affairs that she does not have brown hair;

4. the propositions that she does have brown hair, and the proposition that she doesn't.

I think situations are the most concrete objects, and objects and properties are uniformities across them. States of affairs are abstract objects that situations make factual or not factual. States of affairs give us the basic propositions, but propositions also include more complex conditions such as, for example, there being more than one philosopher who has owned a 1939 Pontiac.

The issues in this paper do not depend on accepting all of these objects and distinctions, however. I am concerned with belief in propositions of a simple kind I call *R-propositions*. These can be identified by a sequence of an n-ary relation and n objects of the appropriate sorts. A proposition $\langle R; a_1, \ldots, a_n \rangle$ is true if $a_1, \ldots, a_n$ stand in the relation R, false otherwise. R-propositions are what Kaplan calls *singular propositions* (1978, 16). As he points out, sentences using indexicals and demonstratives seem to express R-propositions. If I say, "I wrote this paper," and you say to me, pointing at the same thing, "You wrote that paper," we have said the same thing. We have both expressed the same

R-proposition, even though we identified the individuals in it differently.[21]

I use the term *R-proposition* as short for *Russellian proposition*. The identity of these propositions depends on the identity of the individual in them, not on the way it is identified. ⟨Has brown hair; my wife⟩ is the same as ⟨Has brown hair; Frenchie Perry⟩. This means that the proposition does not contain the *mode of presentation* or *cognitive fix* that the believer has on the individual. Russell thought that these sorts of propositions were expressed by sentences with real names in them. Still, it might be misleading to call these Russellian propositions. He did not think there were very many real names, and in the history of the philosophy of language he is most famous for his theory of descriptions, which is a way of avoiding R-propositions. A sentence with a definite description in it will not express an R-proposition, according to Russell. It will express a proposition that is true if there is someone who satisfies the description and has the predicated property. Propositions of this latter kind are close in spirit to what Frege called *thoughts* (although the theoretical apparatus of Frege and Russell differs a lot). Frege thought that R-propositions were a rather weird idea. (See Essay 13 for more discussion of these issues.)

Role and Proposition

Once my older brother told me "I will give you five dollars tomorrow." I believed him, and asked him for money the next day. He said, "I said I will give it to you tomorrow, and I will." This kept up for a couple of days until I got the message. At the time, I thought the message was that tomorrow never comes. Now I realize that it does, though when it does, we do not call it "tomorrow." The real point my brother was trying to get across was this: Do not confuse sameness of text accepted (or asserted) with sameness of R-proposition believed (or asserted).

Each day my brother induced me to accept the same text: "He will give me five dollars tomorrow." By accepting this, each day I believed something dif-

---

[21]In Essays 1 and 2, I argued that we need to adopt some such notion to handle thinking and speaking that makes use of one's identity and position in the world. These were called "thoughts" in the first paper and "objects of belief" in the second. But the nonindividual constituents of thoughts or objects of belief were not properties. In the first paper, they were to be Fregean senses of predicates, and in the second paper, the matter was left obscure. It now seems clear to me that we want properties and relations, not senses or other kind of meanings as constituents of what is believed. We may say that situations are composed of references and not senses, thus describing in Fregean terms a notion Frege did not adopt. Here it must be remembered that Frege took properties—not extensions—to be the references of predicates, and that properties are distinguished by Frege from the senses of predicates. (See Frege 1891/1960 and 1892/1960a.) (There is a tendency on the part of Fregeans to let senses of predicates do the work traditionally done by properties, and move extensions into the position of the reference of predicates. This tendency has a basis in Frege's own practice for his concepts may be thought to differ from extensions—more precisely, courses of values—only in being unsaturated. But in fact, he did distinguish concepts from senses and from extensions, and did call them "properties" on occasion.)

ferent. On Sunday, I believed $\langle x$ will give y \$5 on z, my brother, me, Monday$\rangle$; on Monday, $\langle x$ will give y \$5 on z; my brother, me, Tuesday$\rangle$; and so forth.

So we can believe different R-propositions in different contexts, in virtue of accepting the same text. We can also believe the same R-proposition, in the same or different contexts, by accepting different texts. I may believe $\langle x$ has brown hair; my wife$\rangle$ on a given occasion both in virtue of accepting "my wife has brown hair" and "the person on my left has brown hair," and I might do so whether or not I accept "the person on my left is my wife." And you may also believe this very same object, in virtue of accepting yet another text, say "His wife has brown hair."

Behind this picture of belief are some semantical notions, which I want to make a bit more explicit. Expressions are thought to have *roles*, which are taken to be an important aspect of their linguistic meaning. A role is a rule that takes us from a context to a reference. A context is identified by a person and a time—the speaker or thinker and the time of the thinking or speaking. Thus the meaning of "I" is given by the rule that it stands, each time it is used in thinking or speaking, for the thinker or speaker. Given the context—say, President Carter on some given day—the rule gives us the referent of a use of "I": President Carter. "Is red" has a role that takes us from any context to a certain color property, while "is the color of the typewriter I am now using" takes us to different color properties from different contexts. A simple atomic sentence, like "I am sitting," takes us to an R-proposition.

This semantical picture is an embodiment of some ideas of David Kaplan, in his extremely important studies of the logic of context-sensitive expressions (1978 and 1979). But it differs from his system of *characters* and *contents* in crucial ways, and since "character" and "content" are precisely defined notions, it seemed best to adopt some new terms. Kaplan's characters are functions from contexts to contents, and so start off very much like roles. The important difference comes when we get to the contents. Kaplan's contents are *intensions*. They are explications of, or at least descendants of, Frege's absolute senses.[22] Thus for Kaplan "I" takes us from a context with me as speaker to a constant individual concept of me, an intension that takes me as extension in each possible world (1979, 403). A role, however, takes us directly to me, with no intervention of an intension.

Now these differences may be simply terminological[23] and in any case, what will be said about continued belief does not turn on the difference between role and character. But I suspect the difference is more than termino-

---

[22] Frege's senses were absolute in the sense that their reference was not relative to a speaker or context.

[23] I say this because Kaplan 1975 suggests adopting a Russellian approach to intentional logic. I am not sure where this would leave the system in Kaplan 1979, but it seems it might lessen the differences just mentioned.

logical, and so would like to briefly explain my revisionism. It seems to me that Kaplan has not made radical enough changes in the Fregean system; like many who hit upon revolutionary ideas, he hesitates at completely uprooting the structures within which he grew up. Kaplan sees character as an aspect of sense that Frege missed, something that needs to be added on top of sense. So in his system we have, for each possible use of an expression, its character, its content in the given context, and its reference, determined by the content. Contents, like Frege's senses, will not determine references relative to a context, but absolutely.

But I think Frege's notion of absolute sense was a *mistake*. We need something like character *instead of* absolute senses or intensions. By "absolute" I mean that Frege's senses have a reference independent of context. My picture is this. Frege introduces senses, in the first instance, to serve as ways of apprehending references. We need the notion of a way of apprehending a reference, but Frege's notion of sense will not do, because absolute. He cannot bring out the difference between the way you think of me when you think "you" and the way I think of me when I think "I." That is because these ways of thinking do not correspond neatly to what is thought about. Ways of thinking cut across what is thought about. The way I think of myself when I think "I" is just the way you think of yourself when you think "I." Only the way of thinking plus a context determines a reference. And that means we need something like character or role, something that takes us from the subject's identity and position in the world to reference, to serve as ways of thinking.

However, because he took senses to be absolute, Frege was free to use them in ways in which characters or roles could not be used. The additional uses for senses become an integral part of Frege's system, so we cannot make his senses nonabsolute without altering it in important ways. The relation *sense of* provides a homomorphism from the realm of sense into the world of things and properties, allowing the former realm to do much of the semantical work of the latter. Belief is a case in point. That one may believe that *a* is a featherless biped without believing that *a* is human, even if the featherless bipeds are just the humans, was explained by Russell in terms of two different properties having the same extension. But in Frege's system, it is explained by the different senses of "human" and "featherless biped." We no longer need to address the question whether different properties can have the same extension. Fregeans cease to distinguish it from a question about expressions and senses. Most importantly, the system of absolute senses allows Frege to take sentences to stand for truth-values, and ignore R-propositions altogether. There are properties in Frege's system—they just are not given much to do. But R-propositions are not even part of the system. It does not matter that in the reference of the sentence "all that is specific is lost," as long as the specificity is retained in the sense of the sentence.

I think that Kaplan has shown that absolute senses cannot by themselves handle the ubiquitous phenomena of context-dependence. I think attention to the epistemology of context-dependence suggests that the phenomena are not only ubiquitous but ineliminable. So senses cannot do what they were introduced to do—serve as ways of believing. And I think that, by recognizing properties and R-propositions, the remaining work for absolute senses is removed. We can let the objective world handle the work of absolute senses. (See Barwise and Perry 1981, 1983.)

Belief States

While I have spoken, and will continue to speak, of believing an object in virtue of accepting a text, this is misleading. I think texts accepted are of interest as a way of characterizing *belief states*. One may think of belief states as brain states, perturbations in mind-stuff, or whatever—right now I do not care.

My point is that *texts accepted* is a useful notion for classifying believers, when we want to look for plausible general principles with which to explain and predict human behavior, and that this is clearly because roles correspond to internal states. My own view is that belief states are multiple manifested dispositions, and that with the notion of a text we label the state in virtue of one of its manifestations. But in any case, I want to emphasize that I do not think of texts or their roles as "direct" objects of belief. They are not, ordinarily, objects of belief at all, but objects produced by one who is in a belief state, under certain conditions.

So, strictly speaking, it is not partly in virtue of text accepted, but partly in virtue of one's belief states, that one believes the objects one does. The other factors are positional and causal factors.

In the case of texts containing indexicals, this basically means the context of the belief: the identity of the believer and the time at which the believing occurs.

In the case of texts involving proper names—and, as we shall see, other cases—it includes the causal history of one's use of the name. Suppose there are two English speakers whose texts include "David Lewis has a beard." There is a belief state they both are in. Given that each hated anyone with a beard, both would be unhappy if told "David Lewis is here to see you." Nevertheless, on the assumption that David Lewis the philosopher and David Lewis the railway magnate are different men, their beliefs are about different people.

So, in virtue of being in a belief state in a certain environment, we believe a certain object. Because the same object can be believed in different ways, from different environments or "points of view," classifying people by the objects believed is not always particularly useful.

Both you and I may believe ⟨x will get hit if he does not duck; John Perry⟩.

I duck, you shout. Why the difference in behavior, if the same object is believed? Because what is important is *how* it is believed. I accept "I will be hit if I do not duck," you accept "He will be hit if he does not duck." But I act just as you would if you accepted what I did.

There is a traditional view according to which what one does is explained in part by what one believes. Now the view I am putting forward is different. What one accepts explains in part what one does; what one accepts plus the context in which one accepts it, determines what one believes. This can seem very puzzling. If what one does does not depend on what one believes about the world, why expect it to be appropriate to one's situation in the world? There seems to be a sort of preestablished harmony involved. Another way of approaching the same question is to note that the accepted sentences really have two roles. What I have been calling their role is their *semantical* role. But they also seem to have a *cognitive* role. How do the two connect?

While I cannot here develop an answer to this question, I want briefly to suggest one. Consider the sentence "There is a hungry lion coming towards me." Now consider the contexts relative to which this sentence is true. They all consist of persons and times such that the person is being approached by a hungry lion at the time. It is a good idea for all of these people to run like crazy. In a sense they do not need to know what they believe. Even if they have forgotten who they are and lost track of time, they know enough to run. (In another sense, they do know what they believe even then.) Most of these people will not believe the same thing. But each of them will believe in *something* that provides *them* with good reason to run.

Kaplan develops the idea of a "theorem in the logic of demonstratives." This is a character that, though it may lead to different contents from different contexts, and may not lead to anything necessarily true, always leads to a content that is in fact true. His favorite example is "I am here, now."

I am relying on a notion with a similar structure. "If I am approached by a hungry lion, I should run like crazy" is *reliable advice*. Each person who accepts it will be well served. But in a sense, each person who accepts it is not getting the same advice. I am adopting the strategy of running when I am approached by a hungry lion, while you are adopting the strategy of running when you are approached by a hungry lion, And the advice I am adopting *would not* be good for everyone to follow. Why should you run when I am approached by a hungry lion?

This all suggests a way in which the cognitive role and the semantical role of a sentence are related. In a sense it is a preestablished harmony. But it is not a mysterious preestablished harmony.

Preservation of R-Proposition Believed and Continuity of Belief

I will now return to the topic of continuity of belief. The picture of belief sketched suggests two obvious conditions for it. The most natural, perhaps, is that it consists in preservation of the R-proposition believed. A second and different hypothesis is that continued belief is simply retention of text accepted (that is, retention of the belief-state that is a disposition to accept a certain text). It seems our ordinary notion of continued belief might be either one of these notions, or some combination thereof.

Variations on the Morning Star/Evening Star case seem to show that preservation of R-proposition believed is not a sufficient condition of continued belief. Suppose I ask two friendly Chicagoans which building is Union Station. One points to a building the three of us are standing beside, the other to a building some distance away, across a street. Both are correct, as Union Station is mainly under the street, rising up on either side of it. But I do not know this. My mind changes as I turn to each of the honest-looking natives. First I accept "This is Union Station," and then "That is Union Station." The R-proposition believed remains constant: $\langle x$ is Union Station; Union Station$\rangle$. But this does not seem to be a case of what we would ordinarily call continuing to believe the same thing.

We might think that the case of continued belief in Santa Claus' white beard shows that preservation of R-proposition believed is not a necessary condition either, for here we have continued belief with *no* R-proposition believed. But this is pretty indecisive. We might say instead that the R-proposition is *nothing*, and is preserved, or perhaps that the R-proposition is $\langle x$ has a white beard; the null set$\rangle$. If we had good general reasons for thinking that preservation of R-proposition was a necessary condition of continuity of belief, we would try to handle this sort of case one way or another.

A more convincing case comes from Pendlebury (1980, 1982).[24] Someone being driven around the environs of Bloomington, Indiana, retains the text "This is Monroe county." Unknown to her, she leaves and reenters Monroe County several times in the course of the drive. So the R-proposition believed changes. But isn't this a case of continued belief?

I find that different people say different things about this example. Philosophers (with exceptions, including Pendlebury) tend to think that as she moves in and out of the county, she acquires new beliefs. Nonphilosophers (e.g., my wife), whom we may think of as having purer linguistic intuitions than philoso-

---

[24] I read Pendlebury's paper and discussed these issues with him while writing this paper and this was very helpful and illuminating. Pendlebury uses this example as an argument against the notion of an object of belief, and develops an account of belief that takes belief to be mainly (in the terminology I am using) a matter of what goes on inside, with no important role for external objects of belief.

phers, tend to agree with Pendlebury, that the person in the example continues to believe the same thing, although what she believes changes truth-value. For the moment, I will simply leave this disagreement, and the question of whether preservation of object believed is a necessary condition of continued belief, unresolved.

Retention of Text and Continuity of Belief

The results of the last section suggest that continued belief does not have just to do with the outside factors in belief, so we should look inside. But the simplest hypothesis, that continued belief is just continued acceptance of the same text, is quite wrong. Retention of text is neither a sufficient nor a necessary condition of continued belief.

My brother showed that it is not sufficient. I continued to accept "He will give me five dollars tomorrow," but did not thereby continue to believe what I first believed. Another example: Suppose I am tied to a chair, waiting for the time bomb on the table to explode. At each time I accept "It is going to explode an instant from now." This is not continued belief, but continuously changing belief.

Nor is it necessary. The case described at the beginning of the paper, where I believed a certain man to be a dean, is one of continuous belief. Yet no text is retained. First we have "That man is a dean" and then "You are a dean" and then "He is a dean."

Preservation of R-Proposition by Retention of Text

Suppose Julius had said, "That man next to the bar is Halsey, and Halsey is a dean." I retain the text "Halsey is a dean" throughout the party, and up to the day I meet him on the quad. Surely this is a paradigm case of continuing to believe something. And it suggests at least a sufficient condition: we continue to believe when we continue to believe a given R-proposition by continuing to accept the same text.

If this suggestion were correct, it would be tempting to try to use it to reply to the last claim of the last section, that retention of a text is not a necessary condition of continued belief. After all, that I thought of Halsey in different ways during the period of time in question—as "that man" and "you" and "he"—does not show that I did not also think of him in some other way the whole time. If Julius had told me his name, I would have thought of him as "Halsey" throughout, even though I also thought of him as "that man" and "you" and "he." Yielding completely to this idea, we might argue as follows. Clearly what we call continued belief is just preserving the R-proposition believed by retaining a text. Since in the original Halsey case (where I did not have a name for him) I continued to believe, we know that there must be a text

I continued to accept. I just did not look hard enough for it.

Tempting as this is, I do not think it can be correct, if to have such a text I must have some way of thinking of or referring to Halsey of the ordinary sort, which I can use throughout the period I believe him to be a dean. I would have to possess some singular term A that designates Halsey all along. But what could A be?

A might be a context-insensitive definite description that denotes Halsey. Indeed, the meaning of such a thing is just what would have been taken, combined with the meaning of "is a dean," to compose a traditional proposition. Such propositions, on the traditional theory, serve the purposes of both my texts and belief objects: they are the bearers of truth and the classifiers of belief states.

But I see no reason whatsoever to suppose that I could produce, or have in my possession in any manner, however implicit, such a definite description for Halsey (or for that matter for any other object).[25]

For the purposes of the temptation at hand, however, such a context-insensitive definite description is not needed. A singular term, like a context-sensitive definite description, or an indexical, or a proper name, would do as well. The designation of A need not be Halsey from anywhere at any time, just from those places I occupy between the party and the day on the quad. "The man on my left" would do, if Halsey happened to be the unique individual on my left throughout the episode.

Even so, I cannot see that I need to have such a singular term in my repertoire to continue to believe what Julius told me. Someone might argue that my problem is an insistence that the singular term be one that can appear in a public text—that perhaps an "inner name" of some sort is being employed instead. Little as I understand it, I have no objection to introspection as a pastime or even as a method for doing philosophy. I just can find no inner name that I would have to have or be likely to have in the sort of R-proposition described.

In any case, I do not think preservation of R-proposition believed by retention of text accepted is even a sufficient condition of continued belief. It is almost sufficient. When we see what else is required, we will have a clue for handling cases in which a single text is not retained.

The example I have in mind to show nonsufficiency is yet another variation on the morning Star/Evening Star case. Smith, whose watch is an hour fast, accepts "Today is my husband's birthday." Just very shortly before eleven, she looks at the calendar and realizes that she had it wrong. It is March 1 and not March 2. Just as this sinks in, she glances at her watch—precisely at eleven, so it shows precisely midnight—and thinks to herself, "so *today* is my husband's birthday." And by doing that she preserves the R-proposition believed, for in

---

[25]I now think this is much too strong. See the last section of Essay 13.

this case she does believe ⟨*x* is my husband's birthday; March 1⟩ even though she also believes ⟨*x* is my husband's birthday; March 2⟩ and even though she does not accept "March 1 is my husband's birthday." So she preserves the R-proposition of belief by retaining a text. But she does not continue to believe the same thing. She changed her mind.

Retaining a Text in Order to Preserve R-Proposition Believed

The problem here is that Smith was not trying to preserve object believed: indeed, she was trying not to. This suggests the following view.

We have a (fairly) clear notion of preserving R-proposition believed. This is an "external" notion, having to do with the R-proposition believed, however it may be believed. But we have a device for generating an internal notion from the external one. We suppose that there is such a thing as *trying* to preserve R-proposition believed—or, to diminish the suggestion that conscious effort need be involved—retaining one's texts *in order to* preserve R-proposition believed. This is an internal notion, for one can retain one's texts in order to preserve R-proposition believed, but not succeed. Let us call this internal notion *internal continuity of belief*.

Now perhaps we really have two ordinary notions of "continuing to believe." One is just internal continuity of belief. This is the one Pendlebury and my wife employed, in their reaction to the episode in (and out of) Monroe County. The other is *successful internal continuity of belief*. This suggestion won't quite do, however, for it implies that retention of text is a necessary condition of continuing to believe the same thing, but we have already seen that it is not.

Change in Text in Order to Preserve the R-Proposition Believed

Consider the original case, which was used to show that retention of text is not a necessary condition of continuity of belief. I first accept "That man near the bar is a dean" and then, after Halsey has left the bar and walked over to me, "You are a dean." It seems to me this is not only a clear-cut case of preserving the object believed, but also a case of internal continuity of belief. This is what it is like to try to continue to preserve the R-proposition believed, when one is aware that a constituent of the R-proposition believed is moving around.

So it seems that not even our internal notion can be identified simply with retaining a text. Rather, the general case of continued internal belief is changing the text in order to preserve the R-proposition believed, where we understand that change includes retention as a limiting case.

So now we have three notions:

    (i) preservation of R-proposition believed, or external continued belief;

(ii) changing (or, in the limiting case, retaining) the text *in order to* preserve R-proposition believed (internal continued belief);

(iii) successful internal continued belief (ordinary continued belief).

The Problem of Internal Identity

Now I finally reach the problem of the title. I have said that we have the notion of *internal continued belief*. Thus far, I have assumed that the internal states are displayed by the structure of texts accepted. It seems then that continued internal belief should be displayed by relationships among the texts accepted. But saying how it is displayed is a problem, one that will lead us to a new theoretical notion, that of a file.

In the example concerning Halsey, I used "you" at the later time in order to refer to the same person I had used "that man near the bar" to refer to earlier. I shall call this a case of *internal identity*. Internal continued belief in the Halsey case requires internal identity and what we might call internal sameness of attribution. I ignore the conditions for the latter, and spend the remainder of the paper on internal identity.

We might suppose that internal identity would be displayed by identity texts. But neither at the earlier or the later time do we find me accepting "You are that man near the bar." At both times, this would have involved me in the belief that Julius and Halsey are one, which I never had.

At the later time we would have found "You are the man I referred to as 'that man near the bar' a moment ago." The presence of this text does seem to show, in a sense, that at the later time I am trying to refer with "you" to the person I earlier referred to with "that man near the bar." But it is not the right sense for internal identity.

Suppose Lew was near the bookcase while I was talking to Julius, and Julius pointed to him saying, "That man near the bookcase is a historian." At the later time, while talking to Halsey and pointing to Lew, I accept these texts: "You are a dean, and were standing by the bookcase a moment ago" and "He is a historian and was standing near the bar a moment ago." Both texts are false, for I have become confused. Perhaps there are different ways I could have gotten confused, but one way seems to be this. I come to believe and continue to believe both $\langle x$ is a dean; Halsey$\rangle$ and $\langle x$ is a historian; Lew$\rangle$. But I misremember where each man had been standing earlier.

In this case, I would accept "You are the man I referred to as 'the man near the bookcase' a moment ago." This would be false, of course, but that is not my point. I would also not display internal identity. Just because at the end of the later time I accept "A is the person I referred to as B a moment ago," it does not follow that my earlier use of B and later use of A constitute internal identity. In this case, my earlier use of "that man near the bar" and later use of "you" are a case of internal identity, even though I accept "You are not the man I referred to as 'the man near the bar' a moment ago."

I do not think that the solution to the problem of internal identity involves finding identities among the texts. And even if, contrary to what was claimed earlier, we could find, whenever we have a case of continued belief, a retained text, our problem would not be solved. Suppose we had found the mythical A, the singular term with which I referred to Halsey throughout the episode. Then we might suppose we could reconstruct the process of internal continued belief as a sort of inference:

(Earlier time)   That man near the bar is a dean.
                    That man near the bar is A.
                    So, A is a dean.

(Later time) A is a dean.
                    You are A.
                    So, you are a dean.

But now we are assuming that the use of A at the earlier and later times is an instance of internal identity. But we cannot assume that, as was shown by the case of Smith and the birthday.

Internal Identity Without Singular Terms

Moreover, another kind of case will show that any reliance on identity of singular terms from the earlier to the later time, or identities formed with singular terms formed at the earlier or later times, must be misguided. For we can have internal continued belief and internal identity when I have no singular term at all to refer to the thing I continue to think about.

Consider the period of time after the party, and before I saw Halsey again on the quad. I think it is perfectly possible that I continue to believe $\langle x$ is a dean; Halsey$\rangle$ during the interim, even though I have no way of referring to him at all. He is indexically inaccessible—"you" and "he" and "that man" will not reach him. I know nothing about him that does not apply equally well to many others. I might, of course, remember enough about the circumstances to think of him with a description like "The man who was near the bar while I was talking to Julius," but I need not remember this, so far as I can see.

In order to make the phenomenon of recognition intelligible, we shall have to suppose that I believe more about Halsey than merely that he is a dean. Let us suppose that, as Julius directs my attention towards Halsey, I come to accept "That man near the bar is a dean, wears a bolo tie and a rumpled suit, smokes a pipe, and has a mathematical demeanor." Seeing a man on the quad with a pipe, and this sort of suit, tie, and demeanor, I say "Ah, yes. You are a dean." If this is the man Julius pointed at, then we have a case of recognition.

The information about Halsey seems to have been retained in my mind without benefit of singular terms. So it cannot be the singular terms that are the key to internal identity. It seems, instead, to be just what was retained in this case, the cluster of predicates, that provides the internal identity.

Predicates do not need a singular term to be knitted together. A quantifier phrase serves this purpose: "Some man wears bolo ties, rumpled suits, smokes a pipe, has a mathematical demeanor, and is a dean." Such a sentence among my texts we would naturally think of as that in virtue of which a general belief would be held, rather than a belief about a particular person. Yet this seems a mistake (or perhaps better the phrase I use next can be considered a singular term). Consider the phrase "A certain man"—described in the dictionary as meaning "not further described or more specifically named but assumed to be known." If I say "A certain man wears a bolo tie and rumpled suits," I would be ordinarily thought to have someone in mind and not merely to be making a likely guess that at least one person in the world dresses in this way. "A certain man" functions here, I shall say, as an ersatz name.[26] In virtue of accepting the sentence, I believe of some specific individual that he dresses in the manner described. But how does this man get involved in the belief?

Files

I believe the solution to this problem lies in the adaptation of some ideas from Keith Donnellan's account of proper names (1970 and 1974). This adaptation leads to a new theoretical notion, that of a file.

On Donnellan's account, a proper name refers to an entity on a given occasion of use if that entity occupies a unique position in the correct historical account of that use. Suppose, for example, a student in a seminar tells me her name is "Phyllis." Later on, in talking to a colleague, I say "Phyllis has studied Frege's writings with great care." A complete account of the factors that led up to this utterance would mention many people, including me and my colleague. But it seems that the student would figure into the account in a certain way that others would not. That is what makes her the referent of my use of "Phyllis."

Now it seems to me to be helpful to speak of causal chains here (though I doubt that it would seem so to Donnellan). The property is having a certain role in a causal chain that led up to my use of "Phyllis." One may object to this account because it is vague, for Donnellan says very little about what this role is. This seems to me not a good objection, but simply a suggestion for further research. Suppose there were a debate about whether "is red" stands for a color property or a shape property. Close study of a number of examples chosen to minimize color/shape correlation would convince us that it stood

---

[26]The view that an indefinite description like "a man" can function semantically as a referring expression is defended in Wilson 1978 and in Chastain 1975.

for a color property. This would be quite clear, even while we remained quite unable to say much about which color property it was, other than by pointing out instances of it. Examples Donnellan provides convince me that for any proper name A and any person Q, "Q refers to x with his use of A" stands for a historical or causal property, and not the property of satisfying a set of descriptions held by Q or even Q's linguistic community.

It may seem that Donnellan's account cannot be adapted for ersatz names, for the history of my uses of "a certain man" would not be of much interest in determining whom I had in mind on a given occasion. That phrase has nothing in particular to do with Halsey. But as Donnellan emphasizes, it is not the history of the use of the name, but the events that lead to a given use of the name, that are important (1974, 19). Donnellan's theory is compatible with a name being used for the first time in history referring to a long-dead individual. In the example, my use of "Phyllis" might be the first time the student had ever been referred to by a use of that name—if, for example, her name was "Philo" and I had simply heard it wrong. It might also be the last, if my colleague says, "You must be referring to Philo—there is no one named 'Phyllis' in your seminar." That I refer to Philo as "Phyllis" on this occasion does not make it her name, of course.

Thus we can apply Donnellan's account to ersatz names. Doing so leads us to see that it is not the name itself (ersatz or proper) that is of interest, but the grouping of predicates. It is the predicates grouped that lie at the end of a causal chain originating with the person I am thinking about.

Suppose then that on Wednesday I accept "Halsey wears a rumpled suit and a bolo tie and has a mathematical demeanor." By Friday, I have totally forgotten the name of the dean, but still accept "A certain man wears a rumpled suit and a bolo tie and has a mathematical demeanor." If the earlier acceptance and the later acceptance are parts of the same causal chain of the right sort, then we have internal identity. And if the chain leads in the right way back to a unique individual, that is the individual I think about on both occasions.

Of course, there are many ways we might have internal identity without there being a single person, in any clear sense, thought about. There might be no individual initiating the chain in the right way. Causal chains might merge, so that a week or so after meeting Halsey and Lew I accept "A certain man named Lew—or maybe Halsey—wears a bolo tie and is a historian." Although the facts are clear enough, there will no longer be a straightforward answer to the question "Who is this belief about?"

Let us say that the set of sentences a person accepts at a given time is their doxastic profile at that time. We are now supposing, then, that linking various entries in the doxastic profiles of a given person at various times are causal chains, and the entries so linked we shall say belong to a single *file*. Files are clearly theoretical notions, even relative to profiles, internal identity is not *displayed* in the profiles. In this respect, this adaptation of Donnellan's ideas deviates significantly from the kinds of R-proposition he deals with. In his examples, it seems clear that we would know what to say about what a given use of a name refers to, given the sort of information we can readily imagine having, about who first said what, point at whom, and the like. But here we do not have this feeling. Given all the information about the goings-on in someone's brain for a period of time, I would have no idea what to say about whether two uses of a name were due to an entry in a single file. This seems to be a case in which we have mastered all sorts of indirect tests for a phenomenon without having the foggiest idea what we are testing for. But this is not an unusual situation. I know how to test to see if my television is tuned to the same channel as last night—even if the channel selector knob is slipping and the numbers on it are no sure guide, I can figure it out pretty well. But I have only the foggiest idea what being tuned to the same channel really is, and would be quite helpless if confronted by the inner works of a television and asked to explain the conditions under which we have the same channel tuned in.

Although I have no idea how a system of files might be instantiated in a brain, I can give an analogy that shows how such a system could be instantiated with a much more primitive information-storage system. Let us suppose that on the first day of class I carefully note down features of the various students around the table. I use full sentences, for example, "The student in the seat first to my left is a woman, has blonde hair, is short, was born in Ottumwa, is a psychology major, and has on a red sweater." I call this "opening a file." I do not use names (perhaps for religious reasons). Later in the day I look at the cards. I erase or alter some phrases. I erase "the student in the first seat to my left" and change "has on a red sweater" to "once wore a red sweater." At the next lecture, I use the remaining predicates for purposes of recognition. For example, to the student first on my right I say "Weren't you born in Ottumwa?" for she is a woman, blonde, short, with an *Advanced Psychology* text at her side.

There are no singular terms left on my card. The predicates remaining might allow me to construct one, perhaps "The only student ever to wear a red sweater and be a psychology major and be from Ottumwa." But I need not do this; it serves no purpose, and it would not change things if the description did not fit the student for whom I opened the file (maybe I heard wrong and it was Omaha, not Ottumwa). Although I could have done this in a more orderly way, assigning each student a number, or using their names, or assigning them a name of my own, I need not. The work that would be done with these devices is done by the predicates being written on a single card.

Now each such file card offers me, at each seminar, a profile, a set of predicates. Whom does this profile stand for? We clearly must make a distinction between the persons, if any, of whom the profile is true, and the source of the

profile. The source is the student my perception of whom led to the establish-
ment of the file (it need not have been perception, though, as far as I can see).
The predicates on the file may or may not be true of her. I update the cards
after each class. Old entries are changed, new entries are made, the writing
fades, I may have made mistakes recording the data, and so forth. I have come
to believe something false about a certain student—a student I may no longer
have any way of recognizing.

Instead of writing on a file card, I might have taken a photograph. The
distinction between whom a photograph is *of* and whom it might resemble is
familiar. (See Kaplan 1969.)

I think our notion of internal identity is based on thinking of the mind as
working in this way. In the analogy, if the same file card has "is F" on it at
one time and "is G" at another, then according to my files a certain person was
F at the earlier time and G at the later time. This is the analogue of internal
identity.

If we think of the mind as a storehouse or a filing cabinet, the relation
would be between the stored items that correspond to predicates, say, being
stored in the same room or in the same file drawer or folder. What is essential
in these metaphors and analogies is a path from the production of texts at one
time back to the original perception of (or other introduction to) the source at
an earlier time. This path in the mind plays the role of an object in the world.
So our notion of internal identity, and so ultimately of believing the same thing,
depends on the identity of the internal causal path or chain.

Now it may be that in the mind the work of files are done by something
like proper names. It is important to stress that identity of proper names does
not constitute internal identity, and so we need the notion of a file to explain
what would be special about these names.

One advantage of filing with proper names is the ease with which one can
handle relational predicates. In the analogy I have presented, there is really no
provision for handling such predicates. I'd like to end by pointing out how considerable relational information can nevertheless be handled in such a system,
for this is a point that seems importantly related to the study of what it is to
think from a position in the world.

First, the order of the files might be significant. Thus, in the seminar case,
I might keep the cards stacked in the order in which the students are seated
throughout each seminar. Second, context-dependency itself provides a way
of embodying relational information in a system of one-place predicates. Consider the fact that a student wears a red shirt on a certain day. This is a relational
fact, involving the student, the day, and the relation "x wears a red shirt on y."
But on that day I can believe that fact simply by accepting "α is wearing a
shirt." The fact that the student is to *my* left, *I* can believe simply by accepting
"α is to the left." I do not need a file for the day, or for myself; I finesse the

need for such files by setting up the system on the day, and by being me.

We may think of the final product, at the end of the quarter, as a pack of bundles of ten cards each, each bundle giving information about what has been taken to be one student, the order of the cards in each bundle showing what I observed the first week, second week, and so forth. Through exploitation of context, and arrangement of the files, considerable relational information is embodied, without using names or other than one-place predicates. There are, of course, a lot more efficient ways to encode such information, but that we can, by using our position in space and time get by with monadic predicates seems to me to be a fact that may be of some importance, both in understanding thinking as a phenomenon that exploits our position in the world, and in understanding how such thinking can lead to increasingly objective conceptions of the world.

Afterword

The first three essays do not say much about what is involved in continuing to believe the same thing. When I was working on the first two essays, I assumed that belief consisted in (what is here called) accepting a text in a context. I was inclined to think that continuing to believe the same thing must involve adjusting the text accepted to suit change of context so as to preserve what is believed. This view is suggested by Frege's remark:

> If someone wants to say the same today as he expressed yesterday using the word "today," he must replace this word with "yesterday" (1918/1967, 24).

In "Demonstratives," David Kaplan brought up this issue under the heading of "cognitive dynamics":

> Suppose that yesterday you said, and believed it, "It is a nice day today." What does it mean to say, today, that you have retained *that* belief? It seems unsatisfactory to just believe the same content under any old character—where is the retention? You *can't* believe that content under the same character. Is there some obvious standard adjustment to make to the character, for example, replacing *today* with *yesterday*? If so, then a person like Rip Van Winkle, who loses track of time, can't retain any such beliefs. This seems strange (1989, 537–38).

He elaborated on this theme in some lectures he gave at Stanford in fall quarter 1978, discussing several examples of conversations involving continued reference to individuals who had become indexically inaccessible. These brought up the problems of "internal identity" very forcefully. This paper was written for the Oberlin Colloquium in winter 1979. I am grateful to many participants, particularly John Heinz, for comments.

In the original version, I eschewed the notion of a proposition, taking what is believed to be "situations." The notion of a situation I had in mind was essentially what Jon Barwise and I called "abstract situations" in *Situations and Attitudes*. In the present version, I have instead used the terminology and notation of the later essays in this volume, so that what is believed, in the cases under consideration, is an "R-proposition." I have come to think that both the motivation Barwise and I have for situations, and the difficulties our approach presented with respect to propositions, are not directly relevant to the main point of this paper.

5

Castañeda on *He* and *I*

In a series of thoughtful, original, and thought-provoking papers published in the late 1960s, Hector-Neri Castañeda brought forcefully to the attention of analytical philosophers the importance of indexicals and demonstratives in thought and in descriptions of thought (1966, 1967a, 1968, 1968a). Castañeda put forward a theory to deal with these phenomena; in this paper I explain and criticize basic parts of his original theory, restricting myself to issues associated with the first person.

I allow myself great liberties in the exposition. Castañeda wrote these papers in a manner neutral among several philosophies of language. This hinders comprehension at times. The more central aspects of his theory are also easily lost in a barrage of detail and argument. I present his theory as an attempt at a conservative revision of a Fregean theory of language, thought, and action, in response to discoveries about indexicals and demonstratives. This may produce some distortion and unfairness; I hope it does not.

Elsewhere, I have argued for an account of the issues discussed here that goes along different lines from Castañeda's (Essays 1–4). This account also began as a conservative revision of Frege, making a different choice of what to save and what to give up (Essay 1). But it has led to an increasingly radical departure from the Fregean approach, most recently in joint work with Jon Barwise, who had come to a similar skepticism about the Fregean perspective through his work on definability and on the logic of perception (Barwise and Perry 1980, 1981; Barwise 1981; Essay 6). I do not develop these views here. Rather, in writing this paper, I have tried to recapture the Fregean spirit from which I originally approached Castañeda's pioneering work, in order to indicate as clearly as possible the reasons Castañeda's approach seems to have difficulties, even from within a basically Fregean perspective. In the last section, however, I offer a diaphilosophical fantasy intended to suggest some grounds for dissatisfaction with the entire approach.

77

The Original Position

I shall describe as a starting point a theory of thought, language, and action that I characterize as "Fregean." I believe most of its elements are found in Frege, particularly in his later essays on the philosophy of logic (1892/1960, 1918/1967). But there are differences of emphasis, of detail; points of great importance to Frege are not mentioned, and so forth.

There are senses that, though not mental, can be directly grasped by the mind. Senses are wholes determined by their parts, called constituents.[27] Some senses are propositions. Minds can have the attitude of belief, as well as other attitudes, towards propositions. Belief in a proposition is a mental state; the propositions a person believes are an important fact about her or him, which, together with other facts, including facts about other propositional attitudes, are the basis of our explanations and expectations of purposeful actions.

Senses have unique references. Some senses have objects as references, others, properties;[28] propositions refer to truth-values. The reference of a complex sense depends on the way things are in the world. We shall use "ref" for the function that assigns a reference to a sense.

Expressions in a language express senses and are the means by which thoughts, including beliefs, are communicated. We shall use "sen" for the function that assigns to each expression its sense in English. Thus,

ref(sen(*The President of the U.S.*)) = Reagan.

We shall say that expressions *designate* objects, properties, etc. When an expression α has a sense, its designation must be the reference of that sense:

des(α) = ref(sen(α)).

des(*The President of the U.S.*) = Reagan.

But we shall not assume that expressions only achieve designation by having sense.

Sentences that do not embed other sentences, like *The President of the U.S. is a Republican*, we shall call simple. Those that do, like *Agnes believes that the President of the U.S. is a Democrat* and *The President of the U.S. is a Republican or the President of the U.S. is a Democrat*, we call complex. The sense of a simple sentence is a whole made up of the senses of the expressions in the sentence. The reference of such a sentence is determined by the references of the senses of its parts. But with some types of complex sentence, these principles do not hold.

---

[27]This useful notion of a *constituent* of a proposition is probably one Frege did not have, and one of which he would not approve, since it suggests that a given proposition ("thought") would be the value of a unique set of arguments.

[28]I ignore the differences between Frege's *Begriffe* and more traditional properties, and, in particular, the idea that they are functions.

In particular, *A believes that S* does not have the proposition expressed by *S*, but a sense of the proposition expressed by *S*, as a constituent; this seems quite reasonable, given what was said above, that belief reports describe the relations minds have to senses.

A problem must be noted here. Each successive embedding of a sentence brings in a new level of senses. Thus the proposition expressed by *S* is just sen(*S*). The proposition expressed by *A believes that S* has, as a constituent, a sense that has sen(*S*) as reference. The proposition expressed by *B believes that A believes that S* has, as a constituent, a sense that has as reference a sense that has sen(*S*) as reference. The problem is the use of the indefinite article in the last two sentences. Which of the indefinitely many senses that refer to sen(*S*) is to be a constituent of the proposition *A believes that S*? Any serious Fregean theory must solve this problem, which involves, in this case, providing a route from a reference (sen(*S*)) to a sense of it.

Beliefs affect action. Most obviously, beliefs affect how one describes the world. Let us say that a person *accepts* a sentence when that person uses it, or is disposed to use it given appropriate conditions, to sincerely describe the way things are. Then, in general, a person's acceptance of *S*, which is a disposition to act in a certain way, is explained by the person's belief that *S*. But acceptance is only the most obvious way in which beliefs affect action; beliefs, together with other propositional attitudes, explain purposeful actions in general.

Similarly, we can perceive that the conditions for the truth of a proposition are met, and this results in belief. Thus propositions, and the senses that constitute them, have psychological roles. These would be difficult to articulate, given that action depends not just on belief, but belief together with various other propositional attitudes. But in our ordinary explanations of belief in terms of perception, we show great familiarity with, and facility in, dealing with the psychological roles of senses.

The fact that senses have unique references provides a method of individuation. If $\text{ref}(s) \neq \text{ref}(s')$, then $s \neq s'$. But the psychological roles of senses require and provide a more finely grained principle of individuation. In particular, even if $\text{des}(\phi) = \text{des}(\psi)$ where ϕ and ψ are sentences, it is entirely possible that both

> *A* believes that ϕ.
>
> Not-(*A* believes that ψ).

In this case, ϕ and ψ must have different senses. Acceptance is a test for belief, so we can speak of the acceptance test for sense identity.

Given the distinction between sense and reference, we get two concepts of the truth conditions of a sentence. Consider these sentences

> The editor of *Soul* smokes cigars.

The author of "It" smokes cigars.

Given a grammatical analysis of each sentence into a noun phrase and a verb phrase, we can ask (i) what conditions the truth of the sentence imposes on the references of the expressions, or (ii) what conditions the truth of the sentence imposes on the senses of the expressions. We shall call (i) the referential level of analysis of truth conditions. Given that the editor of *Soul* is the author of "It," we get the same condition for both sentences at the referential level. But when we rise to (ii), the sense level, we get different conditions of truth for the two sentences.

The linchpin of this theory is sense. Reading, writing, hearing, speaking, and thinking with expressions play a big role in our lives. All of the properties of expressions that make this so derive from the fundamental property of having a sense. We might represent this central role of sense in the theory with a diagram:

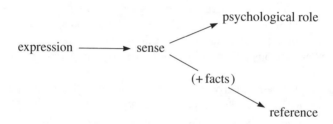

The Problem Posed by *I*

This theory needs revision or supplementation to deal with indexicals (*I, now, you, here, today, yesterday*, etc.) and demonstratives (*this, that*). Here is a simple, intuitively plausible candidate for a rule that gives the meaning of *I* in English:

K-I: In any statement in which it occurs, *I* designates the speaker of the statement.[29]

---

[29]I use the expression "K" for David Kaplan, not the first to state such a rule, but deserving credit for *pondering* it so fruitfully (1979). Note that in Kaplan's formal theory, we do not quite have the K-I rule, for "I" gets us to a "rigid" intension, not an individual. Indeed, given the way I have set up Castañeda's theory (benefiting, of course, from Kaplan 1969 as well as 1979), it is strikingly similar to Kaplan's. With Kaplan, character and context yield content, a rigid individual concept; with Castañeda, meaning and (something like) context yield a rigid special sense. The great difference is the importance accorded to the "intermediate" property of character or meaning. The step Kaplan took, which Castañeda did not, is developing a theory of character. This allows

From this we see immediately that something has to give in the original theory. There we had

meaning of $(\alpha) = \text{sen}(\alpha)$.

$\text{des}(\alpha) = \text{ref}(\text{sen}(\alpha))$.

According to K-I, the designation of *I* varies from speaker to speaker. Therefore, the sense must vary. Therefore, the meaning must vary. But K-I appears to give a perfectly general meaning for *I*; the same rule applies when you use it as when I use it.

Castañeda's approach is best represented as recognizing a break between meaning and sense. *I* has the same meaning, no matter who uses it, but picks up a different sense, with a different reference, and so designates someone different. This result can be achieved by a rule like this:

C-I.1: In a statement made by speaker a, *I* expresses a sense s such that $\text{ref}(s) = a$.

Rule K-I follows from this rule, so its apparent plausibility is explained.

But this won't quite do. It does not explain the fact that *I* has a definite psychological role. The sentence *I am wanted on the telephone* has a definite psychological state associated with it, one that, in conjunction with the other beliefs, desires, and values of most of us, would lead us to go answer the telephone. If *I* can express any of the countless senses that have the speaker of a particular statement as reference, this would be mysterious.

Furthermore, none of the senses already in the theory, to serve, for example, as the senses of definite descriptions or proper names, will work. This is shown by the acceptance test. Given any name or description α that does not contain the first-person pronoun, Castañeda can invent a story in which a reasonable person, who is the reference of α, accepts a sentence containing *I* but not the sentence just like it containing α, and another in which the opposite happens.

To solve this problem, Castañeda postulates a realm of *special senses*, as I shall call them. Each person's special sense has, for him, the psychological role one associates with *I*. We shall use "ego" for the function that takes us from any person to that person's special sense. Then Castañeda's basic rule for *I* is:

C-I.2: In a statement of speaker a, *I* expresses ego(a).

Kaplan to avoid taking the step Castañeda did: Kaplan's rigid contents need not be *special*; they can be the same contents used, for example, with proper names. The difference is at the intermediate level. Which step was an opportunity missed, and which a cul-de-sac avoided can be argued; my view, in the papers cited, is that it is Kaplan's step that we must take before we can get clear about the psychological role of indexicals. We should also mention A. W. Burks' important work here; in particular, the use of duplication arguments to demonstrate the indispensability of indexicals and demonstratives (1949).

K-I is also a consequence of this rule, so its intuitive plausibility is still explained.

This account of the meaning of *I* leaves a gap in the theory of belief reports, and Castañeda sees that it also must be revised. Suppose that i = ego(Ivan). How do we report that Ivan has the belief

that i am wanted on the telephone

(i.e., the proposition consisting of i combined with the sense of *am wanted on the telephone*)? We do not say, *Ivan believes that I am wanted on the telephone*. Instead, we would say, *Ivan believes that he is wanted on the telephone*. But this, as Castañeda brings out by a number of delightful examples, need not be taken to absolutely require that Ivan believes the proposition indicated. To bring out the reading in which it does absolutely require this, Castañeda introduces the term *he**. This word disambiguates *he*; it is only a linguistic accident that we use the same word for imputing self-knowledge as we use for other purposes. Castañeda calls *he** a *quasi-indicator*.

The most straightforward way to interpret what Castañeda says about *he** is embodied in this rule:

C-He*.1: With antecedent α, *he** expresses the sense ego(des(α)).

Thus,

Ivan believes that *he** is wanted on the telephone

attributes to Ivan just the belief we wanted,

that i am wanted on the telephone.

Here des(*Ivan*) is Ivan, and ego(Ivan) is his special sense, i.

*He**: Some Problems

Consider,

(1) *Ivan believes that he* is wanted on the telephone.*

As I have stated the theory, (1) expresses the proposition that Ivan believes a certain proposition, namely,

(2) that i is wanted on the telephone,

where i = ego(Ivan). This theory seems to have grave difficulties.

First, note that on this theory, anyone who can believe anything about Ivan can believe (2). Suppose, for example, that this is true:

(3) *Sheila believes that Ivan believes that he* is wanted on the telephone.*

And suppose further that Sheila believes the proposition

(4) that Ivan is wanted on the telephone.

(3) tells us that Sheila believes a proposition with a sense of the sense i as a constituent.

It seems that if the belief of Sheila's reported by (3) leads her to expect Ivan to go answer the phone, as it surely might, she *must* believe (5).

(5) that Ivan is i.

But from (5) and (4), (2) follows. So it would be very surprising if Sheila did not believe (2).

Some things that Castañeda says have led readers to suppose that this is not possible on his theory, that "first-person propositions," like (2) are private, that only those referred to by the special senses therein can grasp them, much less believe them. But this is a misreading; Castañeda quite explicitly says the opposite, in his reply to Kretzmann 1966.

Kretzmann claimed that since there are certain propositions only one person can know, as when Jones knows that he (himself) is in the hospital, there are things God cannot know, and so there is no omniscient God. This seems like a pretty good argument, if there are private first-person propositions. But Castañeda says, in his comments on Kretzmann's paper, that Kretzmann's view does not follow from his theory. The example in question is

(7) *Jones knows that he (himself) is in the hospital.*

Castañeda says,

> The expression "he (himself)" in sentence (7) is a quasi-indicator. It cannot be eliminated from (7) by any name or description of Jones that includes no first-person quasi-indicator. It is this fact that leads Kretzmann to say that the statement expressed by the occurrence of "he (himself) is in the hospital" in (7) cannot be known by any other person. But this does not follow. If Kretzmann, or the reader, knows that Jones knows that he (himself) is in the hospital, then, by principle (P) above, Kretzmann or the reader know the very same proposition that by (7) Jones knows to be true. Hence, theism is not, by the present route, incompatible with omniscience (1967a, 209).

Principle (P) is,

> If a sentence of the form "X knows that a person Y knows that ..." formulates a true statement, then the person X knows the statement formulated by the clause filling the blank "..." (1967a, 209).

Castañeda is using *statement* here as I am using *proposition*.

Thus it seems clear that Castañeda intends it to be possible for Sheila to believe exactly what Ivan believes, when Ivan believes that *he** is wanted on the telephone.

(He does maintain that there is no simple way in unadorned English to state the proposition that Sheila believes (2); the relevance of this is discussed below.)

There seem to be at least three fairly serious difficulties with this theory.

First, suppose that Sheila and Ivan both believe (2). If the theory is to explain the data, this belief must have different psychological roles for Sheila and Ivan. Ivan should accept *I am wanted on the telephone* and be disposed to answer the phone but Sheila should not be disposed to speak or act in these ways. What is to explain the difference?

It does not seem an adequate explanation to say that i has Ivan, but not Sheila, as reference. It seems that it would have to be added that Ivan was aware that he^* was the reference of i. But in what could this awareness consist? It cannot simply be his belief in the proposition,

> that i is i

for there is no reason to doubt that Sheila has that belief also.

The second problem has to do with reports like (1). This belief report seems like the sort of thing that might explain Ivan's moving towards the telephone to answer it. But it is not at all clear why it should do so. What (1) says, on this theory, is that Ivan believes a certain proposition,

(2) that i is wanted on the telephone.

Now if the first difficulty can be solved, then it must be that not everyone who believes (2) accepts *I am wanted on the telephone* and tries to answer the telephone. One only does this when it is one's own special sense that is a constituent.

Therefore, reporting that a person believes a first-person proposition does not provide any explanation of that person's accepting the relevant *I*-sentence, or performing the appropriate actions. The information that it is his or her *own* special sense that is a constituent of the believed proposition must also be conveyed. On the theory being considered, (1) does not provide this information. Remember that the meaning of he^*, given by rule C-He*.1, is not a constituent of the proposition expressed by (1). The proposition expressed by (1) says nothing about the expression he^*, or its meaning, or about i being the value of the function ego for the argument Ivan. It simply says that Ivan believes (2).[30]

---

[30]This is really an ad hominem argument. One is inclined to say that one simply sees the he^* in the sentence, and realizes that since it can be used to identify Ivan's belief, *his* first-person sense must be a constituent of the proposition he is said to believe. We pick up the crucial information from *how* a certain proposition is expressed—by use of he^*—even though the information is not part of what the proposition says. I think this a fine reply, but anyone who uses it is on the verge of accepting the point of view suggested later on anyway.

The reply in effect countenances a third level of truth conditions, in addition to the referential level and the sense level; it is by understanding these that we *see* that it must be Ivan's special sense that is involved.

The third difficulty is provided by Castañeda himself (1966). It is also brought up by an example due to Rogers Albritton, which I have altered somewhat (Adams and Castañeda 1983).

Suppose that Ivan has just been appointed the editor of *Soul*, but does not know it, although he has heard that *Soul* has once again appointed a male editor. The following might be true:

(6) *Ivan believes that the editor of Soul believes that he* is alive.*

Where e = ego(the editor of *Soul*), it follows that Ivan believes the proposition

(8) *that e is alive.*

The reasoning is similar to that credited to Sheila above. Ivan believes the proposition

(9) that the editor of *Soul* is e

and the proposition

(10) that the editor of *Soul* is alive.

So he concludes (8). But Ivan surely also believes the proposition that *he** is alive, that is,

(11) that i am alive.

But since Ivan is the editor of *Soul*, ego(Ivan) is the same sense as ego(the editor of *Soul*), that is, $i = e$. Therefore, (8) = (11).

It seems that if Ivan would but reflect upon (8) and (11), he would realize that they are one and the same proposition. But then he would know the proposition

(12) that $i = e$.

But then he would believe that *he** has been selected editor of *Soul*, for this follows from (12) and (9). But this is contrary to the original hypothesis.

Castañeda considers the possibility that "the heaviest man of Europe could come to know that *he** weighs more than anybody else without resorting at all to the scales and comparison of weights" (1966). Castañeda says that "This absurdity arises simply from allowing the tokens of '*he**' to function as independent symbols, i.e., as referring expressions in their own right, without the need of a grammatical and logical antecedent" (152). Castañeda says, "Propositions about a given I can be the full objects of belief (knowledge, assumption, assertion, etc.) only if the belief (knowledge, etc.) in question belongs to that same I" (1968a, 263). And in reply to Kretzmann, Castañeda says, "an omniscient being does not know every proposition in *oratio recta*: indexical propositions he must know in *oratio obliqua*, in the form of quasi-indexical propositions ..." (1967a, 210).

I believe these remarks may be responsible for some people taking Castañeda to be asserting that persons cannot grasp first-person propositions other than their own. But, as we saw, this is not his view.

In these remarks, Castañeda is drawing our attention to the fact that in English there is no simple way of reporting, say, that Sheila believes (2). Neither of the following will do:

> *Sheila believes that I am wanted on the telephone.*
> *Sheila believes that she* is wanted on the telephone.*

The first seems like it ought to work, according to the theory, as long as Ivan is the speaker. But, as we shall see below, Castañeda amends the rule for *I* so that in such sentences it does not express a first-person sense.

(3) reports that Sheila believes a proposition of which a sense of (2) is a constituent; but there seems to be no straightforward way to report her belief in (2).

In the remarks quoted, this apparent fact about English seems to somehow be used to resolve the third difficulty. But if this is the strategy, I do not believe it succeeds.

There is nothing in Castañeda's theory to explain why English has no way of saying that Sheila believes (2). To stipulate that since English has no way to report such beliefs, there are none to report, would be at best an ad hoc way of solving the problem. But even this is not available to Castañeda; he maintains, in the reply to Kretzmann, that we can have such beliefs and that we can have such beliefs does seem to follow from the theory by two good arguments, the one I gave and the one he gave. So if English has no way to express such beliefs, that just seems to be an odd fact about English. If it is a deep fact about English, it seems an embarrassment to the theory that it provides no explanation of it.

My argument that the editor of *Soul* could figure out virtually a priori that *he** was the editor of *Soul* did not depend on allowing *he** to function as an independent symbol, as examination of it will show. But, in fact, the theory seems to give us no reason not to introduce a perfectly intelligible close relative of *he**. We simply let *he*(Ivan)* do, in a sentence where *Ivan* is not available as an antecedent, just what *he** does when it is available. In this slightly augmented English, we can say

> *Sheila believes that he*(Ivan) is wanted on the telephone*

and

> *God knows that he*(Jones) is wanted on the telephone*

to express Sheila's belief and God's knowledge. Finally, the phrases "*oratio obliqua* knowledge" and "*oratio recta* knowledge" seem to me misleading in the quote given above about what an omniscient being can know. Castañeda has argued, against Kretzmann, that an omniscient being can know Jones' first-person propositions in the way of knowing a proposition that is usually reported with *oratio recta*. That unaugmented English has no way of reporting such knowledge does not seem to change this.

So I conclude that appeal to these facts about English will not provide a solution to the third difficulty I have raised.

*He**: A Revised Theory

I believe the account of *he** can be amended in a way that takes care of the three difficulties I have raised. The theory as so amended is one that, I think, people have often taken Castañeda to be putting forward, and is in the spirit of a suggestion made by Carl Ginet (Castañeda 1966, 143). This account is compatible with first-person propositions being accessible only to those to whom the special senses in them refer.

Consider,

(3) *Sheila believes that Ivan believes that he* is wanted on the telephone.*

On the revised theory the proposition

(2) that *i* is wanted on the telephone

is not a constituent of the proposition expressed by (1). Instead, (1) says that Sheila believes that Ivan believes the proposition resulting from combining his special sense with the sense of *is wanted on the telephone*.

Let *s* be a variable ranging over senses. Then we can say such things as,

For some *s*, Ivan believes that *s* is wanted on the telephone.

This does not mean that Ivan thinks someone wants to talk to a sense, of course. It means, rather, that there is a proposition, resulting from the combination of some sense *s* with the sense of *is wanted on the telephone*, that Ivan believes.

To achieve the desired effect, we need to treat *he** as an expression that abbreviates a construction that binds such sense variables. The rule may be put as follows:

He*.2: With α as antecedent,

> *A believes that he* is so-and-so*

has the sense of

> *There is an s such that s = ego(α) and A believes that s is so-and-so.*

Using this rule, (3) says,

> *Sheila believes that there is an s such that s = ego(Ivan) and Ivan believes that s is wanted on the telephone.*

On this theory, i, Ivan's special sense, is not a constituent of the proposition Sheila believes, but is a constituent of the proposition she believes that Ivan believes. On the other hand, the sense of the expression

(13) *ego(Ivan)*

is a constituent of the proposition Sheila believes. It is easy to get confused here, since (13) has a sense and designates another sense. Only the former is a constituent of the proposition (3) expresses.

Let us turn to (1). We want (1) to attribute to Ivan not simply the belief that a first-person proposition of his is true, but belief in that proposition. The proposal gives this result. (1) says,

> *there is an s such that s = ego(Ivan) and Ivan believes that s is wanted on the telephone.*

Although (2) is not a constituent of the proposition expressed by (1), Ivan has to believe (2) for (1) to be true.

Given this account of *he**, the arguments for the possibility of believing (3), or God's believing Jones' first-person proposition in Kretzmann's example, do not work. This undercuts Castañeda's criticisms of Kretzmann, but it allows Castañeda to claim that the special senses are private. He can then claim, against the first objection raised, that any normal person who believes (2) will accept "I am wanted on the telephone" and go to answer the telephone. He could claim that it is intrinsic to (2) that belief in it has this role. But since Ivan is the only person who can believe it, there is not a general rush to the telephone.

The second objection, that (1) does not explain Ivan's telephone-answering behavior, is also now answered. The sense of the expression (13) is a constituent of the proposition expressed by (1), although not of (2), the proposition Ivan must believe for (1) to be true. So (1) now tells us what the connection is between Ivan and the special sense that is a constituent of the proposition he is said to believe. Given general knowledge of the psychological role of first-person propositions, (1) does tell us that Ivan may be expected to accept *I am wanted on the telephone* and to go to answer the phone, assuming he is relatively normal.

The a priori argument by which anyone who is editor of *Soul* could figure out that fact will not now pose a problem. (6) now attributes to Ivan a belief that has the sense of the expression

ego(the editor of Soul)

as a constituent, but not e (the editor's special sense) or i (Ivan's special sense). The argument by which Ivan was to overcome his ignorance of his appointment does not get started.

Toward the Unity of *He*

Once we have adopted the revised theory of *he**—and I am not saying that Castañeda ever has or will—certain questions naturally arise. On the revised theory, *he** does not seem so distinct from other uses of *he* as Castañeda argued. But when we pursue this, we find ourselves wondering whether there really is a separate sense of *he* corresponding to *he** after all.

Castañeda isolates what he calls the "(F)-use" of *he*:

> (F) "He" is often employed as a place-holder for some *unspecified* description which refers to a previously mentioned object. . . . Examples are "Paul said (believes, knows) of (someone who in point of fact is) Mary that she is happy." . . . and, of a different linguistic form "Paul saw Mary and believes that she is happy" (1966, 133).

Castañeda gives an analysis of such uses. Consider,

(14) *Paul believes of Mary that she is happy.*

Castañeda's analysis is

> There is a sense s such that ref(s) = Mary and Paul believes that s is happy.

Consider (1) once more,

(1) *Ivan believes that he* is wanted on the telephone.*

If we were to take the *he** in (1) to be simply an (F)-use of *he*, the analysis would be

> There is a sense s such that ref(s) = Ivan and Ivan believes that s is wanted on the telephone.

This is not so far off; if we could restrict the domain of senses to the special senses, we would have just what we want. But then, why not simply treat *he** as complex; *he* is an (F)-use of *he*, while * restricts the domain of senses to the special senses?

The relevant rules look like this:

(F).1: With α as antecedent,

> B believes that he is so-and-so

has the sense of

> there is a sense s, such that ref(s) = α and B believes that s is so-and-so.

(*): Appended to an F-use of *he*, * restricts the domain of senses to special senses.

(Note that Castañeda's explanation of (F)-uses mentions unspecified *descriptions* of previously mentioned objects. But there is no obvious reason why we should limit ourselves to senses of descriptions.)

Castañeda 1966 gives arguments against treating *he** as an (F)-use of *he*. But I do not believe these arguments are effective against the present proposal. The first argument (135–36) is directed against an attempt to treat uses of *he** simply as uses of *he*, not against a proposal like the present one, which treats *he** as semantically complex, built from the (F)-use of *he*. Arguments that show that uses of *he** do not go proxy for nonspecial senses (senses of names or descriptions not containing *he**) are irrelevant, so long as rule (F) is not limited to such senses.

Castañeda says,

> It is only a linguistic freak that "he" in the sense of "he*" looks exactly like the third-person pronoun "he," which occurs, for instance in "Arthur came, but he knew nobody he saw; he left early" (1966, 132).

For those who are skeptical of such linguistic freaks, the present suggestion may seem plausible. And perhaps we can go further.

There seem to be many useful restrictions on the domain of senses that could be combined with (F)-uses of *he* for various purposes. Indeed, Castañeda suggests one, by way of an alternative treatment of (F)-uses. On rule (F), or at least analogous rules for *it*, we can say of *B* that he believes of the morning star that it is the evening star, so long as *B* believes that the evening star is the evening star. To avoid this result, Castañeda suggests incorporating into (F) a requirement that restricts the domain of senses to those not expressed by expressions in the relevant embedded sentence, in this case eliminating the sense of *the evening star*. And Castañeda notes that he "can easily conceive of" other implicit restrictions of this sort.

Here are some examples in which it seems plausible to appeal to such implicit restrictions.

Suppose I am explaining why Albert went over and asked Mary if he could borrow her copy of *Word and Object*:

> *Albert wanted to look up something in Word and Object, and he knew, of Mary, that she had a copy, so he walked up to her.*

This is really an incomplete explanation, as it stands. To make it work we need to assume that the sense with Mary as reference that is a constituent of the proposition Albert knew is, say, the sense of *the woman I see in the corner* and not, say, the sense of *the person I met last week who is now in Madrid watching a bullfight, for all I know*. Why do we assume this? One explanation is that there is a special *she* quasi-indicator, whose meaning forces the restriction to senses whose constituency in the proposition believed by Albert explains his actions. Another is that we simply have an (F)-use of *she*, but that its occurrence in the context of explanation and common sense force the assumption. It is not the *she*, but the *so*, that forces it. One argument in favor of this is that we might criticize the explanation by saying, "That is not why he walked up to her, because although he did know that, he did not recognize her." We would be allowing that the part of the sentence before the *so* was true, but denying that the facts that made it true are explanatory. If *she* were a quasi-indicator, we should deny that Albert knew what he is said to know.

You ask me why I have bet so much money on the outcome of the Orange Bowl. I say, *Jimmy the Greek has seen the team from my state play, and said that it would win the Orange Bowl.* This would be rather misleading if what Jimmy the Greek had said was,

> *The next winner of the Orange Bowl will win the Orange Bowl*

or

> *The best team will win the Orange Bowl.*

It would be misleading even if the team from my home state is the best team and the next winner of the Orange Bowl. We assume that he expressed a proposition with a sense that would give me some reason for betting on the team from my home state. We do not assume this because of any special meaning of the word *it* contained in my sentence, but simply because unless he expressed such a proposition my explanation is stupid.

Or consider: *Ivan saw Sheila from a distance, and believed she was not Sheila.* Here we assume that Ivan thought something like *That person is not Sheila.* Suppose Sheila is also the new editor of *Soul*, but Ivan did not know it. He sees her from a distance, recognizes her, but thinks, *The new editor of Soul is not Sheila.* It would be very misleading to report this last incident with the sentence indicated. We restrict the candidates for the proposition Ivan believes to those with "demonstrative senses" as constituents, but the restriction is an assumption guided by common sense, not sensitivity to a special meaning of *she*.

I think, in fact, that nearly all (F)-uses of *he*, *she*, and *it* would naturally be regarded as placing some implicit limitations on the senses that can be parts of the incompletely specified propositions. The limitations are not placed by a number of different senses of these pronouns, but by common sense and explanatory relevance. The restrictions seem to come in *not* when we understand the proposition expressed by the sentence containing the pronoun, but when we figure out how the facts would have to be to make the proposition true and explain what is in question.

It is a very natural step to begin to think of *he** not as marking a separate sense of *he* at all, but as an important use of *he*, conforming to a well-known pattern of implicit restriction to special senses.

That is, we might conjecture that where the antecedent of an (F)-use of *he* is an expression that designates the believer of a proposition expressed by a sentence in which it occurs, we always assume, unless the suggestion is cancelled, that the domain of senses is restricted to the special senses. This is not a matter of entailment by a special sense of *he*, but a matter of common sense and Gricean implicature.

Suppose I say,

> *Privatus believes that he is rich.*

I think one would ordinarily expect that I intended to imply that Privatus accepted "I am rich." But this suggestion can be cancelled:

> *Privatus believes that he is rich, but in an odd way, since he is one of Castañeda's characters.*

The additional information cancels the expectation; instead one expects Privatus to accept something like *The editor of Soul is rich* or *The man in the mirror is rich*.

This is not to say that one cannot *introduce* an expression that works as we have defined * to work. But it is an interesting fact that English can get by without it, and, as we shall see, a fact that leaves the way open for more drastic revisions.

Himself

We do have in English the expressions *herself* and *himself*. And Castañeda often inserts *himself* after *he* in his initial explanations of quasi-indication. One might conjecture, then, that *himself* in ordinary English does just what we imagined * to be doing in the last section, systematically restricting the domain of senses. Note that it is treating *he** as complex that makes this suggestion possible.

I do not think this is the way *himself* works, however.

First, note that this expression can be used in nonepistemic contexts:

(15) *Elwood bites himself.*

(15) may be contrasted with

(16) *Elwood bites Elwood.*

(15) seems to involve an intransitive verb phrase, *bites himself*; (16) a transitive verb phrase, *bites*. A natural proposal is that *himself* is governed by these syntactic and semantic rules:

(Himself):

(i) Where δ is a transitive verb, δ *himself* is an intransitive verb.

(ii) $\alpha \delta$ *himself* is true if and only if $\alpha \delta \alpha$ is true, and α designates a male.

The device *himself* thus gives us two ways of stating what is intuitively a single fact, that Elwood bites Elwood. Why should we want two ways of saying this?

Note that the intransitive verb phrases, *bites himself* and *bites Elwood*, give us two quite different principles of classification. The class of dogs that bite themselves may have interesting attributes in common, and so may the class of dogs that bite Elwood, but they are probably not the same attributes. The real point of *himself* shows up in sentences like

(17) *Like every dog that bites himself, Elwood is covered with sores.*

(18) *Like every dog that bites Elwood, Elwood has broken teeth.*

Similarly, the class of people picked out by the verb phrase,

> *believes himself to be rich*

differs from that picked out by

> *believes Privatus to be rich.*

This makes it quite easy to see why

(19) *Privatus believes himself to be rich*

generates quite different suggestions than

(20) *Privatus believes Privatus to be rich.*

In day-to-day discourse, sentences are often proffered as explanations in a way that requires a lot of filling in by a listener. Even if (19) and (20) are both true just in case Privatus believes Privatus to be rich, they naturally answer different questions. Suppose that the generalizations *Everyone who believes himself to be rich is a snob* and *Everyone who believes Privatus to be rich is amazed* have both been asserted and left unchallenged in a conversation. Then (19) would be a good answer to the question *Why is Privatus so snobby?* and (20) would be a good answer to *Why is Privatus so surprised?*

There is, in fact, a very common and important way of believing oneself to be rich, which, on Castañeda's theory, involves believing that *s* is rich, where *s* is one's special sense. It is not surprising then, that the use of the verb phrase *believes himself to be rich* so strongly suggests that Privatus believes it in this way.

It does seem to me that the suggestion is still cancelable, however. Here is an example from Jon Barwise. The dean has been complaining that professors who publish less than ten articles per year on the average are overpaid. He has particular ones in mind, Professors *A*, *B*, *Q*, and *Z* in the blind sample he has been studying. Then one day he counts the articles he has written and finds only ninety-three articles over the past ten years, agreeing exactly with the figure for Professor *Z*, which could not be a coincidence.

We say,

> *The dean was surprised to find that he believed himself to be overpaid.*

Toward a Little More Unity

Besides the quasi-indexical and (F)-uses of *he*, Castañeda distinguishes five other uses. Three of these are, roughly speaking, demonstrative uses. The other two are often grouped together by philosophers and linguists, as the use of *he* as a variable of quantification:

> *Somebody came when I was out and he returned my book.*
> *If Arthur comes late, he will call.*

Both of these can easily be translated into the predicate calculus in a way so that the function of the *he* is taken by a bound variable. One way to handle the second sentence is

> *There is an x such that x = Arthur and if x comes late, x will call.*

But it is much simpler to simply regard proper names, as Montague does, as capable of binding variables,

> *If Arthur x comes late, x will call.*

Those who find this strange should recall that in English *somebody* and *everybody* do not come equipped with variables any more than *Arthur* does, and that most quantifiers in English cannot be treated as logical expressions (Barwise and Cooper 1980).

Suppose we think that there is such a bound variable use of *he*. Can we see the (F)-use of *he* as simply what happens to the bound-variable *he* when it finds itself in a sentence embedded in a propositional attitude sentence?

When variables or pronouns regarded as variables are found in such embedded sentences, there is a familiar problem for Fregean theories. Within such embedded sentences, expressions are to refer to their usual senses, and contribute senses of those senses to the propositions expressed by the embedding sentence. But, on the usual treatment, variables have no sense, only designation. Castañeda's analysis of (F)-uses is in fact very similar in spirit to attempts to solve this problem. (Cf. Kaplan 1979.) The basic idea is that we go from the designation of the variable or pronoun to the set of senses that have that object as reference, usually restricted in some way or other. One of these senses has to be a constituent of the proposition, belief in which is attributed.

Two sections back I advocated seeing the *he* in

> *Ivan believes that he is wanted on the telephone*

as an (F)-use of *he*, which picks up, as virtually all (F)-uses do, commonsense restrictions on the domain of senses. In this case, the natural restrictions are to special senses, unless something to the contrary is indicated. Now we can regard this as simply a use of the bound-variable use of *he*.

I

Rule C-I.2 actually oversimplifies Castañeda's treatment of *I*. Consider Ivan's remarks:

(21) *Sheila believes, of me, that I am wanted on the telephone.*

(22) *Sheila believes that I am wanted on the telephone.*

In these cases, *i* clearly need not be part of the proposition Sheila is reported to believe.

Castañeda calls the use of *I* exhibited by (21) an (F)-use. Like an (F)-use of *he*, he regards it as a "place-holder for some unspecified description or name of the person" to whom the antecedent refers. This result is obtained by an additional rule:

> (P′) A statement of the form "X E's of me that ϕ (I)" is the same as the statement of the corresponding form "There is a way of referring to a certain person as Z, I am that person and X E's that ϕ (Z)" (1966, 147).

On rule C-I.2, *I* does provide a sense, unlike a variable or a use of *he* as a bound variable. The problem that arises with (21) cannot, then, be the same problem that arose with *he*. It is not that *I* provides no sense to serve as the reference within the embedded sentence, but that it provides the wrong one. Rule (P) is simply an additional rule, in no way motivated by C-I.2; Castañeda recognizes this fact when he says that this use of *I* "... is at bottom not an authentic first person use of *I*" (1966, 147).

Note that the rule K-I would leave us in exactly the same position with an *I* in an embedded sentence as we are with a *he*; designation but no sense. The fact that in both cases we seem to be left with an unspecified sense for the proposition expressed by the embedded sentence would be no accident.

(22) has to be treated differently, since there is no authentic use of *I* or *me* to serve as antecedent. Castañeda introduces a third rule for it:

> (P″) A statement of the form of "X E's that ϕ (I)" is the same as the corresponding statement of the form "There is a way of referring to a certain person as Z, X can identify Z (in the relevant respect, or knows who Z is), I am Z and X E's that ϕ (Z)" (1966, 149).

Now consider

(23) I believe, of me, that I am wanted on the telephone.

(24) I believe that I am wanted on the telephone.

I do not sense much difference between these. But it seems that either of them might be used, by Ivan, to explain his acceptance of *I am wanted on the telephone* and his rising from the table to answer the phone. Principles (P′) and (P″) do not explain this, for according to them, the proposition in which Ivan expressed his belief has not been specified.

Now one might reply, at this point, that although the exact proposition has been left unspecified, one can see what it probably is. We naturally assume, when someone says (23) or (24), that it is their own special sense that is a constituent of the proposition they are reporting their belief in. Since this is exactly the sort of reasoning I have been advocating, in arguing that we only need *he* and not *he**, how could I object to this reply?

I do not object, but I wish to draw a moral from this reply. On the Fregean view, the role of attributions of belief is to tell us which propositions the believer has the attitude of belief toward. This knowledge then can play a role in forming expectations or explanations of the believer's actions, in conjunction, of course, with other knowledge.

On the original view, the attributions told us directly which proposition was believed. It was simply whatever proposition was the sense of the embedded sentence. On the accounts of *he* and *I* that we have arrived at, however, things do not work this way at all. The expressions, embedded in a belief report, designate entities referred to by their antecedents. We ask ourselves, based on a number of factors, including the relation of the person to whom belief is attributed and the designation of the antecedent, and the purpose for which the belief report was given, which sense or senses are reasonable completions of the proposition. Then we take the report to attribute belief in one of those propositions.

In this process, we go from designation to sense, but never from sense back to reference.

To see how this is so, first reconsider rule C-I.2. This rule tells us that each time *I* is used, a sense that refers to the speaker will be expressed. But to get to this sense, we must first identify the speaker. The speaker does not get into the picture through his special sense, but the other way round. To use rule C-I.2, we would first have to use K-I to find the speaker.

Now consider Ivan's use of (23). Rule K-I gives us Ivan as the designation of the first *I*. Rule (P′) tells us that Ivan believes some proposition with a sense that refers to him as initial constituent. Common sense, or Gricean implicature, or some mixture, leads us to suppose that it is Ivan's special sense that is needed. *This is the first use we have had for this sense.*

I think that, if we look closely at the way the theory would actually work in figuring out what people believe on the basis of belief-attributions, we would find that this result is quite general. What is important about special senses is that they are expressed by the use of *I* and that they have a certain psychological role. Their reference is immaterial.

Once we see this, certain alternatives to Castañeda's view present themselves. One is that we need nothing in our theory except the meaning of *I* and the designation of *I* on specific occasions of use. The former would be the same for everyone, and correspond to the same psychological role for everyone. It would therefore not be what determines reference, since it would no more refer to one person than another. But it would not *need* to determine reference, since *I* designates without sense—but not without meaning.

Can we get by without special senses? I think so. When I think to myself, *I need to do the taxes*, the meaning of *I*, and the fact that I am doing the thinking, suffice to make the thought about me. No special sense is needed. *I*, of course, must have a meaning, but the K-I rule will do.

One might ask how *I* can have so crucial a role in the thinking of each of us, if not through expressing a special sense. But I do not think that one need look beyond the K-I rule for an answer. It insures that *I* will have a definite psychological role, the same for everyone who understands it.

These ideas have been developed in the series of articles mentioned at the beginning of the paper. I will not pursue them here, but rather, in the next section, try to put the basic point in a rather different way.

But first I would like to leave those who would still like to pursue Castañeda's line with a couple of challenging examples to chew on that have not otherwise come up:

(25) *Sheila and I both believe that I am wanted on the telephone.*

(26) *Sheila and I each believe that she and I are wanted on the telephone.*

(27) *I believe that I am wanted on the telephone and Sheila believes it too.*

A Fantasy

Let us suppose that God has created the heavens and earth, and populated the latter with humans. These humans have the powers of perception and movement, and there are wired-in connections between the two. When they see a carrot they grab it and eat it, for example. But they do not get enough carrots during the day to thrive. God assigns a very astute angel, Michael, to develop the capacity of belief for them. The idea is that having this capacity will help them: perceptions that do not immediately lead to action will lead to beliefs; later these beliefs may lead to effective actions that would not be occasioned by the perceptions they had then. They will be able to eat carrots they see during the day when they get hungry at night. Michael is given instructions to work out such a capacity and instill it in the humans.

Michael has read Frege, and proceeds as follows. He creates a realm of senses and creates in the humans the power to grasp those senses. By decree, the various senses stand for various conditions, with certain complex ones standing for the unique objects that meet the complex conditions, all this being done in a nicely compositional way. Some senses he calls propositions. He gives humans the power to have the attitude of belief towards propositions, and programs them to believe the propositions that correspond to what they see, and to take actions that according to the beliefs will satisfy their desires.

(He plans to give them the capacity for more complex desires once he has solved the problem of belief.) He puts all of this into effect. Nothing happens.

Then Michael reads Castañeda. He diagnoses his problem as follows. The humans perceive and act from a certain position in space and time. The belief that a certain type of perceptual experience should lead a given individual to have, and the actions that certain beliefs should lead that individual to perform, depend on this position. When Ivan, the king of France, perceives a carrot in front of him, he needs to be led to a belief that there is a carrot in front of the king of France. But Sheila, the editor of *Soul*, should be led to the belief that there is a carrot in front of the editor of *Soul*, when she sees a carrot in front of her. And the king of France, when he believes that there is a carrot in front of the king of France, and becomes hungry during the night, should reach out and grab the carrot in front of him. The editor of *Soul*, if she believes there is a carrot in front of the king of France, should not reach out, even if she is quite hungry, but she should if she believes there is a carrot in front of the editor of *Soul*. Michael realizes he has not given humans enough to use their beliefs in this way. The king of France's perceptions do not tell him who the carrot is in front of; he does not know whether to believe that there is a carrot in front of the king of France or one in front of the editor of *Soul*.

Michael decides to give each human a very special sense, which will refer to them, by his decree, no matter where they go or whether or not they become the editor of *Soul* or the author of *Waverly* or the king of France. All they have to do is be who they are. He puts such a sense into the system for each created person and resolves to create more as necessary. Ivan and Sheila and all the humans grasp these senses, as well as the old ones. Still, nothing happens.

Thinking this over, Michael sees the problem. There is still nothing in perception or action to tie each person's special sense into an effective network of psychological states. Ivan's special sense i refers to him; Sheila's special sense s refers to her. But this is not the sort of specialness that is important. This specialness guarantees that once they form the belief he wants them to, it will be true. But he has not done anything to get it formed, or to make it effective.

Michael decides he overdid things. He makes each person's sense graspable only by them; this was something that Castañeda sometimes seemed to suggest. It is not clear why this would help, but it does make each person's special sense even more special, so he gives it a try. Still, nothing happens. People are grasping sentences and entertaining propositions. Perhaps they are even writing novels in their heads. But they are not forming beliefs and eating carrots at night.

Michael thinks things over, and finally sees what must be done. He calls upon his subordinate, Penelope. Penelope is to take a list of each person and their special sense, and retool their minds so that their perceptions lead to right beliefs and the beliefs lead to the right actions. When Ivan sees a carrot, he will believe that there is a carrot in front of i,

and when Ivan believes this, and is hungry, he will reach out and grab the carrot. In this way, Michael explains, the system of beliefs each person has will be oriented to the objective world, in the way that their perceptions and action have been all along.

"That is a very long list," Penelope says. "Days are getting short, and these people are going to be dropping off like flies if they do not start getting some carrots down at night. I have an idea that will save some time."

Penelope's better idea is very simple: "We choose one special sense, Ivan's, perhaps, and retool everyone so that they form the belief

that there is a carrot in front of i

when they see a carrot. And we retool everyone so that when they have this belief and are hungry, they reach out." She points out that this will make psychology possible, since there will be systematic connections between perceptual states, belief, and types of action, rather than separate link-ups for each person.

Michael is worried. "That is going to knock hell out of reference and truth," he observes. "Everyone but Ivan will be having false beliefs about there being carrots in front of Ivan, when they actually see carrots in front of themselves."

"Granted," Penelope observes. "But their false beliefs will lead systematically to effective action. Those people are starving. We can worry about reference and truth when I get back."

Michael agrees reluctantly. But when Penelope returns, a simple solution to the problem of reference is found. Michael, by decree, makes the sense i no longer stand for anyone. "We will say that the person's belief is true, when they believe

there is a carrot in front of i

if there is a carrot in front of them," he adds, as an afterthought. This change seems to have no effect on the nocturnal carrot-eating, which is now proceeding apace.

Later, pleased with their success, God charges Michael and Penelope with giving humans language. They are apprehensive that their rather rushed solution to the carrot-eating problem will wreak havoc with this project.

The problem is this. Their strategy for language is to have words associated with senses, sentences with propositions. Sentences are true if the associated propositions are.

But there in the middle of the system is a sense with no reference. What is worse, Michael's decree that when someone believes,

that there is a carrot in front of i

they believe truly if and only if there is a carrot in front of them, has somehow to fit in.

Again, Penelope has a promising if rather ad hoc idea. So far, they have been assigning senses to expressions, and letting reference take care of itself. This will not work with i; the word used to express it will not stand for anything, since i does not have a reference. Penelope suggests simply having the word governed by two separate rules,

(i) I expresses i.

(ii) Whenever it is used, I stands for the user.

She explains: "Although i does not refer to anything, and thoughts with i in them are not true or false, it has a definite cognitive role, as a result of all those connections between i, perception, and actions that I built into humans. So humans have to have a word to express i, to explain their actions. Now they can say 'I reached because I believed there was a carrot in front of I'. But your hastily drawn rule says that they believe truly, in such a case, if there *is* a carrot in front of them. When it comes to truth, we need a reference. The same sense cannot have different references; that is clear. So we cannot have I's reference determined by the sense it expresses. We will just have it determined by who uses it, and this is what (ii) does." Again, Michael and Penelope give in to expedience.

But later Penelope reasons as follow.

"Just look at part (ii) of our rule for I. Now suppose a human learns to use the word correctly *just insofar as its use is governed by rule (ii)*. That means that a human will say

I am planting a carrot patch

if and only if they believe

that i am planting a carrot patch

and so forth. Rule (i), the rule that allows I to express a certain special cognitive role in human psychology, will be conformed to automatically by anyone who masters rule (ii)!"

"Do you suppose," Michael ruminates, "that if I had started with language and exploited the systematic links God had wired in between perception and action to give words a use, the way we did with I, we could have just worried about reference, and left sense out of it?" [31]

―――――――――
[31] Many of the points herein doubtless had their origin in the many conversations Michael Bratman and I have had about Castañeda's work over the last several years. The paper was written while I was collaborating with Jon Barwise on another project; he was patient and helpful when I diverted our discussions to *he**. Conversations with John Etchemendy were also very helpful.

This paper was completed while I was a Fellow at the Center for Advanced Study in the Behavioral Sciences and on sabbatical leave from Stanford University. I am grateful for financial support from these institutions, and from the National Endowment for the Humanities, and the Andrew Mellon Foundation.

6

Perception, Action, and the Structure of Believing

Psychology has its beginning in ethological observation, Grice says. Systematic philosophical psychology appropriately enough has its beginning in ethological fiction, Grice's Toby and his fellow squarrels (1975). Toby and the other squarrels often gobble nuts in front of them, particularly after doing without nuts for some time. The theoretical apparatus we use to describe this in an explanatorily promising way allows us to say such things as *Toby prehends nuts as in front of him* and *Toby judges on nuts in front, for squarrel food*. Appeal to certain laws or near-laws then allows the explanation of Toby's gobbling. Prehending is a type of protoperception, and judging a type of protobelief. *Prehending nuts as in front of him* and *judging on nuts in front, for squarrel food* are states instantiated at different times, in front of different nuts, by different squarrels; gobbling is a type of act, similarly instantiated by different squarrels at different times; when successful, different nuts are gobbled. Thus the laws relate (proto) perceptual states, (proto) belief states, and types of action.

This is all, I think, just as it should be, not only for squarrels, prehension, judging, and gobbling, but also for humans, perception, belief, desire, and action. Psychological theory must deal with perceptual states, belief states, desire states, and types of action if it is to be general and systematic. The laws that relate these states and types of actions and their combinations to one another as typical causes and effects must square with ethological observation and make ecological sense.

A widely held conception of the structure of belief makes this impossible. The conception is the progeny of an inadequate semantics for attitude reports due to Frege but attractive to many. This, in turn, is the result of an inadequate semantics for the sentences embedded in canonical attitude reports. The inadequate theory has been and is being developed in great complexity and detail, with impact on disciplines from metaphysics to syntax. When Grice's program of creature-construction reaches the point where it can give us a "genitorial" justification for the psychological laws or near-laws that govern us, we should have a reasonably clear idea of what these laws are. This requires, I think, a new semantic perspective.

I explain the problem and show how a new semantical perspective, situation semantics, promises a solution. Situation semantics, developed by Jon Barwise and me (see Barwise and Perry 1981, 1981a, and 1983),[32] brings back into semantics a notion banned by Frege (1892/1960, 64ff), the idea that sentences stand for something like facts.[33] It incorporates many of the insights of David Kaplan's three-tiered semantics, with its formal recognition of the sort of meaning that demonstratives and indexicals have (1978, 1979, and 1989). The importance of this type of expression has long been championed by a distinguished minority of philosophers of language, including C. S. Peirce, Arthur Burks, and Hector-Neri Castañeda (Burks 1949, Castañeda 1967). It is not surprising that a philosophy of language and mind that wishes to take our relation to the environment seriously must also take seriously *this, that, I, now,* and *here.*

This paper began as a discussion of the role of *I* in memory, occasioned by certain theses advanced in Grice 1941. A bit like the *monstera gigantea,* a vine mentioned later, the paper grew toward a nearby protuberance that cast a shadow on the original enterprise, leaving its roots behind. The protuberance was the semantics of indexicals and demonstratives. I end, however, with some remarks about *I* reminiscent of the themes that were once the core of the paper.

The Two Faces of Belief

Reports of the form *X believes that S,* where *X* designates a person and *S* is a sentence, appear to be of subject/object form. The subject is a believer, the object an entity designated by the that-clause, and the transitive verb is *believes.* We can speak of *X* and *Y* believing the same thing, of there being something that *X* believes, and so forth. The identity of the object believed or *proposition* seems to have much to do with the embedded sentence *S.*

---

[32]The present paper was actually written in the fall of 1980, before the last two items mentioned, while actively working out the ideas of situation semantics with Barwise. It was heavily revised in the spring of 1982, incorporating some developments made in the theory in the meantime. The following papers, although not very up-to-date as far as situation semantics goes, explain the basic ideas and motivations reasonably well: Barwise 1981; Essays 1–4; Barwise and Perry 1980.

[33]Many authors have seen the need for facts or at least events in philosophy generally and semantics in particular. Our real situations are in many ways similar to Davidson's events, or at least are motivated by many of the same considerations and in response to Davidson's many insights concerning the need for events. Davidson was convinced by an argument we call the "slingshot" that events or situations could not serve as the semantic values of sentences, as they do in situation semantics; we discuss the argument in Barwise and Perry 1981. Our abstract situations are close to the Brandt/Goldman/Kim notion of event; see Goldman 1970 and Kim 1966.

Traditionally, propositions have been expected to play two roles. On the one hand, they identify states of the world. *It is true that Caesar was a Roman* makes a claim about the world, a claim that is either right or wrong depending on what the world is or was like. But propositions are also thought to identify belief states. Thus *Smith believes that Caesar was a Roman*, tells us something about the state of Smith's mind.

The dual role is connected with two uses we make of belief reports. We can use them as *evidence* about what the world is like: Turvey, a reliable authority on lunch, believes that lunch is served. So we believe it too, and go to lunch. We also use belief reports as parts of *explanations* about how people act: Turvey believes lunch is served; that is why he is leaving his office and running towards the cafeteria.

Propositions are identified by sentences, and thus seem to reflect logical relations among sentences (or perhaps impose them). So, using propositions to characterize the world, we can infer the truth of *that ψ* from the truth of *that φ* and *that φ only if ψ*. But this logical structure is also useful in characterizing beliefs. I appeal to authority:

> Our attitudes fit into a causal network. In combination, they cause much of our behavior; they are caused in part by the stimuli we receive from our surroundings and in part by one another. In attempting to systematize what we know about the causal roles of the attitudes, we find it necessary to refer to the logical relations among the objects of the attitudes (Lewis 1979, 514).[34]

The phrases *objects of the attitudes* and *objects of belief* have three possible uses (at least). The ambiguity would be harmless, at least in the case of belief, if propositions really had the dual role envisaged. The phrase *object of belief* most naturally means those entities designated by the direct-object phrases in belief reports. So the object of Elwood's belief that Caesar was a Roman is whatever *that Caesar was a Roman* stands for. The phrase might mean those

---

[34]In this typically subtle and elegant paper, Lewis describes an alternative treatment of what I called a "self-locating belief" in Essay 1.

Then, exploiting his modal realism, he treats all beliefs as self-locating. The modal realism does make a lot of streamlining possible. But I think our views on the structure of believing are very close. I suspect I do not agree with his remark in the footnote on page 541, that it is "unfortunate that the study of the objects of belief has become entangled with the semantic analysis of attributions of belief." This is supported by reference to the claims that "belief is in the head," and that "the main purpose of assigning objects of attitudes is ... to characterize states of the head ..." (526). Given the difference between belief as evidence about the world and belief as explanation of the believer's actions, these claims suggest an oversimple picture, which too easily leads us to think that our way of reporting beliefs is not "straightforward." Compare, "Vision is in the head." Surely, in some sense, true. The eyes and visual centers are all in the head. It does not follow that the point of saying what people see is mainly to describe their heads, or that, to the extent that we do report perception for that purpose, the expressions used will refer to what occurs in the head.

entities we are interested in when we use belief as evidence, the states the world either is or is not in. Or it might mean those entities that characterize our belief states in a way that allows us to systematize their causal roles, those entities in terms of which we should characterize states of the believer for purposes of explaining behavior. If propositions are the designata of that-clauses, identify states of the world, and identify states of believers, then propositions are the objects of belief in all three senses.

Experience with perception should raise doubts about this comfortable convergence of theoretical roles. Like belief reports, canonical perception reports identify a perceiver, a relation, and an object. But the point of the traditional arguments from illusion and perceptual relativity (properly construed) is just that the objects of perceptions in the first two senses are not the objects of perception in the third.

Suppose Smith says "Elwood sees Hoover Tower." *Hoover Tower* stands for Hoover Tower. That Elwood sees it might tell us something important about the world, most obviously that wherever Elwood is, Hoover Tower is there to be seen. But the facts of the relativity of perception show that there are countless ways to see Hoover Tower. The states we are in when we see Hoover Tower depend on our perspective and other conditions of perception, not just what we see. The actions that are appropriate for us, given certain desires, also vary with our position, relative to the object seen. So we should expect the ways of seeing Hoover Tower, and not the mere fact of seeing it, to be linked systematically with action and desire. A person who wants to reach Hoover Tower will turn one way if he sees it the way one does when one stands on the north side of it, and another way when he sees it as one does when one is to the south side of it.

Not only are there many perceptual states one could be in when seeing Hoover Tower, those same perceptual states could conceivably be involved in seeing something else. The perceptual state one is in when one sees Hoover Tower from one hundred yards on a foggy day in Palo Alto is quite a bit like that which one is in when one sees the Nebraska State Capitol Building from one hundred and fifty yards in Lincoln. We could use this fact to fool someone, were we so inclined and adequately funded.

Objects perceived, physical objects for the most part, do not serve well to classify perceivers for the purpose of explaining their behavior. This is recognized in commonsense psychology. We could never expect to explain what a person does just in terms of what they see, without, at least implicitly, considering the spot from which they see it. If I tell you that Smith wanted to get to Hoover Tower, and saw it from the Athletic Department, then I have given a reasonable explanation for his walking south. If he saw it from an airplane, I have not given a reasonable explanation for his walking south. It is also recognized that what is seen and the place from which it is seen sometimes give the wrong suggestion. If conditions are abnormal, one may not see things one usually does from that spot. In that case, we expect behavior appropriate to the spot from which things would ordinarily look that way.

In ordinary language, we have a variety of devices for describing our perceptual states independently of what we see when we are in them on a given occasion. For example, we explain mistakes by saying one thing looked like another; this can mean that we were in the state one is usually in when one perceives a thing of the latter sort. One can imagine a very systematic attempt to describe perceptual states, however. One might have a catalog of photographs, taken of various objects from various angles, and have people pick out one that shows "what things look like." Such a system of identifying perceptual states, though less than the last word scientifically, might have its uses. Then the system of photographs used to individuate the perceptual states would be the "objects of perception" in the third sense indicated. This would be a very dangerous usage, however. For confusing the usages, but keeping the system of identifying perceptual states, one might begin to think of the photographs, or something akin to them, as what we *really* see. The third use of *objects of perception* seems best avoided altogether.

I think an approach similar to that described for perception (which is intended to be relatively noncontroversial), is needed in the philosophy of belief. The reason is that nothing can play both of the roles that propositions are supposed to play in the traditional theory.

The states an object is in at a time are distinguished from the relations in which it stands to other things at that time. That grass is green is a true proposition. It is not true just for certain persons or from certain positions, it is simply true. Its being true, we might think of as a state of the world, rather than a relation that the world stands in to certain people, or certain positions within it. But if propositions correspond to such states of the world (and this is how I shall use the term), then there are no general and systematic links between belief in propositions, perception, and action.

To "systematize what we know about the causal role of attitudes," we need states that are typically caused in normal perceivers by certain perceptual states and states that typically cause, in normal believers, certain kinds of actions. Belief in a proposition will not fill this theoretical need, so long as propositions identify states of the world. The propositions one comes to believe through perception will concern the objects in one's environment; someone in some other place, looking at other objects, will not acquire belief in the same proposition, even if his perceptual state is the same. And the proposition, belief in which leads me to run or to reach out for a morsel of food, will not lead someone else, in some other place at some other time, to act in the same way.

Consider the proposition that the door to Building 90 at Stanford is open. Belief in this proposition can have no systematic and general links with action.

Even holding desires constant for the general population, what one should do depends not just on the fact that the door is open and one's desire (say) that it be shut, but where one is. Some with this desire and belief should walk downstairs and shut it. Others should phone and ask Julius to close it. A monk in Tibet, who has been apprised of the situation and desires that all doors be shut, really has no appropriate course of action open to him. Aristotle, who was awfully smart, may have foreseen that the door would be open, and have thought that philosophers should be kept warm. Apart from adding a footnote "Close the door!" to his *Ethics* (much studied in Building 90), it is hard to imagine what he could have done about it.

Standing in front of Building 90, one comes to believe that the door is open by seeing it open. But given the uniformity of Stanford's inner quad, one would be in the same perceptual state when looking at Building 30's open door (the numerals are obscured when the doors are open). But one would thereby be led to a different belief, that *that* door was open.

What we perceive—Building 90 or Building 30—is a matter not just of how we see things, but also of our position in the world. What we do—close the door of Building 90 or close the door of Building 30—is a matter not just of how we move but also of where we are and what we touch. If psychology, commonsense or otherwise, is to be systematic and general, it will be concerned with ways of perceiving and ways of acting, the same theory applying to the philosophy major in front of Building 90 and the English major in front of Building 30. A similarly two-faceted account of the structure of belief is needed.

Acceptance and Belief

Consider this unlikely conversation:

> Sarah: It is Tuesday. So you should empty the trash.
> Joe: I agree. I should empty the trash.
> Jim: So you both believe that Joe should empty the trash.

I shall say that Sarah *accepts* the sentence *You should empty the trash*. By *sentence*, I mean the meaningful English sentence. Joe accepts *I should empty the trash*. Sarah does not accept *I should empty the trash*, but she thinks that when Joe says it, he says something true. And Joe does not accept *You should empty the trash*, although he thinks that when Sarah says it, she says something true. The sentences one accepts at a given time are those one uses or would use to describe the world to oneself and others. But description is just one activity among many; the sentences one accepts are those that guide one's actions generally. Some sentences, like *Caesar was a Roman* one usually accepts for a long time if one accepts them at all. Others, like *I should empty the trash*, one usually does not accept for long.

I suggest that the sentences one accepts give us a pretty good way of identifying the belief states one is in. I take belief states to be dispositions to do various things, including use various sentences in various ways, and so this is a case of identifying a multiply manifested disposition by one of its upshots. Thus belief states are identified by the behavior they cause in articulate adults in suitable circumstances. But belief states and belief are attributable to prelinguistic children and animals insofar as we are motivated to identify the states they are in with those of articulate adults. This is conceivable because the disposition to accept a sentence may be the disposition to do much else that is more important. This approach not only does not preclude the attribution of belief states to organisms without language, it facilitates it. Individuation of belief state by sentence accepted, rather than propositions believed, makes it possible to link some of these states systematically with perceptual situations on the one hand and environmental threats and opportunities on the other. This is precisely the step that is needed to make sense of belief without language.

Acceptance must be distinguished from belief. Belief is an attitude we have towards propositions in virtue of accepting sentences, or being in the states that dispose us to accept them. Propositions I take to be abstract complexes of objects and properties; details are found in the next section. As Jim points out, Sarah and Joe believe the same thing: the proposition that Joe should empty the trash. The fact that they believe it in virtue of accepting different sentences manifesting different belief states, I shall put as they believe it *in different ways*. Of course, they both accept *Joe should empty the trash*, so there is a way they both believe it. But this is not necessary: one or the other might not know Joe's name. They might also accept the same sentence, and thereby believe different things. For example, if they both accepted *You should empty the trash*, there would be a sharp disagreement.

Acceptance is not belief that a sentence is true, although one will believe that one's uses of the sentences one accepts will be true, if one reflects on it. The analogy with perspective may be helpful. I have a certain perspective on Hoover Tower from my office. I realize that other positions give other perspectives, and I can imagine having those perspectives, and might even produce some rough drawings. I believe that those are how Hoover Tower looks from various angles. Of the drawing from the angle I have, I believe that it shows how Hoover Tower looks from where I am. And I can focus on the way it looks to me now, even without a drawing, and if I reflect upon it, I will certainly agree that this is how Hoover Tower looks from here, now. But believing that about how it looks should not be identified with its looking that way to me, now. Similarly, my acceptance of *Hoover Tower is over there*, should not be confused with my belief that the sentence, as uttered by one in my position and looking in the direction I am, is true. Accepting it is not thinking that it is true, but being in a certain kind of state identifiable by it.

When we describe beliefs, we usually identify the believer, the time at which the believing occurs, and the proposition believed. This is what Jim does in the example. A sincere first-person present-tense belief report—*I believe that such and such*—will embed in the that-clause a sentence accepted by the believer. But this is the exceptional case. Thus if Joe were to say "Sarah believes that I should empty the trash," his belief report would be true, but he would not have embedded the sentence that Sarah accepts, which is not *I should empty the trash*, but *You should empty the trash*.

This may lead us to suppose that how a person believes a proposition is not very important. But often it is crucial. When we seek to explain a person's behavior by their beliefs it is ultimately the way they believe, not what they believe, that is important.

In the example, we may confidently expect Joe to collect the trash and head for the door, while Sarah continues her studies. Their behavior thus differs dramatically. But their beliefs are the same. It is the difference in what they accept that appears to coincide with the difference in behavior. All well-behaved children will behave as Joe does when they accept *I should empty the trash*, even though each will believe something different.

Consider the English major and the philosophy major of the last section. They are in the same perceptual state, the one a normal perceiver is in, looking at a building of a certain type with an open door. But, of course, they see different things. One sees one open door, the other sees the other. Each is led to a belief state that is systematically and generally tied to such a perceptual state in a wide range of human beings, that state identified by acceptance of *That door is open*. They believe in the same way, though, of course, they believe different things. The one believes the one door is open, the other believes the other door is open. The belief state, given certain desires (where a similar distinction will have to be made), is linked with a certain type of action: closing that door. They both perform actions of this type, but, in so acting, close different doors.

The sentences whose acceptance will be systematically linked to perception and action typically contain demonstratives and indexicals: *That rock is coming at me, I'd better duck, This door is open*, etc. We need an account of meaning that comprehends such expressions.

Situation Semantics

The framework I shall use is situation semantics, the theory that Jon Barwise and I are developing. The basic idea of situation semantics is that the meaning of a sentence is a relation between situations. First we shall look at the notion of a situation, then at the relation theory of meaning.

Situations

The basic metaphysical idea is that reality consists of real situations, objects having properties and standing in relations at space/time locations. But we should not think of real situations as made up of separately existing objects, relations, and locations standing in some higher-order relation. Rather, objects, relations, and locations are abstractions from the flux of real situations, from what there ultimately is. They are at the most basic level of abstractions, but the are abstract. Such abstraction is the only way we have of dealing with the uniformities in reality, the recurring pattern of adjustment to which, whether through Divine Plan, evolution, or practical reasoning, is a precondition to effective action.

We assume that each situation $\mathbf{s}$ has a location l ($l = loc(\mathbf{s})$) and a type s ($s = type(\mathbf{s})$). The type is a relation between n-place relations, n individuals, and 1 and 0 (whose role in this scheme will be explained shortly). Where we have a real situation $\mathbf{s}$ with $loc(\mathbf{s}) = l$ and $type(\mathbf{s}) = s$, then if

s(runs, Albert) = 1,

Albert is running at l. Situation types, like objects and properties and locations, are abstract; they represent *uniformities* across real situations. The type s just mentioned represents what all situations in which Albert is running have in common, while s' represents what all situations in which Albert is not running have in common, where

s'(runs, Albert) = 0.

Now one can see the point of the 1s and 0s. They allow us to distinguish situation types that represent Albert as not running from those that are merely silent on the matter. Consider these two situation types:

s(barks, Mollie) = 1
s(barks, Fido) = 0
s'(barks, Mollie) = 1.

The first represents Mollie as barking and Fido as not barking; the second represents Molly as barking but does not represent Fido as doing anything.

A pair $\langle l, s \rangle$ of a location and a situation is an *abstract* situation. An *actual situation* is an abstract situation that corresponds to a real situation. That is,

$\langle l', s' \rangle$ *is actual if there is a real situation* $\mathbf{s}$ *such that* $loc(\mathbf{s}) = l'$ *and* $type(\mathbf{s}) = s'$.[35]

Other abstract situations are nonactual. Actual and nonactual situations are just set-theoretical objects that do or do not correspond to real situations. In

---

[35]This way of putting things builds in a decision about the question of how many situations there are at a location. If we think there is only one, whose type includes everything that is going on at a location, then we should want to require that s' be part of $type(\mathbf{s})$.

particular, nonactual situations fail to correspond to real ones, rather than corresponding to nonreal ones.

There is, then, a gap between real situations, the stuff of the world, and abstract situations, actual and nonactual. The difference is obscured by calling them all *situations* and also by using, as I shall, the variable **s** to range over both. *Situations* will usually be used for abstract situations, with *real* added when needed.

Linguistic Meaning

In situations semantics, the linguistic meaning of a sentence is a relation between situations, between an utterance on the one hand, and a described situation on the other. Suppose someone says, "This table was built by you." For this *utterance* to be true, a certain relation will have to hold between the utterance of it and another situation. Let us call the utterance **u** and the situation it describes **s**. Then the relation in question is this one:

There are objects a, b, c, locations l, l', and types u and s such that:

   (i) $\mathbf{u} = \langle l', u' \rangle$

  (ii) $\mathbf{s} = \langle l, s \rangle$

 (iii) l temporally precedes l'

 (iv) $u(\text{speaks to}, a, b) = 1$

  (v) $u(\text{demonstrates}, a, c) = 1$

 (vi) $u(\text{table}, c) = 1$

(vii) $s(\text{builds}, b, c) = 1.$

This is a complex relation that holds between abstract situations, involving many different individuals and locations. A true utterance occurs when there are situations in this relation that each correspond to reality: an actual utterance of *This table was built by you*, and an actual, properly related episode of table-building.

A theory of linguistic meaning assigns to expressions of a language relations between utterances and elements of described situations, in such a way that the correct relations for sentences emerge.[36] We indicate the meaning of an expression α with $[\![\alpha]\!]$. This is a relation between utterances and situations if α is a sentence, otherwise, elements of situations. Thus

    $\mathbf{u}[\![\alpha]\!]\mathbf{s}$

is an instance of the form

---

[36]I am simplifying here, by sticking to situations, rather than bringing in *courses of events*. A course of events is a set of situations, hence a set of pairs of locations and situation types, hence a relation in extension between locations and situation types. Such a relation can be thought of as a partial function from locations to situation types. So a course of events is a dynamic version of a situation, it represents what is going on at locations, or, more precisely, part of what is going on at some locations.

aRb.

Here are some semantic rules of this form,

(a) $\mathbf{u}[\![built\ by]\!]r$
iff
r is the relation of being built by.

(b) $\mathbf{u}[\![you]\!]b$
iff
there is an individual a, a location l, and a type u such that
(i) $\mathbf{u} = \langle l, u \rangle$
(ii) $u(\text{speaker},a) = 1$
(iii) $u(\text{addresses},a,b) = 1$.

Note that "$\mathbf{u}$" does not appear on the right-hand side of (a). *Built by* stands for a certain relation, independently of the facts of the utterance.[37] But *you* works very differently, since whom a use of *you* stands for depends on whom the speaker is addressing.

Here are the rest of the rules we need to handle our simple sentence.[38]

(c) $\mathbf{u}[\![table]\!]p$
iff
p is the property of being a table.

(d) Where α is a common noun, *this α* is a noun phrase;
$\mathbf{u}[\![this\ \alpha]\!]c$
iff
there is a location l, a type u, a property p, and an individual a such that
(i) $\mathbf{u} = \langle l, u \rangle$
(ii) $u(\text{speaker},a) = 1$
(iii) $u(\text{demonstrates},a,c) = 1$
(iv) $\mathbf{u}[\![\alpha]\!]p$
(v) $u(p,c) = 1$.

(e) Where α is a transitive verb and β is a noun phrase, $\alpha\beta$ is a verb phrase;
$\mathbf{u}[\![\alpha\beta]\!]a, \mathbf{s}, l$
iff
there is a relation r, an individual c, and a type s such that
(i) $\mathbf{u}[\![\alpha]\!]r, \mathbf{u}[\![\beta]\!]c$
(ii) $\mathbf{s} = \langle s, l \rangle$
(iii) $s(r, a, c) = 1$.

---

[37] Although we could treat the language spoken as an additional parameter of the utterance, and for certain purposes this is useful.

[38] Of course, these rules are not intended to be the final word, just to give the flavor of what a theory of meaning looks like in situation semantics. Rule (f), for example, would not fare very well as the fragment got larger.

(f) Where β is a verb phrase, *was β* is a full verb phrase;
$$\mathbf{u}[\![was \ \beta]\!]a, \mathbf{s}'$$
iff
there are locations l, l', and a type u such that

   (i) $\mathbf{u} = \langle l, u \rangle$,
   (ii) l' temporally precedes l, and
   (iii) $\mathbf{u}[\![\beta]\!]a, \mathbf{s}', l'$.

(g) Where α is a noun phrase and β is a full verb phrase, $\alpha\beta$ is a sentence;
$$\mathbf{u}[\![\alpha\beta]\!]s$$
iff
there is an individual a such that
$$\mathbf{u}[\![\alpha]\!]a \text{ and } \mathbf{u}[\![\beta]\!]a, s.$$

Meaning, Interpretation, and Information

Utterances are ways of conveying information, and although there are all sorts of information that an utterance can convey, the central case is that in which the utterance is true, and the information conveyed is that the conditions for the utterance's being true are met. On the relation theory of meaning, the truth conditions of an utterance pertain to two situations, the utterance and the subject-matter situation. They must be related in a certain way, and both be actual, for the utterance to be true. And there are cases in which the information we gain is limited to this. Suppose I get a postcard in the mail, with no signature, no return address, no picture to indicate where it came from, and the postmark blurred. Written on it are the words *I am having a good time*. What constraints are placed on the world if I assume that the writing of this card was a true utterance? Just this,

> There are actual situations $\mathbf{u}$ and $\mathbf{s}$, a type u, location l, and an individual a such that
>
>   (i) $\mathbf{u}\ [\![I \ am \ having \ a \ good \ time]\!]\ \mathbf{s}$
>   (ii) $\mathbf{u} = \langle l, u \rangle$
>   (iii) $u(\text{writes, this card}, a) = 1$
>   (iv) l temporally precedes the present moment.

By knowing the conditions under which an utterance is true, and knowing something about the utterance, we learn about the subject matter, the described situation. Thus, if I know that you wrote the card last week, I learn that you were having a good time last week. This is clearly the normal pattern, knowing about the utterance, and learning about the subject matter. By fixing the facts of the utterance, and only allowing the situation to vary, we get the notion of interpretation:

> The interpretation of an utterance $\mathbf{u}$ of an expression α, is the set
> $\{\mathbf{s} \mid \mathbf{u}[\![\alpha]\!]\mathbf{s}\}$.

Consider my utterance to Jane, of *This table was built by you*. There are many situations in the interpretation of this utterance. The utterance is true if any of them are actual. They all have Jane building this table at some time previous to my utterance, but they vary in every other conceivable way. Some have World War II avoided by timely diplomacy, others have it happening as it did, others do not consider it.[39] Each of these situations has a type that is defined upon Jane and this table; these objects are the subject matter of the utterance. Nothing else makes it into the subject matter, not even me.

This last point is important. When we use natural language, we tend to focus on interpretation. The most common notion of saying the same thing is just uttering something with the same interpretation. If you say, pointing at Jane, and picking up a reference to the table, *She built that table*, we would ordinarily say that you said just what I did, that Jane built the table. The meaning of the sentences we use is not the same. And if it were the same, we might not have said the same thing. If you were talking to Albert and used the sentence *That table was built by you*, you would not have said what I did, but something quite different. Even in reporting utterances, it is the interpretation we worry about, not the meaning. You could report what I said as *He said that Jane built that table*, or even *He said that Jane built the table in the living room by the fireplace*. You are not reporting the meaning of the sentence I used, but the interpretation of my utterance.[40] This point carries over into the other propositional attitudes, such as belief and knowledge. Given this focus on interpretation, it is natural to capture one thing that has been meant by *propositions* with the interpretation of the utterance of a declarative sentence, a set (or class) of situations. This is how I shall use the term in this essay. So used, it conforms to the first two uses of *object of belief*, propositions are the designata ($\approx$ interpretation) of that-clauses, and are the entities we are interested in when we use belief reports as evidence about the world. But the propositions in this construal do not give us the fine-grained way of classifying belief states that we would need to systematize their causal role. That job, as we shall see, is played by meanings.

This focus on interpretation in natural language leads one into thinking that all of the information we get from an utterance is information about the subject matter. But this is just not so. When we hear or read sentences that we take to be making true statements, we must simultaneously build up a picture of the utterance and of the subject matter. Often what we learn about the utterance, the general situation of the speaker, is more important than what the speaker says. A hostess hears a child say "This chair is funny looking." She knows a little about the utterance situation from the fact that she can hear the voice. Taking

---

[39] Here the lack of courses of events in this exposition makes accurate statement of the point impossible.

[40] This thesis is defended at length in Barwise and Perry 1981a and at greater length, with changes, in Barwise and Perry 1983.

the statement as true, she can fix the interpretation of *this*; there is only one funny looking chair in the house. This, together with the meaning of *the chair*, fixes the utterance situation in more detail, and she shouts, "Do not sit on that chair, it is a valuable antique." What she learned was not that a certain chair was funny looking, which she already knew, but that a child was near her favorite antique. Another example. Elwood's brother has made it to San Francisco, but is lost. He calls and says, "This phone booth is next to a large tower that looks like a fire-hose nozzle." Elwood learns where his brother is—near Coit Tower—although his brother has not *said* anything about himself at all.

If the normal focus on interpretations is not properly understood, the other ways of getting information can seem mysterious. Sentences like *I am Elwood Fritchey* and *This city is San Francisco* can seem rather odd. If Elwood says the first one, he has said something necessarily true. If anyone else says it, they have said something necessarily false. And when Elwood says the first, it seems to have the same interpretation as *Elwood Fritchey is Elwood Fritchey*, when anyone else says it. And yet when he says it, I learn something, for I learn who I am talking to.

Let us introduce the notion of the inverse interpretation:

The inverse interpretation of a use of α relative to **s** is that set $\{u \mid u[\![\alpha]\!]s\}$.

Relative to any actual situation **s**, the only utterances in the inverse interpretation of *I am Elwood Fritchey* are ones in which Elwood Fritchey is the speaker, and the only utterances in the inverse interpretation of *This city is San Francisco* are ones in which the speaker is demonstrating San Francisco. If you and I are at Powell and Geary, and you say "This is San Francisco," not pointing to a place on a map, but just the area around you, I learn that we are in San Francisco.

If we equate meaning and interpretation, perhaps lumping them together under something called "truth conditions," then information of the sort just noted will be hard to deal with. We may deny it any semantic status, but this is a mistake because the constraints placed on the identity of the speaker and other aspects of the utterance situation are as closely related to the meaning of the sentence used as the constraints its truthful use places on the described situation. We may shove all the information we can get into the interpretation so that we think that what is said contains implicit reference to the speaker and so forth. These strategies are both instances of what we call the *fallacy of misplaced information*. Given a relational perspective on meaning, we do not need to misplace information. The truth of an utterance of a sentence with a given meaning puts a set of interrelated constraints on two situations, the utterance and the subject-matter situation. When we recognize a truthful utterance, or take one to be true that is not, we pick up information, or misinformation, about both situations. The usual case is to know a lot about the utterance and learn about the subject matter, but cases where the basic drift of information is in the other direction are quite common.

So far, we have taken one thing about the utterance, the expression, to be given. But this is not always so. Indeed, when you report my utterance of *This table was built by you* by saying "He said that Jane made that table," your auditor learns the interpretation of my utterance without learning which expression I used. But the expression is constrained to be one that would have that interpretation, as used by me, in the situation I was in. Given further knowledge about that situation, you may be able to figure out just what words I uttered. This sort of reasoning, and its analogues with reports about what a person believes or knows, is very important, as we shall see.

Perception, Acceptance, and Action

This account allows us to see why the acceptance of certain sentences can be systematically linked with perception and action. By a *context* let us mean a situation like an utterance, except for the speaking or writing of a sentence. Given the way we have been using *utterance*, there are still a lot of facts left: who and where the potential speaker is, and how he or she is connected to the wider world.[41] A context belongs to the inverse interpretation of an expression relative to a situation just in case the utterance gotten by adding the productions of the expression would. Finally, let us say that a context that belongs to the inverse interpretation of an expression relative to some actual situation belongs to the *actual inverse interpretation* of the expression.

The acceptance of a sentence φ will be systematically and generally linkable to one's perceptual situation, if one's situation can often be determined to belong to the actual inverse interpretation of φ perceptually. This does not require that all situations in the inverse interpretation of φ be perceptually similar, but that there be a subset of those that are. Thus *This is a fir tree* can be directly linked with perception, even though some situations in its actual inverse interpretation could not be perceived to be in it because it is dark or the fir tree is disguised as an elm.

---

[41] The facts about an utterance that are relevant to interpretation can be divided in various useful ways. We have generally divided them into facts about the discourse situation and connections. The former are publically observable facts such as the identity of the speaker and the time and place of utterance. The latter are basically causal connections to objects in the wider world. The interpretation of a use of *I* requires only the first sort of facts, the discourse situation. The interpretation of a use of a proper name requires the latter sort of fact, a lesson to be learned from the theories of Donnellan and Kripke. Some kinds of expression require both sorts of facts for their interpretation, but they still are relevant in ways worth keeping separate. For example, the object demonstrated may be constrained by facts about the discourse situation but further causal facts are probably also relevant; which of the various chairs in a room a speaker refers to with *this chair* may turn on which one the speaker is attending to.

The beliefs that can be acquired directly through perception seem to be those that are about the perceptible properties of objects in one's environment. This can be so because there are sentences whose acceptance for each person guarantees a belief about just those objects in that person's environment, and whose acceptance therefore can be directly and systematically linked to the perceptual states one is in when one is in certain kinds of situations.

Let us distinguish between sentences with bland and rich inverse interpretations. Those with bland inverse interpretations are those that are, or come close to, being eternal sentences. Their utterance has the same interpretation, no matter who says them and where and what they are attending to. Their meanings are insensitive to the context. Such sentences cannot be linked with perception in a systematic way. This can only happen if the sentence has a rich inverse interpretation, if its meaning puts heavy restrictions on the kinds of situations in which it can be uttered truly.

Similarly, the acceptance of φ will be linkable with action if there is a type of action that is generally advisable for speakers in situations in its actual inverse interpretation. For example, every speaker in a situation in the actual inverse interpretation of *There is a rock coming at me* should duck. Again, we get at the truth of a simple idea, that beliefs about the threats posed and opportunities afforded by objects in one's environment lead directly to action.

From this perspective, we can see the source of the tension created by the notion of the "objects of the attitudes." If they are to be true or false, corresponding to states the world might or might not be in, the common objects of belief of various people in various places and times, they correspond to interpretation of utterances. If they are to serve the purposes of psychological classification, they should correspond to meanings of sentences with rich interpretations. The class of those who accept as I do is not the class of those who believe as I do. Many believe that I have a deadline; many of them are fishing, attending plays, and the like. But most of those who accept *I have a deadline* sit in front of their typewriters, thinking hard, and feeling pressure.

From this point of view, the importance of sentences with bland interpretations may seem a bit of a mystery. This is because to see how the acceptance of sentences can be linked to perception and action, we have had to ignore, in thinking about language, the very thing that makes language so important to us, the ability it gives us to communicate and hold information in ways that are not tied in any very immediate way to perception and action. An animal or a child will duck if a ball is thrown at them; there seems little point in attributing an intervening belief state. The perceptual states can lead to ducking through the design of the organism without belief intervening. If the only sentences we had were those capable of being directly linked to perception and action, those sentences would be useless. Their having a use requires two things. There must be some natural dispositions to act in certain ways, given certain perceptual states;[42] the acceptance of sentences can be seen as taking over this causal role. Second, there must be some other way besides perception of the objects in one's environment to come to accept these sentences. The acceptance of sentences puts another node in the network of psychological states, one that can have the effect of perception without all of its risks. It is this second factor that makes sentences with constant meanings so important.

On Interpretation

Sentences, or tokens of them, travel. They travel quickly through the air as sounds, and slowly through the mail as marks. They are published, stored away in libraries, and sometimes read, at later times and far-away places. The utterance is in general not the same as the situation of interpretation, the time and place when the utterance is understood, and information gained from it.

Let us say that to interpret a sentence heard or read or otherwise apprehended is to find a sentence with the same interpretation in one's own situation, as the apprehended sentence had in the utterance of origin.[43]

We can distinguish several kinds of interpreting.

Interpreting up. This is to find an interpreting sentence with a less sensitive meaning. My friend in San Francisco sends me a card on which she has written, "This city has dilapidated cable cars." I write in the draft of my travel guide: "San Francisco has dilapidated cable cars." Note that the sentence I find is not insensitive. It has tense and a proper name. But it is less sensitive than the sentence I read on the card; it has a constant or near-constant interpretation over a wider range of change in the context.

Interpreting down. This is to find a more sensitive sentence with the same interpretation. On a trip to San Francisco, I read in my Mobil Guide, "San Francisco has dilapidated cable cars." I write on my notepad, "This city has dilapidated cable cars." Or I think it. But I do not get on the cable cars I see.

Lateral interpreting. This is to find a sensitive sentence to interpret a sensitive sentence. My friend shouts, "You are about to be hit by a rock." I think, "I am about to be hit by a rock."

---

[42]The term *state* suggests much too static a way of looking at things, particularly things having to do with perception; I use it in spite of that, because of another set of suggestions it has, where the states of a thing at a time are contrasted with a wider set of properties dependent on its relations to the wider world.

[43]This is a dangerous usage. Sentence-*types* do not have interpretations, but meanings; they have interpretations relative to contexts. But we can think of sentence-*tokens* as having interpretations in an extended sense, the interpretations of the utterance that produced them. Xerox machines and other things complicate the latter notion, but I shall ignore such complications. This may be the point to indicate that I try to italicize mentioned sentence-types, but use quotation marks with verbs like the *says* of direct discourse. There is a theory of indirect discourse, which is that it is the mention of a sentence-type, but I am not at all sure that theory is right. It must have something to it, however, or I would not have so much trouble adhering to the convention I have described.

We can always interpret a sentence, if we know its meaning. I get the post-card described above with no signature, no postmark, and no picture. I inter-pret: *The author of this postcard was having a good time when he or she wrote it.* Such a sentence is pretty useless in forming expectations or guiding action. Theoretical semantics is the systematic development of a theory of such (prac-tically) useless interpreting sentences, in some language previously explained, of an appropriately formidable appearance.

These three types of interpreting have different purposes, different advan-tages, different disadvantages, and different requirements, even within the gen-eral project of gathering information.

Upwards interpretation allows the retention of information through change of discourse situation. *San Francisco has dilapidated cable cars* will have the same interpretation as I move about the world and for others reading my guide book. *This city has dilapidated cable cars* does not have this virtue. Upwards interpreting requires relatively insensitive expressions for the subject matter and knowledge of the utterance.

Downwards interpreting is used to generate expectations and guide actions. It requires knowledge of one's own situation. I could go from accepting *San Francisco has dilapidated cable cars* to accepting *This city has dilapidated cable cars* because I accepted *This city is San Francisco.* Having done so, I expect to see such cable cars, and avoid getting into them.

Thus it is the very blandness of inverse interpretation that makes insensitive sentences unsuited for direct linkage to perception, that makes them eminently suited for storing information thus acquired.

These reflections lead to the following picture of the structure of accepted sentences, or *doxastic structure*, in a normal believer. It has three levels. At the top are the insensitive sentences. At the bottom are those suited for direct linkage with perception and action. Tying these two levels together are the orienting sentences like *This city is San Francisco* and *That person is Richard Sklar* and *I am Elwood Fritchey.* Such a structure may be said to be in *perfect equilibrium* when the structure is closed under strong logical consequence.[44] This happens only rarely, one assumes, but I use *equilibrium* loosely, to mean approaching perfect equilibrium. For example, if *That person is Richard Sklar* is accepted and so is *Richard Sklar helps tourists in distress*, then *That person helps tourists in distress* is accepted. A structure is properly oriented when the orienting sentences are true in the context, and more or less fully oriented when there are a good number of them.

Given these rather vague notions, we can list some vague expectations we have about doxastic structures: program stability and generality, relative full-ness and stability of orientation, relative stability of belief.

---

[44] φ is a *strong logical consequence* of ψ when the interpretation of ψ in any context is included in the interpretation of φ in the same context.

Program Stability and Generality

The program of an individual relates perceptual states to doxastic or belief states, doxastic states to each other, and doxastic and affective states to types of expectation and action. This is our loose version of Lewis' vision, a picture that the Gricean program in philosophical psychology can help bring into focus.

A program is reliable if it takes us from perceptual states to the acceptance of sentences that are true in the contexts in which the speakers are likely to be in those perceptual states, from sentences that are true in contexts to others that are, and from accepted sentences to appropriate actions. I think of the notion of a reliable program as a generalization of David Kaplan's concept of something true in virtue of the logic of demonstratives. The latter is a sentence true in every context, even though it does not have the same true content ($\approx$ interpretation) in every context. *I am speaking* is such a sentence. It is true, whoever says it, although what they say varies from speaker to speaker and time to time. A reliable program need not be so flawless, just something that works out in most contexts. And truth is not always the relevant measure of success. Consider *Never do today what can be put off until tomorrow*. It gives us different advice every day, usually good.

A more sophisticated notion of a reliable program would consider changes from state to state that are reliable as one's discourse situation changes in automatic ways, as time passes.

We expect such programs to be stable within individuals and across members of a species, and to make ecological sense. The first attribute makes the elucidation of such programs a reasonable part of empirical psychology, the latter accounts in part for the illumination provided by Grice's program.

Relative Fullness and Propriety of Orientation

We expect people to recognize the objects in their environment, by and large, to know who they are and approximately where they are, and the like. This requires changes in the doxastic structure as time passes and they and other objects move about and change. If they are aware of the passage of time, and little else, there will be an orderly transition of the whole structure. If aware of their own movement, local changes occur at the top level where their own name occurs, and massive changes at the bottom two levels. If aware of changes in other objects (of a relatively noncatastrophic nature), local change occurs at all three levels. (Compare Gibson 1979.)

Relative Stability of Beliefs

We expect beliefs by and large to remain the same, except as necessitated by changes in accord with the principles just adumbrated. Thus we expect the doxastic structure to change so as to preserve what is believed, the interpretation of the accepted sentences. But we do not expect generality of belief. We expect different individuals to have different beliefs, not mainly because of disagreements about what the world is like, but because different individuals interact with, and are concerned about, different parts of the world.

Commonsense psychology is a psychology of differences. It has locutions built to focus on the way in which individuals differ; this means it focuses on what is believed, and not just what is accepted, because by the first two principles it assumes that difference of belief gives rise to appropriately different action. Given the assumptions of normal programming and relative full and proper orientation, classification by what is believed, the interpretation of the accepted sentences, rather than the accepted sentences themselves, makes sense. Relative to these assumptions, what is believed isolates a deeper dispositional property than what is accepted does; the latter changes to accommodate the former. (See Essay 4 for more about this.) We also have a reasonably rich vocabulary for describing orientation or lack of it: *recognizes, knows who, where*, and the like. And we have ways of cancelling the presumption of orientation when disorientation occurs.

When we speak of orientation, we have in mind, first and foremost, orientation towards objects in the environment. This is the requirement for making effective use of beliefs held at the upper level of our doxastic structure. But it is a fact of human life that we have many ways of designating individuals and the modes of designation are tied to actions directly and indirectly through different parts of our doxastic structure. We can speak of orientation here too.

Elwood is at a party and wants to look up a passage in *Word and Object*. He stands next to Marcia. I say, "Elwood believes that Marcia has a copy of *Word and Object* in her backpack." I know he believes this because I said to him "Marcia has a copy of the book you are looking for," just before the party. You expect him to ask her for it, and are puzzled when he does not. But Elwood is not fully oriented; he does not know who Marcia is. He cannot downward interpret in an effective manner, and so he cannot use his belief effectively.

Later Elwood is at home. He wants to call the person whom he was first told about, and later came to learn was standing next to him, who knew so much about Quine. But he does not know who that woman is; that is, he cannot interpret upwards in the way necessary to use the information, stored in an insensitive way in the phone book, which has a lot of Marcias in it. It has often been noted that *knowing-who* and like expressions seem to vary a lot in their applicability depending on context. But there is a system behind it. These expressions are used to describe an interpretive ability suitable for the task at hand.

Knowing-who is being able to interpret information effectively for the task at hand. So knowing-who is a species of knowing-how. As used with reference to humans, it is usually a knowing-how that is supported by acceptance of some sentence. But such interpretive ability is not always based on acceptance. We should add three more species of interpretation.

Interpreting in: Interpreting information made available in ordinary perception (as opposed to perception of sentences) into accepted sentences.

Interpreting out: using information in accepted sentences to act effectively in ways directed towards objects in one's environment.

Interpreting through: acting on objects as a direct result of perceiving objects.

The concept of orientation is applicable here also. A shark that perceives a flounder by detecting a change of ionization in the water through which he swims turns towards the flounder, gives chase, and eats it. A tree casts a shadow on a *monstera gigantea*. The vine grows towards the tree and then climbs it, leaving its roots behind. In both cases, it is natural to speak of orientation: information about environmental objects was converted by a reliable program into action, or something like it, directed towards the same object. These programs are very reliable, but by taking the shark or the vine out of its ecological niche we could produce something resembling disorientation; language is not necessary for identity problems, although it helps.

Neither the shark nor the vine need to interpret up. In each case, the constant presence of the object throughout the episode eliminates the need for anything like a constant expression. *Information that is always available in the environment need not be retained in the head.* Intentionality has its origins in the ecological description of organisms, the borrowing of terms for environmental objects to describe states of the organism. Such descriptions require systematic interaction with the environment, not internal representations of it.

If the tree towards which the vine grows is cut, the vine has to wait until a different tree casts a new shadow before it changes direction. The shark we can imagine to be more sophisticated. After chasing one flounder, it heads back towards another, through whose perimeter of ionization it passed during the chase. To make sense of this, we have to attribute a little more to the shark, something a little like our doxastic structures, that enable it to continue to believe in a perceptually inaccessible flounder.

When the shark perceived the flounder, the information it picked up was as much about it as about the flounder; it is its direction and distance from the flounder that is crucial, not the absolute location of the prey. And in returning to the flounder of second choice, the shark had to keep track of where it had gone, not just where the flounder had stayed. Does this mean that the shark needs also to be credited with some primitive precursor of *I*?

Some Remarks About *I*

The shark needs no precursor of *I*, no self-referring perturbation of shark consciousness, no self-specifying blot in shark vision. It needs none because it has no access to information about itself except through perception, and no use for the information, except in action. The difficulty in grasping this point has less to do with the difficulty of imagining what it is like to be a shark, than with seeing clearly the connection between the meaning of *I* and its role in perception, cognition, and communication.

I stands for the person who uses it. This simple rule hardly seems to invest *I* with sufficient meaning to give it very special place in self-knowledge that philosophers have accorded it. There seems to be an immediacy and salience to knowledge that we formulate with *I*. Most famously, Descartes begins his climb out of the pit of doubt with *I think*, not *Descartes thinks*, or *The author of the Meditations thinks*. Hector-Neri Castañeda has enriched philosophy with many examples of importance (1966, 1968). A version of one: Ivan Tovar, heir to a famous fortune, does not claim it, in spite of reading accounts in the papers of the search for Ivan Tovar, the riches that await him, and so forth. Why? Because he has amnesia, and does not accept *I am Ivan Tovar*. He does accept *Ivan Tovar has many riches awaiting him*, but not *I have many riches awaiting me*. So he does not act.

Some philosophers have thought such importance shows that the rule cited cannot be the whole truth about *I*, perhaps not even an important part of it. Frege thought that *I* must have a special sense for each of us, a sense that determines that person as reference when he uses *I* (1918/1967). Anscombe suggests that *I* should not be thought of as a referring expression at all, for she feels that to suppose that it is leads us to take it not to refer to persons but to selves, a metaphysical nuisance (1975).

The special importance of *I* is easily accounted for in terms of our framework. Those who accept *I have many riches awaiting me* do not all believe the same thing, they may even disagree. But they all believe something that makes it reasonable for them to take steps to obtain their riches. Membership in this class of people projects onto behavior, more or less. But membership in the class of people who believe that Ivan Tovar has many riches awaiting him does not project onto obtaining behavior. So, Ivan's membership in the second class leaves him just like a lot of other people, while his membership in the first would lead us to expect him to seek his riches.

We can get a lot of knowledge about ourselves through perception. And knowledge about ourselves is quite relevant to action. The meaning of the word *I* makes it peculiarly appropriate for identifying a certain causal role. Acceptance of *I*-sentences, although determining different beliefs for each of us, plays a very similar role for all of us. That is why the first person is indispensable for philosophers who want to isolate an important class of doxastic states.

But indispensable as *I* is for philosophers in identifying such states, it is not necessary for someone to have mastered *I* to be in them. Children learn to use their own names before they master the intricacies of *I* and *you*. Katie may respond to *Katie get in here* and insist *Katie wants a cookie* long before she masters the first person.

It is not surprising that use of one's own name precedes the use of *I*, or can. *Katie wants a cookie* is not in general an effective thing to say if one wants a cookie. But for Katie, it works well. If she gets in the habit of using it whenever she is cookie-deprived, it will work well. We can make the same point about an expression like *this city*. As long as Katie does not travel, sentences like *It is raining in Palo Alto* can be linked to her perceptual state. When she begins to travel, we will have to break this link.

Katie won't ever cease to be a Katie. But she may meet other kids with the same name. She may meet adults who do not know her name, and whose names she does not know. In these situations, *I* and *you* must be mastered.

When a perceivable entity a is constantly in X's environment, X can link a sentence with an insensitive expression for a to her perceptual states. The constant expression can play the role of a demonstrative or indexical. But the opposite is also the case. An indexical or demonstrative phrase can play the role of a constant expression in the retaining of information in just such a case. The distinction between a reliable sentence—one that makes a truth whenever uttered, but not always the same one—and an insensitive sentence becomes blurred. *This planet is not a bad place to live, all things considered* has a very secure place in the doxastic structure of all but the pickiest nonastronauts. Does it belong at the top level of our doxastic structure or at the bottom?

I has a similarly blurred status, even for astronauts. Wherever I go, I am always there, standing right behind whatever is in front of me, the one with a head I cannot see, and a body that disappears under a mustache.

The fact that we can get by with our name and not *I* is based on the same fact as that we can get by with *I* and not our name. Both are needed for more complicated forms of life. I need my name to look up my own phone number. But I need *I* to engage in Cartesian doubt. Among the things I might doubt is whether my parents fooled me as to my name. They might have trained me to say *Thomas E. Dewey wants a cookie* when cookie-deprived, as a sort of misguided patriotic joke. It seems easier to worry about this than to worry about whether I got fooled or confused about the meaning of *I*, but if I wanted to worry about that, my name might come in handy. But suppose I wanted to worry about both at the same time. How could I think of myself?

Even a name is not necessary. The gannet folds its fragile wings gracefully to its sides just before it hits the water, when it dives for a fish. It does not fold its wings when it sees other gannets about to hit the water. It knows the difference between *its* hitting the water and *that bird's* hitting the water. But it seems wrong to think of the gannet really receiving or using information that makes specific reference to itself at all. It has no use for *I*. Indeed, the gannet, a bird with rather a long protruding neck, usually does not even have a decent amount of itself in its own visual field. If we wanted to paint a picture of what the gannet sees, it would just be a picture of water, with the faint outline of a fish below the surface. And what seems true for the gannet seems true for us. We often see parts of our body. But we do not need to see parts of our body to know where we are in relation to the objects we see in the environment.

In just those cases in which either a name or a constant expression will do, because what is designated is always there, neither is really needed. The entity can be built into the semantics of the informational medium, without any perturbations in the medium, any name or indexical or disruption in the sensory field to designate that entity.

Consider the language I use with my dog: *Come, Go, Food, Sit, Stop that.* The dog interprets these; her actions and expectations vary (somewhat) with what I shout. Quite apart from whether this or anything like it could qualify the dog as penetrating the essence of language, the dog surely gets information from my verbal activity. We could take the meaning of each of these expressions to be a relation between an utterance of mine and situations involving my dog. This would be reasonable, in that the dog takes those to be commands for her. It would be misleading in that she has no apparatus for taking them in any other way.

We might say that my commands are preinterpreted for the dog. She does not need to interpret them up, down, or laterally. Perception is kind of like that. The information that we get at a certain spot in the world is information about objects in the neighborhood of that spot in a form suitable for the person in that spot. As long as this is the only source of information we have about ourselves, we need no way of designating ourselves, indexical or insensitive. Our entire perceptual and doxastic structure provides us with a way of believing about ourselves, without any expression for ourselves. As soon as we begin to get information about ourselves in other modes that need to be laterally or downwards interpreted to be effectively used, we will need to take some expressions as standing for us; to do so will be to interpret the information in a certain way. If Katie comes when we call *Katie*, she has it right. She still does not need *I*. She only really needs that to produce information about herself, not to interpret it. The first indexical she will take to designate her will probably be *you*, as said by her mother, standing before her, posing some threat or affording some opportunity.[45]

---

[45]Jon Barwise and Michael Turvey gave me a lot of help on this. Various parts of this paper were included in talks at Stanford University, Harvard University, the University of Washington, and the University of British Columbia. I am grateful to the philosophers of those places for a number of probing questions and helpful comments. This paper was first completed while I was at the Center for Advanced Study in the Behavioral Sciences. I am grateful for financial support from the center, the National Endowment for the Humanities, the Andrew Mellon Foundation, and Stanford University. Revisions have been influenced by comments from Michael Bratman, Hector-Neri Castañeda, Julius Moravcsik, Howard Wettstein, and others, including someone who returned a copy of an earlier version with very useful comments, but no name.

7

From Worlds to Situations

In this paper, I argue that it is reasonable and useful for one who has adopted a certain conception of possible-worlds theory to extend that theory until it becomes a version of situation theory.

The conception of possible worlds I have in mind is that developed by Robert Stalnaker (1984). I shall first explain what I take the Stalnakerian conception to be, and then list a number of additions that seem to be in the spirit of this conception, to make it more useful, and to have the cumulative effect of making it into a version of the theory of situations. Basically, possible worlds are seen as a special case of situations, so none of the power of possible-worlds semantics should be lost, while the flexibility of situation semantics will be gained.

In speaking of a version of the theory of situations, I make a distinction between the theory and the most extensive formulation of it to date in Barwise and Perry 1983. There were formulations before this one, and new and improved ones are being developed (Barwise 1985, 1985a, 1985b). The apparatus I develop here of issues, answers, ways, and propositions is in some ways a hybrid, but I think it works well for purposes of comparison with Stalnaker.

I shall not be talking about semantics, per se, but its foundations. Semantical suggestions are made only for the purposes of motivating or illustrating the additions to Stalnaker's theory I suggest. If semantics consists in studying truth and similar relations between linguistic elements and the world, then it requires some systematic way of classifying language, some systematic way of classifying reality, and some systematic way of matching them up. It is the second issue that concerns us here: finding a way of classifying reality.

Stalnakerian Possible Worlds

In chapter 3 of *Inquiry*, Stalnaker introduces his conception by contrasting it with that of David Lewis.[46] Lewis says that it should be uncontroversial that there are ways things could have been other than the way they are. The way things might have been are possible worlds. So far, Stalnaker agrees with Lewis.

But Lewis goes on to take these possible worlds to be alternative concrete realities, just like the actual world in every deep metaphysical respect, except that we are in *it* and not in *them*. "Actual" is really an indexical. Other worlds are as real for their inhabitants as ours is for us. There is no additional status our world has over theirs. (Lewis thinks that no one is in more than one possible world; in the world in which I fall off the stage at this point, it is really not me that falls, but a "counterpart" of me.)

Stalnaker does not share this view of possible worlds. He points out that there is a considerable step from thinking of possible worlds as ways the world might be, to thinking of them as concrete alternatives to it. He does not take that step.

Rather, Stalnaker makes a sharp distinction between what he usually calls the world, something concrete, and possible worlds, including the actual one, which are abstract entities—ways the world might be. I will usually call possible worlds, so conceived, *total ways*, since to me the word "world" has concrete implications. There is one world, which might be of any one of a variety of total ways. I shall call the total way it is the *actual* total way, rather than the actual world.

Stalnaker, like Lewis, takes a proposition to be a function from possible worlds to truth-values. This is why I call his possible worlds *total* ways. Each world provides a truth-value for every proposition, in effect, an answer to every question.

But Stalnaker's worlds are not total in another, more metaphysical sense, in which Lewis' are. Stalnaker considers possible worlds theory as a formal or functional tool—a philosophical apparatus, as he calls it—rather than a metaphysical theory. He does not assume, for example, that there is a single set of all total ways. A set of total ways is an analytical tool, and which set is appropriate depends on the purposes at hand. Since propositions are defined in terms of sets of total ways, the same holds for them. So, in this sense, possible worlds are not total. I shall use "comprehensive" for this notion. So, Stalnaker's possible worlds are total, but not comprehensive.

For example, suppose we are interested in the beliefs of a dog and its master (Stalnaker 1984, 63). They both believe that a bone is buried in the back yard.

---

[46]For Lewis' view, see Lewis 1973. In addition to Stalnaker's criticisms, one should consult Adams 1974.

But the master has the concept of an ersatz bone and the dog does not have this concept. In representing the master's beliefs, we would want to include, among the possibilities his belief might rule in or out, or leave open, the bone in question being ersatz. But we would not want to do this in the case of the dog, or at least might not want to. In the first case, we should take the set of total ways to separate the two cases; in the latter, we should not. Given these different sets of total ways, the propositions believed will differ also, since propositions are functions from sets of total ways to truth-values.

Since I want to recommend some additions to this theory, and an alternative notion of proposition, I need a way of talking about some properties of total ways and propositions that is, so to speak, outside of the theory. For this purpose, I shall use the notions of basic issues and answers.

An n-adic relation R and appropriate objects $a_1, \ldots, a_n$ determine a basic issue, the issue whether the world is such that R holds of $a_1, \ldots, a_n$ or not. A basic issue has an answer; yes or no.

It seems that total ways provide answers to issues. This is not to say that we should *define* them as functions from issues to answers. That would be contrary to the spirit of Stalnaker's enterprise; total ways are the basic primitives. Even thinking in terms of issues may infect my analysis with an atomism that distorts Stalnaker's view. Still, I think we can productively use this feature of total ways to study them, for at the very least, we will put ourselves in a position to learn how this perspective distorts things. So I shall represent total ways as (total) functions from sets of issues to answers.

Then it seems to me that we can present both sides of Stalnaker's perspective. On the one hand, the relativity to interests corresponds to the different sets of issues that might be relevant to a given analytical task. On the other hand, the total nature of these ways is reflected in the fact that given a set of issues, the worlds or ways for that set of issues are represented by total functions, functions that provide an answer for every issue.[47] So, as I understand Stalnaker, here are the basic points of his view, explained in terms of the notion of an issue and using the term "total way" instead of "possible world":

There is an important, unique, concrete object, the world.

Relative to a given set of issues, there are a number of ways the world might have been. These are total ways relative to those issues.

The world has a special relation, which I shall call *making actual* to one and only one of the total ways in such a set of alternatives. This is the actual total way, relative to the issues under consideration.

---

[47]Note that on this conception there is a kind of proposition that is closely connected to total ways, the proposition that returns truth for only a single total way. Stalnaker calls these basic propositions (56).

A total way provides an answer to every issue under consideration, that is, provides a total function from issues to answers.

Hence, the world determines an answer for each issue, the answer provided by the total way it makes actual.

Stalnaker singles out two features of his view for special mention. The first is that the propositions lack the structure of sentences. The second is the language-independence of propositions. Propositions are not sentences or statements or eternal sentences or abstract entities built up from sentences.

Although I agree with both points, they can help us identify some areas of disagreement. As to the second point, it is worth emphasizing that even if propositions are not intrinsically linguistic, certain parts of language might be made to order to express them.

The first point implies that there could be two statements, which make use of sentences with different structures, but nevertheless express the same proposition. One example of this might be the active and passive; one might well suppose that *Tom kissed Mary* and *Mary was kissed by Tom* express the same proposition. But, in enunciating the principle, Stalnaker has especially in mind the doctrine of the identity of necessarily equivalent propositions. On this doctrine, *George is sleeping* and *George is sleeping and Mary is weeping or Mary is not weeping* express the same proposition as do $7 + 5 = 12$ and $45/5 = 9$.

While agreeing with the first point, I reject the doctrine of the identity of necessarily equivalent propositions. The doctrine does not follow from the point, because there are factors other than the sentence used, which can account for the difference between the propositions. In cases of necessary equivalence, unlike the case of the active and passive, the objects the statements are about differ, as well as the structure of the sentence used. Thus there is room for a principled rejection of the doctrine, without individuating propositions linguistically.

I think the doctrine of the identity of necessarily equivalent propositions is an unnecessary weakness of Stalnaker's theory, one not required by the language-independent nature of propositions. It is unnecessary because the theory admits of a straightforward extension, requiring no doctrines except some rather commonsensical ones, that allows us to distinguish among necessarily equivalent propositions without taking propositions to be linguistic.

From Total Ways to Partial Ways

The first addition I want to suggest to possible-worlds theory is to allow partial ways in addition to total ways. A total way provides answers to all of the issues under consideration, while a way of this new sort I am suggesting provides answers to only some of the issues. It is the common part of all the total ways that provide its answers to its questions. So we have ways, some total, others partial.

Each way will provide answers to some of the issues under consideration. The world will make actual any number of ways, but still only one total way.

If we think of total ways as functions from issues to answers, then the existence of the more general class of ways would seem to be pretty uncontroversial. They would just be parts of total ways, in the sense in which one function can be part of another. But as I said, the representation of total ways as functions may be distorting. There may be a reason to be skeptical about the existence of the wider class of ways, given some other conception of the total ways. However, I do not see such a reason, so I shall assume that this is a small unobjectionable addition to the system.

In fact, Stalnaker already recognizes these entities. Consider the set of total ways we use for the master, each of which has the bone being ersatz or not. It looks like the total ways we use for the dog, which do not provide an answer for the issue of whether the bone is ersatz, are just what we want. These entities are total ways, relative to the issues we consider in the dog's case. But it looks like they are just parts of the entities we call total ways in the master's case. That is, it seems that the very entities that are total ways relative to the issues relevant to the dog, are partial, relative to the issues relevant to the master. So, it seems like Stalnaker has recognized all the ways I want. From this perspective, all that I am suggesting is to allow, as an additional analytical tool, a set of ways or alternative possibilities that is the union of sets of ways Stalnaker already recognizes separately as analytical tools.

The second addition, which also seems to be small and unobjectionable, is a wider class of propositions. Let us call the propositions Stalnaker has defined, those that are functions from total ways to truth-values, Stalnaker-propositions or S-propositions. I want to suggest that we recognize a wider class of propositions: partial functions from ways generally to truth-values, not just total functions and not just from total ways.

Consider again the proposition that George sleeps. The relevant S-proposition is that function that takes us from a total way to truth if the total way provides the answer yes to the issue of whether George is sleeping, and from a total way to falsity if the total way provides the answer no to that issue. Since these ways are total, every one of them will provide one answer or the other to this issue.

The proposition of the more general sort I am now introducing, will be a quite different function. It is that partial function P from ways w to truth-values, such that

$P(w) = T$ if w provides the answer yes to the issue of whether George is sleeping.

$P(w) = F$ if w provides the answer no for that issue.

$P(w)$ is undefined if w provides no answer for that issue.

In this more general sense of proposition, propositions that are expressed by statements that are necessarily equivalent do not always turn out to be identical. For example,

> that George sleeps and Mary weeps or Mary does not weep

is that function P' such that

> $P'(w) = T$ if w provides the answer yes to the issue of whether George is sleeping, and provides the answer yes or the answer no to the issue of whether Mary is weeping.

> $P'(w) = F$ if w provides the answer no to the issue of whether George is sleeping, and provides the answer yes or the answer no to the issue of whether Mary is weeping.

> $P'(w)$ is undefined otherwise.

P and P' are not identical.

To return to the case of the master, the dog, and the bone, we can now, in terms of this wider class of propositions, consider the difference between their beliefs. Suppose the master has the concept of an ersatz bone, but does not have an opinion as to whether the buried bone is ersatz or not. Then we can say that the master believes,

> that the bone is buried and it is ersatz or it is not ersatz

while the dog does not believe this, but only,

> that the bone is buried.

It seems that we might find it useful to be able to make the distinction between these two propositions, within one set of alternative possibilities, in giving semantics for something like:

> The dog believes the bone is buried, while the master believes that and, in addition, that it is ersatz or not ersatz.

Thus, having the more general sort of proposition available, in addition to S-propositions, seems to add structure, and hence flexibility, to our available semantical tools, and at no real cost. Nothing has been lost, for one still has the S-propositions, if they should be needed. S-propositions might be crucial, for example, in thinking about necessity and possibility.

Here is another example of where this flexibility might be useful. Consider the following two courses of action one might contemplate:

> bringing it about that George sleeps

> bringing it about that George sleeps and Mary weeps or Mary does not weep.

It seems to me that these are quite different things to consider doing. The decision to do the first, for example, would not require a further decision before it is carried out, while the second would; once one had decided to bring it about that George sleeps and Mary weeps or she does not, one would have to decide which of the latter two alternatives one was going to try for. Now, one might want to handle the difference in a variety of ways, but I cannot see the harm in having available the tools that allow for a relatively straightforward differentiation, in terms of the difference in the propositions expressed by the embedded sentences. Even if that is the wrong way to handle it, it seems to me that a semantical system that can consider and reject it is better off than one that cannot even consider it.

Finally, we now have a possible explanation for the fact that it might be true that Elwood believes that $2 + 2 = 4$, but not true that he believes that $367 + 345 = 712$. The embedded expressions, "$2 + 2 = 4$" and "$367 + 345 = 712$" express different propositions, defined on ways that provide answers to different arithmetical issues, and Elwood can believe one without believing the other.

Now, once again, this explanation might well be wrong. Stalnaker offers another, that the objects of belief and doubt in mathematical inquiry are propositions about the relation between statements and what they say. I do not think I need to criticize Stalnaker's proposal, or defend the one just mentioned, to make my point. An apparatus for semantics should give us the flexibility to consider both explanations. The reasons for taking the objects of mathematical inquiry to be propositions about the relation between statements and what they say should not have to rely on the semantical apparatus leaving out partial ways.[48]

Instead of introducing the general class of ways as entities that are in some sense parts of total ways, we might try introducing them as sets of total ways. The idea would be that we would represent a partial way that is undefined on a subset of the issues at hand as a set of total ways that give different answers to these issues, while agreeing on the issues on which the partial way is defined. Then we could introduce propositions as partial functions from ways, so conceived, to truth-values, where the proposition is undefined on those ways all of whose members (which will be total ways) do not provide the same answer to the issues at hand.

One then might ask, would this not be a more acceptable way of introducing ways than the one I have suggested? Might there be reasons for taking ways as sets of total ways rather than as parts of them? Again, if total ways are regarded as functions from issues to answers, the answer to this question

---

[48] See Barwise 1985 for a discussion of mathematical conditionals, and the problems raised for the doctrine that there are only two propositions for mathematical statements to express.

seems pretty clearly no, however we conceive of functions. Suppose first that we conceive of functions as sets of pairs of argument and value. Then a part of a function will just be a subset of the original function—a perfectly good entity. There seems to be no particular reason to prefer working with a set of sets of pairs, that all include this subset, and differ with respect to the other pairs they contain, rather than working with the subset itself.

Suppose now that we conceive of functions rather as rules. Consider the rule that says I put a book on shelf 1 if it is about philosophy and on shelf 2 if it is about linguistics. It does not say anything about what to do if it is a recipe book. What reason would there be to take this rule to be a set of more detailed rules, some of which have me putting recipe books on shelf 1, some on shelf 2, some on shelf 3, and so forth? There are many surprises in logic and set theory—at least for me—so I cannot be sure there is no good reason for this, but I admit I cannot see what it would be.

Finally, introducing ways as sets of total ways would not be equivalent to introducing them as partial. All total ways will agree on issues with only one possible answer, as for example the issue whether seven plus five equals twelve. So all ways introduced the second way will be defined on such issues, since all of their members will agree. But if we introduce ways directly as partial, there is no problem in having ways that do not provide answers to mathematical issues, and the flexibility thus obtained is just what we might want to deal with partial knowledge of mathematical truth.[49]

But as I said, the representation of total ways as functions may be distorting. So, it might be that on certain conceptions of total ways, taking ways to be sets of total ways would be less objectionable or more practical or rigorous or precise than taking them to be parts of total ways. So here, again, all I can say is that I do not yet see why this should be so.

So, to sum up the recommended additions so far: we introduce partial ways, providing partial rather than total functions from issues to answers. We introduce a more general class of propositions, as partial functions from ways to truth-values.

Stalnaker on Necessary Equivalence

Stalnaker gives an independent argument for the desirability of identifying the propositions expressed by necessarily equivalent statements (1984, 24). According to this argument, the causal pragmatic account of intentionality that he offers provides a deep philosophical motivation for the identity of necessarily equivalent propositions. In this section, I want to express some reserva-

---

[49]In the lecture on which this paper was based, I said the two methods for introducing ways were equivalent; the nonequivalence was pointed out to me in a letter from Richard J. Hall and Herbert E. Hendry.

tions about this argument. These are not reservations about the general idea of a causal pragmatic approach to intentionality, but about the step from such an approach to the identity of necessarily equivalent propositions. These may not be definitive counterarguments, but I think they should at least provide some motivation for not ruling out more "fine-grained" objects for the attitudes in the very way we set up our semantical apparatus. It seems that the restriction of the objects of the attitudes to S-propositions, if correct, should come as a (surprising) result of analysis of the attitudes, not a limitation forced upon that analysis by only having S-propositions available in the first place. But I think Stalnaker only provides the second sort of motivation, not the first.

First we must be clear about the sense in which Stalnaker holds the doctrine of identity of necessarily equivalent propositions ("the doctrine," for short). I want to distinguish two senses of the doctrine, one which Stalnaker does hold and one which he does not hold. To make this distinction, we first need to make another one, between propositions that are *true of* the same total ways, and those that are *the same function* from total ways to truth-values. By saying that a proposition is true of a way, I mean simply that if that is the way the world is, the proposition is true.

Consider two partitionings of the space of possibilities, one a finer-grained version of the other. For example, consider again the ways we partition the space of possibilities for the master and his dog. Now consider the statement that a bone is buried in the back yard. Depending on which partitioning we use, we will take this statement to express two quite different propositions. They will be different, because they are different functions, with different sets of total ways as their domains. Call these P_M and P_D. Now it seems to me that P_M is true of the total ways, in the dog's partitioning, in which a bone is buried. But it is not a function that returns true for these ways, for it is not defined on them, but only on the finer-grained ways emerging from the master's partitioning. And similarly, it seems to me that P_D is true of those ways, in the master's partitioning, in which either kind of bone is buried, although it is not a function that returns true for these ways, since it is not defined on them.

Now let us distinguish two senses of necessary equivalence of propositions P and Q. One is that P and Q are true of the same ways. The other is that P and Q are the same function from ways to truth-values. I think it is clear that Stalnaker means the latter when he advocates the doctrine, for in the former sense, the doctrine is clearly false. Each way of partitioning the space of possibilities will give us its own necessary proposition, the function from all of the ways in the partition to true. These will all be necessarily equivalent in the first sense, but not identical.

The form of Stalnaker's argument is that on the causal pragmatic account of the attitudes, we can expect the attitudes to share features with other, nonattitudinal relations between individuals and propositions, such as x *tends to bring about that* P and x *indicates that* P. Stalnaker claims these relations (and some others cited in developing the causal-pragmatic view) are such that if they hold between x and P, and P is necessarily equivalent to Q, they hold between x and Q. Given the causal pragmatic approach, we can expect the attitudes to behave the same way. That is, we can expect that the attitudes cannot discriminate between necessarily equivalent propositions, and this provides a motivation for taking such propositions as identical.

Now consider the relation x *tends to bring about* P, where P is a proposition. On Stalnaker's definition, this relation holds only if P is a logical or causal consequence of x being in its equilibrium state.

But why should we define *tends to bring about* in this way? It seems like a poor definition. I tend to bring it about that I have food in my stomach, for this is a causal consequence of my being in my equilibrium state. But do I tend to bring it about that $7 + 5 = 12$, or that Cicero either did or did not like Caesar? It does not seem to me that I have ever done so. But unless we are convinced that a definition of *tending to bring about* that has these consequences is correct, the causal pragmatic account of the attitudes will not support the doctrine.

Similarly, consider *indication*. The definition is as follows: an object indicates that P if and only if, for some state a in the relevant set of alternative states of the object, first, the object is in state a, and second, the proposition that the environment is in state $f(a)$ entails that P. State $f(a)$ is the state the environment will be in if fidelity conditions hold and the object is in state a.

On this definition, a tree having 100 rings indicates not only that it is 100 years old, but also that $7 + 5 = 12$ and that it is 100 years old and $7 + 5 = 12$. Again, being impressed with indication as a model for, or component of, belief will motivate us to accept the doctrine that necessarily equivalent propositions are identical only to the extent that we think a definition with these consequences is acceptable.

One might respond that although the consequences are not obviously correct, they might be inevitable, and hence have to be accepted. Suppose our basic idea is that relations to propositions are derivative. In all of the cases of "relations to propositions," attitudinal and nonattitudinal, the basic facts are that some state of an object determines a set of ways that the world must be, given that the object is in that state, and certain assumptions hold (causal principles in the case of tending and indicating, something more complex and counterfactual in the case of the attitudes). Propositions will come in derivatively; the ways that are compatible with the object's being in the state, given the assumptions, will determine a set of propositions, the ones those ways make true. But then propositions that all ways make true will always "come along for the ride." Given the strategy, it seems inevitable that our definitions of tending or indicating will imply that a thing tends or indicates all necessary propositions as well as the conjunctions of those necessary propositions with the contingent propositions that the thing tends to make true or indicates.

But this result is not inevitable, given the distinction between a proposition's being true of a way, and a proposition's returning truth for the way. It might be that the way of partitioning, suitable for the definition of tending or indicating, simply does not provide the materials required, for the definition of all necessary propositions. In fact, it is a consequence of Stalnaker's view that those propositions that are defined on more fine-grained partitions are not definable in terms of less fine-grained partitions. One might still maintain that for each statement of a necessary truth and each partitioning, no matter how coarse, there is a proposition definable in terms of the partition that can be regarded as what the statement expresses. However, I cannot see why, except for the desire to create problems for oneself, one would think that this was so. For example, take a partitioning of possibility into two total ways, relative to the single issue of whether Ronald Reagan dies his hair. I see no reason why the function from these two ways to truth should be a reasonable candidate for the interpretation of, say, "There is no largest prime number." So, it seems to me that the notions that we tend to bring about all necessary propositions, and that tree rings indicate all necessary propositions, are not only unintuitive consequences of the suggested definitions of tending and indicating, but also are avoidable, even if we accept Stalnaker's version of possible-worlds theory and the general approach to the definitions that he takes.

So, in conclusion, I do not see that Stalnaker has provided us with a deep enough reason for identifying objects of the attitudes expressed by necessarily equivalent statements, to motivate building such an identity into the very notion of a proposition provided by our semantical apparatus.

Bivalence

In order to get a grip on the effect of the recommended additions to Stalnaker's system, let us focus on the impact of the addition on the issue of bivalence of propositions.

Recall Stalnaker's approach to truth:

S is true, iff $S(w*) = T$, where $w*$ is the actual total way; otherwise, S is false.

Since each proposition is defined on all total ways, each one will be defined on $w*$, and so each will have at least one truth-value. Since there is only one actual total way, each one will have only one truth-value. So we will have bivalence.

Now let us see what happens when we add partial ways, and the more general class of propositions, to our semantical framework. Recall that a proposition is now a partial function from the set of ways (total and partial) to truth-values. The intuitive idea is that we give the conditions under which propositions are true and false. So we should handle truth and falsity as follows:

> P has truth-value v, iff there is a way w such that w is a way the world is, and $P(w) = v$.

We assume that for any way, the world is that way or it is not, and the world is not both of two incompatible ways, where ways are incompatible if they return different answers for the same issue. These metaphysical assumptions, our conception of a proposition, and the treatment of truth and falsity are not enough to guarantee bivalence. For example, a proposition that was defined on only one way w, returning T, would not have a truth-value if w was not actual. To get bivalence, we need a narrower class of propositions.

Let us say that a way is *basic* if it is defined on a single issue, and that ways are *opposite*, if they provide opposite answers for exactly the same issues. We use $w \sim$ for w's opposite.

Let us define a focused proposition as follows:

> P is focused iff
>
> (1) there is a basic way w such that $P(w) = T$ and $P(w \sim) = F$;
> (Call w and $w \sim P$'s T-Core and F-Core.)
>
> (2) For all w, $P(w) = v$ iff P's v-core is a part of w.

Focused propositions will be bivalent. By (1) and our metaphysical assumptions either the proposition's T-core or F-core will be actual, so it will have at least one truth-value. Suppose a focused proposition has both truth-values. Then there are actual ways w and w' such that $P(w) = T$ and $P(w') = F$ and P's T-core and F-core are parts of w and w', respectively. But then P's T-core and F-core are both actual, which cannot be, since they return opposite answers to the same issues.

This is all an illustration of the general theme of the paper. By making the additions to Stalnaker's semantical apparatus I suggest, we do not lose anything. We have a coherent notion of a bivalent proposition, supporting whatever intuitions there are behind classical propositions. But we could also explore, within the semantical apparatus, propositions that are not focused, and the logics to which they give rise.

Types of Nontruth-Functionality

If the classical propositional logic were the issue, of course, we would hardly be motivated to consider Stalnaker's theory, much less the revisions I am suggesting. We could rest content with a semantical apparatus that provided us two truth-values. The need for more fine-grained objects to serve as the interpretations of statements arises with nontruth-functional phenomena, various linguistic contexts O such that

$O(S)$

S and S' have the same truth-value

So, $O(S')$

is not a valid argument. Of course, there are many such linguistic contexts.

I think it is plausible that the propositions provided by possible-worlds semantics are successful in explaining the nontruth-functional nature of the notions of absolute necessity and possibility found in philosophy, theology, and elsewhere. The relevant linguistic contexts discriminate between statements with the same truth-value, but, so far as I know, there is no good reason to take them to discriminate between statements that are necessarily equivalent. S-propositions explain this behavior.

The attitudes, on the other hand, do seem to discriminate between statements that are necessarily equivalent. The revisions of Stalnaker's theory I am recommending, and other versions of situation theory, account for this. However, the attitudes also seem to discriminate between statements that differ only in having different names for the same object. The amendments considered so far do not explain this. As Hall and Hendry say,

> It would seem that the issue of whether Venus is a planet is the same as the issue of whether the morning star is a planet. But if they are the same issue, then it would appear impossible for a way, total or partial, no matter how defined, to give a different answer to whether Venus is a planet than to whether the morning star is a planet ... we will not be able to distinguish these issues, and the corresponding propositions, much as we would like to.

Does this mean that our exploration of partial ways was a waste of time? I think not, for two reasons. The first is the spirit of partiality; there is nothing wrong with a partial solution, which may turn out to be part of a full solution. The second reason is that there is a class of linguistic contexts that do seem to discriminate between necessarily equivalent statements, but do not discriminate between statements differing only in the names used for the same object. One example are the expressions we use to express causation. Suppose the bed's collapsing made it the case that Cicero lost sleep. It seems that, on the one hand, it does not follow that the bed's falling made it the case that $7 + 5 = 12$. And, on the other, it surely did make it the case that Tully lost sleep. If Cicero lost sleep because the bed fell, and Tully is Cicero, then Tully lost sleep because the bed fell.

Conditionals are another example, although intuitions are not always as sharp as with causal notions. Suppose we have taken a cheap flight to Boston, with stops in Omaha, Bloomington, and Ithaca. I wake up as the plane lands in Ithaca and say, "If this city is Boston, we have no further to go." It seems that what I have said is true. But if I had said instead, "If this city is Amherst, we have no further to go," you would correct me by reminding me that our goal is Boston and not Amherst. Now there is no possible world in which Ithaca is Boston. And similarly there is no possible world in which Amherst is Boston. So if conditionals were insensitive to change of necessarily equivalent statements, both conditionals should be true or both should be false. Of course, there are many things that could be said about this example, concerning as it does such mysterious things as the relation of identity and Boston. But there seems to be an advantage in being able to at least consider the most straightforward approach, that the change of antecedent statements produced a change of propositions, and hence a change in the truth-value of the conditional.

Given this conjecture, that the most natural application of the benefits of partiality is the realm of causal and conditional notions, it is surprising more time was not spent on them in *Situations and Attitudes*, and less on the attitudes. Barwise is now making amends, however, and since he discusses Stalnaker's views on conditionals in the papers cited earlier, I will not dwell on these issues further.

I believe the problem of substitution of names in attitude reports can be dealt with, in a straightforward way, within situation theory. The strategy is explained in *Situations and Attitudes*, but not in a way that makes it seem very straightforward. However, I have neither the space nor wit to do better here.

The World and its Parts

Stalnaker's version of possible-worlds theory has two main sorts of entity, the world, of which there is only one, and total ways, of which there are many. The first additions I suggested to his theory came from recognizing partial as well as total ways as legitimate entities that ought to be available for semantics. The second set of additions come from recognition of parts of the world as similarly legitimate.

I think it is very natural to suppose that there are parts of the world. For example, what has happened so far seems to be only a part of all that has happened and will happened; I would find it very distressing if this were not so, though not for long. What happens in this room, between midnight yesterday and midnight today, again seems a part of the world, not the whole.

In fact, it seems that all that would ever be needed, in any account of anything, would only be a part of the world. Even if one is very Whiteheadian about how the understanding of anything that happens really involves a great deal else, most of us would put some limits on this.

It seems in the spirit of Stalnaker's theory that just as the set of total ways, and hence the propositions, relevant to a given analytical task can vary, so too might that stretch of reality that counts as the world. If so, then the same sort of unification of tools across tasks, which seemed to motivate inclusion of partial ways that are partial relevant to a given task, seems also to motivate the inclusion of stretches of reality than are less than what is taken to be the complete world for a given analytical purpose. We gain flexibility, and lose nothing.

There are two kinds of parts that I think we need to keep in mind. First, and perhaps most naturally, there are the parts that correspond to everything that happens in some continuous spatiotemporal location. Both of the parts I mentioned, everything that has happened up until now and everything that happens in this room in a 24-hour-period, are of this sort.

Second, there are parts of the world that determine the answers to a certain set of issues. Consider the set of people listening to me now in this room, and the property of being asleep. This set of individuals and this property give us a certain set of issues: whether or not each of these individuals is asleep. Then we have a somewhat different notion of a part of the world: that part of the world that determines the answers to this set of issues. This part of the world will not be everything that happens in a continuous spatiotemporal location.

I will call parts of the first kind chunks of the world and parts of the second kind aspects of the world. Aspects of the world are more closely connected to ways than are chunks, and one might wonder whether we need aspects at all in addition to ways. I think we do need them. That is, we should distinguish between that aspect of the world that makes it the case that a certain way is actual, and that way itself. The way would exist, even if it were not actual. It would be there, an unactualized possibility. On a Stalnakerian conception, these unactualized possibilities seem no more objectionable than other uninstantiated properties. But the aspect or aspects of the world that make the way actual would not be there if the world were not the way it is in these respects.

Earlier, we recognized a relation, *making actual*, between the world and total ways. Then we extended that relation to partial ways. While the world makes only one total way actual, it makes many partial ways actual. Now I suggest a further extension, allowing that parts of the world make partial ways actual.

Let us assume, as an example, that George Washington had false teeth. Now it seems to me as clear as anything can be that this issue was settled by a part of the world that occurred before the twentieth century. The world is a certain way, being such that George Washington had false teeth, because a certain part of it, say, the world up until 1850 (to be cautious) was this way.

Suppose some obscure piece of reasoning of Bradley's or Frege's yet to be understood will eventually show us that no issue is settled except by the whole of the world. Still, this seems like a very significant fact, one we want to be in a position to state. So it seems a good idea to recognize parts of the world, and the relation of *making actual* between them and ways, even if no part of the world ever has made or ever will make a way actual by itself.

Let us call all parts of the world *situations*. For a given analytical purpose, we may suppose that some situation is large enough to include everything relevant to the tasks at hand; it is the world. Its parts are the rest of our situations, and represent the second addition I am suggesting to Stalnaker's theory.

Now what will recognition of these situations add to our theory that might be useful for semantics? Before answering this, let us make an important distinction between persistent and nonpersistent properties of parts and wholes, and consider the general point of recognizing parts when we already have the wholes.

There are properties that the parts and the whole can share. For example, I have a weight, and so does my right arm. Note, however, that my weight will not be that of my right arm. I weigh about 190 pounds. I do not know how much my right arm weighs, but if I caught a fish the size of my right arm I would expect it to weigh at least four or five pounds. So let us suppose that my right arm weighs five pounds. Now from this it follows that I have an arm that weighs five pounds, and that I weigh at least five pounds, but it does not follow that I weigh (exactly) five pounds.

The property of weighing (exactly) five pounds is not persistent along the relation of physical part to whole. Some properties, though, are persistent, such as weighing at least five pounds.

The ways we have so far are all persistent properties of situations. If a situation settles a number of issues in a certain way, then every larger situation of which it is a part will settle those issues in the same way. Now, if all properties of situations were like this, there might be little point in recognizing situations in addition to the world. It is nonpersistent properties that make parts of interest. My dining room table, for example, has a leg that in an extreme emergency could be used as a baseball bat. It has a certain weight and size and shape, and heft. The table of which it is a part does not have that size, weight, shape and heft, and would not make a good baseball bat. When the emergency comes, I will be better off for having recognized the part as well as the whole, because by doing so, I was able to recognize one of its important nonpersistent properties.

It seems clear that situations have many nonpersistent properties, as well as the persistent ones. The property of not settling an issue one way or the other, for example, is clearly not persistent, for the issue will be settled by some larger situation. Also, insofar as we interact with situations, or they interact with other objects, or with each other, they will have nonpersistent properties. For example, I now see a certain situation, with various people doing various things—nodding, yawning, looking at their watches, and the like—but I do not see every situation of which this situation is a part. So being seen by me is a nonpersistent property of situations.

Here is another example. If a situation makes it the case that George Washington had false teeth, then any larger situation of which it is a part must also settle that issue in that way. But suppose a situation has only one person in it that has false teeth. Consider the situation in George Washington's bedroom at Mount Vernon. On certain assumptions about Martha's teeth, this situation has only one person in it having false teeth. But other situations of which it is a part, such as the world as a whole, do not have this property.

These nonpersistent properties of situations can seem sort of puzzling. They must be reflected somehow in the way the world is. The persistent properties of situations end up being ways the world is. Are the nonpersistent ones in danger of being left out?

They are not left out, because by recognizing situations, we generate a whole new set of issues. Some situation s must settle the issue of whether I see a given situation s' or not. That it settles this issue in the way it does will be a persistent property of s. So the nonpersistent property of s', being seen by me, is reflected in the persistent property of s, of settling the issue of whether I see s' positively, and hence in a property of the world. (The reader can see that the issues generated in this way can quickly make things quite complicated. In Barwise and Perry 1983, we represented real situations, within the formal theory, with what we called abstract situations. But abstract situations were also used to represent the real uniformities across situations that I am here calling ways. This led to some difficulties, and a failure to realize the importance of the new issues that are generated by taking situations to be objects. This is one of the main reasons we are working on yet new versions of the theory of situations, much to the frustration of some who have worked hard to understand the versions already put forward.)

It seems reasonable, then, that if there is a world, it has parts. And if it has parts, these parts have nonpersistent as well as persistent properties. And if this is so, it would seem wise to have these entities, and their nonpersistent properties, available for semantical analysis.

Barwise and I think that many of the topics that have been puzzling in the history of semantics revolve around situations and their nonpersistent properties. In fact, we think that the problem highlighted in the previous section, of contexts that are sensitive to substitution of names for the same object, is such a topic, but as I said, I will not try to explain our approach in this paper. (See Barwise and Perry 1983, part IV.) But I will mention a couple of other examples.

Consider a statement like "The man in the red coat is asleep." A straightforward Russellian analysis seems to make this a claim that implies there is one and only one person in the whole world that has a red coat, but this is not usually what is intended. Another approach is to suppose that we are not trying to describe the world, but just a part of it: a situation in which there is only one man with a red coat, and he is sleeping. This property of the situation is not persistent.

Here is another example. Suppose that after my talk the program committee, Barwise, Feferman, and Israel, say to me, "Everyone was asleep during your talk." Of course, they do not mean that everyone in the whole world was asleep. Nor do they even mean that everyone in the room was asleep, because they do not think I was asleep. Rather, there is a certain set of issues in question: whether each member of the intended audience was asleep or not. These logicians are describing that part of the world that settles the answers to those issues. Their statement is about that part of the world. The semantics of "Everyone was asleep" should provide for this; that is, it should identify a property of situations, of everyone in them being asleep. And it should allow that a statement can be about a part of the world, a situation, rather than the whole of the world, and can be true if it describes that part of the world correctly.

There are, of course, other ways of dealing with these examples. We might suppose that the context supplies some extra descriptive material, which, together with that which is explicitly articulated, yields a persistent property of situations, a way the world might be. I am inclined to think that the strategy of requiring the context to supply a situation to be described will be more workable. But for present purposes, I only want to claim that we want our semantical tools to be rich enough to consider this treatment as well as others.

So, my final suggestion for an addition to Stalnaker's possible-worlds theory is a class of propositions that are true only relative to situations. These propositions will be functions from pairs of nonpersistent properties and situations to truth-values. We might call the propositions nonpersistent too, since the fact that such a proposition is true relative to a given situation, will not insure that it is true relative to other situations of which that situation is a part.

So I have argued that certain additions to Stalnakerian possible-worlds theory, which do not strike me as contrary to the spirit of the theory in any obvious way, will provide us with a richer and more flexible foundation for semantics. By recognizing parts of possible worlds (considered, as Stalnaker does, as ways or properties of the world, and not alternative realities), we make available structured propositions, whose conditions of identity are more fine-grained than those provided by Stalnaker's theory unamended. By recognizing parts of the world, we are able to recognize discourse that attempts to characterize those parts directly, and the world as a whole only indirectly.

Let me end on a modest note. Stalnaker emphasizes that he does intend his possible-worlds theory to be a metaphysical theory, but a semantical apparatus. But what then is the underlying metaphysics, implied by our ability to partition possibility in different ways for different purposes? I believe that situation theory, considered as a metaphysical theory, provides Stalnaker with all he needs for possible-worlds theory, considered as a semantical tool: a world and total ways, and the relevant S-propositions, *given a fixed set of issues*. And it will also support Stalnaker's skepticism about there being a set of total ways apart from any fixed set of issues. That is, my final conjecture is that situation theory is the right metaphysics for one who wants Stalnakerian possible-worlds theory as a foundation for semantics—even for one who wants it unsullied by situations, in spite of all my good advice.[50]

---

[50]This is an expanded version of a paper prepared for a symposium at the 1985 CSLI Summer School/ASL Meeting. Certain examples reflect the fact that the paper was originally prepared to be read to an audience. The thoughts recorded here reflect many conversations over a period of years with Jon Barwise on the topics of situation theory and possible worlds, as well as participation in a seminar on *Inquiry* with John Etchemendy, Robert Moore, David Israel, Ned Block, and others.

8

Possible Worlds and Subject Matter

Introduction

Barbara Partee emphasizes two contributions possible-worlds semantics has made to linguistics (1989). First, possible worlds have helped to provide an appropriate structure on the space of meanings. Second, the possible-worlds conception helps relate linguistic meaning to other kinds of informational content.[51] She believes that these contributions are "largely independent of metaphysical issues" (1989, 107).

I agree that possible worlds have helped to provide a *more* appropriate structure on the space of meanings than that provided by extensional semantics. But I do not think the structure it provides is fully adequate to the needs of a general theory of informational and intentional content. The basic problem is that the notion of a proposition that is suitable for modality is not suitable for all informational and intentional contexts. In this paper, I argue that versions of possible-worlds semantics that limit themselves to the structure of intensions needed for the semantics of modality face serious problems, and that the assumptions at the root of these problems are metaphysical.

The problems I list are instances of what I shall call "the subject-matter problem." These problems are not new. They all are instances of a category of problems that Partee describes as the crucial ones facing possible-worlds

---

[51] I have one reservation about how Partee puts the point about the benefits for linguistics of a general account of meaning and information. She says this benefit has not so much to do with linguistics proper, but with the linking of linguistics to other disciplines. But this general conception of meaning and information is needed within linguistics proper, too, in at least two ways. First, the concept of meaning that is used by formal semanticists should connect up with the concepts of meaning used in the rest of linguistics—in the study of meaning change, for example. Second, it seems plausible that the information content that phonological, morphological, and syntactic aspects of an utterance contain about each other should be understood within the same general framework of meaning and information as the content of the utterance as a whole. Thus, a substantive theory of meaning and information should be useful not only for understanding how linguistics connects with other disciplines, but for understanding how the parts of linguistics connect with each other.

semantics (1989, 119). These are cases in which we substitute cointensional statements within an informational or intentional context, but do not preserve truth-value for the embedding statement.

I think the full force of the subject-matter problem has not been appreciated, however, because it has been assimilated to another class of problems in the same category, which are not specific to strong possible-worlds theory. This is the "mode-of-presentation" or "Cicero/Tully" problem. I argue that the subject-matter problem is distinct, and related to the metaphysical principles characteristic of strong possible-worlds theory.

I end by arguing that there is no very strong motivation for the metaphysical assumptions that underlie possible-worlds semantics, and hence every reason to explore alternative frameworks that do not rest on these assumptions and do face the difficulties they bring.

Strong Versions of Possible-Worlds Theory

The versions I have in mind share the following assumptions:

(1) Possible worlds are *total* possibilities.

(2) Intensions may be set-theoretically defined as functions from possible worlds to extensions.

(3) Possible worlds and the intensions definable from them provide us all that we need for a theory of informational and intentional content.

David Lewis and Robert Stalnaker are among those who hold strong versions of possible-worlds theory (Lewis 1973; Stalnaker 1984, 1985). But these two theorists are in radical disagreement as to the metaphysical nature of possible worlds. In the terminology of Robert M. Adams, Lewis is a *possibilist* and Stalnaker is an *actualist* (Adams 1974). Lewis asserts the existence of an infinity of equally real possible worlds, of which our world, the one *we* call "the actual world," has no special status other than our presence. In Lewis' theory, truth is relative to possible worlds in just the way it is relative to times and places and inertial frames. Possible worlds are simply an often unnoticed parameter of all empirical relations. Stalnaker does not believe in these other equally real possible worlds, but he does believe in other ways things might have gone, other ways the one actual world might have been. These ways the world might have been are what *he* calls possible worlds.

Principles (1)–(3) do not, then, really delineate a metaphysical doctrine, but only a metaphysical schema—something that provides a doctrine, once we are told what a possible world is. Even so, it may be the case that the various strong versions have enough in common for there to be common problems for them. I shall argue that this is the case.

Before considering the objections, however, let us say a bit more about what principles (1)–(3) come to.

Possible worlds are total possibilities

Both actualists and possibilists hold that possible worlds are "total" or "complete," but actualists have a little more flexibility here than do possibilists.

Let us say that for any n-place relation and sequence of n appropriate objects there is an *issue*, which has one and only one answer (or one per world, at any rate), yes or no. (This is just an apparatus for discussing things; neither the reader nor the scholars discussed will be assumed to be committed to it without warning.) Possible worlds supply answers to issues, somehow or other, depending on the conception of what a possible world is. By saying that possible worlds are total, I mean that each possible world provides an answer to each issue in the relevant universe of issues. I distinguish being total from being comprehensive, which is to provide an answer to every issue, period. Actualists may deny that worlds are comprehensive, while maintaining that they are total. The idea is that for a given analytical project, only some issues may be relevant. Also, there may not be a complete set of issues (Stalnaker 1984). So, each possible world in a "partitioning of the space of possibility" will provide answers to all of the issues that the others in the same partitioning do.

Intensions may be set-theoretically defined in terms of possible worlds and individuals

This may seem like a truism, for "intension" is now widely used to mean just a function from possible worlds to extensions. But the word "intension," and the view that language was basically intensional, is older than possible-worlds semantics.

Basically, intensions are entities that provide some principle of classification, and that have an identity, independently of the objects so classified. So the intension of a term, which determines whether it describes an object or not, is contrasted with its extension, the set of objects it describes. Properties are intensions, for we can classify objects into those that have them and those that do not. Concepts are intensions, for we can classify objects into those they fit and those they do not. Words are intensions, when we consider them with their meanings intact, for we can classify objects into those they describe or are true of, and those they do not describe or are not true of. The notion of an intension can be found in a wide variety of theories; we might say, for example that the classical debate between nominalists, conceptualists, and realists pertained to which intensions were needed.

The idea that most discourse was "intensional," in the sense that intensions, and not just the actual extensions determined by them, were relevant to truth, is quite old. For example, it is the view of Whitehead and Russell in the introduction to the first edition of *Principia Mathematica* that it is the extensionality of mathematical discourse that requires explanation.

The thought that all intensions are set-theoretical constructions out of possible worlds is thus a substantive thesis. It is one that many philosophers reject who nevertheless find possible worlds good entities to have when thinking about theological, metaphysical, and semantical issues connected with necessity. Adams and Plantinga, for example, fall into this category (Adams 1974, Plantinga 1974). Thus they are not adherents of strong possible-world semantics, in my sense.

Possible worlds and the intensions definable from them provide us all that we need for a theory of informational and intentional content

Informational and intentional notions are often expressed by constructions that embed statements, as in "Harold said that Mary was crying," "Tom knows that Mary wasn't crying," and "The tree rings indicate that the tree is over one hundred years old." Philosophers commonly suppose that such statements express *propositions*, and that the propositions expressed by the embedded statements are the objects of belief, assertion, knowledge, etc. From this point of view, providing a satisfactory notion of a proposition is a key test for strong possible-worlds semantics.

Strong possible-worlds theorists take propositions to be the intensions they assign to statements, functions from possible worlds to truth-values. I shall argue that this notion of a proposition is inadequate, and that its inadequacies are related to the metaphysics that leads to strong possible-worlds theory.

Two Problems

Functions from possible worlds to truth-values surely provide a more appropriate structure for the space of meanings of statements truth-values by themselves do. By taking propositions to be such functions, and to be the semantic values of statements embedded in modal and intentional contexts, we can explain their nonextensionality.

Still, one might well suspect that such propositions, motivated by the needs of modal contexts, might prove less than completely successful for intentional contexts generally. In particular, the possible-worlds treatment of propositions requires that propositions that are necessarily equivalent are identical, and one might suspect that this notion is too coarse-grained for many purposes. It is natural to suppose that propositions that are true in the same possible worlds have their modal properties in common, so that exchange of logically or necessarily equivalent statements in modal contexts preserve truths. But it is not at all obvious that propositions true in the same possible worlds have *all* properties in common. So it seems that this way of individuating propositions might give us problems, in dealing with nonmodal contexts.

A variety of cases, in which substitution of cointensional statements within an informational or intentional context does not seem to preserve truth-value for the embedding statement appear to justify this worry. Partee identifies such cases as the crucial problem facing possible-worlds semantics (1989, 119).

I maintain that the problems in this category fall into two quite different subcategories. Problems in the first category are not specific to strong possible-worlds theory, while those in the second category are.

The mode-of-presentation problem

The first kind of problem involves statements that differ only in the proper names used to designate some individual, such as "Tully was a Roman orator" and "Cicero was a Roman orator." Such statements will be cointensional. Given that Tully and Cicero are the same person, the possible worlds in which Tully was a famous orator will be just those in which Cicero was a famous orator. But substitution of one of these statements for the other in reports of belief, knowledge, assertion, and the like does not always preserve truth-value. In certain circumstances, we would be very reluctant to infer from "Smith believes that Cicero was a Roman orator" to "Smith believes that Tully was a Roman orator."

I call this the "mode-of-presentation problem." The change from "Cicero" to "Tully" does not alter whom we are talking about, only how that person is presented. This problem is not specific to possible-worlds theories. Any semantic theory that takes propositions to be nonlinguistic intensions, so that the interchange of two codesignational names determine the same proposition, has the same problem, whether propositions are taken to be states of affairs or worlds, sets or functions, primitive or constructed, partial or total.

A natural reaction to this problem is to suppose that somehow language is relevant to our reluctance to allow substitution in these contexts. After all, language is explicitly involved in assertion, and is intimately associated with the higher cognitive states and activities reported by "believes" and "knows." One might suppose that the objects of these attitudes are not propositions at all, but statements. Or one might suppose that the objects of these attitudes are not propositions, but some "hybrid" entitity. Or, taking the assertion case as one's model, one might suppose that there is an implicit parameter for linguistic entities. One does not simply say that so-and-so, one does so *by* uttering a certain statement in a certain context. Our reluctance to substitute one name for another might be due to the affect on the implicit parameter, rather than on the proposition. (See Barwise and Perry 1983, 262ff.) While no solution along any of these lines has won universal acclaim, the line of attack is plausible enough to make it unreasonable to reject the possible-worlds notion of a proposition because of the mode-of-presentation problem.

The second kind of example presents a problem that is specific to strong possible-worlds semantics, however. I call this the "subject-matter problem."

The subject-matter problem

We have a fairly coherent and intuitive notion of what things various propositions are about. If you ask me to tell you about Martha, and I say, "The sea is salty," or, "I really like macadamia nuts," you will think I am dotty or run and reread Grice on conversational implicature in hopes of finding some clue as to what I am getting at. The propositions that the sea is salty and that I like macadamia nuts are not about Martha, even though, if they are true, Martha lives in a world in which the sea is salty and in which I like macadamia nuts.

The notion of aboutness may not be as crucial as belief or necessity, but it is quite useful and we have pretty clear intuitions about it. I think the following informally stated conditions could be considered the beginnings of a theory of aboutness:

(a) A simple statement that contains a name for an individual expresses a proposition that is about the individual named. For example, "David is clever" expresses a proposition about David; "Ruth threw Paul over the fence" expresses a proposition about Ruth and Paul.

(b) If P is about a, then $not\text{-}P$ is about a.

(c) If P is a proposition about a and Q is about b, then P and Q is about a and about b. So "David is clever and Ruth threw Paul over the fence" expresses a proposition that is about Ruth and Paul and David.

(d) If P is about a and Q is about a, then P or Q is about a. So, "David is clever or Ruth threw David over the fence" expresses a proposition that is about David, whether or not it is about Ruth.

(e) If P is about a, and $P = Q$, then Q is about a.

Item (e) is simply an application of the indiscernibility of identicals. But it creates a problem for strong possible-worlds theory. For, given the coarse-grained way in which possible-worlds theory individuates propositions, we get the consequence that every proposition Q is about every object that any proposition P is about.

(1) Assume that P is about a.

(2) P or $not\text{-}P$ is about a, by (b) and (d)

(3) Q and $(P$ or $not\text{-}P)$ is about a, by (c)

(4) $Q = Q$ and $(P$ or $not\text{-}P)$, by the possible-worlds theory of propositions

(5) Q is about a, by (e)

Which is to say, strong possible worlds cannot capture the notion of a proposition's being about an object.

The problem can be traced to the mechanism, in strong possible-worlds semantics, of obtaining propositions that focus on any particular matter of fact, such as, say, whether Peter is picking peppers. Each individual possible world provides an answer to every such issue. One focuses on a particular issue, by cancelling out answers to other issues. The proposition that Peter is picking peppers is the set of possible worlds that give an affirmative answer to that issue, and cancel out each other's answers to every other issue. One possible world has Sally selling seashells by the seashore; another one has her selling peaches instead, and so forth. The only thing that they agree about is the target issue, that Peter is picking peppers.

That, at any rate, is the strategy, but it doesn't quite work. Some issues, such as whether 7 and 5 add up to 12, have only one possible answer. And other complex things, such as that Sally is either selling seashells by the seashore or she is not, will be true throughout the set of worlds. Since they are true in all worlds, they cannot be separated one from another; since they filter out no worlds, the conjunction of statements that express them with simple empirical statements are true in the same worlds as those simple empirical statements by themselves.

A natural reaction to this problem is to suppose that the real culprit is not the possible-worlds notion of a proposition, but, as with the mode-of-presentation problem, some implicit linguistic parameter. One might suppose that propositions are really not about anything in and of themselves (just as the possible-worlds theory predicts), but only relative to some statement by which they are expressed, and that when we work out the nature of this relativity to language, the coarse-grained nature of the possible-worlds propositions will be no problem. This approach is exemplified in Stalnaker's treatment of attitudes towards mathematical truths in *Inquiry*.

However, I do not think that this defense works.

We have basically two paradigms of nonextensional, statement-embedding contexts. The first, modal contexts, are insensitive to shifts in mode of presentation and shifts in subject matter. The second, the cognitive attitudes, are sensitive to both. These latter are intimately involved with language, which suggests that the sensitivity may be due to an implicit linguistic parameter, rather than with the coarseness of possible-worlds propositions.

But a great many informational and intentional concepts fit neither of these paradigms. They are insensitive to shifts in mode of presentation, but sensitive to shifts in subject matter. These concepts typically do not have much of anything to do with language, so that the strategy of protecting coarse propositions, by finding an implicit linguistic parameter, is not very promising. I now turn to a number of examples of such concepts.

More problems

These examples canvass a broader range of states and activities that are usually considered in discussions of intentionality. On the one hand, a number of the examples have to do with *information*, what an inanimate object indicates or shows. On the other, a number have to do with *action*, what an intelligent being does in virtue of the way it moves. The important connection between intentional notions and informational notions has been stressed by Dretske, and that between intentional notions and action is part of the functionalist perspective, whose relevance to semantical issues Stalnaker has stressed. I do not think it has been sufficiently recognized that the logical behavior of informational and pragmatic concepts deviates from both the modal and the cognitive paradigms.

Causation and action

Caesar brought it about that Tully fell out of bed.

Caesar made Tully fall out of bed.

The collapse of a defective bedpost caused Tully to fall out of bed.

In each case, the substitution of "Cicero" for "Tully" will not have any conceivable effect on the truth-value of the embedded statement or clause. A man made to fall out of bed by any other name is still a man made to fall out of bed. Note here that we are not talking of what a man tried to do or thought he was doing or formed an intention to do, but just what he in fact did. It seems quite odd to suppose, say, that just because Caesar made Tully fall out of bed, he made Tully fall out of bed *and* $7 + 5 = 12$, or that he made Tully fall out of bed *and* Peter pick or not pick his peck of pickled peppers.

It is true that when a person performs an action the whole world, in some sense, changes. One might then think of modeling the results of an action as the set of worlds that might be actual given that it is done. I think it is clear, however, that some alternative, more *incremental* notion underlies the way we actually think about the effects of action. We are interested in those things about the world that would not have been as they were, without the action: the issues, on whose answers the action had some effect. That $7 + 5 = 12$, that Peter did or did not pick his peck of peppers, and much else about the world is unaffected by Caesar's overturning of Cicero's bed.

Perception and memory

Harold saw Mary cry.

Harold remembers Mary crying.

We use a variety of constructions for perception and memory, with interestingly different properties. The statement that Harold saw *that* Mary was crying seems sensitive to exchange of names, as does the statement that he remembers that she was crying. There are many contexts in which we would use these locutions, in which the information Harold sees, or needs to produce, is linguistic in form. In these cases, the exchange of names seems to imply a difference in abilities to interpret or produce information. But the constructions we have used do not seem sensitive in this way. Any inclination to say that Harold saw or remembers "under a description," seem to disappear once we have reminded ourselves that we are speaking of seeing and remembering, not seeing-that and remembering-that.

Yet it would be strange indeed, to reason from the fact that Harold saw Mary cry, to the conclusion that he saw her cry and Peter pick his peppers or not. After all, if Harold saw Mary cry and Peter pick his peppers or not, then he saw Peter pick his peppers or not pick them. And if Harold saw Peter pick his peppers or Peter not pick his peppers, then he saw one or the other. But we cannot conclude, from the fact that Harold saw Mary cry, that he either saw Peter pick his peppers or not pick them. (See Barwise 1981, Barwise and Perry 1983.) Analogous reasoning applies to "remembers."

Information and meaning

These tree rings show that this tree is more than 100 years old.

The height of the mercury in the thermometer indicates that Freddy has a fever.

In the old days, "Ken is starving" meant that Ken was dieting.

"IV + III = VII" means that four plus three equals seven.

The principle that if X shows that P & Q, then X shows that P and X shows that Q, seems pretty plausible. So, given the possible-worlds notion of a proposition, everything shows that R, for any necessary truth R. One might respond, "Why not? It seems pretty harmless to let tree rings show 'the necessary proposition'."

The problem again is that our ordinary devices for dealing with information, and for dealing with devices, like ourselves, that deal with information, are interested in increments. In the typical case we have a system that can vary along a certain dimension or dimensions; in this case, the number of rings the tree has. This systematically depends on, and so carries information about, some other dimension of variation of the system or its environment. Our concept of information, of what is shown, wants to focus on these variations and dependencies. Our ordinary notion of a proposition, what is said or shown or indicated, seems to have built into it a notion of subject matter, of focus on definite objects and issues about them.

This seems most clear in the case of meaning, a notion with which possible-worlds semantics must come to grips, if it is to provide a framework in which the activities of the natural-language semanticist cohere with empirical studies about meaning conducted in other parts of linguistics. We are interested in the increment the truth of a statement makes to the totality of what is true, not that totality. It is not correct that in the old days "Ken is starving" meant that Ken was dieting and $7 + 5 = 12$.

Necessary truths and conditionals

The principle that there is only one necessary proposition causes havoc with conditionals.

> If this is Stockholm, we are in Sweden.

> If Nixon bet on ODD and won when the ball landed on 7, then 7 is an odd number.

> If 387 is a prime number, Jack owes Jill $5.

Again, there is no way that exchange of codesignative names could affect the truth-value of these statements. But, at least to untutored intuitions, changing the subject matter makes quite a difference, even if the resulting proposition is necessarily equivalent to the original.

Suppose the first statement is made when a plane lands in Oslo. The antecedent is then false, and necessarily so. But in possible-worlds semantics, there is but one necessarily false proposition, so we should be able to exchange this way of expressing it for any other. But this seems clearly wrong; the statement in question seems true, while, say "If $7+5 = 13$, then we are in Sweden" does not seem true at all. One might point out that, on most possible-worlds analyses of conditionals, conditionals with necessarily false antecedents are true, so this second conditional would also be true. But this latter doctrine seems just more reason to look for some other notion of a proposition.

The second conditional seems true enough, but if we replace the consequent with, say, "41 is a prime number," the conditional does not strike me as true at all. The third conditional seems like the sort of thing that becomes true when Jill bets Jack that 387 is a prime number. But, given that 387 is not a prime number, so that the antecedent is a necessarily false proposition, the conditional is true on the standard possible-worlds analyses, quite independently of any wager between Jack and Jill, which seems quite implausible.

It can seem odd that things might depend on one necessary truth, but not depend on others. Odd or not, we talk this way all the time. Logicians who teach less mathematically oriented philosophers are always saying things like, "That depends on the fact that addition is associative." This is not confused, although it can be confusing. As Jon Barwise has emphasized, use of conditionals in mathematical pursuits is not an isolated language game, but continuous with their use for other purposes (1985). The notion of propositional content bequeathed to us by strong possible-worlds semantics is simply not flexible enough to cope with such conditionals.

All of the problems I have mentioned are but putative problems; that is, one way or the other of treating them within the framework of strong possible-worlds semantics may, in the end, when all the costs and benefits of the approach are summed, be reasonable. My point is that it is not semantics, or possible worlds, but only the strong view that creates the problems in the first place, so the approach needs to have some benefits to counterbalance the costs.

Towards Intensional Tolerance

The source of these problems is the basic thesis of strong possible-worlds semantics, that all intensions are to be built up from total possible worlds. If we drop this thesis, we could take propositions to be more "fine-grained" entities. There are a number of ways of doing this available to the tolerant intensionalist. Here is a simple one, designed to keep as close as possible to the possible-worlds idea of taking propositions to be sets of possibilities.

We start by taking relations and objects as primitives, rather than possible worlds. From these we can build up "issues"; the answers can be 0 and 1 or any suitable set-theoretic entities. We can introduce worlds as further primitive entities, associating with each a total function from issues (whatever universe of issues is relevant to our linguistic or philosophical project). Call this the world's "issue profile." Then we can focus on simple facts by subtraction rather than addition. That is, augment the total functions from issues to answers with partial functions, which only provide answers for some of the issues. The limiting case would be a function defined only on a single issue, say, whether Peter was picking peppers. We introduce entities, perhaps "partial worlds" or "partial ways," with these partial functions from issues to answers as their profiles. Then, we take propositions to be functions from the worlds *plus* these new partial entities to truth-values.[52]

Where an issue consists of the relation R and the sequence of objects $a_1, \ldots, a_n$, I shall say that the members of the sequence are constituents of the issue. The constituents of a (partial or total) world w are the constituents of the issues on which the associated function is defined. A proposition is about those objects that are constituents of every (partial or total) world that is a member of the proposition.

So, the proposition expressed by "Peter is picking peppers" will consist of all (partial or total) worlds that provide the affirmative answer to this issue, including the limiting case, the one defined only on this issue. The proposition that Peter is picking peppers will be about Peter, but not about anyone else.

This suggestion fits with the intuitive principles about aboutness that we noted above. A conjunction will be about the objects the conjuncts are about, since the proposition expressed by the conjunction will be the intersection of those expressed by the conjuncts. But a disjunction may not be about the objects the disjuncts are about, since the ways in the union of two propositions may not all be defined on issues with the constituents the original propositions were about.

---

[52]Partee claims that Stalnaker shows in the ms. of "Possible Worlds and Situations" that "there is no obstacle in principle to identifying a situation with the set of all possible worlds that have that situation as a part" (1989, 104). This argument did not make the final version of the paper, and I do not have the ms., so I am not sure exactly what was shown. The difficulties in question stem from the basic strategy of modeling something partial with a set of totalities. Some of them were spelled out in Barwise and Perry 1980.

The more fine-grained notion of a proposition we have just considered does nothing directly to solve the problems connected with the mode-of-presentation problem. But it does solve the problem of subject matter, in that it blocks the inferences that depended on the strong possible-worlds treatment of propositions. We need not infer that Caesar made it the case that Peter was or was not picking peppers, simply because he played a trick on Tully, or the tree rings indicate all of the truths of logic and mathematics, simply because they indicate the age of the tree. Conditionals can be taken to express relationships between partial worlds, and not simply total worlds. (See Barwise 1985.) It is, then a partial solution in two senses, to some putative problems for possible-worlds semantics. I am not claiming, of course, that the apparatus just sketched is one that will meet all of our needs. My point is simply to suggest how limiting the strong possibilist possible-worlds position is. *The problems that derive from the identity of necessarily equivalent propositions are not inevitable or based on any principle of technique or methodology; they are simply the results of a metaphysical commitment to reduce all intensions to functions on the domain of total possible worlds.*

Motivations for Strong Possible-Worlds Semantics

So what motivation is there for strong possible-worlds semantics?

Here, again, there seems to be a large difference between the possibilist and the actualist.

Although possibilism is often characterized as some sort of extreme realism, there is a pretty clear sense in which the possibilist is not, or need not be, a realist at all. According to Lewis, for example, possible worlds are not properties or relations or universals or abstract entities of any kind. So possible worlds are not intensions. Traditional intensions, or replacements for them, are built out of possible worlds and other nonintensions. These "new" intensions are all just sets of various sorts. As far as I can see, there is nothing in the ontology of Lewis' theory that someone like Quine should object to, except the possible worlds. Each of them is a desert; it just turns out that there are more deserts than one counted on. From the perspective of someone who likes desert landscapes, but is not put off by needing a lot of them, strong possible-worlds semantics is perfectly natural. The problem of change of subject matter is difficult to avoid, because the only intensions he can fairly avail himself of are those built up out of possible worlds. But these difficulties might be a fair price to pay for a theory that can be at once so scrupulous about abstract entities and generous in providing interpretations for intensional constructions. It all depends on how one feels about alternative concrete realities, about living in a possibluum of equally intrinsically real worlds as well as a continuum of equally real locations.[53]

For the possibilist, then, possible worlds are not intensions at all, but concrete objects. For an actualist, possible worlds are intensions of a special kind, sort of like properties of the entire universe. There is clear motivation for recognizing this new sort of intension, for they deal well with necessity and possibility. But what is the motivation for an actualist to adopt strong possible-worlds semantics, forsaking all intensions but these?

A possible reason is that one believes that possible worlds are in some metaphysical sense the fundamental intensions. Stalnaker disavows this reason. He points out that taking possible worlds as primitive and other intensions as derivative, in one's formal semantics, does not preclude thinking that possible worlds are definable or analyzable in terms of other sorts of entities, and that the possible worlds needed for various analytical enterprises might be analyzable in various ways. (See Stalnaker 1985.)

A reason Stalnaker does give is that, by working in a framework basically the same as that of the possibilist, technical points can be debated without getting enmeshed in philosophical issues. This point is not compelling. Lewis and Stalnaker agree that conditionals describe an abstract relation between total worlds. One can hardly compare their theories in a system that has no total worlds, but there seems to be no motivation for excluding partial worlds.

Stalnaker's most important reason, which he has advanced and defended in a number of places, has to do with intentionality and the nature of informational content:

> The picture is this: to have the capacity to represent, an organism must be capable of being in each of a set of alternative states ... which will, under ideal conditions, reflect corresponding states of the environment ... the state of the environment tends to cause the organism to be in its state.... Now we can ask, what must informational content be if this is what it is for an organism to be in states that have informational content? What is essential to contentful states is that they distinguish, in some way or other, between alternative possible states of the world ... what any representer must do—what it is to represent—is to locate the world in a space of alternative possible states of the world. It is appropriate to begin with possibilities because that is the level of abstraction that captures what is essential to representation (1986).

This argument seems to beg the question. If we use total possible worlds to model environmental states, then this picture will lead us to use total possible worlds to model intentional states. But if we use some partial technique for the

---

[53]I would feel better about rejecting this out of hand, if I understood better how equally real I think the past and future are, and why.

former, we may also do so for the latter.

Consider a simple case. The waiter brings it about that there is a milk shake in front of me. I see that there is a milk shake in front of me, believe that there is, and drink the milk shake. We can represent what the waiter brings about as the set of total possible worlds, whose issue-profiles disagree about everything except necessary truths and the relative position of me and the milk shake. Or we can represent it by the set of partial worlds, whose issue profiles have the milk shake in front of me. Whichever we choose to model the state of my environment, we can use to model my intentional states. Choosing sets of total worlds, the route of strong possible-worlds semantics, will enmesh us in the putative problems listed above. Choosing to use partial objects, will mean that our theory of informational content cannot simply rely on the structures bequeathed to it by the semantics of modal logic. The picture sketched by Stalnaker does not provide an argument for the first choice over the second.[54]

Afterword

Essay 8 was my contribution to a session on Barbara Partee's "Possible Worlds in Model-Theoretic Semantics: A Linguistic Perspective," which was held at the Nobel Symposium on Possible Worlds in Humanities, Arts and Sciences, in Stockholm in 1988 (1989). In her "Speaker's Reply," Partee took issue on two counts (1989a).

First, she claimed that strong possible-worlds semantics can capture a semantic notion of aboutness, which she calls pw-aboutness:

> An empirical proposition can be said to be *about* a particular individual (or property, etc.) if the truth of that proposition varies systematically with the properties of that individual (or property, etc.).... Let the worlds in which proposition p is true be p's T-set and those in which p is false be p's F-set. Then a proposition p is pw-about Jones if there is some systematic difference between the properties Jones has in the worlds in p's T-set and the properties Jones has in the worlds in p's F-set. This will be the case for the proposition expressed by the sentence "Jones is bald" but not for the proposition expressed by "Smith is bald"; Jones's properties in various worlds will presumably not have any systematic correlation with whether those worlds are in the T-set for "Smith is bald" (1989a, 153).

[54]The research reported in this paper was supported by a grant from the System Development Foundation to the Center for the Study of Language and Information. Many at the center have contributed to the paper through discussion on possible worlds and related topics. Of course my views about possible worlds have been heavily influenced by Jon Barwise. John Etchemendy, David Israel, Ken Olson, and Dagfinn Føllesdal also provided many ideas and useful suggestions.

Unless I am mistaken, the presumption made in the last sentence is one a strong possible-worlds semanticist should not make. There are actually a number of properties, of the strong possible-worlds variety, that Jones has in all and only the worlds in which Smith is bald. Consider the function f:

$$f(w) = \{\text{Jones}, \text{Smith}\} \quad \text{if Smith is bald in } w$$
$$f(w) = \emptyset \quad \text{otherwise}$$

f is a function from worlds to extensions, hence a property on the strong possible-worlds account. $f(w)$ contains Jones in all and only those worlds in which Smith is bald, so Jones' having this property in a world varies systematically with whether the world is in the T-set for "Smith is bald." We might express this property as "being such that Smith is bald and one is Smith or one is Jones."

It seems that the properties that Partee must have been thinking of, in the quoted sentence, are not functions from worlds to extensions, but good old-fashioned properties. Being bald is such a property, but being such that Smith is bald and one is Smith or one is Jones is not. Given this old-fashioned kind of property, Partee's concept of pw-aboutness is fine. But Partee's semantic concept of pw-aboutness does not belong to strong versions of possible-worlds semantics.

The second point on which Partee takes issue is whether there really is a "relatively clear and robust pretheoretic notion of aboutness that a semantic theory *should* enable us to capture." I always get a little nervous when philosophers claim it is our concepts that are at fault, and not their theories, when their theories cannot take account of the concepts. But in this instance, the main point Partee makes seems to be correct. This point is that we do not have very clear intuitions on the cases on which her notion of pw-aboutness and my notion of aboutness differ. "Jones is bald" is about Jones (by my principle (a)), and pw-about Jones, since it is empirical and its truth varies systematically with the properties of Jones. "Jones is Jones" is also about Jones by principle (a), but it is not pw-about Jones. Do we really have clear pretheoretic intuitions about this necessary truth being about Jones? I agree with Partee that we do not.

I do not have very clear pretheoretic intuitions the other way either, though. The idea that the proposition that Jones is Jones is about Jones in some semantic sense in which it is not about Smith does not seem incoherent, even if it is not a blue-ribbon intuition. It would be nice if our semantics could give us two concepts, so we could compare them. So we might consider whether pw-aboutness could be strengthened so as to apply to necessary and impossible propositions by dropping Partee's requirement that the propositions in question be empirical. But this seems hopeless. In possible-worlds semantics we have only one necessary proposition (the set of all worlds) and one impossible one (the empty set). So if the proposition that Jones is Jones is about Jones, so is the proposition that Smith is Smith.

This may not be all there is to say, though. Stalnaker has made an important distinction between taking worlds to be total and taking them to be comprehensive. I think this is a good distinction, and Partee agrees. As she puts it, "total possible worlds may be totally specified alternatives within some very small domain of possibilities, such as the distinct possible outcomes of a sequence of three coin-flippings" (1989a, 153). But I think this distinction means that there is not just one necessarily true proposition, and one impossible one.

Given the distinction, it does not seem quite right to talk about the set of all possible worlds except relative to a range of possibilities under discussion. In Partee's coin-flipping example there are eight possible worlds. The universal set of worlds, relative to this range of possibilities, includes these eight. This will yield us 256 propositions, one of which is the necessary proposition for this range of possibilities.

Obviously none of these 256 propositions can reasonably be taken to be the proposition that Jones is bald. Can we then reasonably take the one of them that contains all eight worlds to be the proposition that Jones is Jones? If not, then there seems to be room in possible-worlds semantics for more than one necessary proposition, without resorting to syntactically inspired internal structure.

In any case, the intuitions Partee had about pw-aboutness suffice to make the main point of my paper. This is the intuition that Smith and his properties have something to do with which worlds get into the T-set of "Smith is bald," while Jones and his properties do not. The concept of property that honors Partee's intuition will not be that of a function from possible worlds to extensions. Only metaphysics, not methodology, prevents us from countenancing such properties and propositions. It still seems to me that for a possible-worlds semanticist with no metaphysical commitment to limiting intensions to functions on possible worlds, the problem of necessary equivalent propositions is simply a fly bottle that did not have to be flown into. The solution is to fly out, not to argue that, all things considered, maybe it is not such a bad bottle to be in.

9

Circumstantial Attitudes
and Benevolent Cognition

An agent's beliefs, desires, and other cognitive attitudes depend not only on the agent's mental states and various necessary (or at least universal) facts connecting mental states with the rest of the world, but also on contingent circumstances that vary from individual to individual.

This circumstantial nature of the attitudes is a more or less direct consequence of the circumstantial nature of reference. If the object an idea is about depends on such circumstances as the causal paths leading to its occurrence, the identity of the agent, and the time and place of cognition, then what the agent believes or desires in virtue of the cognitions of which that idea is a component will vary with these contingent facts too.

The circumstantial nature of the attitudes strikes many philosophers as puzzling, inappropriate, or even unacceptable. Sometimes it is thought that there must be a layer of noncircumstantial attitudes underlying the circumstantial ones; this is one thought behind the *de dicto* vs. *de re* distinction. Sometimes it is supposed that the whole line of reasoning that leads to the circumstantial nature of the attitudes must be confused.

A central cause of puzzlement is the idea that the circumstantial nature of the attitudes would render inexplicable the regular nomic links between what we believe and desire and what we do. But these nomic links are a central part of commonsense psychology, our conception of how we work.

In this paper, I claim that the circumstantial nature of the attitudes does not threaten, but rather renders intelligible, this insight of commonsense psychology. I do this by showing how an appreciation of the circumstantial nature of the attitudes allows us to state a central principle of the commonsense view. The basic idea is that it is a complement to the long-recognized circumstantial nature of action.

Benevolent Cognition

Fairly often, what we do helps us get what we need. This fact is the result of two others. First, our beliefs often correspond to the facts fairly well, and our desires often correspond to our needs fairly well. Second, the actions that we perform because we have certain desires and beliefs, are often of a sort that will promote the satisfaction of the desires if the beliefs are true. It is this second fact on which I shall focus.

It requires that two aspects of our beliefs and desires be coordinated, their content and their effect. Suppose I believe that the glass in front of me contains water, and I desire to drink. The content of my belief is that a certain glass contains water, and the content of my desire is that I get a drink. Some actions I might perform will satisfy my desire if my belief is true, and others will not. So the contents of my desire and belief determine a certain class of actions: those that are appropriate or reasonable given the contents of the desire and the belief. But the desire and belief themselves are, it seems, mental states. And these mental states are related by laws of nature to certain behavior. Because I believe and desire as I do, I act in a certain way. I reach out, grab the glass, raise it to my lips, and swallow. This is an appropriate action, one that will lead to the satisfaction of my desire, if my belief is true. So the two aspects of my cognitive state, its doxastic and appetitive contents, on the one hand, and its effects, on the other, are coordinated.

This coordination suggests a certain benevolence on the part of God or Mother Nature. If this belief and desire resulted in my emptying the water on my head, or singing the National Anthem, then attribution of malevolence or a sense of humor might be more appropriate. But the evidence is in favor of benevolence, although perhaps of a rather grudging or parsimonious variety.

The principle that these two aspects of cognition are thus coordinated I call "efficient and benevolent cognition." By "efficient," I mean to express the idea that we do work in a lawlike way. Other things being equal, others in the same cognitive states that I am in will behave or act as I do.

In this paper, I begin by putting before the reader a straightforward version of the principle, whose conflict with the circumstantial nature of the attitudes will be fairly apparent. I show how appreciation of the circumstantial nature of action raises problems for this version. I then state a second version, which accommodates the circumstantial nature of action and the attitudes, explains it, and defends it against a possible criticism.

First Version

Here is the first version:

> (1) If (i) believing P and desiring Q cause A,
>   then (ii) A promotes Q, given P.

The idea is very simple: (i) envisages that there is a certain psychological law, connecting the property of believing P and desiring Q with the property of performing action A. If God or Mother Nature has wired us up in this way and is benevolent, our environment must meet certain conditions; (ii) gives those conditions.

P and Q are propositions.[55] The notion of proposition I have in mind is based on the theory of situations, but the ideas presented here do not require exposition of that theory. It comprehends both objectual and qualitative propositions. That is, propositions may have objects as constituents in some sense, as is natural to suppose, given circumstantial theories of reference; for example, "President Reagan is asleep" expresses a proposition with Reagan himself as a constituent, rather than some properties he uniquely instantiates. But propositions may also have only relations and properties as constituents, as seems natural for "every President is asleep" and some uses of "The President is asleep." For the purposes of this paper, the crucial property of propositions is that they are true or false absolutely, not relative to the circumstances of the agent.

A is an action; I take actions to be properties of a certain sort. As I use the terms an action is a uniformity across acts; that is, if you and I both raise our right hands, the acts are different, but the actions are the same.

I take causing and promoting as primitive. The first is a relation between properties. The latter, in this version, is a relation between a property (performing a certain action) and two propositions. A strong construal of an action promoting Q given P is that it guarantees Q given P; a weaker construal is that it merely makes Q probable, given P. For the purposes of this paper, this difference will not matter.

So the principle tells us that if things are benevolently organized, then a desire and a belief will cause an action, only if the action promotes the satisfaction of the desire, given the truth of the belief. That is, if (i) is a psychological law for a class of agents, (ii) should be a principle that governs the environment of the agents.

Version (1) strikes one, at first, as surely too simple, but headed in the right direction. But if the attitudes are circumstantial, it will not work at all. If what I believe and desire depends, not just on the internal mental states that we can conceive as leading, in lawlike ways, to actions, but also on the external circumstances in which those mental states occur, then the efficient benevolence envisaged by (1) looks impossible. For why should the actions, caused by those mental states, be appropriate to the attitudes one has in virtue of the

---

[55]It is a fact of some interest, I think, that we ordinarily take actions or other properties of individuals as the objects of desire, rather than propositions. We are much more likely to say "x wants to go to the store" or "x desires to be at the store" than "x desires that he be at the store." I think reflection on this point would strengthen the arguments I make here. But for simplicity I take propositions to be the objects of both belief and desire.

mental states plus these additional, contingent circumstances, that can vary among cognitively similar individuals? It seems like God or Mother Nature would be faced with the choice of varying the action to suit the circumstantially determined attitudes, and so abandoning efficiency, or letting the actions vary only with the mental states, abandoning benevolence. We must either give up (1), or give up the doctrine of circumstantially determined attitudes.

Actions and Circumstances

We should give up (1), for it does not have things right. It envisages too simple a relation between actions and the propositional contents of beliefs and desires.

It is a familiar point that there are different ways to individuate actions. Suppose you move your right hand in a certain manner, thus grabbing the glass in front of you and bringing it to your lips, and I move my right hand in the same manner, thus grabbing the glass in front of me and bringing it to my lips. Have we performed the same action or not? It depends on how we individuate actions. Our acts were behaviorally similar, and if we use this as our criterion of individuation, we may be said to have performed the same action: moving in the way one does when one grabs a glass in a certain direction and at a distance in front of one with one's right hand and brings it to one's lips. But we can also individuate actions by their results, by reference to the propositions they make true. Given this criterion of individuation, we did not perform the same action. You made it the case that the glass in front of you was at your lips, but I did not. I could have done so, by moving my arm in a different way, which would have resulted in grabbing the glass in front of you and moving it to your lips. But, had I done that, I would not have performed the same action on the first criterion, for quite different behavior is required for me to get the glass in front of you to your lips than is required of you to get it there.

When we think of actions as being caused by cognitive states, we must have a behavioral notion of action in mind. We expect agents that are cognitively similar to move their body and limbs in the same way. There is no reason to expect these movements to make the same propositions true, since this will depend not only on the behavior, but also on the circumstances in which it occurs. Thus *making true* does not have as parameters only behaviorally individuated actions and propositions, but also agents and their circumstances.[56]

---

[56]Note that to take into account bodily differences, we need to make a further distinction between behaving in the same way and moving in the same way. Extending one's arm fully will not, with individuals of different arm lengths, lead to the same movements, if these are individuated in terms of the number of inches over which the arms move. In an earlier version of this paper, I added another parameter to the promoting relation discussed below, having to do with bodily characteristics, and another parameter to the causing relation. The idea was that a cognitive state caused behaviors depending on psychological type, and where things are benevolent, the psychological type accords with the bodily characteristics. This approach was taken because of a background

Similarly, *promotes* is not simply a relation between behaviorally individuated actions and a pair of propositions but also requires agents and their circumstances as parameters. The movement we are imagining me to make may guarantee or make probable that I get a drink from glass G, given that G contains water, if I perform it when G is exactly twenty-three inches in front of me in a certain relative direction. The same movement, made by you, with G twenty-three inches in front of you, will not guarantee or make it probable that I get a drink from G, given that G contains water. Nor would my making that very movement promote my getting a drink from G, in slightly different circumstances, with G, say, twenty-nine inches away instead of twenty-three. In those circumstances, the movement would merely make me look silly, as if I thought my arms were longer than they are.

So, given that it is behaviorally individuated actions we need for the psychological principles, the promotion relation (whether it is construed as guaranteeing truth or something weaker), must be made relative to agents and circumstances. Version (1) simply will not work.

An Improved Version

I now put forward and explain an improved version of the principle, which accommodates the circumstantial nature of action, by exploiting the circumstantial nature of the attitudes.

First some preliminaries. The principle will be put forward in the form of a necessary condition for a relation of benevolence holding between three items: a psychology, a projection relation, and an environment. A psychology is a system of psychological states, behaviors, and causal principles governing them. In (1), it was assumed that cognitive states can be directly assigned pairs of propositions, which a person in those states believes and desires. Now we make the weaker assumption, that they can be assigned such propositions relative to circumstances. We break the circumstances into the context and the wider circumstances. The context includes both the agent and his spatiotemporal location—although here I am ignoring the latter. The wider circumstances are properties, including complex relational properties to other objects that an agent might have. These assignments are made by a projection relation:

Projects (a, C, S, Q, P)
iff
a desires Q and believes P in virtue of being in state S in circumstances C.

I use "cognitive states" for those psychological states that have this relation to

---

assumption that perceptual states should be individuated in terms of objectively determined circumstances, and so this should also be true of cognitive states. However, I do not now feel very clear about how things should be handled, and so ignore the issue in this paper.

some agents, circumstances, and propositions.

I leave it open just what underlies the projection relation. It might be an additional fact about agents that God or Mother Nature establishes, in addition to the facts of the psychology. Or it might be an artifact of our commonsense theory for dealing with the facts of psychology for the various purposes for which we need to deal with them. Something like the former is, I take it, Searle's view, while the latter I take to be common to various forms of the identity theory and functionalism. I am inclined to favor the latter view, and think that the considerations brought forward in this paper are relevant to arriving at a plausible version of it, but this topic is not further considered here; indeed, couching the project in terms of benevolence—either the real benevolence of God or the metaphorical benevolence of Mother Nature—fits most easily with the first view. If we hold the second view, this benevolence becomes something like a postulate underlying the commonsense theory.

Here then is the improved version:

(2) Let Ψ be a psychology, E an environment, and Proj a projection relation. Let a, S, and A range over agents, states, and actions of Ψ respectively, and C range over circumstances of E. If Ψ is benevolent for E according to Proj, the following must hold:

Whenever

(i) an agent a is in circumstances C such that Proj (a, S, C, Q, P), then

(ii) a is also in circumstances C' such that some action A caused by S is such that Promotes (a, A, C', Q, P).

In my example, my circumstances included seeing a glass that was in front of me, call it G. In virtue of being in the cognitive state I was in, I believed, of this glass, that it had water in it. Had a different glass, G', been in front of me, I would have then believed that G' had water in it, even though I was in exactly the same cognitive state. The possibility of this sort of relativity to circumstance is built into (ii).

Someone else in the same cognitive state would have desired that they get a drink from G, not that I do so. This involves relativity to context; that is, this difference would remain even if this other person were assumed to be in exactly my circumstances. Thus we need both the agent and the wider circumstances as parameters of the projection relation.

In my example, my being in this cognitive state causes me to move my hand and arms in a certain way, which works effectively to get me a drink. This would only work if I do it, and only in certain circumstances, as we discussed above. So now promoting has become a more complex relation. However, the circumstances that are relevant to my attitudes and those that are relevant to my action are not the same.

In the example, there is a certain glass, G, that I both have a belief and desire about, and act upon. The circumstances that determine that my belief is about G have to do with the fact that I am looking at it, and it is the cause of certain aspects of my perceptual and cognitive state. The circumstances that determine that my movement intersects with the position of G at about the right point, and thus promotes my drinking rather than spilling water on myself or missing the glass entirely, have to do with the distance and position of the glass relative to me, and also the length of my arms and other such facts.

For this reason, we do not cite the same circumstances in (i) and (ii). Rather, we place a requirement on the environment E, that when an agent is in circumstances that determine, together with his cognitive state, certain attitudes towards an object, he will also be in circumstances that determine, together with the behavior caused by the cognitive state, actions that are reasonable given the attitudes.

Note that it would be much too stringent to require that every action caused by S stand in the promotion relation. S may cause actions that have parts that are also actions, but which, considered in isolation from the larger wholes, do not promote anything helpful. And S may cause irrelevant actions, like fidgeting. All of this is compatible with benevolence, so analyzed.

The sort of benevolence for which we have evidence is hardly as perfect as this might suggest. Sometimes our beliefs and desires cause behavior that does not promote satisfaction of the desire, even if the belief is true. We might weaken the conditions by saying "typically when" or even "sometimes when." The last alternative might be appropriate for Mother Nature, if her ambition is really just to allow a few agents enough freedom from total frustration that they reproduce. Or, rather than explicitly weakening the conditions, we may think of the analysis as providing us with a constraint that, like most conditionals, holds only relative to certain assumed background conditions (Barwise 1985).

How benevolent are things? Suppose an experimental psychologist puts spectacles on me that make G appear closer than it really is, so when I reach for it I miss it and look silly. In this case, the environment has not lived up to the demands of unconditional benevolence, given my psychology. So, the presence of experimental psychologists is enough to disprove unconditional benevolence, in this strongest sense. But unless they are allowed to take over the world, a more modest form of benevolence is still a possibility. And, to be fair, various odd circumstances that lead to illusions and clumsy behavior occurred even before the advent of experimental psychology. Note that the effect of insisting on unconditioned benevolence would be to insist that all such instances of illusion and ineptitude are instances of false belief. An insistence of this sort would lead to a criticism of version (2) that I now consider.

(Over) Burdening Belief

The objection is that (2) is motivated by a misdiagnosis of the problems with (1), and as a result brings in circumstances twice over. The critic[57] would maintain that while action is circumstantial, the attitudes are only contextual. That is, the projection relation should be relative to context, but not to wider circumstance: only the context, the identity of the agent, is needed to intervene between cognitive state and attitude. And, furthermore, the job of closing the gap between the behavior a cognitive state causes and the goal it is to promote, should be mainly borne by the proposition believed. That is, the truth of the proposition believed should guarantee that the agent is in those circumstances in which the behavior caused promotes the goal desired.

On this view, our example is diagnosed as follows. I must have believed not simply that the glass had water in it, but also that it was a certain distance and direction from me—exactly the distance and direction it had to be for my action to promote my getting a drink.

On this view, we replace projection with a simpler relation:

Projects$'$ (a, S, Q, P)
iff
a believes P and desires Q in virtue of being in state S.

On this conception, one can represent cognitive states by pairs of properties of agents. The cognitive state I was in is represented by the pair: being such and such a distance and direction from a glass full of water; drinking a glass full of water from which he is such and such a distance and direction. To get from the state so represented to the proposition, we need only the context.

However, *projects$'$* can be defined in terms of *projects*:

Projects$'$ (a, S, Q, P)
iff
for every C, Projects(a, S, C, Q, P).

Not all cognitive states that bear the projecting relation to some agents, circumstances, and pairs of propositions will bear the projecting$'$ relation to agents and pairs of propositions, only those for which the wider circumstances are irrelevant, in that once a is fixed, the content of belief and desire is also fixed. We can call this subclass of contextual but noncircumstantial cognitive states *merely contextual*. There is no need for me to deny the possibility of cognitive states that are merely contextual, and the analysis of benevolence in (2) ex-

---

[57]The critics I have in mind are Robert Moore, David Lewis, Roderick Chisholm, and Hector-Neri Castañeda. The first three have independently developed conceptions of the attitudes as relations to properties of the agent, and Castañeda's inclination to suppose that all indexicals and demonstratives can be analyzed in terms of "I" and "now" makes me think he would also make a criticism of this sort.

tends to them. So the possibility of such cognitive states does not count against (2). We can retain (2) and entertain the possibility that all cognitive states are merely contextual as a hypothesis. A psychology with only merely contextual and not circumstantial cognitive states would be benevolent, but a benevolent psychology need not be of this sort. It is just a matter of how much God or Mother Nature wanted to make use of the stabler aspects of our environment.

To see what sorts of issues are relevant to this hypothesis, let us first note how unrealistic it would be to suppose that the content of our beliefs fix all of the circumstances relevant to the success of our action. Consider the force of gravity. If I am in space or on the moon or in some other situation where gravitational forces are much diminished, the movement we envisage me making in the example will not lead to getting a drink; the water would fly out of the glass all over my face—or perhaps I would not even grab the glass, but instead propel myself backwards. If all possible failures are to be accounted for by false beliefs, the corresponding true beliefs must be present when we succeed. So, when I reach for the glass, I must believe that the forces of gravity are just what they need to be for things to work out right.

But it hardly seems probable that everyone, even those with no knowledge of gravity, believes, when they reach for a glass of water, that the gravitational forces are what they are; such an attribution would drain the word "belief" of most of its content. Benevolence certainly does not require such omnidoxasticity, to misbeget a phrase. A more efficient way for Mother Nature to proceed is to fit our psychology to the constant factors in our environment, and give us a capacity of belief for dealing with the rest. She could have been confident that by the time we achieve space travel and have some need for action-affecting beliefs about gravity, we will have developed the concepts required to do so.

There are countless other circumstances necessary for our action to be successful that are constant throughout the normal range of humans. One might conjecture a general belief, that things are normal, underlies much of our action. But if we distinguish believing that things are normal from not believing that things are abnormal, this conjecture seems groundless.

These reflections do not decide the issue, for the hypothesis in question requires only that all of the nonconstant circumstances relevant to action be comprehended by what is believed; the constant factors can be dealt with by admitting our psychology is benevolent only for environments that embody them.

It does, however, suggest where the issue does lie. Let me suggest a crude picture of psychology and projection that motivates my skepticism about the hypothesis.

Suppose that, although there being a glass twenty-three inches in front of me is hardly a constant circumstance in my environment, there is a constant relation between a certain perceptual state and this circumstance. And suppose that there is a similar but different perceptual state that is similarly related to there being a glass twenty-nine inches in front of me. Suppose further that these states have the property of referring to the object that plays some prominent role in their causation: in these cases, the glass in question. Finally, suppose that cognitive states are complex, that perceptual states of this sort can be components of them, and that the projective properties of cognitive states are systematically related to the referential properties of their components.

Given this picture, we may expect that different cognitive states, with different components, may project the same beliefs and desires, in slightly different circumstances. In one case, I am twenty-three inches from G. In the other, I am twenty-nine inches from it. My perceptual states are different. But both perceptual states are of the same glass, G, and the cognitive states of which they are components project the same desires and beliefs, that I get a drink from G and that G contains water. Still, given the different components of the different cognitive states, their causal roles may differ, even though their projective properties do not. The first cognitive state gives rise to behavior suited to the circumstances stably related in the environment to its perceptual component— that is, my arm moves to a spot twenty-five inches away—and the second gives rise to behavior suited to the circumstances stably related to it—I extend my arm a bit further.

If this were the way things worked, the hypothesis in question would be incorrect. To understand the relation between cognitive states, the beliefs and desires to which they give rise, and the actions they cause, we would have to recognize circumstances as a significant parameter of the projection relation.

While the picture sketched is crude, it seems the principle it illustrates could survive in more sophisticated accounts. It seems then that version (2) can at least claim the virtue of not ruling out such accounts a priori, so that the contextualist hypothesis can be weighed against alternatives.[58]

[58]Research on this paper was begun while on sabbatical leave from Stanford University. It was also supported by a grant from the National Science Foundation and a grant to the Center for the Study of Language and Information from the System Development Foundation.

This paper owes a great deal to a seminar on planning and practical reasoning, held at the Center for the Study of Language and Information during winter quarter 1984. Thinking about Bob Moore's theory of knowledge and action was particularly helpful. While the ideas in this paper are basically in the spirit of Barwise and Perry 1983, the seminar and other discussions with Michael Bratman, Stan Rosenschein, John Etchemendy, Ned Block, David Israel, and others led to an increased appreciation of the importance of action in thinking about the attitudes. Both Jon Barwise and I have been thinking a great deal about such matters, and hearing his ideas on the semantics of OLP, a simple programming language based on English commands, was extremely helpful. Other developments in the theory of situations are reported in Barwise and Perry 1985.

10

Thought Without Representation

I see a cup of coffee in front of me. I reach out, pick it up, and drink from it. I must then have learned how far the cup was *from me*, and in what direction, for it is the position of the cup relative to me, and not its absolute position, that determines how I need to move my arm. But how can this be? I am not in the field of vision: no component of my visual experience is a perception of me. How then can this experience provide me with information about how objects are related to *me*?

One might suppose that while no component of my perception is of me, some component of the knowledge to which it gives rise must be. Perhaps I am able to infer where the cup is from me, because I know how things look, when they are a certain distance and direction from me. Without a component standing *for me*, how could this knowledge guide my action, so that it is suited to the distance the cup is *from me*?

But some philosophers think that our most primitive knowledge about ourselves lacks any such component: basic self-knowledge is intrinsically self-less. Something like this was presumably behind Lichtenberg's remark, that Descartes should have said "It thinks" rather than "I think." And according to Moore, Wittgenstein approved of Lichtenberg's remark:

> The point on which he seemed most anxious to insist was that what we call "having toothache" is what he called "a primary experience ...'"; and he said that "what characterizes 'primary experience' is that in its case, " 'I' does not denote a possessor." In order to make clear what he meant by this he compared "I have a toothache" with "I see a red patch"; and said of what he called "visual sensations" generally ... that "the idea of a person does not enter into the description of it, just as a (physical) eye does not enter into the description of what is seen"; and he said that similarly "the idea of a person" does not enter into the description of "having toothache." ... He said that "Just as no (physical) eye

171

is involved in seeing, so no Ego is involved in thinking or having toothache"; and he quoted, with apparent approval, Lichtenberg's saying, "Instead of 'I think' we ought to say 'It thinks'" (Moore 1959, 302–03).

I am sympathetic with Wittgenstein's view as I interpret it. There is a kind of self-knowledge, the most basic kind, that requires no concept or idea of oneself. The purpose of the present paper, however, is not to argue directly for this view, but to try to see how it could be so, by seeing how it is possible to have information about something without having any "representation" of that thing. I begin by studying something a bit more open to view, the possibility of talking about something, without designating it.

I

It is a rainy Saturday morning in Palo Alto. I have plans for tennis. But my younger son looks out the window and says, "It is raining." I go back to sleep.

What my son said was true, because it was raining in Palo Alto. There were all sorts of places where it was not raining: it does not just rain or not, it rains in some places while not raining in others. In order to assign a truth-value to my son's statement, as I just did, I needed a place. But no component of his statement stood for a place. The verb "raining" supplied the relation $rains(t, p)$—a dyadic relation between times and places, as we have just noted. The tensed auxiliary "is" supplies a time, the time at which the statement was made. "It" does not supply anything, but is just syntactic filler.[59] So Palo Alto is a constituent of the content of my son's remark, which no component of his statement designated; it is an *unarticulated* constituent. Where did it come from?

In approaching this question, I shall make five initial assumptions, which together will provide a framework for analysis. First, I shall assume that the meaning of a declarative sentence S can be explained in terms of a relation between uses of S and what is said by those uses—the propositional content of the statement made. Consider the declarative sentence *I am sitting*. Different people at different times say quite different things by using this sentence. What they say depends in a systematic way on the *context*—the facts about the use. The pertinent facts in this case are the user and the time of use. An explanation of the meaning of *I am sitting* quite naturally takes the form of a relational condition:

---

[59]Note that if we took "It" to be something like an indexical that stood for the location of the speaker, we would expect "It is raining here" to be redundant and "It is raining in Cincinnati but not here" to be inconsistent.

A use u of *I am sitting* expresses a proposition P iff there is an individual a and a time t such that

(i) a is the speaker of u
(ii) t is the time of u
(iii) P is the proposition that a sits at t.

The second assumption is that the propositions expressed by statements—at least the simple sorts of statements we shall consider here—have *constituents*. Their constituents are the objects (relations, individuals, times, places, etc.) that they are about. Thus the constituents of my statement that I am sitting are me, the present moment, and the relation of sitting.

The third assumption is that a declarative sentence has significant components, the meanings of which can be explained in terms of the relations between uses of these components and the objects those uses stand for or designate. Let us suppose that in our sentence the components are the three words, *I*, *am*, and *sitting*. We can explain their meanings as follows:

A use u of *I* designates an object a, iff a uses *I* in u; a use u of *am* designates a time t, iff t is the time at which u occurs; a use u of *sitting* designates a relation R, iff R is the relation $sits(a,t)$.

In the first two cases, facts about the use affect the object designated. This is not so in the third case; no variable for the use appears on the right of the "iff." Expressions of the first sort we call "context-sensitive"; those of the second we call "context-insensitive," or "eternal." In this example, each of the components is a separate word, but this is not necessary, and is not even plausible in the case of this simple sentence. A more plausible syntactic analysis would also find the component verb phrase *is sitting*. This we could take to designate a more complex object, say, a propositional function:[60]

A use u of *is sitting* designates a propositional function $P(x)$ iff there are u', u'', R, and t such that

(i) u' is a use of *is* that designates t, and u' is the initial part of u
(ii) u'' is a use of *sitting* that designates R, and u'' is the second part of u
(iii) for any a, $P(a)$ is the proposition that $R(a,t)$.

The fourth assumption is that the meaning of a sentence is systematically related to the meanings of its components. In the simple example I have given, we can see what the relationship is (ignoring the verb phrase, for simplicity):

A use u of *I am sitting* expresses the proposition P iff there are u', u'', u''', a, t, and R such that:

---

[60]That is, a function whose values are propositions, not one whose arguments are, as the phrase might suggest to those outside philosophy.

(i) u' is a use of I that designates a

(ii) u'' is a use of *am* that designates t

(iii) u''' is a use of *sitting* that designates R

(iv) u consists of u', followed by u'', followed by u'''

(v) P is the proposition that $R(a, t)$.

The fifth assumption is that a statement made by the use of a sentence is true, just in case the proposition the statement expresses is true.

The picture presented by this approach suggests a principle, which I shall call *homomorphic representation*:

> Each constituent of the proposition expressed by a statement is designated by a component of the statement.

It is this principle, to which my son's remark is counterexample. The propositional content of his use of *It is raining* was that it was raining, at that time, in Palo Alto. But no component of his statement designated Palo Alto.

II

We saw that there were basically two ways in which an articulated constituent is supplied. It can be built into the meaning of the expressions that it supplies with a given constituent in any context of use, as we supposed to be the case with *sitting*. Or the meaning can simply identify a certain relationship to the speaker, a role that different objects might play, in different contexts of use. In the case of I the relationship is that of identity.

I suggest that unarticulated constituents are also supplied in these two ways. They can be fixed by meaning, once and for all, or the meaning may just fix a certain relationship that the unarticulated constituent has to the speaker. That is, we can have eternal, and context-sensitive unarticulated constituents.

To this remark, one might reasonably ask what meaning it is that either fixes the unarticulated constituent or fixes the relationship it has to the speaker. After all, the problem is that there is no component of the sentence that designates the unarticulated constituent; hence, it seems inappropriate to begin by dividing the ways that it gets designated.

The unarticulated constituent is not designated by any part of the statement, but it is identified by the statement as a whole. The statement is *about* the unarticulated constituent, as well as the articulated ones. So, the theory is (i) some sentences are such that statements made with them are about unarticulated constituents; (ii) among those that are, the meaning of some requires statements made with them to be about a fixed constituent, no matter what the context; whereas (iii) others are about a constituent with a certain relationship to the speaker, the context of use determining which object has that relationship.

It is raining clearly has a meaning of the second sort. Let us assume, for a moment, that the unarticulated constituent for any use of this sentence is simply the place at which the use takes place. Then an analysis of its meaning would be:

A use u of *It is raining* expresses a proposition P iff there are u', u'', u''', t, p, and R such that

(i) u' is a use of *It*

(ii) u'' is a use of *is* that designates t

(iii) u''' is a use of *raining* that designates R

(iv) u occurs at p

(v) u consists of u', followed by u'', followed by u'''

(vi) P is the proposition that $R(p,t)$.

Clause (iv) pertains to the unarticulated constituent. Unlike clauses (ii) and (iii), it does not pick up a constituent designated by a component, but simply goes straight to the context, in this case, the facts about where u occurred.

It will be useful, to have a term for that part of the context, which determines the unarticulated constituent. I shall use the term "background" for this. The background facts in this case are those about the location of the statements.

An analysis of *It is raining here* would differ, just that instead of clause (iv) we would have:

(iv) u'''' is a use of *here* that designates p

(with the rest of the condition changed as necessary to accommodate u''''). The place would then be an articulated rather than an unarticulated constituent of the proposition.

The supposition that *It is raining* simply leaves unarticulated what *It is raining here* articulates is not very plausible, however. Suppose, for example, that my son has just talked to my older son in Murdock on the telephone, and is responding to my question, "How are things there?" Then his remark would not be about Palo Alto, but about Murdock. All we should probably say as part of our analysis of the meaning of *It is raining* is simply:

(iv) u is about p.

This is not to deny, of course, that a good deal more could be said concerning the factors that determine which places a use of this sentence is about. The intentions and beliefs of the speaker are clearly key factors. My son's belief was about Murdock, and his intention was to induce a belief in me that was about Murdock by saying something about Murdock. Here it is natural to think that we are explaining which unarticulated constituent a statement is about, in terms of something like the *articulated* constituents of the beliefs and intentions it expresses.

My example of context-free provision of an unarticulated constituent is somewhat fanciful. Suppose there is a dialect, spoken only by very chauvinistic San Franciscans. In this dialect, the sentence *It is raining* is used to state the proposition that it is raining, at the moment of utterance, in San Francisco. (*It is raining here* is used for other locales the speakers of this dialect might find themselves in.) This is the proposition a speaker of this dialect asserts with *It is raining*, no matter where in the world it is spoken. San Francisco is then an unarticulated constituent of the propositions expressed by statements using this sentence. It is determined in a context-insensitive way.

III

Simple-minded as it is, this little theory establishes, I think, that there is no basic problem with a statement being about unarticulated constituents. In particular, we do not need to first find an expression, hidden in the "deep structure" or somewhere else and then do the semantics of the statement augmented by the hidden expression. Things are intelligible just as they appear on the surface, and the explanation we might ordinarily give in nonphilosophical moments, that we simply understand what the statement is about, is essentially correct.

Still, it might seem that to correctly use and understand statements with unarticulated constituents, we must have, or be able to provide, expressions that designate them. When I hear my son say "It is raining," and learn thereby that it is raining in Palo Alto, it seems I must have understood that his remark was about Palo Alto. And to do this, it seems I must have in my mind some concept or idea of Palo Alto, with which I can identify it as the right place. And as we noted, it seems that what made his remark about the weather in Palo Alto, in one case, and the weather in Murdock, in the other, was his intentions and beliefs—what he had in mind, as we might say.

I shall argue that this is not quite right, although not quite wrong, either. We can imagine linguistic practices that do not require their participants to have any way of articulating some of the constituents of the propositions we would take to be the content of their statements. The basic idea is that the unarticulated constituents earn their role in the interpretation of statements by their place in the role of the thoughts that such statements express and give rise to, rather than by being designated by components of those thoughts. But once we have imagined all of this, a slightly different way of handling things will suggest itself.

Consider a small isolated group, living in a place we call Z-land. Z-landers do not travel to, or communicate with, residents of other places, and they have no name for Z-land. When a Z-lander sees rain, he will say to others not in a position to look outdoors, *It is raining*. His listeners then act appropriately to there being rain in Z-land: they close the windows in Z-land, cancel plans for

Z-land picnics, and grab umbrellas before going into the Z-land out-of-doors. They have no other use for "It is raining." They do not call their sons in far-off places, or listen to the weather news, or read newspapers with national weather reports.

It would be natural to treat Z-landers' uses of the sentence *It is raining* as having Z-land as an unarticulated constituent. But what secures Z-land, rather than, say, San Francisco, as the unarticulated constituent of their discourse about rain? It is simply that the perceptions that give rise to the beliefs that *It is raining* expresses are perceptions of the weather in Z-land, and the activities, to which the belief gives rise, are suited to rain in Z-land. Z-land is a constituent of the practice, or language game, in which the sentence *It is raining* plays a role. There is no need to postulate a concept or idea of Z-land as a component of their thought, to secure the connection to Z-land. The connection is secured by the role of the whole belief in their lives.

In the transaction we imagined with my son, there were three places that were relevant. First, there was the place his remark, my source of information, was about. Second, there was the place the belief I acquired from hearing him was about. Finally, there was that place rain in which would make appropriate the action to which my belief led me. As imagined, Palo Alto played all three roles. My son's remark was about the weather in Palo Alto, I took it this way, and going back to sleep was appropriate to rain in Palo Alto. But each of these connections might be broken. In a slightly different example, I would be misinterpreting a remark of my son's about rain in Murdock. His remark would be about one place, my belief about another. A little bit more elaborate change is required to break the second connection. Suppose we have spent the night in Sacramento, with the intention of driving back to Palo Alto early in the morning, so we can play tennis. My son looks out the window, and says "It is raining." I take him, correctly, to be telling me about the weather where we are. But I have forgotten where we are. The action I take is appropriate to there being rain in Palo Alto, for if it were raining there, there would be no reason to leave early. But it is not appropriate to there being rain in Sacramento.

Given that we get information about the weather in various places, and have a repertoire of actions appropriate to weather in various places, our weather beliefs have a coordinating job to do, a job mine did satisfactorily in the original case, and unsatisfactorily in those we have just imagined. If our beliefs are to successfully guide our actions in light of the weather information we receive, they must reflect not only the kind of weather but also the place of the weather.

The Z-lander's beliefs have a simpler job to do. All of the information (or misinformation) they get about the weather, through observations or reports of others, is about Z-land. All of the actions they perform, in light of their weather beliefs, take place in Z-land, and are appropriate or not depending on the weather there. The connection between the place about which they receive weather information, and the place whose weather determines the appropriateness of their actions, is guaranteed by their life-style, and need not be coordinated by their beliefs.

Some psychologists and philosophers find it useful to postulate a "language of thought," a system of internal representations, with a syntactic structure and a semantics that is involved in belief, desire, and other mental activities and states. One goal of the present investigation is to develop concepts that will help us to understand the motives for attributing structure to thought, and the extent to which linguistic structure is the appropriate hypothesis. So I do not want to commit myself to any very determinate version of the language of thought. Still, we can use this hypothesis, bracketed, so to speak, to make the present point: there is no reason that thoughts that employ representations in the language of thought should not have unarticulated constituents, just as statements that employ sentences of natural language do.

IV

Still, it does not seem quite right to treat Z-landers' discourse about weather just as we treated our own. A Z-lander semanticist would look at things differently. Having himself no concept of other places it might rain, he regards *rain* as a property of times, not a relation between times and places, as we do. He treats Z-landish discourse about the weather as homomorphic. What he provides as that which Z-landers believe and assert about the weather, the content of their discourse and thought, is something that to *us* seems to be but a function, from places to propositions.

There is something right about our Z-lander's point of view that we have not yet captured, and something right about ours that we do not want to lose sight of. There is some distortion in treating the Z-landers' uses of *It is raining* just as we treat our own, as if there were a range of possibilities left open by their language that they simply fail to consider. Nevertheless, the possibilities we see, and they cannot yet express or think, are real.

Suppose we accept the Z-lander semanticist's opinion as to the objects of the Z-landers' attitudes—what they assert with a use of *It is raining* and what they believe when they hear such a statement from a reliable source—but stick to our view of what those objects are. Then we would say that the Z-landers assert and believe propositional functions, rather than propositions. What would be wrong with this?

Let us back up for a moment. Beliefs have a semantic and a motivational or causal aspect: they are true or false, and they guide our action in achieving our goals. The two aspects are connected. The action to which a belief leads us, given our goals, should promote those goals if it is true. Thus my belief that it is raining in Palo Alto leads me to go back to bed, given my goal of sleeping late unless I can play tennis without getting wet. And if the belief is true, going back to bed will promote this goal.

Similarly, the Z-landers' beliefs about the weather lead them to actions that make sense if it is raining in Z-land. So, it seems that those beliefs ought to be true, depending on how the weather is in Z-land. And so it seems that the objects of the belief should be about Z-land, so that they will be true or false depending on the weather there. This last step leads us to attribute content to their beliefs nonhomomorphically, for if we took the content to be a propositional function, rather than a proposition, it seems like the connection between the semantic and the motivational aspects of their beliefs would be mysterious.

But this last step is not really necessary. There is another way to make Z-land relevant to truth of the Z-landers' assertions and beliefs. We can give up our fifth assumption, that a statement made by the use of a sentence is true, just in case the proposition the statement expresses is true. For the Z-landers' discourse about weather, a statement is true if the propositional function it expresses is true relative to Z-land. Z-land comes in not as an unarticulated constituent each Z-landish weather statement is about, but a global factor that all Z-land discourse about the weather concerns.

The point is to reflect, in our semantics, the lesser burden that is put on the Z-landers' assertions and beliefs compared to ours because of their impoverished sources of information and their limited repertoire of weather-sensitive actions. The only job of their assertions and beliefs concerning the weather is to deal with the nature of the weather in Z-land. Their assertions and beliefs are satisfactory, insofar as their "weather constituent"—rain, snow, sleet, etc.—matches the weather in Z-land, were our need also to register the place of the weather. By taking the propositional content of their beliefs to be propositional functions, rather than complete propositions, and taking them to be true or false relative to Z-land, we mark this difference.

Let us develop a little more vocabulary to mark this distinction. We shall reserve "about" for the relation between a statement and the constituents of its content, articulated and unarticulated. We shall say a belief or assertion *concerns* the objects that its truth is relative to. So the Z-landers' assertions and beliefs *concern* Z-land, but are not *about* Z-land.

V

As an alternative to this approach, we might consider taking Z-land to be a context-insensitive unarticulated constituent of Z-landish weather reports and beliefs. This would be plausible, insofar as it makes the relevance of Z-land a fact about the whole linguistic system, rather than about individual assertions and beliefs. It does not seem quite right, however. Suppose the Z-landers become nomads, slowly migrating westward. If their uses of "It is raining" is keyed to their new surroundings, we would either have to say its meaning had changed, or that their reports were now false, whenever the weather in their new environs deviated from that in Z-land. Neither of these steps seems plausible. What we have contemplated is a change in their surroundings, not a change in the meanings of their sentences.

We can handle this under the approach of the last section, however. We can say that the place Z-landers' weather assertions and beliefs *concern* changes, as they move west. Or, if a schism develops, and different groups of Z-landers move off in different directions, severing connections with their old comrades, we can say that the different groups, though continuing to speak the same language, come to be concerned with different places. What is "built into" Z-landish, at the current stage of its development, is that those who speak it are concerned with the weather where they are, and their assertions and beliefs about the weather are true or false depending on the weather there.

VI

Could we apply this analysis to my younger son's remark? That is, could we interpret it homomorphically, taking it to express a propositional function, and say that it is true, because it concerns Palo Alto? But this would not be an accurate remark about English. Weather discourse in English does not uniformly concern the place where the discussants are.

Still, there is a little of the Z-lander in the most well-traveled of us. Talking on the phone and reading the national weather reports are one thing, talking to someone in the same room about the weather is a bit different. Our reaction to the local statement "It is raining" is to grab an umbrella, or go back to bed. No articulation of the fact that the reporter's place and our place are the same is really necessary.

Something like the Z-landers' way of looking at things may be regarded as an aspect of our way of dealing with information about the weather, in circumstances in which the weather information we get is guaranteed either to be about or to concern our own location. And something like the semantics provided for the Z-landers' weather discourse is an aspect of the meaning of sentences like *It is raining* in our language.

To borrow a phrase from Wittgenstein, we might say that the sentence *It is raining* has a role in a number of different language games. In those parts of our life where there is an external guarantee that the weather information we receive be about and our actions will concern our own locale, there is no reason for our beliefs to play the internal coordinating role they need to at other times. When I look outside and see rain and grab an umbrella or go back to bed, a relatively true belief, concerning my present surroundings, will do as well as a more articulated one, about my present surroundings.

VII

There is a stronger point to be made, however. The weather in one's locale plays a special role in the life of humans. This is not necessarily the case for all agents that deal with information about the weather; the local weather of the National Weather Service Computer need have no special significance for it. But humans are affected in important ways by the weather around them, no matter where they happen to be. It is important that we be able to pick up information about the local weather perceptually, as we are able to do, and to act appropriately to it, by dressing warmly, taking an umbrella, or grabbing the sun-tan oil, as the case may be. These actions, which help us deal with the local weather, need to be under the control of beliefs that are formed through perception of the local weather. Efficiency suggests that there should be states of belief, typically caused by observations of the weather around one, and typically causing behavior appropriate to that weather. That is, there should be a belief state[61] that intervenes between perception of rain and behavior appropriate to rain. But if beliefs involving this state are required to be *about* the place of the believer, then they must differ from person to person, depending on where they are, and even in a mobile individual, from time to time. Those in Phoenix should have their rain-behavior controlled by beliefs about Phoenix, those in Palo Alto should have their rain-behavior controlled by beliefs about Palo Alto, and so forth.

This could happen in two ways. One is that those belief states that directly control behavior for local weather merely *concern* local weather, rather than being about it. All believers who had just seen rain and were about to open their umbrellas would be reckoned as believing the same propositional function, but the truth conditions of their beliefs would differ with their location. The other would be to have these belief states correspond to a sentence like *It is raining here*. This sentence makes a statement about the local weather, no matter who says it and where; an analogous belief state would be about the local weather, no matter who was in it and where. On this view, the believers would be in the same state, but would not believe the same thing, because the state contains an "indexical" component.

We need both alternatives. An internal "indexical" component of weather beliefs, which makes them *about* the weather where in one's locale, is not necessary to understand beliefs with the causal role we have envisaged, intervening between local observations and actions appropriate to local conditions. It

---

[61] The term "belief state" suggests to many the total doxastic state of the agent, but I do not use it in that way. Two agents, each of whom has just looked outdoors and seen rain, could be in the same belief state, in my sense, in virtue of the common aspect of their total states that would lead each of them to say, "It is raining," even though there is little else they would both be disposed to say.

suffices that one's beliefs *concern* the local weather. Furthermore, using the indexical correctly is the same sort of ability as that grabbing an umbrella when one sees rain. "It is raining here" is an assertion appropriate when one sees rain, no matter where one is.

But a state corresponding to *It is raining here* also has an important role to play. For those who have access to information about weather in various places, and reason to communicate facts about their own local weather to others elsewhere that have such access. Such a state is best conceived as one that can be nomically tied to beliefs *concerning* the local weather and nonnomically tied, via beliefs about one's location, to beliefs *about* the local weather. I hear on the radio, "It is raining in Palo Alto." I believe that it is raining here, for I know that I am in Palo Alto. As a result, I believe that it is raining, a belief at a more primitive level that concerns Palo Alto. As a result, I get my umbrella.

The suggestion is, then, that our beliefs about the weather have a certain structure. At the bottom, there are what we might call "primary beliefs" about the weather, which are like the Z-landers' beliefs. These concern the local weather, and are true or false depending on it. They are typically caused by observations of local weather, and typically lead to action appropriate to local conditions. This is all our hypothetical Z-landers have, perhaps all that children have at certain stages of development, and often all that we need. Above these are indexical beliefs, which are *about* the place that the more primitive beliefs merely *concern*: It is raining here.

At the top are beliefs that correspond to more sophisticated forms of getting information about the weather: reading or listening to news reports, talking on the phone, and so forth. These beliefs are about various places, in virtue of relatively context-insensitive components of belief: it is raining in Palo Alto, it is raining in Murdock, and so forth. At the middle level are identificatory beliefs that allow information at the top level to be translated into action at the bottom level: this place is Palo Alto.

VIII

This all suggests, I hope, a possible approach to the problem sketched at the beginning. What each of us gets from perception may be regarded as information concerning ourselves, to explain connections between perception and action. There is no need for a self-referring component of our belief, no need for an idea or representation of ourselves. When a ball comes at me, I duck; when a milk shake is put in front of me, I advance. The eyes that see and the torso or legs that move are parts of the same more or less integrated body. And this fact, external to the belief, supplies the needed coordination. The belief need only have the burden of registering differences in my environment, and not the burden of identifying the person about whose relation to the environment perception gives information with the person whose action it guides.

Lichtenberg's original remark was that one should say "There is thinking," just as one says "There is lightning" (von Wright 1972, 464). I have picked a somewhat less dramatic type of weather to serve as an analogy to self-knowledge, and developed it at somewhat greater length. Such analogies can carry us only so far, of course, but that is as far as I shall try to go in this paper.[62]

Afterword

This paper was presented to the Aristotelian Society in 1986 in a symposium with Simon Blackburn. In his contribution, "What About Me?" Blackburn is sympathetic with the framework of propositions and constituents that I use (Blackburn 1986). He agrees that speakers need have no representation of a thing to talk about it, in my sense. He agrees that the most fundamental level of thought requires no idea or representation of ourselves. So far, so good.

But Blackburn keeps his enthusiasm under control:

(1) He thinks that my sense of "about" is attenuated; with a stronger more intuitive notion, there are no convincing examples of a speaker talking about a thing with no representation of it.

(2) He does not think that it is correct to take propositional functions as the objects of the Z-landers' thoughts.

(3) He does not understand why we should say, about the fundamental level of thought that requires no idea or representation of ourselves, that it involves information *concerning ourselves*. I say we need to attribute the information to explain something, but he does not see what.

(4) He does not think that I have provided any reason to be sympathetic to Wittgenstein and Lichtenberg; towards the end of his paper, he surveys some other reasons for sympathy that might be given, and finds them wanting.[63]

I will consider issues (1)–(3) in reverse order, but leave (4) for another occasion.

(3) Suppose that a ball comes at my head and I duck. Or suppose that I am hungry, see a milk shake and reach for it. In all likelihood, the perceptual and

---

[62]Recognition of the need for a distinction between what I here call *concerning* and *being about*, and the necessity to investigate nonhomomorphic representation, were forced upon me by Joseph Almog and Robert Moore in the course of conversations about the motivation for propositions with truth-values relative to times, as found in David Kaplan's work on demonstratives. The present approach is the result of conversations with Jon Barwise, David Israel, Bob Moore, John Etchemendy, and others.

[63]I do not claim that this is an exhaustive list of the reservations Blackburn presented.

cognitive processes involved in these events will be integrated into my more or less adult-like system of self-consciousness and explicit self-representations. I will remember that a ball came at my head, readily infer that at least once a ball has come at a philosopher's head, and so forth. Or I will remember that I am overweight and should not be drinking a milk shake, and then remember that I am overconscientious and should not be worrying about something as trivial as a milk shake, and so forth. These episodes would no doubt involve explicit self-representation and even self-recrimination. But, I argue, simply to understand the fact that I duck when I see the ball, or the way hunger and perception of a milk shake leads me to move my arm, we need not postulate a self-representation. With this Blackburn agrees: "It is fact external to the belief—facts about the integration of our control systems—which as he puts it, supply the needed coordination. There need be no self awareness, and no self knowledge ..." (161). But, given this, he is somewhat mystified as to why I want to attribute the possession of information concerning myself to me: "Perry does however suggest that even at the fundamental level, what we get from perception may be regarded as information *concerning* ourselves, to explain the connections between perception and action. I am not clear how this works ... why we need a reference to myself in the identification of any belief state, even if the reference is external ..." (161).

I do not claim that we need a reference to the believer in the identification of the belief state in question. When a ball approaches me, I can be in just the state that Blackburn or anyone else is, when a ball approaches them. We need a reference to the believer to specify the conditions under which the belief is true. Without this, we will not be able to understand the belief as part of a benevolent psychology, in the sense of Essay 9, and we will not be able to understand the logical connections between thought concerning an object and thought about an object.

This takes us to point (2) and the question of how it is best to describe episodes of language and thought whose truth conditions depend on objects of which they do not contain representations.

There are lots of cases of this. The general phenomenon is using an n-place predicate or concept to deal with an $n+1$-ary relation. Suppose I judge perceptually that two events happen simultaneously, and I am right. The fact that makes me right is that those events were simultaneous relative to my certain frame of reference. "Is simultaneous with" is a 2-place predicate that we use to deal with a 3-ary relation, that of one event being simultaneous with another relative to a frame of reference. The frame of reference in question is not determined by a representation in my thought, but by the broader situation in which my judgment takes place.

A theorist who is analyzing the way an agent handles information and uses it to guide action may have to pay attention to factors the agent cognitive's system can safely ignore. The theorist's interest may be precisely how these factors can be ignored—how architectural or external constraints make internal representation unnecessary. It is the speed of light that allows us to get by with a 2-place concept of simultaneity. It is the shortness of our arms compared to the width of time-zones that allows us to ignore the latter when we read our watches. But where should the extra parameters come into the theorist's account?

My suggestion was that, in cases in which same unrepresented parameter is relevant to a whole mode of thinking or discourse, we should classify each specific belief or utterance with a propositional function. The truth-value would be that of the proposition obtained by applying the function to the value of the parameter fixed by facts about the whole system. Blackburn objects that this proposal leaves in the sphere of the Z-landers cognition "something which should not be—namely understanding of a general property (it raining at a place), which introduces exactly the possibilities which they cannot 'express or think' " (158).

But I do not think that having a cognitive relation to a family of properties requires one to understand that there are a range of things that can have or not have the properties. It may be that if one does not realize that, one is not properly appreciating the property-like nature of what one is cognizing. But that seems exactly the situation the Z-landers are in. If we think of propositions as 0-ary properties, we can say that they are in the same situation we are, most of us most of the time, with respect to simultaneity. We perceive and make judgments about a tertiary relation, while conceiving it to be a binary one; they perceive instances of and make judgments about unary properties (raining or not raining at particular times) while conceiving them to be 0-ary ones.

(1) Consider someone who is lost in Palo Alto. This does not prevent them from noticing that it is foggy, and they say "It is foggy here." Should we say that the content of their remark is the singular proposition individuated by Palo Alto and the property of being foggy? Blackburn thinks, correctly, that this is what I would say, and agrees that attributing this content might be reasonable for some purposes, such as understanding connection of utterances with truth and information. But, he says, "the notion of a proposition which is at this much distance from understanding ... is evidently not quite the notion—or at least not evidently quite the notion—with which to think about understanding. And thought, surely, goes with understanding" (155).

The problem, according to Blackburn, is not the very notion of a singular proposition, of a proposition with constituents. It is that certain constraints on the use of this apparatus come with the goal of understanding thought. In particular, the "metaphor" of a constituent should be constrained by the principle:

> You can identify a proposition only if you know which each of its constituents is.

Identifying the proposition one expresses is a condition for "fully understanding" one's own remarks. The person lost in Palo Alto fully understands what she says when she utters "It is foggy here." That means she can identify the proposition she expresses. By the principle, that means she knows which each of its constituents is. This means that, if that proposition has constituents, she is "knowingly denoting" them. But she is not knowingly denoting Palo Alto. Hence it is not a constituent of the proposition she expresses, given the notion of expressing a proposition that conforms to the principle, and is appropriate to the study of thought.

I believe the issue here is between a one-tiered and a two-tiered theory of the contents of thoughts. My approach is based on the extension of Kaplan's two-tiered theory of character and content to the realm of beliefs. It is in the interaction of the two levels that thought is to be understood. Singular propositions only indirectly characterize thoughts, in ways dependent on the circumstances of the thinker. Episodes of thought that are quite different in their nature and their cognitive and causal roles might all have the same singular proposition as their content, due to different circumstances. The thought naturally expressed with "It is foggy in Palo Alto" differs from one that is naturally expressed with "It is foggy here," even if the thinker of the latter is in Palo Alto. The present paper assumes this basic point of view, claims there is a further distinction to be drawn between the latter thought and one naturally expressed with "It is foggy," and seeks to understand that difference in the way the circumstances of the thought determine its interpretation.

As I understand Blackburn, he is approaching things a bit differently. He supposes that the the "metaphor" of constituents captures something about a certain kind of thinking, the kind of thinking that involves knowing denotation of certain objects, which are then (given the principle above) eligible for constituency in fully understood propositions. This is not the sort of thinking our person lost in foggy Palo Alto has. Rather than crediting them with the expression of a singular proposition they do not fully understand, we should admit that they fully understand what they say, but it is not such a proposition.

I do not want to deny that this is a reasonable approach, for it is surely one that has enabled philosophers such as Evans and Blackburn to say illuminating things and make useful distinctions. They see the object-individuated proposition as the hallmark of a certain very special kind of thinking, whereas I see it as that which is common to quite different forms of thought, and allows us to understand their different functions and connections.

From my point of view, Blackburn's principle does not so much hew out a clear notion of full understanding, as to illuminate one of the consequences of admitting singular propositions. Individuals, locations, and times have a plethora of properties and stand in a multitude of relations; for different purposes, different types of properties and relations are relevant to identification.

It seems to me that the right moral to draw from the principle is that the concept of identifying a proposition is susceptible to the same sorts of relativity as the concept of "knowing which thing." The concept of identifying a proposition has the delightful murkiness that is characteristic of good philosophical problems, but not of good philosophical tools.

Consider an admirer of Quine's, at a party where he knows Quine to be present. Does he know who Quine is? Yes, for he can say, "Quine is so and so," providing rich and interesting information. No, because he is standing next to Quine without realizing it. Does he know what proposition he utters when he says to Quine, pointing to Stuart Hampshire, "That man wrote *Word and Object*." Yes, because he can identify it: "It is the proposition true if and only if *that man* wrote *Word and Object*." No, because he can misidentify it— "It is true if and only if Quine wrote *Word and Object*"—and it is only this misidentification of it that leads him to say it. Which answer takes precedence in determining whether the fellow was knowingly denoting and fully understanding or not?

In the paper, I suggest a metaphor for thinking about the ways we think about things, a sort of three-story house. At the top, we store information in ways that are relatively unaffected by context. There we would find thoughts naturally expressed as "It is foggy in Palo Alto" or "Quine wrote *Word and Object*." At the bottom, tied to specific ways of picking up information about objects around us and specific ways of acting on them, are the thoughts naturally expressed as "It is foggy" and "That man looks distinguished." In the middle are orienting thoughts: "This city is Palo Alto," "That man is Quine." When we are correctly oriented, upper-story beliefs are altered based on what we find going on around us, and actions directed at things around us are guided by the information stored upstairs. When we are not oriented, the upward and downward flow of information is blocked. Central to this picture are the different ways we have of dealing with the same objective facts.

Singular propositions came to us from the theory of "direct reference." On Kaplan's theory, for example, the same singular proposition about Palo Alto is the content of "Palo Alto is foggy" and "This city is foggy," said by a person lost in Palo Alto. I take this to show that we ordinarily describe linguistic and cognitive activity in ways that focus on the things cognized and referred to, and not the ways we do so. This system works most smoothly when we are talking about well-oriented agents, for the lack of connection between "cognitive fixes" on the same object at different levels (as well as the possibility of multiple fixes at each level) is just what comes into play when people get disoriented and confused about where they are, who they are, and which things and individuals they find around them. A system of description that abstracts from the differences among them is not well-suited to describe confused thought. Should we abandon this commonsense system of description for one that describes thoughts noncircumstantially? Or should we merely reserve attribution of singular propositions to well-oriented agents? Or should we exploit them to help us compare, contrast, and understand the interrelations among the various ways we have of dealing with things? Blackburn's approach, as I understand it, is something like the second, and I admit is has a certain appeal. Mine is the last, and I admit that it is the product of confusion. But I hope that it is this only in the sense of being motivated by examples of confused people.

11

Cognitive Significance
and New Theories of Reference

Consider these utterances:

(1) "Pete Rose lives in Cincinnati," said by Roger Craig.

(2) "I live in Cincinnati," said by Pete Rose.

(3) "That star lives in Cincinnati," said by a fan to a child, pointing at Pete Rose.

(4) "You live in Cincinnati," said by Will Clark to Pete Rose.

Lessons learned from the works of Donnellan, Kaplan, Kripke, Putnam, Wettstein, and other New Theorists of Reference have convinced me to accept two theses with respect to (1)–(4).[64] First, the references of the singular terms do not depend on Fregean senses, or identifying descriptions in the mind of the speaker. The expressions used do not have such senses attached to them by the conventions of language. The beliefs of the speaker need not supply conditions that single out a unique individual. Even if the speaker has such beliefs, the reference is not determined by those beliefs. Second, each of these utterances expresses what David Kaplan has called a "singular proposition," a proposition that contains Pete Rose as a component or constituent, and so the same proposition is expressed by all of these utterances.[65] Each of these folks said, in their different ways, that Pete Rose lives here.

---

[64]I borrow the term "New Theory of Reference" from Wettstein 1986. Page numbers in parentheses refer to this article.

[65]Russell believed in propositions individuated in this way, even for entities as complex as Mt. Blanc. See Russell's letter to Frege of December 12, 1904 (Frege 1980, 169). As he developed his philosophy, though, he tried to replace propositions of this sort, in his analysis of cognitive activity, with general propositions, by exploiting his theory of descriptions to show that we only had denotation where we might have thought we had reference. In criticizing Russell's theory of descriptions, Strawson developed the notion of a statement and making the same statement, where statements are individuated by the individuals to which referring expressions refer, rather than the conditions used to refer to them (1950).

Wettstein argues that New Theorists cannot explain certain puzzles about the cognitive significance of language that are due to Frege, and so cannot meet certain Fregean conditions on a theory of linguistic meaning (1986). I think, in this respect, many philosophers agree with Wettstein. His article would be the classic Fregean critique of New Theories of Reference, except for one thing. Wettstein himself accepts a New Theory. From its correctness, and the inability of a semantical theory based on it to resolve Frege's puzzles, he concludes that it is not part of the business of semantics to deal with them.

The Problem of Cognitive Significance

Wettstein develops a number of theses and examples in his paper. I am going to attempt to deal with one central argument developed in the following quotes. Although Wettstein makes a number of points in the text between these quotes, I think they faithfully represent this central argument:

> Gottlob Frege motivates his famous distinction between sense and reference by formulating what amounts to a Fregean's idea in that any such account must provide an answer to a crucial question concerning the cognitive significance of language: the question of how identity sentences in which proper names flank the identity sign can both state truths and be informative (185).

> The new theorist holds that "Cicero was an orator" and "Tully was an orator" express the same propositions, that believing what the first sentence expresses just is believing what the second expresses. This seems plainly wrong, since the cognitive contents of the two sentences seem very different. One can understand both sentences, accept the first as expressing the truth, while not accepting the second. Similarly, the new theorist is committed to the view that "Cicero = Cicero" and "Cicero = Tully" express the same proposition. This seems wrong, however, since it is surely plausible to suppose that virtually everyone believes the first proposition, but only a select few believe the second.... The new theorist's difficulty here ... has nothing essential to do with proper names (187–88).

> Imagine two utterances of "He is about to be attacked," where a single individual is being referred to, but where it is not at all obvious that this is so. Indeed, let us suppose it appears to both speaker and his auditors that two very different individuals are being referred to. No doubt the cognitive significance of these utterances is dramatically different. One who understand these utterances might take only one of them to express a truth.... The same problem arises with regard to Frege's original problem about in-

formative identities (195).

Imagine that our speaker is watching a rock singer from the hall-way outside an auditorium. The singer is so outfitted and made up that one cannot tell from his right profile and from his left profile that the same person is in question. Our speaker first observes him from a small window in a door on the side of the auditorium and then walks to another doorway and sees what he takes to be an entirely different performer, performing in what he takes to be a different auditorium. We point out to him, "He (dragging our orig-inal speaker down the hall) is the same person as he is," or "That one is none other than that one." The cognitive significance of the first "he" is clearly different than that of the second (196).[66]

As I construe Wettstein's argument, it goes like this:

(1) If a person who understands the meaning of sentences S and S' of lan-guage L can accept as true an utterance u of S, while not accepting as true an utterance u' of S', then the cognitive significance of u differs from the cognitive significance of u'.[67]

(2) A person who understands both sentences could accept as true an utter-ance u of "Cicero was an orator," while not accepting as true an utterance of "Tully was an orator." Similarly for "Cicero = Cicero" and "Cicero = Tully." Also, a person who understands the sentence "He is about to be attacked," could accept as true an utterance u of it, while not accepting as true an utterance u' of it, even though the reference of "he" in both utterances is the same person.

(3) According to New Theories of Reference, in each of these three cases the proposition expressed by utterance u is exactly the same proposition as the proposition expressed by u'.

(4) The proposition expressed by an utterance is its cognitive significance.[68]

---

[66]Wettstein lists three problems, but he grants that what he calls the "Perry/Kaplan" approach can handle the first and third. The third problem, incidentally, was not a puzzle Frege posed, but one posed for both Fregean and New Theories in Essay 1, drawing on ideas and examples of Hector-Neri Castañeda's 1968 and other writings.

[67]Wettstein sometimes talks about the cognitive significance of a sentence, but when he has the general case in mind, he fairly consistently talks of the cognitive significance of an utterance.

[68][A number of people have pointed out to me that I seem to imply here that Wettstein accepts (4), which he does not. He spends a considerable amount of time, in "Has Semantics Rested on a Mistake?" and elsewhere, developing points about cognitive significance that would not make sense if (4) were true. I apologize for misleading people about Wettstein's view. What (1)–(5) are intended to represent, however, is the argument Wettstein develops in the first part of his paper, which he takes as a motivation for abandoning the attempt to give a semantic account of cognitive significance. A key step in this argument occurs in the second paragraph quoted above, where he says,

(5) So, either New Theories of Reference are wrong, or it is not the business of semantics to understand cognitive significance.

Semantics and Cognitive Significance

Wettstein's argument presents New Theorists with a dilemma. Wettstein takes the second horn and accepts that cognitive significance is not the semanticist's worry. Is this reasonable?

What the semanticist should worry about depends on what the semanticist is trying to do. A logician who is trying to come up with a semantic account of some logic that will enable the construction of a completeness proof should be relieved of worrying about cognitive significance. But this is not the sort of project Wettstein has in mind. By "semantic theory" he means a theory of linguistic meaning for natural languages. Wettstein is interested in how demonstratives, descriptions, and proper names work in English, not how variables, iota operators, and individual constants work in languages for quantification theory. If this is the semanticist's interest, then he has picked a subject matter that, whether he likes it or not, ties in with a number of other subject matters, including the study of cognition.

After all, our main interest in language is the way its use can communicate beliefs, inspire action, and have other effects on what we think and do. In these uses of language, it is aspects of the meaning of the language used that are crucial. A theory of linguistic meaning should help provide us with an understanding of the properties sentences have that lead us to produce them under different circumstances, and react as we do to their utterance by others.

If I were to divorce semantics from these interests, many of my reasons for adhering to the two principles Wettstein takes as definitive of being a New Theorist would be undermined. One reason we need singular propositions is to get at what we seek to preserve when we communicate with those who are in different contexts. Fregean thoughts will not do, and neither will mere truth-

---

The new theorist holds that "Cicero was an orator" and "Tully was an orator" express the same propositions, that believing what the first sentence expresses just is believing what the second sentence expresses. This seems plainly wrong, since the cognitive contents of the two sentences seem very different. One can understand both sentences, accept the first as expressing the truth, while not accepting the second.

This step of Wettstein's argument seems to turn on equating cognitive content or cognitive significance (which I took to be stylistic variants) with the proposition expressed. I don't see, without step (4), how the examples Wettstein gives constitute a problem for the new theory of reference.

This does not imply that Wettstein accepts (4). It is perfectly possible that Wettstein thought that giving up (4), and giving up the view that it is the business of semantics to understand cognitive significance, amounted to the same thing. I think this would be a natural view to take, if one accepted the new theory of reference, and thought that theories of this sort could produce no semantical property of an utterance of a sentence other than the proposition expressed to serve as its cognitive significance.]

values. Another reason is to get at the structure of belief. Philosophers who are bothered by singular propositions often complain that individuals cannot be "inside the mind." But, of course, the properties and relations that are constituents of "general propositions" are no more in my mind than individuals are. Minds evolved in a very Strawsonian world, where the ability to reidentify individuals and to use information picked up in one encounter to guide action in a later encounter is crucial. That we can usefully describe minds by reference to the individuals they have acquired information about, and that our concepts of belief and the other attitudes embody such a way of describing minds, should not be especially perplexing. New Theories are better suited for dealing with cognition than the alternatives.

The semanticist or philosopher of language does not need to carry the whole burden of responsibility for the philosophy of mind or cognitive science. Compare the problem of the perception of color. It is by no means obvious what physical property of objects we are reacting to when we distinguish them by color. It now appears that the property in question is the relation between the wavelength of the light that hits the object, and the percentage of light that is absorbed. (See Hilbert 1987.) This property stays constant throughout changes of lighting in the ways that colors do. It is a physical property of objects, of interest because of its effect on a certain special type of cognitive system, the visual systems of animals that can discriminate colors. Now I think it would be rather parochial or precious for physicists working on the physical properties of light and reflective properties of substances to say that locating this property was none of their business. They cannot be expected to take upon themselves the whole burden of explaining color vision, but, as physicists, they should be able to provide a theory of physical objects, within which the properties crucial for perception can be found.[69]

In the puzzle cases Wettstein has provided, the problem really comes down to explaining action. In the first version of the puzzle, we have two pairs of sentences, "Cicero was an orator" and "Tully was an orator." The New Theory holds that they both express the same proposition: "This seems plainly wrong, since the *cognitive* contents of the two sentences seem very different. One can understand both sentences, accept the first as expressing the truth, while not accepting the second." What is at issue is *accepting as true* a cognitive act. A person sees or hears a sentence uttered, and comes to believe a proposition; she hears another sentence uttered, and does not. The person is rational; her acts of acceptance and rejection were based on her beliefs and goals, and what she perceived about the sentences. It was not the spelling or the sound or the number of characters in "Tully was an orator" that she reacted negatively to.

---

[69]Of course, a physicist who said, "I cannot find the properties in question, so color vision must be a fiction of folk-psychology," should not be taken seriously at all.

Don't New Theorists have the responsibility to find that semantic property she did note, and in virtue of which her behavior towards the two utterances differed? It seems to me that we do.

I accept, therefore, some version of Frege's conditions. Here is a formulation that seems to come close to what Wettstein has in mind.

> *If there is some aspect of meaning by which utterances u of S and u' of S' differ, so that a rational person who understood the meaning of both S and S' might accept u but not u', then a fully adequate theory of linguistic meaning should assign different propositional contents to u and u'.*

To accept this formulation, however, would be to abandon hope for New Theories. That merely shows, I think, that this formulation begs the question. The semanticist need not assign different propositional contents to the discriminated utterances, if he can find some other aspect of their meaning that explains the differing effects on the beliefs of a rational, competent listener. The formulation I accept, then, allows a little more room for maneuver:

> *If there is some aspect of meaning, by which an utterance u of S and an utterance u' of S' differ, so that a rational person who understood both S and S' might accept u but not u', then a fully adequate theory of linguistic meaning should say what it is.*

The Cognitive Significance of Utterances

Since as New Theorists we can embrace neither horn of Wettstein's dilemma, we must avoid his conclusion. The way to avoid it is to reject step (4), by finding some other candidate for the cognitive significance of an utterance than the proposition it expresses. The first step, in doing this, is to isolate what other requirements Wettstein's argument puts on the concept of cognitive significance. As I understand his argument, there are five:

    (a) The cognitive significance of an utterance S in language L is a semantic property of that utterance.

    (b) It is a property that a person who understands the meaning of S in L recognizes.

    (c) The cognitive significance of an utterance of S in L is a proposition.

    (d) A person who understands the meaning of S in L, and accepts as true an utterance of S in L, will believe the proposition that is the cognitive significance of the utterance.

    (e) A person who understands the meaning of S in L, and sincerely utters S, will believe the proposition that is the cognitive significance of his utterance.[70]

---

[70]This last point actually relies on Wettstein's first puzzle.

I think this analysis of "cognitive significance" fits well with Wettstein's usage, and the common philosophical usage of this term. It fits well, also, with the ordinary meaning of the terms. The cognitive significance is "significance," that is, a semantic property, having to do with meaning, reference, truth, and so on. And it is "cognitive," that is, that aspect of meaning which is cognized by those who understand the sentence.

Given this analysis of cognitive significance, the identification in step (4) is mistaken, for the proposition expressed by an utterance does not fit these criteria. I think step (4) is an instance of what Jon Barwise and I have called the "fallacy of misplaced information":

> Construing the meaning of an expression as a multiplaced relation is what lets us account for information, since information is available about any or all of the coordinates, not just about the coordinate that gives us the [proposition expressed]. The idea that all the information in an utterance must come from [the proposition it expresses] we call the fallacy of misplaced information (Barwise and Perry 1983, 38, 164–66, 264; Essay 6, passim.)

Seeing and accepting this point does not require a grasp of situation theory or situation semantics, much less acceptance of those doctrines. It does require adopting a certain perspective, one that we basically derived from Kaplan 1979, and which we called the "relational theory of meaning." Let me explain that point of view by considering an example.

Suppose Ellsworth and McDuff are standing in the lobby of the hotel talking philosophy. Ellsworth is talking passionately about reference while holding a cup of coffee in his hand, and because he is so animated, coffee is sloshing over the sides of the cup and spilling on the carpet. I notice this, and say to Ellsworth, "You are spilling coffee on the carpet." This utterance expresses a certain proposition, that Ellsworth is spilling coffee on the carpet, in virtue of the following relevant features: (i) it is the production by a speaker at a time of a certain pattern of sound, (ii) that counts as a sentence of a certain type in English, (iii) with which English conventionally associates a certain meaning, (iv) that takes place in certain circumstances, one of which is that the speaker is addressing Ellsworth.

My utterance has the propositional content it does because of the other features, (i)–(iv). If English associated with the word "you" the meaning it actually associates with the word "I," then the propositional content would have been that I was spilling coffee. But even with English fixed, the other factors affect the content. If I had been addressing McDuff, then the propositional content would be that McDuff was spilling coffee. So, the content of an utterance is a property it has in virtue of various factors. We can think of this in the following way. What language associates with sentences is a certain relation among the contextual factors and the proposition expressed. The meaning of "You are spilling coffee" is a relation between speaker, time, circumstance, and propositional content. If this relation obtains, then the speaker, by uttering "You are spilling coffee" at the time, in the circumstances, expresses the propositional content.

Given this analysis, what our semantics should associate with the sentence "You are spilling coffee" is a a relation between the various factors:

> An utterance u of "You are spilling coffee" by an agent a at a time t in circumstances C expresses singular proposition P,
>
> iff
>
> There is an individual x such that (i) a's addressing x at t is part of C; (ii) P is the singular proposition that x is spilling coffee.

From the perspective of any theory along these lines there is a clear distinction to be made between the proposition expressed by an utterance and the proposition that the truth conditions of the utterance are satisfied. The former, in our example, is that Ellsworth is spilling coffee. This could be true if my utterance had never occurred. So the proposition I express has Ellsworth and not my utterance as a constituent. But my utterance could have been true, even if Ellsworth never spilled coffee in his life, as long as I was speaking to someone who was spilling coffee. So the proposition that the truth conditions of my utterance are satisfied has my utterance as a constituent, but not Ellsworth.

Suppose that you hear my utterance. You think I am eminently trustworthy, and so are sure that it is true. What information would you have? Just that I am speaking to someone who is spilling coffee. That is what you know, and all you know, just on the basis of being linguistically competent and accepting my utterance as true. We cannot, then, equate the proposition that the truth conditions of an utterance are satisfied with the proposition expressed by the utterance. But it seems clear that it is the former that fits the conception of the cognitive significance of an utterance that Wettstein has used in his argument. To carry out the comparison, I shall need a short term for "the proposition that the truth conditions of an utterance are satisfied." Since this proposition has the utterance itself as a constituent, its existence is contingent; it is in a sense created by the utterance. So I shall contrast the proposition expressed by an utterance with the proposition created by an utterance.

The proposition created by an utterance clearly passes criterion (a). I am willing to accept, for the sake of argument, that the proposition expressed by an utterance also passes criterion (a).[71] Surely, however, the truth conditions of the

---

[71] My skepticism on this point is based on skepticism about the whole notion of "the proposition expressed by an utterance." There are many things we do with utterances. We say things, communicate things, express our belief in things, and so forth. These can be quite different. A natural thing to say about the example discussed below, in which Kaplan wants to say something about

utterance are a more direct semantic property than the proposition expressed. The truth conditions of an utterance derive directly from the meaning assigned to the sentence involved, whereas which proposition is expressed depends also on the agent, time, and circumstances of utterance.

Both the proposition created and the proposition expressed meet criterion (c). The proposition expressed by my utterance is that Ellsworth is spilling coffee. The proposition created by it is that its speaker is addressing someone who is spilling coffee. Both can be regarded as singular propositions, one about Ellsworth, one about my utterance.

So far, a close issue. But when we look at criteria (b) and (d), it seems clear that we should equate the cognitive significance with the proposition created by an utterance, not the proposition the utterance expresses. To see why this is so, let me consider a different example.

Ellsworth goes to Hawaii and sends me a postcard. Unfortunately, it gets a bit wet before I receive it. The postmark, return address, and signature are all illegible. The message stays dry: "I am having a good time now."

If I am a competent speaker of English, I will understand the meaning of the sentence written on the postcard and hence the truth conditions of the utterance that produced it. It is true, if the person who wrote the postcard was having a good time at the time he or she wrote it. This is a singular proposition, with the event that produced the postcard as a constituent. If it is is true, the utterance is true, and vice versa. Moreover, Ellsworth, surely a sincere and a competent speaker of English, must have believed this too. No doubt he would not have expressed this by saying, "The current production of this postcard is being executed by someone who is having a good time at the time of said execution." But he was aware as he wrote the postcard that he was doing so, and that he was having a good time. So he and I believed the same thing. The proposition created by the utterance meets conditions (b), (d), and (e).

The proposition expressed, however, clearly does not meet conditions (b) and (d). In the example, I am linguistically competent, and take the postcard to have been sincerely produced by someone capable of telling whether or not she or he was happy. But I do not know which proposition it expresses. Ellsworth could have sent it from Hawaii. Barwise could have sent it from Missouri. My daughter could have sent it from Berkeley. Who knows? But then I do not know which proposition it expresses. The proposition expressed by an utterance is hardly a property of it that can just be read off. One needs to know the relevant contextual factors, in this case, who wrote it.

Carnap, is that what he says and what he communicates are not the same. I am inclined to think that our notion of "the proposition expressed" comes to "what is said," and that saying is a rather complex notion that needs to be explained in terms of intentions to communicate. A relational theory need not be based on the relation of context to what is said, and, in Barwise and Perry 1983, we based it instead on the relation to the information communicated.

I want to emphasize that the postcard is only a somewhat dramatic example of a common phenomenon. Language is a tool for communication, and the artful speaker takes care not to rely on contextual factors that the intended listener will not be able to use. This is the reason behind the familiar points that the expressions used in speech are typically more context-sensitive than those used in writing, and friendly letters, where considerable knowledge of the writer and his circumstances may be assumed, exhibit more context-sensitivity than articles in scientific journals. The point of speech is usually thwarted, unless the listener not only understands the truth conditions of the utterance, but knows which proposition is expressed.[72]

But consider the typical cocktail party, at which a main activity is listening to speech not intended for one to hear. It is common, and frustrating, to understand the truth conditions of overheard utterances, but not grasp the propositions they express. And at such parties, where one is bound to be overheard by linguistically competent persons to whom one does not wish to communicate information, one learns to choose sentences that rely on contextual factors that will only be available to one's intended audience.

Even when one is the intended audience of a remark, however, grasping the truth conditions of the utterance without grasping the proposition expressed is all too familiar. I am sure that others have had experiences like this. One is driving along on a family vacation looking for a place to eat. As an attentive driver, one watches the road, relying on other family members to find an appropriate spot to dine. All of a sudden there is a cacophony of "Stop there" and "That is a good place" and similar remarks. One knows the truth conditions of these utterances. There is a salient to-most-people-in-the-car eatery, and one is being told to stop at it, to turn towards it, and the like. But, as an attentive driver, one does not perceive the relevant circumstances of these remarks. Gestures in the back seat to restaurants visible out the side window just do not help. One does not know which way to turn, the opportunity passes, and an unpleasant silence ensues. An important part of the full mastery of a language is learning to use contextual cues correctly, but it is, in my experience, a skill that deserts people the minute they step in an automobile.

---

[72] All the talk in this paper about knowing which proposition is expressed, has ultimately to be understood, on my view, in terms of ways of believing and the purposes that shape the criteria for being able to identify something that are relevant on a given occasion. For example, in a semantics class, one might give the postcard example as an exercise. If a student can say, "It expressed that the writer was having a good time," in a suitably rigorous way, the professor will say "Good, you know what proposition that expressed." Very roughly, when we communicate, we intend to get our listeners to believe propositions in certain ways, and it is doing that that counts as "knowing which proposition was expressed." Ellsworth did not plan for me simply to be able to think something like "How nice, the writer of this postcard was having a good time when he wrote it," but something like, "That old so-and-so Ellsworth is having a good time in Hawaii," where the belief I acquire is linked (see below) to other beliefs I have about Ellsworth based on past interactions.

The reason that such cases strike us as a bit odd, however common, is that our paradigm is the case of successful communication. The speaker wants the listener to believe a certain proposition; the skillful speaker does not rely on contextual items in expressing that proposition that the listener cannot use in grasping it.

This brings us to criterion (e). I do not think the proposition expressed passes it either, but this question gets us to some interesting issues. For one must surely admit that for a speaker to sincerely and assertively utter a sentence and thereby express a proposition that they do not grasp, would be an odd thing indeed. But there is a familiar example, for which this is one interpretation. This is David Kaplan's example of giving a lecture in a hall in which a portrait of Rudolf Carnap has hung behind the podium for years. Kaplan, pointing behind himself but not looking there, utters "That man is the greatest philosopher of the twentieth century." But someone has replaced the portrait of Carnap with one of Spiro Agnew. Has Kaplan sincerely asserted that Spiro Agnew is the greatest philosopher of the twentieth century?

Wettstein gives us three possible accounts of the semantics of "that": that uses of it refer to the individual that plays a certain causal role, that they refer to the individual the speaker has in mind, and that they refer to the individual that is indicated by the cues available to the audience. The first two theories would have it that the proposition Kaplan expressed was about Carnap, the third that it was about Agnew. If we adopt the third analysis of "that," we will have a case in which one sincerely and assertively utters a sentence, without believing the proposition that one thereby expresses.

Wettstein notes that none of these candidates' rules of reference for "that" specify "the way the speaker is thinking about his referent"; this is one consideration that leads him to suppose that semantics is pretty irrelevant to cognitive significance. But it seems to me that it simply shows that the connection may be more complicated than one might have hoped and hence more interesting than one might have thought.

Wettstein's Examples

Let us now turn to Wettstein's example about the man who is being attacked. There are two utterances in question. Both have the same speaker, employ the same sentence with the same meaning, "He is about to be attacked," and express the same proposition, for, although neither the speaker nor hearer realize it, the two uses of "he" refer to the same person. Wettstein says, "No doubt the cognitive significance of these utterances is dramatically different."

On the approach to cognitive significance sketched here, the cognitive significance of the two utterances of "He is about to be attacked" would be different. Basically, to accept the first utterance as true, the linguistically competent listener has to believe that the speaker is then referring to someone who is about to be attacked. To accept the second utterance as true, the linguistically competent listener has to believe that the speaker is referring, at the second time, to such a person. Even if the speaker is referring to the same person on both occasions, neither the linguistically competent listener nor the linguistically competent speaker need to believe that she is.

Thus Wettstein's version of Frege's puzzle need be no problem for New Theorists of Reference. We admit that the two utterances of "He is about to be attacked" express the same proposition. But the two utterances do not have the same cognitive significance. The fact that a listener accepted one and not the other can be explained by New Theorists, in terms of the difference in beliefs. The explanation is quite natural. The listener believed the speaker was right the first time she spoke, but not the second.

Cicero and Tully

When we use a context-sensitive sentence, there is a clear gap between knowledge of the language, and the proposition expressed by the utterance. So perhaps it is not too surprising that there should be a gap between cognitive significance and proposition expressed. But the same general considerations force a distinction, even when we are dealing with sentences that express exactly the same proposition from context to context.

Let us assume that the rules of English assign Cicero as the reference of both "Cicero" and "Tully." Context-sensitivity is irrelevant. Each utterance of "Tully was a Roman orator" expresses the very same proposition as every other utterance of it, and also expresses exactly the same proposition as every utterance of "Cicero was a Roman orator." [73]

It does not follow from this that a person who has mastered English will know that one person serves as the reference of both names. To understand the name would be to know which object it was assigned to. The criteria that would normally be sufficient to establish this allow for ignorance of coreference. The "Cicero"/"Tully" example, in spite of its venerability, is not the best one to make this point, since "Tully" is not much used as a separate name for Cicero except in philosophy articles. Suppose for a moment that these were instead two names for a river, and that those who are most likely to use "Cicero" for it live along one stretch and those most likely to use "Tully" live along another. A salesman who visited both communities regularly by car might discourse intelligently using both names, be able to carry out the commands "Go to Cicero" and "Go to Tully," and so on, without having any idea that they were names for a single thing.

What does such a competent speaker come to believe, when he accepts an utterance of "Cicero = Tully" as true? He or she surely learns that "Cicero"

---

[73] I am ignoring problems of tense throughout this paper.

and "Tully" stand for the same thing, for this is required for the utterance to satisfy its truth conditions. This bit of knowledge was not, we noted, required for mastery of the language. Nor does it imply mastery of the meaning of "Cicero" and "Tully." Given any nontrivial test for knowing which object the reference of a name is, a person might know that two names had the same one, without knowing which one it is. So there is a separate bit of knowledge that is part of the cognitive significance of "Cicero = Tully," but is not part of the cognitive significance of "Cicero = Cicero." So the New Theorists need not suppose that the cognitive significance of "Cicero = Cicero" is the same as that of "Cicero = Tully," simply because, on the principles of New Theories of Reference, they express the same proposition.

It is commonly thought, I believe, that Frege provided a solution to this problem (1892/1960). But as far as I can see, he does not.

Suppose—to return to the real use of "Cicero" as a name for the Roman—we explain the meaning of "Tully" to Ellsworth by saying, "that was the author of De Finibus" and explain the meaning of "Cicero" by saying "that was Rome's most famous orator." On a Millean theory, we will have assigned the same reference, and no other meanings, to the two names. Our different descriptions merely "fixed the reference" in different ways, in the way that Kripke has explained. (See Kaplan 1989.) On the theory suggested in Frege 1960, we will have assigned different senses to the two names. Which theory fares better on the issue of the cognitive significance of "Cicero = Tully"? It seems to me that the Mill/Kripke theory, combined with the approach to cognitive significance sketched here, fares at least as well as a Fregean theory.

If we now tell Ellsworth, "Cicero = Tully," he will learn two things he did not know:

(1) that "Cicero" and "Tully" refer to the same person;

(2) that Rome's most famous orator was the author of De Finibus.

Both of these changes in Ellsworth's beliefs can be accounted for consistently with New Theory principles. To do so, however, we need to make a distinction between two ways that beliefs can be about the same thing. (See Essay 4.)

Let us return to an earlier example that involved driving while looking for a place to eat. Suppose two children are looking out different windows, but neither of them is paying any attention to that fact. The discussion goes something like this: "That's a Wendy's. Let's stop there," says one child, looking in one direction. "No, it's not, you idiot. Can't you see that it's a McDonald's? Who wants to eat there?" says the other, looking in the opposite direction. The first child's use of "that" and the second child's use of "it" are not coreferential—there is not some thing they both refer to. The use of "that" refers to one restaurant, the use of "it" refers to another. But to understand the internal structure of the discourse, and the emotions to which it gives rise, one must see that the various referring expressions are supposed to be about the same thing. The utterances are not "really" or, as I shall say, "externally" about the same thing. But they are "internally" about the same thing. That is, the utterances bear the relationship that is appropriate in discourse, for utterances that are really about the same thing.[74]

Coreference is not a necessary condition of internal coreference, as this example shows. It is also not a sufficient condition. Two people can refer to the same thing and talk about it for some time, without realizing it. When this happens, the discourse will have a very different structure than it would if they recognized the coreference. The participants may say quite contradictory things about the same object, without correcting each other or feeling any tension. And, of course, one person can corefer to something, without realizing it. That familiar point is what our example above, about the traveling salesman, showed.[75]

In such a case, we need to make the same sort of distinction for beliefs that we make for utterances. Here I am thinking of beliefs not as propositions or meanings, but as changes that occur in minds, typically enduring for some time and then disappearing when it is most inconvenient. On my view, beliefs

---

[74] Internal coreference is handled in logic by sameness of variable, sameness of individual constant, and the identity sign. This might make it seem like a merely syntactic matter. This point of view is promoted when we say that pronouns work like variables, and names like individual constants. But, of course, in a crucial way, they do not. Structural features of an expression like "he" often leave open the question of which referring expressions it has as an antecedent, or is anaphorically connected to, if any. Use of the same proper name does not require identity of referent; within the same sentence, use of the same proper name twice, rather than a pronoun, suggests the opposite. (A real-life example from a department meeting: "If John would quiet down, John might be able to get a word in edgewise.") When we recognize the internal coreference relations in discourse, we are often not recognizing structural relations between linguistic entities, but internal coreference relations in the beliefs and intentions of the speaker. I can imagine a philosopher thinking about anaphora, and saying, "That is syntax," and a linguist agreeing, "Yes, that is syntax." This would not be a refutation of the point, but more like an instance of it. The philosopher means by syntax something like structural features that he, being trained for bigger game, cannot really spot, but is sure must be there, since that is how internal coreference is indicated in logic. The linguist includes as "syntactic" any semantic relationships that could have been explicitly required by syntactic forms, and so can be represented, in a theory, by a sentence of some other language in which they are explicitly required, the "deep structure," or "logical form," or both of the original utterance. The fact of the matter, I think, is that language provides enough structure for us to communicate beliefs, and internal coreference relations will often be clear even though greatly underdetermined by the structure of the language used, meaning here by "structure" the shape of the actual signal that can in principle be perceived independently of recognition of the speaker's intentions.

[75] See also Essay 4, where I motivate the notion of a mental file. Kaplan's theory of concepts provides a notion of internal coreference for thoughts (1979). Donnellan's account provides one for discourse (1974). Irene Heim develops a notion of internal coreference for the semantic analysis of discourse (1982).

are of types, have meaning, and, in virtue of their meaning and the context in which they arise and are applied, have propositional content. But a belief is not a type, meaning, or proposition any more than an utterance is. In the case of the salesman, or Kripke's Pierre, or dozens of other characters from philosophical fiction and real life, we have individuals with different beliefs, formed and applied in different circumstances, that are about the same things, but do not stand in the internal relationship that is appropriate for this.

Consider a simple system for information storage such as the filing cabinet in a philosophy department office. It is easy to imagine a philosophy major who, for some reason or other, ends up with two files, under different names. The entries in these files are about the same person. But they do not stand in the relation that is appropriate, given the way the filing system is designed to store and allow for the utilization of information. Entries about the same person are supposed to be in the same folder. Thus when a query comes from the registrar about this individual, only one of the files may be consulted, which shows only some of the classes taken and requirements completed, and the wrong answer is given. On the other hand, one can also imagine a department ending up with a file for a fictitious major, as a result of a prank. The entries in such a file would be about the same individual in the internal sense, although there is no individual they are both about.

It is very difficult to imagine a system that receives information about individuals outside of it, and stores that information in a way that allows its later usage in dealing with those individuals—a system, that is, fit to be helpful in a Strawsonian world—for which it would not be necessary to make this distinction.[76]

When Ellsworth learned the meanings of "Cicero" and "Tully," he acquired two different beliefs. The content of one was that Cicero was the author of De Finibus and is named "Tully" in English. The content of the other was that Cicero was Rome's most famous orator and is named "Cicero" in English. The relation of internal coreference does not obtain between these beliefs, although they are about the same person. When he hears us say "Cicero = Tully," Ellsworth links these beliefs, so internal coreference does obtain, and he comes to be in a state whose content is (2). On this account, (2) is not part of the cognitive significance of "Cicero = Tully," for someone who was taught the meanings of these words in a different way would not have learned (2).

Frege's views suggest a different account of how Ellsworth comes to believe (2). Because of the different ways Ellsworth learned the references of

---

[76]Note that the problem of making sense of what is going on here, given a reasonable theory of the structure of belief, is not the same problem as that of understanding how reports of beliefs work. A Fregean condition on such a theory might be that it can explain why two belief reports that differ only in having different terms that refer to the same thing, can differ in truth-value. I believe that New Theories can meet this condition also. Exactly how, is explained in Essay 12.

"Cicero" and "Tully," these words have different senses in his language. (2) is part of what gets asserted by a use of "Cicero = Tully."

But Frege's theory of sense and reference offers us no account of (1). The problem represented by (1) seems to have bothered him in the *Begriffsschrift*, for his solution there, to take the content of an identity to be about the referring expressions in it, is responsive to that problem, rather than the one represented by (2). But Frege 1892/1960 says nothing to allow us to explain how Ellsworth comes to know (1).

Basically the same explanation is open to Fregeans as we have offered to the New Theorists. The explanation does not depend on sense, but it also does not depend on absence of sense. I see no other aspect of the theory of sense and reference that allows explanation of the fact that the belief that "Cicero" and "Tully" stand for the same person is clearly one that a linguistically competent person acquires when he accepts "Cicero = Tully."

But if Frege's theory needs to appeal to the difference in the truth conditions of the utterances of "Cicero = Tully" and "Cicero = Cicero" to explain this aspect of the difference in cognitive significance, it can hardly be an advantage for Frege's theory that New Theorists need to do this.

As far as I can see, Frege's puzzles give us no reason to abandon the New Theories, and the New Theories give us no reason to regard Frege's puzzles as irrelevant to semantics.[77]

Afterword

This paper was written for the 1988 Meetings of the American Philosophical Association. I was unable to deliver it because of illness. Leora Weitzman flew to Cincinnati on short notice, read the paper, and ably defended it. I am very grateful to her. I was especially sorry to miss this occasion, because the other speakers in the symposium were Howard Wettstein and Joseph Almog. Almog and Wettstein had spent two years at Stanford in the early 1980s, and I had really been looking forward to the reunion. I learned a tremendous amount from each of them about the philosophy of language.

One thing is rather perplexing, if one reads Wettstein's paper "Has Semantics Rested on a Mistake?" (1986) and then this one. Wettstein praises the ingenuity of a view he calls the "Perry/Kaplan" view of cognitive significance, but says it does not work. I criticize Wettstein's argument, and defend an account of cognitive significance. Am I defending the Perry/Kaplan view? It depends. We might distinguish between a strong and a weak version of the view. The strong version is simply that cognitive significance is character (role, or mean-

[77]The research for this paper was supported by a grant from the System Development Foundation to the Center for the Study of Language and Information at Stanford University. I am grateful to David Israel for helpful comments on earlier drafts.

ing). I am not defending that view. I do not think I ever committed myself to it. If I did not, it was due more to timidity than to anticipation of the problems Wettstein sees.

The weak view is that Kaplan's character/content distinction is the key to unraveling the problems of cognitive significance. I did hold that, and still do. From that distinction, others follow, including the key distinction of the present paper, between the proposition expressed by an utterance and the proposition that the truth conditions of the utterance are satisfied. But it is this latter proposition, not the character, that I take to be the cognitive significance of the utterance. As I note in the Afterword to Essay 2, Stalnaker, and Reichenbach before him, realized that some entity like this was needed.

The term "cognitive significance" has a curious history. I am not sure any such notion as this is to be found in Frege 1892/1960. Herbert Feigl used the term in his translation. It has come to have an enormous intuitive appeal, so that some philosophers just use the term as if it were obvious what it meant. We all know what the problems of cognitive significance are, but that does not mean that we have any clear idea of what "the cognitive significance" of a sentence or an utterance is. Of course, we have an unclear idea: it is whatever solves the problems of cognitive significance.

I think one consequence of Kaplan's distinction is that no one thing will have all of the properties that are associated with this intuitively appealing concept—just as no one thing can have all of the properties associated with Frege's notion of *Sinn*. It seemed to me that the way Wettstein used the term and its close cousins like "cognitive content" in discussing his examples required that a cognitive significance be a proposition, that having one be a property of utterances, and that the cognitive significance of an utterance be something a competent speaker recognizes. Given those requirements, I think the concept I develop in this paper does pretty well. But the concept that meets these requirements will not be the right object to individuate thoughts by their psychological role. This is what character or "role" does on the Perry/Kaplan view, which is why Kaplan said that the cognitive significance of a thought is its character.

Suppose you and I both have beliefs that we express with the words "I am hungry." In Kaplan's terminology, our beliefs are dissimilar, in having different contents. But they are similar, in having the same character. It is this dimension of similarity that Kaplan calls the cognitive significance of our thoughts. This is not the same notion of cognitive significance that is appealed to in Wettstein's versions of Frege's problems. Obviously, one could believe your utterances and not believe mine. If this criteria shows that there are different cognitive significances involved, cognitive significance cannot be character. If we use "cognitive significance" to mean the proposition a competent speaker entertains when they perceive an utterance, it will clearly not be the character of the sentence used, which is not a proposition at all. But it will be, on the account put forward in this paper, a closely related proposition, the proposition that the utterance meets the conditions the character of the sentence used establishes for its truth.

Reasonable as this all seems to me, it seems that my concept does not strike people as fitting their intuitive notion of cognitive significance. I am inclined to think it is the right concept to resolve the *problems of cognitive significance*, but that nothing should be singled out and equated and dubbed "the cognitive significance." In the later papers in this volume I do not use the term, but I do not promise to stick to that.

12

The Prince and the Phone Booth: Reporting Puzzling Beliefs

with MARK CRIMMINS

In Mark Twain's *The Prince and The Pauper*, Tom Canty and Edward Tudor decide to change lives for a day, but fate intervenes, and the exchange goes on for a considerable period of time. The whole story turns on what people believe and do not believe about the two boys; and an intelligent reader, unexposed to recent philosophy of language and mind, could probably describe the key facts of the story with some confidence. Such a reader might explain why Miles Hendon, a penniless nobleman who encounters a boy dressed in rags, does not bow to the Prince, by noting:

(1) Miles Hendon did not believe that he was of royal blood.

And such a reader might ward off the implication that Miles was a fool or ignoramus by noting that Miles shared the dominant conception of Edward Tudor,

(2) Miles Hendon believed that Edward Tudor was of royal blood.

One of our main claims in this paper is that such a reader would be right on both counts. In this we depart from a recent trend to explain the apparent truth of statements like (1) as an illusion generated by pragmatic features of such claims. Accounts of belief reporting given by Jon Barwise and John Perry, Scott Soames, and Nathan Salmon have employed this strategy of denying the accuracy of our strong intuitions about truth and falsity (Barwise and Perry 1983, 253–64; Soames 1987, 1989; Salmon 1986). Here, we shall present an account that does not ignore pragmatic features, but assigns to them a more honorable role. They do not create an illusion, but help to identify the reality the report is about. Our account honors the intuition that claims (1) and (2) are true.

Since "Edward Tudor" in (2) and "he" in (1) both refer to Edward Tudor, this seems to commit us to some version of the doctrine of *opacity*.[78] Specifically, we are committed to the view that, if our reader were to say either of the following, in the same circumstances, he would be incorrect:

(1′) Miles Hendon did not believe that Edward Tudor was of royal blood.

(2′) Miles Hendon believed that he was of royal blood.

The doctrine of opacity has been thought incompatible with two others, to which we also are attracted: the first, *direct reference*, is that the utterance of a simple sentence containing names or demonstratives normally expresses a "singular proposition"—a proposition that contains as constituents the individuals referred to, and not any descriptions of or conditions on them; the second, *semantic innocence*, is that the utterances of the embedded sentences in belief reports express just the propositions they would if not embedded, and these propositions are the contents of the ascribed beliefs.[79]

Direct reference and semantic innocence are well motivated by many considerations in the philosophy of language. But if direct reference and semantic innocence are correct, then it seems that *opacity* must not be: the substitution of "Edward Tudor" for "he" in (1) [or vice versa in (2)] should be completely legitimate. The name and the demonstrative refer to the same object. There is just one proposition, belief in which is denied by (1) and affirmed by (2), the "singular" proposition, which we will represent in this way:

⟪*Being of royal blood*; *Edward Tudor*⟫

The example is typical of many doxastic puzzle cases in the literature—puzzles because they seem to reveal a conflict among the three very plausible doctrines. We hold all three, however.

I

When we substitute "Edward Tudor" for "he," the words change while the proposition expressed by the embedded sentence stays the same. If we think that belief is a relation to propositions and not words, the apparent change in truth-value of the whole report seems puzzling. We are likely to focus on the most apparent change, the change in words, as the clue to the mystery.

---

[78] *Opacity* is the claim that substitution of coreferring names and demonstratives in belief reports does not necessarily preserve the truth of those reports. (Definite descriptions are another matter; it is not nearly as controversial that substituting a description for a coreferring name can influence the truth-value of a belief report.) What "substitution" comes to with respect to utterances (belief reports), as opposed to sentences (belief sentences), is not at all obvious. Our simple notions of substitutivity, opacity and so on are really useful only if sentences are (wrongly) taken as the bearers of truth and content. Here, we will adopt an informal notion of substitution in belief reports, such that the reports (1) and (1′), as well as (2) and (2′), are related by substitution.

[79] For an important qualification, see footnote 8 below.

The most famous doxastic puzzle case, due to Saul Kripke, has nothing to do with substitution, however (1979). Kripke describes a case in which the Frenchman Pierre first hears of London, comes to believe it is pretty, then moves to London, and, not connecting it to the city he's heard about (under the French "Londres"), comes to believe it is not pretty. He does not change his mind about the city he's heard of, but simply does not connect the "two" cities. We have one sentence,

(3) Pierre believes that London is pretty

that we seem to be able to use when reflecting on different parts of the story, to say something true and to say something false. The words have not changed. What has?

What changes in this case, and in every other doxastic puzzle case, is what we are talking about. Pierre has two different notions of London, which play very different roles in his beliefs. An assertion of (3) is true if it is about one of them, false if it is about the other. An ordinary doxastic puzzle case uses a change in words to precipitate the change in the subject matter of the utterance. Kripke spells out the details of his case so clearly that our focus gets redirected without a change in the wording of the report. We shall return to these claims about belief reports in the next section.

One of Pierre's beliefs was caused by his acceptance of the stories he heard about London. It has the content that London is pretty, and it leads him to cherish the prospect of someday visiting that city. This belief also causes him to affirm, in French, "Londres est jolie," in discussions about the city he has heard of.

Also, Pierre has a different belief that was caused by his displeasure with his new surroundings, which has the content that London is not pretty, and which causes him to affirm, "London is not pretty," in discussions about his home.

It is a commonplace to distinguish these two beliefs. We think it is often not sufficiently appreciated, however, that the beliefs so distinguished are concrete cognitive structures. Focusing on this fact provides the basis for our account of belief and for our solutions to the various doxastic puzzle cases.

These are the key features of our theory of beliefs:

(i) Beliefs are concrete cognitive structures: they are particulars that belong to an agent, come into existence, endure, and go out of existence.

(ii) Beliefs are related to the world and to other cognitive structures and abilities in a way that allows us to classify them by propositional content.

Beliefs, since they are cognitive particulars, or "things in the head," are not things that are believed; they are not in any sense the objects of belief. The propositions believed are the objects of belief. An agent believes some proposition in virtue of having a belief with that content. Many agents can believe the same proposition, so propositions are public; they also are abstract. Beliefs are neither public nor abstract; they are concrete particulars that belong to agents just like arms, headaches, and bouts of the flu. A belief comes into existence when an agent forms it; it is not the sort of thing that is around for the agent to adopt. Agents believe the same thing, a proposition p, when each has a belief with p as its content. This is not an analysis of reports of "believing the same thing"—which are not always so simple to unpack—but a clarification of what we mean by objects of belief.

To countenance beliefs as particulars is not to deny that there are interesting systems of abstract objects that might be used to classify them, such as meanings, Fregean senses, intensions, characters, or the like. But in addition to having these abstract features, beliefs, like other concrete particulars, have lots of other features, both intrinsic and relational, many of which can in some cases be relevant to explaining how we talk about beliefs in belief reports. In particular, we often exploit facts about the causes and effects of beliefs, a point to which we shall return.

There are a number of reasons to allow ourselves to speak of particular beliefs, rather than just of a belief relation between a person and an abstract object of some kind. There is, first, the attraction of having entities that can occupy causal roles with respect to perception, reasoning, and action. As Jerry Fodor and others have argued at length, structured concrete particulars or "token" mental entities go a long way toward explaining the roles of belief, desire, and so on, in cognition. There is, second, the fact that the most plausible statements of materialist intuitions about the mind are formulated in terms of particular mental entities. And, third, there is the problem that belief puzzles repeatedly have emphasized: it seems that, for any natural way of classifying beliefs with abstract objects, we can find examples in which a single agent, at a single time, is belief-related to one such abstract object twice over. These are cases, we would like to be able to say, in which an agent, at a time, has two beliefs classified by the same sense, meaning, or whatever. Classifying beliefs only with abstract meanings, senses, and so on, is like classifying drops of water only with intrinsic properties. Kant argued against Leibniz that intrinsic properties of particulars will not always provide us with sufficient material for their individuation. Kant took it as obvious that there can be two exactly similar drops of water; the puzzle cases make it clear that there can be two beliefs sharing the abstract features that one or another theory of belief claims to be central.[80]

Beliefs, then, are particulars that bear complex causal relations to an agent's perceptions, actions, and other cognitive structures and abilities. The story of the causal properties of beliefs will be closely bound to the story of how and why beliefs can be classified with propositional content. A belief constrains an

---

[80]For a fuller defense of the particularity of beliefs, see Crimmins 1989.

agent's reasoning and action in a way that is conducive, if the belief's content is true, to the the agent's getting what she wants.

The ground-level facts behind belief are simply the facts of agents having beliefs. There is a basic relation $B(a, b, t)$ that holds of an agent, a belief, and a time, just in case b is a belief that belongs to the agent a at time t.

Normally, a belief has a propositional content. So there is a partial function $Content(b, t)$ that, for a belief b and time t at which b exists, yields the content of b. The content of a belief will be determined by the "internal" structural properties of the belief plus its real connections to things and circumstances in the world and to the agent's other cognitive structures and abilities.

If an agent a at time t has as an object of belief the proposition p, then there is a belief b such that:

$$B(a, b, t) \; \& \; Content(b, t) = p.$$

So much is all that is really needed for a theory of belief adequate for a broad explanation of the doxastic puzzle cases, and so we are tempted to stick with just the minimal theory of beliefs given so far. The minimal theory is compatible with a wide class of views about beliefs, about propositions (or contents), and about central issues in theories of representation, practical reasoning, and inference. The crucial features of the semantics we give for belief reports, and the resulting solutions for the troubling cases, are therefore to some degree theory-neutral. But we want to present a slightly more detailed, if still simple-minded, theory of beliefs, which satisfies the demands of the minimal theory and which yields a sufficiently rich account of just how the puzzling belief reports work.

Beliefs are structured entities that contain ideas and notions as constituents. Ideas and notions, like beliefs, are on our view concrete cognitive particulars. So there is no such thing as agents having the same idea or notion, but only similar ones. Admittedly, the technical use we make of these terms involves a departure from what we ordinarily say about "ideas" and "notions," or at least represents a choice among the many different ordinary uses of these terms. On our use of the terms, there are no notions and ideas that agents do not have, any more than there are headaches that no one has. The difference between notions and ideas is the difference between an agent's "ways of thinking" about individuals versus properties. The properties and things of which ideas and notions are ideas and notions we call their *contents*. We shall explain in a moment how the contents of ideas and notions help determine the contents of beliefs.

What determines the content of an idea or notion? For example, what is it about Miles' notion of the poorly dressed boy, which causes it to be a notion of Edward as opposed to another boy? The crucial fact is that it was Edward with whom Miles was confronted when he formed this notion. Edward played the right part in the causal origin of the notion; the notion was formed in order to keep track of information about Edward—that is what makes him its content. So the content of an idea can depend on its external properties, like facts about its origin. The very same notion might have been a notion of a different person, had someone other than Edward figured in its origin.

There is a close parallel between this view of the contents of ideas and causal views of the semantics of names. A speaker can refer to an individual with a name, it is held, because that individual figured, in the right way, in the speaker's adoption of the name as a tool of reference.[81]

The content of an idea is not always fixed once for all by facts about the circumstances of the idea's origin. Some ideas are *context-sensitive*, in that their contents change with changes in the agent's circumstances. The context-sensitivity of ideas is analogous to that of demonstratives in language. David Kaplan has proposed that there is associated with each demonstrative a *character*, a function that specifies how the content of a demonstrative depends on the circumstances surrounding its use. (See Kaplan 1989.) The content of a use of the word "you," for example, is the person who is being addressed in the circumstances of the utterance. Analogously, an agent a may have an idea I_{addr} of "being the one I am addressing." The property, which is the content of this idea, changes with changes in circumstances as follows:

> In any circumstances in which a person b is being addressed by a, the content of a's idea I_{addr} is the property of being b.

Undoubtedly, each of us has a "you" idea, the content of which is determined functionally in this way. We do not share ideas, but we have ideas with the same *semantic role*. An idea's semantic role is the function that determines the idea's content based on the agent's circumstances. Semantic roles for ideas are a bit like characters of expressions; some ideas have semantic roles that are context-sensitive, others have semantic roles that are constant functions—their contents do not vary with changes in context.

So there are two ways in which an agent's external circumstances might be relevant to determining the content of an idea. First, the facts surrounding the origin of the idea may fix its content once for all. Second, the idea's semantic role may be sensitive to changes in the agent's circumstances—the content of the idea may vary from occasion to occasion. So an idea may exhibit origin-sensitivity, context-sensitivity, or both.

Miles' idea of red is certainly not context-sensitive. It may be deemed origin-sensitive, whether one supposes that his idea stands for red innately,

---

[81] A speaker can adopt a name (like "John") more than once, to refer to what may be different individuals. Each such adoption creates a type of use to which the speaker may put the name. So a causal analysis of names should look not at names themselves, but at types of uses of names, as the things for which reference is determined causally. An agent may use "John" to refer either to John Dupré or to John Etchemendy. What individuates these distinct types of uses of the name "John"? One answer is that the types of uses of "John" are tied to distinct notions in the agent.

or because of some original assignment of ideas to colors early in Miles' life. Miles' idea of being past, in contrast, stands for different properties as his life unfolds; at each time t, this idea stands for the property of occurring before t. This idea is certainly context-sensitive, and may or may not be origin-sensitive. And Miles' notion of Prince Edward, formed upon hearing of the newborn Prince, is origin-sensitive, but it is not context-sensitive.

Notions are the things in the mind that stand for things in the world. A notion is a part of each of a collection of beliefs[82] (and of other mental structures, such as desires and intentions) that are internally about the same thing. This is not a definition of "notion," but just a central fact about notions—sharing a notion is what it is for beliefs to be internally about the same thing. An agent may occasionally (and will in many of the examples) have several notions of a single individual. This can happen in two ways. First, in cases of misrecognition and "failure to place," an agent may have two notions of an individual, which he does not link or connect; such an agent is guilty of no internal inconsistency. But also an agent can retain two notions of an individual, while linking them, in the way one does when one recognizes that "two" of one's acquaintances are actually a single individual. Why might two notions be retained when such a recognition takes place? One reason for this would be to allow the possibility of easy revision in case the "recognition" was in error. But an agent can also burn his bridges and merge two notions into a single notion. Two beliefs, then, can be internally about the same thing in two ways: by sharing a notion, and by containing notions that are linked.

For the purposes of this paper, we assume that each belief involves a single k-ary idea and a sequence of k notions.[83] To represent the structure of such a belief, we write:

$$Structure(b) = \langle Idea^k, Notion_1, \ldots, Notion_k \rangle.$$

Each belief has as its content the proposition that the objects its notions are of have the property or stand in the relation, that its idea is of:

$$Content(b, t) = \langle\!\langle Of(Idea^k, t); Of(Notion_1, t), \ldots, Of(Notion_k, t) \rangle\!\rangle.$$

The structures of beliefs are individuated not simply by the ideas and notions involved in them, but also by which argument places of the ideas the various notions fill. Thus the order of the notions in our representation of the

---

[82]There is no mystery as to how a single thing can be a part of many different things at the same time (and at different times). One may, for example, be a member of many different committees or clubs.

[83]This is to consider only beliefs of a certain kind of composition. In a more thorough presentation, a discussion of other kinds of belief-structures, perhaps including general beliefs and complex beliefs, might be called for—although the logical connectives and quantifiers can be accommodated within this simple structure. Also, we have chosen to ignore in this paper many subtleties of time and tense.

structure of the belief reflects an assignment of notions to the argument places of the associated idea.

To be clear about the relation between beliefs and their contents, we need to introduce some new concepts.

A belief b associates an idea I with a notion n at an argument place pl:

$$Associates(b, I, n, pl).$$

The belief that Tom fired Mary and the belief that Mary fired Tom differ in which places are associated with which notions, even though the ideas and notions involved are the same.

An argument place of an idea is intimately connected with an argument role of the relation that is the content of the idea, and so with an argument role in the content of the beliefs of which the idea forms a part.[84] If we were to consider complex cases, spelling out this relationship might be a matter of some delicacy, but we shall take it to be straightforward here. We shall say that an argument place pl_I of an idea I generates an argument role r_p of a proposition p (an example below will make this clearer):

$$Generates(pl_I, r_p).$$

Finally, a notion is responsible for which object occupies an argument role of the content of a belief, when the belief associates it with an idea at the argument place that generates the argument role in the content of the belief:

$$Responsible(n, r, b) \Longleftrightarrow_{def} \exists I, pl \; Associates(b, I, n, pl),$$
and $Generates(pl, r)$.

When a notion in a belief is responsible for filling an argument role of the belief's content, it fills the role with its own content, the object of which the notion is a notion.

To give an example: Arthur's belief that Yvain smote Kay involves Arthur's idea for smiting, I_s, and his two notions of Yvain and Kay, call these n_Y and n_K. The idea I_s has two argument places, one (pl_+) for the smiter, and one (pl_-) for the smitten. In Arthur's belief (call it b), the notion n_Y is associated with argument place pl_+ of I_s, and n_K is associated with pl_-. The content of b is the proposition p, where:

$$p = \langle\langle Smote; \; Yvain, Kay \rangle\rangle.$$

The relation "smote" has two argument roles, one (r_+) for the smiter and one (r_-) for the smitten; these are also argument roles of the proposition p. In p, Yvain fills r_+ and Kay fills r_- of the "smote" relation. Since b associates pl_+ with with n_Y, and pl_+ (the smiter in I_s) generates r_+ (the smiter in p), we say that, in b, n_Y is responsible for filling r_+ in p. Arthur's notion of Yvain is

---

[84]Roughly, an argument role of a relation is also an argument role of a proposition (at least) when, in that proposition, the role of the relation is occupied by an object.

responsible in b for determining who fills the argument role r_+ in p. And n_Y provides its content, Yvain, to fill that argument role. Figure 1 should make this clear.

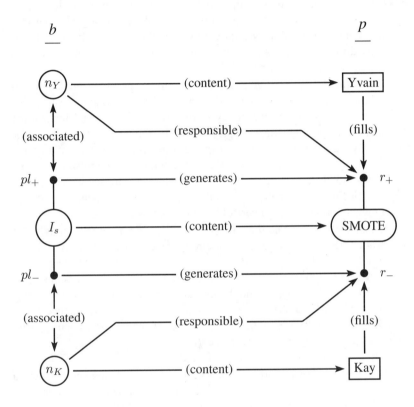

Figure 1: Arthur's belief and its content

Notions and ideas are key figures in our commonsense "folk" model of cognition. The recurring appearance in philosophy of such things as concepts, senses, ways of thinking, names in a language of thought, mental file folders, files and other such devices reflects a firm intuition about the mind, namely, that having beliefs about an individual means having beliefs involving an internal something that is one's cognitive "fix" on the individual. As we have said, we think the correct way to express this intuition demands reference to cognitive particulars that are involved in beliefs, desires, and so on. Now, this leaves a great deal open about just what kinds of things our notions and ideas are. For all we have said, notions and ideas might be—or might have been—particular words in a language of thought, physical objects like file folders, or things with more of a dispositional character, like the process underlying the disposition of an agent to have a specific "pattern of neural activation" in certain circumstances. And, whichever of these kinds of things our notions and ideas are, they certainly may be classifiable with senses, property clusters, intensions, and so on. We want our "notions and ideas" to capture what is in common among all these very different models of cognition: there are things shared by different beliefs that explain the internal way in which beliefs must be about the same object or property.

On this theory, one can have two beliefs with exactly the same content or with diametrically opposed contents, such that there is no significant causal relation between them—because they involve different notions. This is a feature of all of the problematic examples that we shall consider. There is nothing particularly puzzling about this—and, in fact, there is nothing particularly puzzling about any of the examples we discuss, so long as we simply consider the beliefs, and not the reporting of them. Nevertheless, it is a good idea to go over the examples in some detail, for it is these details that our semantic account pays more attention to than others of which we know.

Consider the Prince and the Pauper. Miles Hendon has two notions of Edward Tudor. They have quite different circumstances of origin. One Miles has had for a long time. It is associated (in his beliefs) with such ideas as being a Prince of England, being named "Edward Tudor," being rich, not being a pauper, not looking like a pauper, not being likely to run into (me) on an average day, and the like. The beliefs with this notion as a constituent influence Miles' behavior when confronted with ordinary sorts of information about Edward Tudor. When he reads an article in the *Times*, for example, it is beliefs with this notion as a constituent which are affected.

His other notion was formed when he saw Edward being set upon by an angry mob—angry because Edward, dressed in rags, had been proclaiming himself to be Prince. This notion is associated with ideas of being out of his mind, being dressed like a pauper, and not being of royal blood. The beliefs involving this notion, and not those involving his old notion of Edward Tudor, influence Miles' behavior towards Edward and Edward's assertions during the period he is associated with him as a comrade, until that point, toward the end of the story, when Miles merges his two notions, and comes to believe that Edward the Pauper is Edward the Prince.

Perhaps the ultimate doxastic puzzle case is Mark Richard's puzzle about the woman in the telephone booth:

> Consider *A*—a man stipulated to be intelligent, rational, a competent speaker of English, etc.—who both sees a woman, across the street, in a phone booth, and is speaking to a woman through a phone. He does not realize that the woman to whom he is speaking—

B, to give her a name—is the woman he sees. He perceives her to be in some danger—a run-away steamroller, say, is bearing down upon her phone booth. *A* waves at the woman; he says nothing into the phone (Richard 1983, 439).

The man has two distinct, and unlinked, notions of the woman. Via one, he believes that she is in danger. This is the notion that arose in virtue of his visual perception of her, and that is associated with an idea of being in grave danger. It is this notion that is involved in the beliefs that motivate his waving out the window. The second notion is an older one, assuming the woman is an old acquaintance. It is associated with an idea of being the person addressed, and not associated with ideas of being the person seen or being in danger. Hence, the beliefs involving this notion do not motivate a warning.

Let us return to Kripke's case. Pierre has the same misfortune as Miles and the man on the phone: he has two notions of the same thing. He has one notion of London, which is linked to his memories of the stories and to his use of the word "Londres." He has another, unconnected notion of London, which is influenced by his perceptions and memories about his present surroundings and which influences his use of the word "London." He has a belief associating the former notion with his idea of being pretty, but has no belief associating the latter notion with this idea. In fact, Pierre associates an idea of being ugly with the latter notion.

II

Our basic idea is simple: a belief report claims that an agent has a belief with a certain content. But the basic idea, unembellished, will not allow us to hold the family of views we want to defend. For (2) and (2′) would claim that Miles Hendon had at least one belief with the content

$$\langle\!\langle \textit{Being of royal blood}; \textit{Edward Tudor} \rangle\!\rangle$$

while (1) and (1′) would deny this—thus contradicting our truth intuitions and the doctrine of opacity.

But our embellishment is also simple. When we report beliefs, there is always some further condition that a belief with the specified content is claimed to meet. The belief report is true only if a belief meeting that further condition has the right content. What may be novel is our insistence that this additional requirement is part of the proposition expressed by the belief report. Thus, it is a condition on the truth, not merely the felicity, of the report.

Consider (1). In context, (1) provides an explanation of why Miles Hendon did not treat someone he was looking at in a certain way—a way that would have been compulsory for Miles, given the status of that person. We are interested in the content of only those beliefs that motivated Miles' behavior, the beliefs that involve the notion of Edward, which arose when Miles saw him being threatened and explain Miles' treatment of him. The existence of such a notion is clear from the description of the incident. We know that Miles is perceiving Edward and interacting with Edward on the basis of what he, Miles, perceives. Our view is that, in reporting beliefs, we quite often are talking about such notions, although our belief reports do not explicitly mention them. The general solution to the puzzles is to allow a condition on particular beliefs, over and above a content condition, to be part of the claim made. The version of this strategy we shall pursue here is to take this further condition always to be a specification of the notions that are supposed to be involved in the ascribed belief.

We shall say that a notion that a belief report is about is an *unarticulated constituent* of the content of the report—it is a propositional constituent that is not explicitly mentioned. We shall distinguish another kind of belief report, and say more about the notion of unarticulated constituents in a moment. But first let us see what the semantics of this sort of belief report looks like.

From our account of beliefs, we have the following concepts:

$$B(a, b, t) \quad : \quad \text{b is a belief that belongs to agent a at time t.}$$

$$Content(b, t) = p \quad : \quad \text{p is the content of belief b at time t.}$$

$$Responsible(n, r, b) \quad : \quad \exists I, pl \; Associates(b, I, n, pl), \text{ and } Generates(pl, r).$$

We take a belief report to be an utterance u of a belief sentence, of the form:

A believes that S

where A is a singular term and S is a sentence. We assume a semantics for the use of the embedded sentence, so that $Con(u_S)$ (the content of u_S) is the proposition expressed by the subutterance of u corresponding to S.[85] Where u is a belief report at t, which is about notions $n_1, \ldots, n_k$, and $p = Con(u_S)$,

---

[85] In accord with our simple version of "semantic innocence," we assume throughout that a belief report specifies the content of the ascribed belief by providing a sentence with the same content, as uttered in the report. The puzzle cases that we consider seem to be ones for which this assumption is correct. There are good reasons, however, to think that things do not always work this way. One way of analyzing, "Barbara believes that the Twin Towers are over a foot tall," would involve quantification over contents of beliefs. Other cases of reporting implicit and tacit beliefs might well work similarly. Another case in which a proposition might be "quantified out" is in the use of, "He believes that Russell's yacht is longer than it is." Also, one can use, "Timmy believes that the Tooth Fairy will make him rich," knowing full well that the embedded sentence does not express any proposition (if in fact it does not). These and other cases make us wary of insisting that a content proposition is always specified in a belief report. The present strategy can be extended in relatively simple ways to account for such cases.

$$Con(u) = \quad \exists b \, [B(a, b, t) \wedge Content(b, t) = p \wedge$$
$$\bigwedge_{r_i \ in \ p} Responsible(n_i, r_i, b)]$$

The claim made by the belief report is that the agent a[86] has a belief with the content p, involving the notions $n_1, \ldots, n_k$ (in a certain way).[87] This claim entails the proposition that a has a belief with the content p, but the truth of that proposition is not sufficient for the truth of the report—the report says more than that about the ascribed belief.

We shall say in such cases that the notions that the belief report is about are *provided* by the utterance and its context. Note that the provided constituents of the report's content are not existentially quantified.

Let us see how this theory works with Miles, Edward, and our intelligent reader. We take our reader to be talking about n_{vis}, the notion Miles acquires of Edward from visually perceiving him on the occasion of the rescue. $Con(u_S)$ is just the proposition

$$\langle\!\langle Being \ of \ royal \ blood; \ Edward \rangle\!\rangle.$$

So our reader is saying with (1) that there is no belief that associates Miles' idea of the property of being of royal blood with Miles' notion n_{vis}. He is not contradicting any proposition that Miles has some other notion of Edward Tudor, which is so associated.

And, in fact, a proposition of this latter kind might be just what our reader intends to claim with (2). Imagine the case in which he reads that Miles Hendon is shouting, while treating Edward as a mad fool, "Prince Edward is a man of royal blood, you fool, who would not dress in rags." Our reader might intend to say, of the notion involved in the beliefs that motivate this behavior, that it both

---

[86] Yet another simplification: we ignore the fact that many uses of singular terms, including terms in the subject position of belief sentences, are not directly referential. "Attributive" uses of definite descriptions really should be handled differently. Note also that we really should treat the idea in a belief in the same way we treat notions here; though the puzzles considered here do not turn on this, others certainly do.

[87] Here one major difference from the "official" belief-report semantics in chapter 10 of Barwise and Perry 1983 (256) is apparent. There, a belief report is true if the agent has any belief with the specified content. There is a further crucial difference that is not so obvious. Barwise and Perry countenance beliefs as real, concrete things, as we do here. But these beliefs are represented as situations of an agent being related to an anchored belief schema. Belief schemas are abstract objects in which what we have called notions are represented by indeterminates. Although the way this all works is quite complicated, in the end beliefs are individuated by belief schemas—abstract objects—and the things in the world to which the indeterminates in the schemas are anchored. But indeterminates are not notions, and, we think, relations to anchored belief schemas are not quite fine-grained enough to individuate beliefs in the ways needed for belief reports. So we suggest two major changes to the account in Barwise and Perry 1983: we give ourselves the theoretical machinery to talk about notions and ideas directly; we then claim that these things are among the subject matter of belief reports (via the mechanism of unarticulated constituents), and are not merely quantified over.

is of Edward Tudor and is associated with the idea of being of royal blood.

If so, our reader would surely be consistent, direct, and innocent. On the one hand, the proposition he in turn denies and affirms Miles' belief in is just the singular proposition that contemporary theories of direct reference assign to the utterances of "Edward Tudor is of royal blood" and "He is of royal blood" in the described contexts. On the other, the denial and affirmation are completely consistent.

III

We have claimed that in belief reports, an n-ary relation is reported with an n-minus-one-place predicate. On our account, the complex relation invoked in belief reports is a four-place relation: an agent believes a proposition at a time relative to a sequence of notions. But there is no argument place in the "believes" predicate for the sequence of notions. The notions are unarticulated constituents of the content of the report.

Propositions have constituents. The proposition that Yvain smote Kay has Kay as a constituent—Kay himself is in that claim. When Arthur says "Yvain smote Kay," there is no great mystery about why Kay, rather than someone else, is part of the claim Arthur makes: Arthur uses the name "Kay," which, as he uses it, refers to Kay. Kay is the content of Arthur's utterance of "Kay." This is what it is to be an articulated constituent of the content of a statement.

It is very common in natural languages for a statement to exploit unarticulated constituents. When we consider the conditions under which such a statement is true, we find it expresses a proposition that has more constituents in it than can be traced to expressions in the sentence that was spoken. Each constituent of the content, which is not itself the content of some expression in the sentence, is an unarticulated constituent of the content of the statement.

We report the weather, for example, as if raining and snowing and sleeting and dark of night were properties of times, but they are one and all relations between times and places. If I say, "it is raining," you understand me as claiming that it rains at that time at some place the context supplies. It often is, but need not be, the place of utterance. If I am talking to a friend in Kansas City on the phone, or watching news reports about the continuing floods in Berkeley, you may understand me to be talking about those places rather than the place where we both are.

The phenomenon of unarticulated constituency is similar to that of indexicality in the reliance on context. But the two phenomena should not be conflated. If we say, "It is raining *here*," an expression in our statement identifies the place. The place is articulated in a context-sensitive way. In the case of indexicals, expression and context share in the job of identifying the constituent, according to the conventional meaning or character of the indexical. In a case of underarticulation, there is no expression to determine the constituent in this way.

It would be misleading, however, to say that, in the case of unarticulated constituents, the context alone does the job. The whole utterance—the context and the words uttered—are relevant to identifying the unarticulated constituent. Thus, a change in wording can affect the unarticulated constituent, even though it is not a change in an expression that designates that constituent. Suppose I am in Palo Alto talking on the phone to someone in London; it is morning in Palo Alto and evening in London. If I say, "It is exactly 11 A.M.," I will be taken to be talking about the time in Palo Alto; if I had said, in the same context, "It is exactly 8 P.M.," I would be taken to be talking about the time in London.

The important principle to be learned is that a change in wording can precipitate a change in propositional constituents, even when the words do not stand for the constituents.

Unarticulated constituency is one example of the incrementality of language. In the circumstances of an utterance, there always is a great deal of common knowledge and mutual expectation that can and must be exploited if communication is to take place. It is the function of the expression uttered to provide just the last bit of information needed by the hearer to ascertain the intended claim, exploiting this rich background. What is obvious in context we do not belabor in syntax—we do not articulate it.

This is by no means to transgress the intuition of the systematicity of language, which is commonly reflected in principles of "compositionality." Since we finite creatures are able to make and understand a potential infinity of claims, there must be systematic features of our statements that explain our infinite abilities in something like a combinatorial fashion—in terms of our more finite abilities to understand the contributions of specific features of statements toward the claims made. But there is no reason to assume that these features of statements must all involve syntactic expressions. It is just as systematic for a form of speech, like a belief report or a report of rain, to *call for* a propositional constituent that meets, say, certain conditions of relevance and salience, as it is for a form of speech to have a syntactic expression *stand for* a propositional constituent.[88]

Consider our practices of reporting velocity. A claim that an object is moving at a certain velocity makes sense only if it is understood with respect to what the velocity is to be assessed. We say that velocity is relative to an observer, or a frame of reference—we must count something as stationary. But we articulate this additional parameter of velocity claims only when it is not

---

[88]For more on unarticulated constituents, see Essay 10. There, a systematic semantics for some underarticulated constructions is given, which is connected to a recursive model of syntax in the usual way.

obvious what is to count as stationary. We have in English a number of general-purpose constructions for articulating commonly suppressed constituents of a claim. We say, "with respect to ..." or "relative to ..." or "in the sense that ...." The more likely the unarticulated constituent is to be unclear, the more likely it is that we have a natural way to articulate it.

In the case of belief reports, in which notions are unarticulated, we do have rough and ready ways to clarify just which notions we mean to talk about. We say, for instance, that Miles believes that Edward is a peasant in one way—in the way related to the boy in front of him, not in the way related to the Prince. Or we add to the report, "that is, he thinks the boy in front of him, who really is Edward, is a peasant." Or we specify how Miles would or would not "put" his belief. Or we allude to the evidence that led Miles to form the belief, or to the actions it would be likely to bring about. Each of these devices can succeed in distinguishing among the two notions, which in context can seem equally relevant, thus eliminating possible confusion about which notion we mean to talk about.

We do not, of course, have a very direct way of specifying the notions we mean to talk about in belief reports. This is due to the fact that it is almost always obvious which notion a speaker is talking about. Where it is not, we either use one of the devices just mentioned, or leave the language of belief reporting altogether and talk instead about what the agent would say or would do.

IV

Unarticulated constituency and direct reference are of a single stripe. In fact, if we take the term "reference" in the ordinary sense in which it does not require a referring expression, unarticulated constituency can be seen to result from a kind of direct reference—perhaps, "tacit" reference. When a speaker claims that "it is raining," she is referring to a place, and not to a description of, nor a condition on, a place. In the same way, on our view, a belief reporter refers to an agent's notions. We have chosen not to talk this way in our official account only to avoid being read as claiming that notions are referred to by the reporter's words.

A difficult issue facing all views of direct reference, and ours in particular, is the need to make sense of intuitions about truth and falsity in cases of reference failure. This problem is especially acute for our account in some cases of denials. Consider the following example. A blind man is facing in the direction of a distant building. Someone, unaware of the man's blindness, says, "He believes that building is far away." One normally would take this report to be about the notion the man has as a result of his current visual perception of the building. The speaker is trying to refer (though not with a word) to such a notion, to provide such a notion for the report to be about. But, of course, there is no such notion in this case. Is this report false, or, owing to a failure of tacit reference, does it fail to express a proposition? Certainly, we ordinarily would respond not by saying, "You have failed to express a proposition," but "He does not believe that"—and we have the strong intuition that this denial would be true.

Compare the following case: An astronaut on the moon[89] says, "It's three o'clock." Typically, this sentence would be used to express the claim that it is three o'clock in Z, where Z is the time zone in which the utterance takes place. The confused astronaut thinks that there are time zones on the moon, and he intends to claim that it is three o'clock in "Z," which is the time zone he is in. But there is no such time zone. So he fails to express a proposition. We feel no qualms, however, about denying his claim: "It's not three o'clock. There are no time zones on the moon, you ..."

The present difficulties are often discussed in connection with "negative existential" claims. But the same issues arise with respect to all sorts of denials in which the speaker believes there to be reference failure. A child who sincerely asserts, "Santa will come tonight," fails to refer, and therefore, on most direct reference accounts, fails to express a proposition. But the parent who responds, "Santa will not come tonight," explaining that there is no Santa, makes what seems to be a true claim, despite the fact that the use of "Santa" does not refer.

Note that these examples would present no trouble for descriptional theories of reference. For if in these cases the original speakers are seen not as attempting to provide a specific thing to be a propositional constituent, but merely as claiming that there *is* a thing meeting a certain condition (being the generous elf known as "Santa," being the local time zone, or being the man's perceptual notion of the building), then the claims are straightforwardly false and the denials are true.

The descriptional theories have even more than this kind of extensional correctness going for them; it is because the cited conditions—call them *providing conditions*—are not satisfied that the denials are true. In the child's use of "Santa," the providing condition, of being the generous elf known as "Santa," plays a central semantic role, even though it is not the referent of the child's use of the name. It is a condition that the child expects to be filled as a precondition of successful reference. He expects to refer successfully to a thing in virtue of it meeting the providing condition. His supposed ability to refer to a thing by using the name "Santa" depends on the condition's being satisfied. Similarly, the astronaut takes it that he can talk directly about a time zone, that he can provide one, because it meets the providing condition of being the local

---

[89]John Etchemendy brought up this version of Wittgenstein's example.

time zone. And, we claim, the belief reporter expects to be able to talk directly about a notion because it satisfies the condition of being the man's perceptual notion of the building.[90]

A normal, successful case of direct reference involves a speaker referring to an object in virtue of that object satisfying a providing condition. Reference failure involves failure of a presupposition, namely, the presupposition that a providing condition is satisfied. Now, expressions like proper names and underarticulated phrases that normally invoke devices of direct reference are sometimes used where there is no presupposition that the relevant providing conditions are satisfied. The denials in the cases of the blind man, the astronaut, and Santa are like this. In each of these denials, the speaker does not presuppose that there is a thing meeting the providing condition that is invoked by the utterance. Instead, we claim, the speaker *raises the providing condition to constituency*—he talks about the condition itself rather than about a supposed thing that meets it. The providing condition now plays a semantic role—as a constituent of the proposition expressed in the denial—more central than its usual auxiliary role of providing a propositional constituent.

In particular, the claim expressed by "Santa will not come tonight" (in the described circumstances),[91] is to the effect that there is no generous elf known as "Santa" who will come tonight. And the proposition expressed by "It is not three o'clock" is that there is no local time zone such that it is three o'clock there. And the content of "He does not believe that that building is far away" is the claim that there is no perceptual notion of the building such that the man has a belief involving that notion, with the content that the building is far away. The denials are thus true, and their truth is consistent with our claim that the assertions they deny strictly speaking fail to make claims.

Of course, for each of the original, claimless assertions there is a proposition closely related to the kind of proposition the speaker intends to express, which we can for most purposes charitably treat as the content of the statement. Specifically, we can take the speaker to have expressed the claim that there is a thing meeting the invoked providing condition, such that so-and-so. In fact, the speaker of such an assertion is preassertively committed to this proposition, in virtue of his commitment to the presuppositions that must be satisfied if he is to make a successful claim in the way he intends.

---

[90]Just which providing conditions are invoked in a given case depends on a wide range of circumstances. Also, there usually is more than one such condition for a given use of a term. Providing conditions for a use u of "here" by speaker A at location l, for instance, include the conditions of being the location of the utterer of u, being where A is, and being l. In the "Santa" case, we have the conditions of being the referent of the utterance of "Santa," being the relevant thing known as "Santa," being the generous elf known as "Santa," and so on.

[91]In circumstances where it is presupposed that the providing condition is met, the denial expresses just the negation of the proposition (if there is one) expressed by the corresponding assertion.

Above we analyzed our reader's utterance of (2) in an imaginary case in which Miles has been shouting about the Prince. In fact, Miles was not shouting, "Edward Tudor is of royal blood," at the time he encountered the boy. The reader actually has no specific actions on Miles' part to which he can tie such a notion of Prince Edward. It is obvious from the general tenor of the novel, however, that Miles would have such a notion. Every full-witted adult in England at the time has a notion of Prince Edward—one they acquired shortly after he was born—which motivates their behavior in regard to the Prince of Wales, such as their use of the phrase "Prince Edward," their decorum when the royal procession goes by, and the like. Our reader may not be able to pick out anything very specific in Miles' behavior to serve as evidence that he has such a normal notion of the Prince. But he has every right to suppose that he has one.[92]

It may seem implausible to suppose that our reader, in using (2), can directly provide a notion for the report to be about, since the reader is not directly acquainted with such a notion. If this intuition is right—an assumption we shall question in a minute—our machinery gives us a natural way of respecting it: this is a case in which, instead of a notion, a providing condition becomes a propositional constituent. What our reader is claiming with (2) is that there is some normal notion via which Miles believes that Edward is royal; that is, the condition of being a normal notion of the Prince is the unarticulated constituent. The report, on this construal, is an example of a second kind of belief report—in which notions are not provided, but instead are constrained, by provided conditions; the report is about those conditions, in the sense of "about" appropriate to propositional constituents.

For this (supposed) second kind of belief report we can give the following account. Where u is a belief report at t, which is *about* conditions $C_1, \ldots, C_k$, and $p = Con(u_S)$, where u_S is the subutterance of u corresponding to the object sentence S,

$$Con(u) = \exists b[B(a, b, t) \wedge Content(b, t) = p \wedge$$
$$\exists n_1, \ldots, n_k \bigwedge_{r_i \ in \ p}(C_i(n_i) \wedge Responsible(n_i, r_i, b))]$$

So we have room in our framework for two sorts of belief report, corresponding to whether notions are themselves *provided* or merely *constrained* by conditions. Supposing for now that there really are two kinds of belief report, how can we know, for a given report, of which kind it is? One way, surely, is to look at what would happen if the appropriate notions were to fail to exist.

---

[92]What counts as being a normal notion certainly depends, we think, not only on what is common in a community, but also on other aspects of the background of the discourse, including facts about what is relevant to the goals of the discourse. We would expect an account of "being a normal notion" to exhibit many of the same features as an appropriate account of "knowing who b is," which certainly is background-sensitive in many ways. See, for example, Böer and Lycan 1985.

If the report would then be false, then it is a case of notion constraint rather than provision; if the report would fail to make a claim, then it is a case of (attempted) notion provision.

Of course, we have seen how, in a case where an attempt to provide a notion fails, a proposition closely related to what the speaker is trying to express takes center stage. This is the false proposition to the effect that the agent has a notion that meets the invoked providing condition and that is involved in a belief with such-and-such content. Given this fact, our intuitions about whether a belief report fails to make a claim or is simply false are in the same boat as our intuitions about the truth-value of the child's claim that Santa is coming. The falsity of the closely related propositions, plus the truth of the natural denials of these statements, may well obscure intuitions about the truth of the original claims.

In this paper, we adopt officially the position that there really are belief reports of the second kind (which are about conditions rather than notions). Given our points about providing conditions and propositions to which speakers are preassertively committed in cases of direct reference, however, a plausible case can be mounted for the view that, in all successful belief reports, specific notions are provided for the report to be about.[93]

Assuming, now, that there are two classes of belief reports, there is no reason to suspect that all reports will fall clearly into one camp or the other. For example, if our reader simply assumes that Miles must have a normal notion of King Henry and expects his audience to do the same, then it makes little difference whether he claims that Miles has a belief involving that notion (notion provision) or just a belief involving a normal notion (notion constraint). Since it makes little difference, our reader need not go to any pains to indicate which of the claims he is making; his report simply can land between the two claims.[94]

V

With that out of the way, let us turn to our examples.

First, a recap of the semantics of (1) and (2). We will treat (1) as a case of notion provision. The provided notion is Miles' notion of Edward that is con-

---

[93]This view is argued in Crimmins 1989, though in the end the argument rests precariously on the fact that none of the examples considered as natural candidates for reports of the "second kind" seems clearly to be as required.

[94]There is another way, also, in which a report can land between the notion-provision and the notion-constraint types of report. It is not hard to concoct cases in which one notion is provided and another is constrained; a natural construal of our reader's report "Miles believed that he (Edward in rags) was less noble than Prince Edward" might go along these lines. So in the general case, both notions and conditions may be provided; there are no difficulties in formalizing this along the lines already given for the pure notion-provision and pure notion-constraint analyses.

nected with his perception of and actions toward Edward in the mob incident. The reader claims that Miles does not have a belief involving that notion, with the content that Edward is of royal blood.

With (2), the reader provides a condition on notions, the condition of being a normal notion of Prince Edward. The reader claims that Miles has a belief involving some normal notion of Edward, with the content that Edward is of royal blood.

In the Pierre case, the sentence (3) gets used in two reports, first in a discussion of Pierre's initial acquaintance with London through stories, then in a discussion about Pierre's thoughts of his adopted home. Call these reports u_3 and u'_3. Pierre actually has two notions of London, one relevant to each discussion; call the first n and the second n'. The notion n meets the condition C of being a notion germane to the discussion of Pierre's reaction to the stories; the notion n' meets the condition C' of being a notion germane to the discussion of Pierre's new home.

If one of the two analyses is uniquely correct for u_3 and u'_3, it is perhaps the account in terms of notion constraint. The speaker of the former report is claiming that Pierre has a belief involving some notion germane to the current conversation about the stories, with the content that London is pretty. The speaker of the latter report requires that the belief involve some notion relevant to the conversation about Pierre's new home.

If the circumstances of u_3 and u'_3 are such as to make the notions n and n' clear and present to the speakers and their audiences, then the analysis should be in terms of notion provision. If this is the case, then the speaker of u_3 claims that Pierre has a belief involving the notion n with the content that London is pretty; the speaker of u'_3 claims that Pierre has a belief involving the notion n' with the content that London is pretty. If the circumstances of the two reports are less clear-cut, as they often are, then, as noted earlier, the claims made by the speakers might fall between those offered by the notion-provision and notion-constraint accounts. There just might be no saying.

Note, though, that any of these analyses constitutes a solution to the puzzle. The claim made in u_3 is simply true, and the claim made in u'_3 is simply false.

Kripke presents the puzzle as arising from a few very plausible principles about belief reports, including:

Disquotation: If a normal English speaker, on reflection, sincerely assents to "p," then he believes that p (1979, 248–49).

Translation: If a sentence of one language expresses a truth in that language, then any translation of it into any other language also expresses a truth (1979, 250).

On our account of belief reporting, neither of these principles is at all plausible in general. Each principle presupposes that it is belief sentences that are true or false. On our view, a single sentence, like (3), can be used in both true and false reports. Kripke assumes that, because of the lack of obviously context-sensitive words, (3) can be considered more or less "eternal." But words are not the only sources of context-sensitivity; the presence of unarticulated constituents also can widen the gap between a sentence and the proposition expressed by a statement of it. And that is what happens in the Pierre case.

Richard lists three sentences considered as uttered by A watching B in the phone booth:

(4) I believe she is in danger.

(5) I believe you are in danger.

(6) The man watching you believes you are in danger.

A uses (4), clearly, to make a true report. His notion n_{vis} of B that stems from his view out the window, which is associated with his idea of being in peril, and which causes his waving, is supplied. It is claimed that A has a belief involving n_{vis} with the content that B is in danger. He in fact has such a belief.

The man would not sincerely use (5) over the phone; if sincere, he certainly would deny (5). The natural intuition, we think, is that a use of (5) in the described circumstances would make a false claim. (It is this reaction that Richard sets out to prove mistaken. The very possibility of our semantics shows that his proof is in error.)

The set-up for (6) is as follows. B sees a man, A, in a building across the street waving frantically. Amused, she says (over the phone), "the man watching me believes that I am in danger." Echoing her, A utters (6). Surely B's claim is true. And if so, A's use of (6), which is in explicit agreement with her, is true also.

So we hold that the use of (5) is false while that of (6) is true. But how can this be? The two reports are uttered by the same person in the same circumstances, they ascribe beliefs to the same agent, and they use precisely the same embedded sentence, understood in the same way! The only difference is the way in which the man is referred to—in the one case with "I," in the other with "the man watching you."

Difference enough, we think. The pragmatic principle of self-ascription applies to (5) but not to (6):

> **Self-Ascription:** An utterance of "I believe that ...τ..." provides (or, is about) the notion that is connected to the speaker's use of "τ."

Using "I" in (5), A thus directs attention to the notion (n_{phone}) that is linked to his use, in (5), of "you"—the notion of B that is associated with the idea of being the one he is addressing[95] and not associated with the idea of being in danger. So A's use of (5) makes the claim that he has a belief involving n_{phone}, which has the content that B is in danger. He in fact has no such belief.

In (6), A is discussing those beliefs of the man watching B, that is, of A himself, which explain the frantic gestures directed at B. So he claims that the man has a belief involving n_{vis}, the notion linked to his perception out the window and his gestures of warning, which has the content that B is in danger. In fact, A has such a belief.

Richard's case is especially interesting because it shows how a contextual shift can be brought about by a change in wording outside of the embedded sentence in a belief report. This gives added force to our analysis of substitution worries: the wording changes in the usual cases of reluctance to substitute are responsible, not for changes in meaning or explicitly specified content, but for changes in what is provided by context for the reports to be about.

Our semantics allows that, for a given belief sentence, absolutely any of the agent's notions may be provided—there is no semantic restriction on what notions may be provided in a use of a given sentence. But there are many pragmatic principles, like self-ascription, that constrain which notions can be provided in the normal case. It is semantically but not pragmatically possible for a use of "I believe I am not me," or (normally) "S, but I do not believe that S," to be true. Although it is semantically possible, in Quine's example, for an utterance of "Tom believes that Cicero is Tully" to express a true proposition (say, if Tom's "Cicero" notion is provided twice over), there may be no very natural use of that sentence, which in fact expresses the proposition (although surely we can concoct a Richard-ish example to put this point in doubt). In the normal case, the use of different names for Cicero serves as a strong, though perhaps defeasible, indication that the names have some importance to what is being said over and above just standing for Cicero. Such a difference in names requires a sufficient reason—in this case, a difference in which notions are being provided to play the corresponding roles in the ascribed belief.

VI

The relation of the present proposal to Fregean semantics for belief reports should be relatively clear. The broad similarity consists in the agreement that a belief report specifies, in addition to simply which objects the agent is claimed to have a belief about, also just how the agent is cognitively connected to those objects. On our account, the report specifies (or constrains) the particular notions allegedly involved in the belief. On a Fregean account, "senses" are specified.

---

[95]More precisely, with his idea I_{addr}, the idea that has the context-sensitive semantic role picking out the person being addressed.

Two crucial differences separate the accounts. First, we stress the particularity and unsharability of notions. Since notions are full-fledged particulars immersed in the causal order, they have a great array of different features that we can exploit to provide them in our belief reports. They are involved in beliefs, associated (sometimes) with words, formed in specific circumstances, connected to perceptual situations, reasonings, and actions; they survive the formation and abandonment of beliefs in which they are involved; and so on. We can use each of these kinds of fact to give us a handle on a notion, a way of picking it out. This frees us from a problem often noted about the Fregean strategy; it appears that, on most natural construals of what senses are, we often do not know just what sense an agent attaches to an object (we do not grasp it), and so we cannot know just what we are attributing to the agent with a belief report, which, after all, must be about the agent's ways of thinking.

As we have said, there is nothing in our view incompatible with something like Fregean senses, considered as entities that we can use to classify an agent's notions. A Fregean might well take our talk of "notions" as an account of what it takes for an agent to grasp a sense—agents grasp senses in virtue of having appropriate notions.

The second departure from a Fregean account is in our claim that the agent's ways of thinking about things (her notions), though they are specified in a belief report, are not the referents of the words occurring in the embedded sentence. This difference becomes especially important in the analysis of certain kinds of reports: those with content sentences containing devices of under-articulation, and those with no content sentences at all, but which instead are completed with the likes of "what you said," "the same thing," and "Church's Thesis."

VII

The account of belief reports sketched here closes some doors. If, as we claim, a single belief sentence can be used in both true and false reports, then there can be no simple logic of such sentences. The simplest possible rule,

$$\frac{A \text{ believes that } S}{A \text{ believes that } S}$$

does not hold in general, as we learn from Kripke's puzzle.

Even a logic of belief sentences restricted to a single context will prove difficult.[96] Although a relativized version of the above rule will certainly hold,

---

[96] Here we mean "context" in a sense such that various different statements can be made in the same context. One way of taking our claims in this paper would be as denying the general usefulness in semantics of such a restricted notion of context. Taken this way, we have claimed that such things as the words used in a statement can affect the semantically relevant parts of the statement's context.

this one,

$$\frac{\begin{array}{ll} A \text{ believes that } S & \text{(relative to } c) \\ A = B & \text{(relative to } c) \end{array}}{B \text{ believes that } S \quad \text{(relative to } c)}$$

will not, as we learn from Richard's puzzle.

Also closed is the prospect of a strictly compositional semantics for belief sentences. The semantic values of the subexpressions in a belief report, on our analysis, do not provide all the materials for the semantic value of the report itself. Notions and conditions on notions are not articulated, but end up in the contents of reports; so the semantics of belief reports is in an important way noncompositional.

In addition, our account denies what some have seen as a primary desideratum for theories of belief: that a belief report claims simply that a binary relation holds between an agent and an object of belief.

And, perhaps worst of all, we have given an account on which it appears to be next to impossible to give a complete, systematic account of which claims are made by which belief reports. We have claimed that belief reports are context-sensitive, that they invoke unarticulated constituents, without offering any general method for determining what the relevant contextual factors are, and how they give rise to these unarticulated constituents of belief reports.

Tempted as we are to view each of the above results as an insight rather than a drawback, we realize that we have abandoned many of the issues and goals commonly pursued in this area. But we think the account opens many doors as well.

Whereas there is little possibility of an interesting logic of belief sentences, the logic of beliefs, notions, and ideas is available. Such issues as logical and analytic closure of belief, explicit versus implicit belief, and inferential issues in belief change really belong to the logic of beliefs rather than the logic of belief sentences. We can explore the logic of the relations we have seen as underlying our ordinary talk about beliefs—but this logic will not be a logic of ordinary language.

Of course, we have explained very little about what beliefs, notions, and ideas are. But we think our partial account of them raises obvious questions in theories of representation, action, perception, and the metaphysics of mind.

Our semantics is not compositional, but there is system in the noncompositional mayhem. The ways in which notions and conditions on notions are provided have yet to be explored to any great extent. But the discussions of the belief puzzles suggest several directions from which to look at these mechanisms.

Last, the move to unarticulated constituents emphasizes the importance of pragmatic facts about language to the study of what seem like purely semantic issues. In order to express claims, we exploit a tremendous variety of facts, conventions, and circumstances, of which the meanings and referents of our terms form just a part. So it is a mistake to relegate pragmatics to matters of felicity and implicature. In the case of belief reports, it is central to understanding content and truth.[97]

Afterword

Mark Crimmins came into my office one day when he was a graduate student at Stanford, determined to show me that the account of belief reports Barwise and I had given in chapter 10 of *Situations and Attitudes* would not do. Among other things, he did not like the "bite the bullet approach." And he thought that we needed to interpret the cognitive structures we postulated there as concrete particulars, and bring them explicitly into the semantics rather than quantifying over them. It did not take him long to convince me. At the time, I was thinking rather obsessively about unarticulated constituents, applying and misapplying this idea all over the place. But it seemed to work here, as a natural way of getting Crimmins' concrete cognitive structures into the semantics of belief. The paper we wrote is one of my favorites, and seems to me to fit accord nicely with the view developed in the last couple of papers. The issues are treated more deeply and comprehensively in Crimmins 1992.

[97]This work was supported in part by the System Development Foundation through a grant to the Center for the Study of Language and Information. We would like to thank the Philosophy of Situation Theory group at CSLI; special thanks to David Israel.

13

Individuals in Informational and Intentional Content

> Mont Blanc with its snowfields is not itself a component part of the thought that Mont Blanc is more than 4000 metres high.
>
> —Frege to Russell, November 13, 1904
>
> I believe that in spite of all its snowfields Mont Blanc itself is a component part of what is actually asserted in the proposition, Mont Blanc is more than 4000 metres high.
>
> —Russell to Frege, December 12, 1904[98]

In this paper, I shall defend Russell's view that Mont Blanc, with all of its snowfields, is a "component part" or constituent of what is actually asserted when one utters "Mont Blanc is more than 4000 meters high," and of what one believes, when one believes that Mont Blanc is 4000 meters high. I also claim, however, that a proposition that does *not* have Mont Blanc as a constituent plays an important role in the assertion and the belief that Mont Blanc is more than 4000 meters high.

Taken somewhat out of context, the quotes from Frege and Russell express insights that pull in different directions in the contemporary philosophy of language. Behind Frege's remark is the insight that reference is not direct but mediated. When we think and talk about things, our thoughts and words are not in *direct* contact with the things thought about and talked about. The meanings of our words, and the cognitive roles of our ideas, do not in and of themselves determine their reference. They get at objects via some aspects of the objects; the words directly provide only a *mode of presentation*, an aspect of the object to which they refer. Thus reference depends in part on the properties objects happen to have. Our thought and words could be just as they are, and refer to other things, given different facts about the world.

---

[98]Both quotations are from Frege 1980 (163, 169).

To individuate the thought in terms of the object, passing by the mode of presentation, seems to be to misrepresent its nature and distort its causal role. It makes different thoughts, involving different modes of presentation, come out the same. And it suggests that when a mode of presentation fails to pick out an object, the thought of which it is a part does not exist. The perceptions that lead to a belief, and the actions that flow from a belief, causally mesh with ways of thinking about objects, not the objects themselves.

And yet Russell's remark expresses another insight. We do, in fact, typically individuate the propositions we assert and believe by the objects referred to, not the modes of reference. The evidence assembled for this doctrine of "direct reference"—some of which is sketched below—is extremely persuasive. (See Donnellan 1970, Kaplan 1978, Kripke 1980, Wettstein 1984.)[99] But must we then abandon Frege's point of view?

I argue that the tension between these insights is apparent and not real. In the first place, theories of "direct reference" are misnamed. Kaplan's account of indexicals, Donnellan's account of proper names, and Wettstein's account of demonstratives all see reference as mediated. In each theory, a use of a term of a certain kind refers to an object, because that object plays a certain role relative to that use. On Donnellan's account, a use of a proper name refers to the object that plays a certain role in the historical account of the use. In Wettstein's account of demonstratives, the referent is the object that is salient in a certain way to speaker and audience. In each case, the referent must have a certain property: it must play a certain historical role in the production of the utterance (Donnellan), or be the salient object (Wettstein), or stand in a certain relation to the context of the utterance (Kaplan).[100]

It is important to note that in each of these theories the mode of presentation is *relational*. The object referred to is the one that stands in a certain relation to the use of the word in a specific utterance.[101] The referent of a use of "I" is the person who is the speaker of the utterance. The referent of the word "this" is the object that is salient to the audience of the utterance.

I believe the tension between the two insights disappears when we distinguish the *truth conditions* from the *incremental content* of assertions and beliefs, and distinguish what is central from what is peripheral in Frege's insight. In reporting assertions and beliefs in the normal way, we focus on incremental content. The incremental content of assertions and beliefs often has individuals

---

[99] In my discussions of these theories below I oversimplify; in particular, the simple theory of demonstrative reference in terms of salience greatly oversimplifies Wettstein's increasingly subtle thinking on the complex issue of demonstratives.

[100] Kaplan has emphasized that he did not choose the term "direct reference" to indicate that reference was unmediated, but to indicate that the object referred to, rather than the mode of presentation that determines it, is involved in the proposition expressed by the statement of which the term is a part. See Kaplan 1989a.

[101] In the sense of a certain uttering; a specific event in which a speaker uses the words in question.

as constituents in a clear and intuitive sense, thus vindicating Russell. But to have adequate theoretical accounts of these phenomena, we must also deal with the truth conditions. The truth conditions of an assertion or belief will not have any remote individual like Mont Blanc as a constituent, but only a "mode of presentation" that such an object satisfies. It is thus more Fregean than Russellian. But any reasonable theory of "direct reference" will provide such modes of presentation. The referent will be the object that stands in a certain relation to the utterance itself. A coherent Russellian must be a bit of a Fregean.[102] Frege's own theory ruled out such relational modes of presentation. But this was not a consequence of his insight about modes of presentation, but of other elegant but implausible features of his theory of content.

Propositions

I shall speak of R(eferential)-propositions and A(ttributive)-propositions. An R-proposition is one that has an individual as a constituent—what Kaplan calls a "singular proposition." Conceived as an R-proposition, the proposition that Mont Blanc is more than 4000 meters high might be modeled by a pair consisting of the mountain itself and the property of being more than 4000 meters high. More generally, a simple R-proposition will consist of a sequence of an n-ary relation followed by n objects. An R-proposition $\langle Pxy; a, b \rangle$ is true iff the objects $a, b, \ldots$ stand in the relation $P(x, y)$. The objects and the relation are the *constituents* of the proposition.

Conceived as an A-proposition, the proposition that Mont Blanc is more than 4000 meters high will be modeled by a pair of properties. The first property is being more than 4000 meters high. The second would be some mode of presentation P', the property of uniquely satisfying some condition, which in fact Mont Blanc uniquely satisfies. One might suppose this property is associated, in one way or another, with the speaker's use of the term "Mont Blanc." Perhaps it is a property assigned to "Mont Blanc," by the speaker's "idiolect." Perhaps it is the weighted sum of the properties the speaker would use to identify Mont Blanc. Perhaps it is the property of being the object that plays a certain causal role in the history of the production of the token of "Mont Blanc." Wherever P' may come from, the A-proposition $\langle P; P' \rangle$ is true iff something coinstantiates P and P'.[103]

Properties can also have individuals as constituents. Such properties are sometimes called relational as opposed to purely qualitative properties. Be-

---

[102] Of course, Russell came to be a bit of a Fregean, in the sense that he allowed only individuals with whom one was acquainted to be constituents of the propositions one believed, and became very restrictive about acquaintance.

[103] For symmetry, we should define an A-proposition as consisting of a sequence of properties and a relation, true if some sequence of objects that instantiate the properties, instantiates the relation. But this complication is not needed in what follows.

ing the fountain immediately north of Hoover Tower, for example, is a relational property possessed by Tanner Fountain. As I am using the term, an A-proposition need not be purely qualitative. The properties that are the constituents of an A-proposition may be relational. Consider, for example, the property of being Frege's favorite mountain. This is a mode of presentation, and the proposition $Q' = \langle x$ is more than 4000 meters high; x is Frege's favorite mountain$\rangle$ is an A-proposition.

Now consider these three propositions:

$Q = \langle x$'s favorite mountain is more than 4000 meters high; Frege$\rangle$.

$Q' = \langle x$ is more than 4000 meters high; x is Frege's favorite mountain$\rangle$.

$Q'' = \langle x$ is more than 4000 meters high; Mont Blanc$\rangle$.

Q is an R-proposition with Frege as a constituent. It is true iff he had the property of having, as a favorite mountain, one that is more than 4000 meters high. Q' is an A-proposition, which is true if the properties of being Frege's favorite mountain and being more than 4000 meters high are coinstantiated. It seems that Q and Q' have equivalent truth conditions, even though Q is an R-proposition and Q' is an A-proposition. I shall say that Q' is the result of *refocusing* Q. Assuming that Mont Blanc was Frege's favorite mountain, Q' and Q'' also bear an important relation to one another. I shall say that Q'' results from *loading* Q', *given* the fact that Mont Blanc was Frege's favorite mountain. This is not a very elaborate theory of propositions, but it will do for our discussion.

The terms "referential" and "attributive" come from Keith Donnellan's distinction between two uses of definite descriptions. One way of taking Donnellan's distinction is that statements containing referential uses express R-propositions, whereas statements containing attributive uses express A-propositions (Donnellan 1966).[104] The basic question is whether the properties used in the description are part of "what is said." Suppose Smith says "The tallest mountain in the Alps is over 4000 meters high," and that in fact Mont Blanc is the tallest mountain in the Alps. It is clear that the truth of Smith's utterance requires that there be a tallest mountain in the Alps, and that it be over 4000 meters high. This is so whether we think that Smith is expressing an A-proposition or an R-proposition. Taken either way, if his utterance is true, the definite description must be satisfied, and the object that satisfies it must be over 4000 meters high. So taken either way, the truth of Smith's utterance requires the truth of an A-proposition. But is *this* what Smith has said, the proposition he

---

[104]Donnellan considers this interpretation of his distinction; it clearly does not incorporate everything he has in mind. I am setting aside one important aspect of Donnellan's distinction, having to do with cases in which the description does not really fit the person the speaker intends to express a proposition about. For an important discussion of Donnellan's distinction and a number of related issues, see Neale 1990.

has expressed? Or has he expressed the R-proposition?

To answer this question, we engage in counterfactual thinking. Suppose the Matterhorn to be higher than Mont Blanc, and both to be more than 4000 meters high. In that case, Smith's utterance would have been true. But would he have expressed the same proposition he actually did express? Would the proposition he in fact expressed be true in this counterfactual situation? If we are taking Smith to have expressed the A-proposition, we will be inclined to answer "yes" to both questions. But if we are taking Smith to express the R-proposition about Mont Blanc, we will take the answers to be "no" to the first question, but "yes" to the second. In the altered circumstances, Smith would have referred to the Matterhorn rather than to Mont Blanc, and so would have expressed a different proposition. But the proposition he in fact expressed would still be true in the counterfactual situation, since Mont Blanc would still be more than 4000 meters high. The fact that it would not be the tallest mountain in the Alps is not relevant, since that is not part of the content of the R-proposition.

The results of such a counterfactual test are less clear in the case of descriptions than in that of names, demonstratives, and indexicals, where the distinction between the truth conditions and the proposition expressed is more clear cut. Suppose Smith says, "You are sitting," while addressing Jones, who is in fact sitting, and has been sitting for some time, and is quite unconcerned with Smith. For Smith's utterance u to be true, he must be addressing someone who is sitting. The A-proposition $\langle x$ is sitting; x is the addressee of $u \rangle$ captures this truth condition. But this is not the proposition asserted. Smith has not *said* that he is talking to anyone, and Smith is not *saying* anything about his own utterance. What he said was just that Jones was sitting, something that was true before he began, and would have been true even if he had never spoken. What he said is not the A-proposition just mentioned, but the R-proposition $\langle x$ is sitting; Jones$\rangle$.

Now suppose Smith says, "Mont Blanc is more than 4000 meters high," the case Russell had in mind. Above, we imagined two modes of reference that might be involved. Neither seems to be part of what is said. Suppose the mode of presentation is the weighted sum of properties Smith would use to identify Mont Blanc. Smith has not asserted that Mont Blanc has these properties. Even if Mont Blanc does not have these properties, and Smith would never succeed in identifying it, it does not change what he has said. Suppose the mode of presentation is that property suggested by Donnellan's account of names, of playing a certain role in the history of the production of Smith's token of "Mont Blanc." Smith has certainly not said that Mont Blanc has this property; the proposition he expresses using this token might be true, even if the token had never been produced. So, it seems that Russell is right. It is the R-proposition that Smith expresses. Mont Blanc is a constituent or component part of what is actually asserted in the proposition "Mont Blanc is more than 4000 meters high."

But this view presents a number of problems. Although the notion of an R-proposition is coherent, the notion of asserting or believing an R-proposition can strike us as very odd. For consider an assertion or belief t that expresses the R-proposition $Q = \langle Px, a \rangle$. There must be something about t that makes Q the correct interpretation of it. What could that be? It is not hard to imagine the property P being connected to some aspect of an assertion or belief by some general rule—a convention of language, or a law about how our minds interact with properties in the environment. That is, an aspect or property of an utterance or belief is associated by a general principle with a property of aspect of something else. But how could such a general principle connect an aspect of mind or language with a specific individual? It seems that the connection would have to be mediated by some individuating property the individual has. And it seems that this individuating property is what is important, not the bare identity of the object. This intuition is very strong and has led to the view that there is something about direct reference that defies common sense. I believe things fall into place, however, if we adopt a certain view of meaning—a view I associate with Hume.

A Humean View of Meaning

Although in his *Inquiry* Hume says little directly on the topic of meaning, Hume's point of view lends itself to a simple theory (1748/1975). Hume is concerned with our habit of forming opinions about what will happen at one time, on the basis of perception of what is going on at other times. He sees only one way this might work: we apply general rules or constraints, connecting types of events. We observe these types to be conjoined at the observed times, and assume them to be conjoined at the unobserved times. When one sees an event of one type, one expects an event of the other. I see the ball left unsupported; I expect the ball to fall. I see the man eating bread; I expect he will be nourished. Note that the types are interdefined. It is the very ball I see unsupported that I expect to drop, the very man I see eating that I expect to be nourished thereby.

Hume recognizes a relation between types he calls "constant conjunction." I take this relation to hold if, whenever there is an event of the first type, there is an event of the second type. Of course, no one is in a position to observe that types are constantly conjoined, since everyone's experience is limited. But observing a number of cases of conjunction leads to another relation between one's perceptions (impressions or ideas) of types. I will call this "mental conjunction." When T and T' are mentally conjoined by an individual, that individual will expect an event of type T' after observing, or otherwise coming to believe in, an event of type T.[105] Hume recognizes, and emphasizes, that an individual may mentally conjoin types that are not constantly conjoined. To mentally conjoin T and T' is something like believing that T and T' are constantly conjoined. But it is more primitive than belief; it is not the result of a rational process, but simply of a habit that, if we are optimistic, we may assume nature has built into us because we live in a pretty orderly place where experience of past conjunction is a sign of constant conjunction. (Hume 1748/1975; see especially the last two paragraphs.) In Barwise and Perry 1983, Jon Barwise and I speak of constraints, involving, and attunement. These notions can be understood as generalizations of Hume's point of view. A constraint is a state of affairs in which two types are related: one type of event involves another. Constant conjunction is required for involvement; a thoroughgoing Humean will take it to be *all* that is required, but we left this question open. Hume's theory of habit and custom is a simple theory of attunement. His theory allows attunement to constraints that are not facts; this is what happened to Russell's chicken, who did not expect its head to be chopped off on market day, because it had not happened before then.

Given these ideas, we can introduce the notion of what a fact indicates, relative to a constraint. Suppose we have a constraint that a thing of type T is also of type T'. Relative to that constraint, the fact that x is T indicates that x is T'. I will call these the indicating fact and indicated proposition. A given tree has one hundred rings. That indicates that it is at least one hundred years old. Hume is eating bread. That indicates that Hume will be nourished. The car is making an odd sound. That indicates that it will soon break down. Now consider the indicated propositions in each case: that a certain tree is one hundred and one years old, that Hume will be nourished, that my car will break down. Are these R-propositions or A-propositions? They are R-propositions, with the tree, Hume, and the car as constituents.

In these cases, however, the source of the objects in the R-propositions is straightforward. We are confronted with the indicating fact, in which an object has certain properties. Given various constraints, those properties tell us something further about that very object. The tree that has one hundred rings lived for at least one hundred years; the individual who is eating will be nourished; the car that is making noise will break down. In each case, the proposition captures the further properties indicated about a constituent of the indicating fact, relative to the constraints. There is no mystery about these cases of indication. The object that is a constituent of the R-proposition is a constituent of the indicating fact. The constraint does not have any specific objects as part of its content. But it gets applied to specific objects. It says that if specific objects have one property, they will have another.

---

[105]Note that since the types are interdefined, the mental states will have to be also. That is, there has to be something about a perception of a ball being left unsupported and an expectation of a ball dropping that makes the latter an expectation that the same ball will drop. See Essay 4.

Pure and Incremental Informational Content[106]

Here is another example of indication. The veterinarian takes an x-ray of a certain dog—say, the Barwises' dog Jackie. The x-ray indicates that Jackie has a broken leg. This is a more puzzling case. Jackie is not part of the x-ray. She is not part of the general principles that govern the interpretation of x-rays. So how does Jackie become constituent of the proposition indicated by the x-ray?

We are assuming that there are constraints that limit the possible causes for an x-ray being of a certain type, and further practices that can augment the constraints to get us the information we want. An x-ray of the sort in question, can be brought about only if rays fall in a certain pattern on it. Given the additional regularities that arise from the practices in the veterinarians office—the circumstances under which x-rays get taken—an x-ray can be exposed to just this pattern only if it was produced by the x-raying of such an animal. So, relative to the relevant constraints and practices, this x-ray being of the type it is, carries the information that it was produced by exposure to an animal with a broken leg: ⟨there is a unique animal of which x was taken, and that animal had a broken leg; this x-ray⟩.

We get from this proposition to the one about Jackie by refocusing and then loading. First we focus not on the x-ray itself, but the dog to which it was exposed: ⟨x had a broken leg; x is the unique animal of which this x-ray was taken⟩. Then we load Jackie into the proposition, given that she was that very dog: ⟨x has a broken leg; Jackie⟩. Why do we refocus and load in this way? Because it is Jackie we are interested in. We are ultimately interested in the dog, not the x-ray, and we know which dog is in question. We are interested in the x-ray up to the point at which we have determined what it shows about Jackie; then the x-ray, and Jackie's relation to it, cease to be of interest.

The pattern here is extremely common. We examine one object—call it "the signal"—because of what it shows us about another, already identified, which is connected to it, more or less remotely, in some way or another. We are interested in what additional information the signal has to offer about this connected object. Given that Jackie was x-rayed, what does the x-ray show about her? The R-proposition associated with the signal is simply what it shows about the object whose connection with the signal led to our interest in it.

In these cases, it is natural to think in terms of three interconnected types. There is the type of the indicating fact—in this case that an x-ray exhibits a certain pattern. And there is the type involved in the indicated proposition—in this case that a dog has a broken leg. The third type is the connecting type. It is the type of a fact that connects what indicates and what is indicated. In this case, it is the fact that Jackie was the dog x-rayed. The constraint somehow relates three types:

---

[106]For more on the topics in this section, see Israel and Perry 1990 and Essay 14.

T : x exhibits such and such a pattern.

T' : x was an x-ray of y.

T'' : y has a broken leg.

We can fit these three types into our notion of a constraint in different ways. First, think about the case where you are going through old files and find an x-ray exhibiting the pattern in question. You are sure that this x-ray could only have been produced by exposure to an animal; no x-ray could just accidentally come to look like that. And given that it looks like that, the animal of which it was taken has a broken leg. Here the constraint is that T involves T' and T''. If an x-ray looks like this, there was an animal it was taken of, who had a broken leg. By examining the x-ray, you have learned something additional about it: ⟨there is a unique animal of which x was taken, and that animal had a broken leg; this x-ray⟩. This is the pure information carried by the x-ray, relative to the constraint above. Now you might naturally refocus on the unknown dog rather than the x-ray: ⟨x had a broken leg; x is the unique animal of which this x-ray was taken⟩.

We can also think of the constraint *incrementally*. Suppose we already know which dog the x-ray was exposed to. That is, we know the fact of type T'. What *additional* information does the x-ray's exhibiting such and such a pattern provide us with? Given that the x-ray was taken of Jackie, it seems that the x-ray's exhibiting such and such a pattern indicates that Jackie has a broken leg. It seems this does not even require as strong a constraint as the one above. Perhaps x-rays can accidentally look like that, but in this case you know it was taken of a certain animal, Jackie. You only need the constraint that T and T' involves T''. Every x-ray and dog are such that, if the x-ray looks like this and it was taken of the dog, the dog had a broken leg. This seems like a natural way to look at it—but it is not using quite the notion of indication that we have explained.

Let us introduce the notion of a fact incrementally indicating that P, given another fact. (I use "indicates$_C$" for "involves, relative to the constraint C.")

A fact f incrementally indicates$_C$ that P, given f' iff for some T, T', and T'':

(i) C is the constraint that T and T' involve T''.

(ii) f is of type T.

(iii) f' is of type T'.

(iv) P is the proposition that some event is of type T''.

The notion of incremental indication is doubly relative. One fact carries incremental information *relative* to a constraint, *given* another fact. Thus, in our example, the fact that the x-ray exhibits such and such a pattern incrementally indicates that Jackie has a broken leg, *given* that the x-ray was taken of Jackie, and *relative* to the constraint that if there is an x-ray of such and such a type, then a particular dog has a broken leg, given that the x-ray was taken of that dog.

Now, why would it be useful to think of the x-ray incrementally, rather than purely? Suppose the vet is holding Jackie. Jackie is in pain and the vet wants to help. She plans to put Jackie in a certain room. She knows who Jackie's owners are, and plans to talk to them. So she has access to Jackie via a number of "aspects" or "modes of presentation." The issue in which she is interested is whether Jackie has a broken leg. She knows that the x-ray being developed is of Jackie. But this "mode of presentation"—being the dog that was x-rayed— is relevant only in connecting Jackie with the x-ray. Aside from that it is not as important as the other facts she knows about Jackie in guiding her actions towards Jackie. The vet looks at the x-ray, and says "It shows that Jackie has a broken leg." She is describing the content of the x-ray, *given* that the x-ray was of Jackie, because the fact that the x-ray is of Jackie is only relevant in getting the property of having a broken leg associated with her. Once that has been done, that mode of presentation becomes essentially irrelevant. On the other hand, in order to understand general principles about x-rays and how they work, one has to deal with their pure content. To learn how to take and interpret an x-ray, just about the most basic fact that one has to know is that the developed x-ray contains information about the animal of whom it was taken.

Truth Conditions and Incremental Linguistic Content

The Humean picture is very simple. What gets us beyond the confines of any matter of fact are general principles. Only relative to such principles do we have informational content. To consider the content of a fact, is to consider it in terms of some such principles.

Now think of the conventions of language, as associating types of utterances with the types of situations they describe, and thus as assigning truth conditions to utterances. These conventions also generate "content." This will not be informational content, but *intentional* content. Types of utterances are not constantly conjoined with the situations of the type that language conventionally associates with them. Sometimes people lie, and sometimes they just do not get things straight. But the mechanism of content is the same: general principles that take us from the type of one event to another type of event identified in terms of the objects involved in the first.

Thus abstracted and generalized, the Humean analysis of meaning can be applied to language. The constraints that are relevant to linguistic meaning are not laws of nature, and are not taken to be such, even by the most credulous among us. When we hear an utterance, we do not habitually expect that the proposition expressed will in fact be the case. But we do habitually *entertain* this proposition. The source of the habit is not observation of regularities, but mastery of the conventions of a given language. We are in some sense attuned to them, for our train of thought follows the conventions, even if we do not have the concepts necessary to articulate them.

Suppose the veterinarian says, pointing to Jackie, "This dog has a broken leg." Here the bearer of content is the particular utterance, the veterinarian's production of a token. The content-giving principles are the semantical rules of language that tell us under what conditions utterances of various types are true. If we look at what the vet would ordinarily have been taken to say, it would be that Jackie had a broken leg. That is, if someone were to report the vet's linguistic act by saying, "The vet said that Jackie had a broken leg," that would be an accurate report. Can we analyze this case in terms of pure and incremental content?

Let us develop a fairly plausible although oversimple account of the syntactic, semantical, and pragmatic principles involved here. Here is our account of the sentence the veterinarian used:

(1) Tokens of the form "This X" are noun phrases. Tokens of the form "has a broken leg" are verb phrases.[107]

(2) If a token is of the form XY, where X is a noun phrase and Y is a verb phrase, the token is a sentence.

(3) An utterance of a token of "This X" refers to an object y if y is the object of the kind designated by the utterance of "X" that is most salient to the audience of the producer of the token at the time of the utterance.

(4) Every utterance of a token of "dog" designates the kind, Dog.

(5) Every utterance of a token of "has a broken leg" designates the property of having a broken leg at the time of the utterance.

(6) If a token t is a sentence consisting of a noun phrase followed by a verb phrase, an utterance of t is true iff there is a unique object designated by the utterance of the noun phrase that has the property designated by the utterance of the verb phrase.

I shall use the term "condition of truth" for the condition that an utterance has to satisfy to be true. This is the semantical property associated by the conven-

---

[107] A couple of words about how I am using "token" and "utterance." A use or utterance often involves the production of a token, and tokens are often only used once, by their producers. That is what I am usually assuming here, but it is an oversimplification that ignores important issues. Tokens can be reused for different utterances, even by different agents. In the epistemology of language, tokens are most commonly (more or less) directly perceived, while utterances provide most of the properties crucial for interpretation. To see how important the difference can be, think of receiving a letter in the mail. One perceives the token, but cannot arrive at its content without knowing a good bit about the circumstances of its production or use. The differences between written and spoken tokens, printing, xerography, word-processing, and electronic mail, all raise interesting issues about the relation between utterances and tokens.

tions of English and the general principles of language with indicative uses of sentence tokens of a given form, independently of particular facts about the context. Given this usage, different utterances can have the same condition of truth—even utterances with different truth-values. According to the theory above, the condition of truth for any utterance u of "This dog has a broken leg" are that there be a dog, who is most salient to the audience of the speaker of u, and who has a broken leg. That is, when we fix the facts of language and apply the above rules, this is what is required for truth.[108]

In contrast to "conditions of truth," I shall use the term "pure truth conditions" for the R-proposition consisting of the utterance and its condition of truth. Thus, if C is the condition of truth for a token u, the proposition $\langle u; C \rangle$ is the pure truth condition of u. The truth conditions of an utterance u will be a proposition that is true iff the utterance is. All utterances of the same type need not have the same truth conditions, and, in particular, false and true utterances of the same type cannot have the same truth conditions. Given the theory above, we can distinguish between the pure, refocused, and incremental truth conditions of the vet's utterance u:

Pure Truth Conditions of u:

⟨there is an individual that is the dog that is most salient to the speaker in x and her audience at the time of x and that individual has a broken leg; u⟩.

Refocused Truth Conditions of u:

⟨x has a broken leg; x is the unique dog most salient to the speaker of u and her audience at the time of u⟩.

Incremental Truth Conditions of u, given that Jackie is the unique dog that is most salient to the vet and her audience at the time of u:

⟨x has a broken leg; Jackie⟩.

Our ordinary notion of "what is said" is the incremental truth condition. We do not think that when the vet says "This dog has a broken leg," that she has *said* something about her own utterance, namely, that there is a dog that is most salient at the time it was produced with a broken leg. We think she has *said* that Jackie has a broken leg. But this does not show that the pure truth conditions are not as I have described them. It simply shows we must distinguish

---

[108] Note that I am assuming that the nouns and verb phrases, plus the conventions of language, get us to kinds and properties, independently of contextual facts, while indexicals, demonstratives, and names do not get us to their referents without context. Hence the kind Dog and the property of having a broken leg are "loaded" into the condition of truth, but not the particular dog. This is surely an oversimplification, for there is a great deal of interminacy in our use of common nouns and verbs that must be resolved by context.

between the truth conditions of an utterance and the proposition expressed by an utterance.

The proposition we take to be expressed by an utterance is typically the incremental truth condition, *given* the facts that determine the reference of the indexicals, demonstratives, and names. Above, in giving the incremental truth conditions of u, we fixed the fact that fixes the referent of "this dog," according to the simple semantical theory for demonstratives sketched in rule (3).

Though I have spoken of *the* incremental truth conditions, it is important to note that there is actually a *range* of incremental truth conditions, depending on which facts we fix. Consider an utterance u of "I like that dog." If we fix the facts about the demonstrative and the indexical, we get a proposition of the sort $\langle x$ likes $y; a, b \rangle$. But suppose we fix the facts about the demonstrative but not the fact about the indexical. Then we get a proposition of the form $\langle$the speaker of x likes $y; u, b \rangle$. This is not the pure truth condition, and not the proposition expressed. And yet this proposition might be important, in getting at what a given listener believes on the basis of hearing the utterance. Suppose a person hears u in a situation in which they can tell which dog is being referred to, but cannot tell, without turning around and looking, who is speaking. Perhaps a particularly ugly and mean-looking dog is on a stage, salient to everyone. Someone produces a token, and our listener turns around to see who might have such strange taste in dogs. The proposition above might be important in characterizing the belief the listener acquires from hearing the token that motivates him to turn around. The point is that the "proposition expressed" is not the *only* sort of incremental truth condition that is relevant to the epistemology of language. If we assume that it is, then we shall suppose that theories of direct reference must have difficulties with the problems of "cognitive significance"—with the possibility of different cognitive attitudes towards utterances that express the same proposition. (See Wettstein 1986.) They need not. Theories of direct reference say that modes of presentation are not constituents of the proposition expressed. But they need not deny that modes of presentation are constituents of all sorts of other propositions, including the pure truth conditions that are relevant to the epistemology of language. Theories of "direct reference" will lead one to this denial, only if one assumes what I shall call "the principle of unique content." This is the principle that the only proposition associated with utterances by the semantics of a language is the proposition expressed. (See Essay 11.)

What, then, is special about the proposition expressed? The answer has several related parts. First, in the paradigm case of communication, the audience is in a position to use its own knowledge to "load" the referents of indexicals and demonstratives and names. In a paradigm case of communication, we know who is speaking and are in a position to see to which objects the uses of the demonstratives refer. Second, the paradigm intention in uttering a sentence like

"This dog has a broken leg" is to secure relatively stable belief in a proposition of the form $\langle x$ has a broken leg; $a \rangle$, not in the propositions that constitute the pure or refocused truth conditions of an utterance. This is not to say that belief in, or some other positive cognitive attitude towards, these latter propositions might not be required to get a competent speaker of English to the belief in question. But that is not the goal. If the veterinarian utters "This dog has a broken leg" to her nurse, her intention is that the nurse treat Jackie as a dog with a broken leg throughout Jackie's stay. The nurse will have to have a way of thinking about Jackie that allows her to recognize her in a variety of contexts. The mode of presentation of Jackie that the nurse uses in understanding the vet—being the unique dog salient to the vet and her audience at the time of the utterance—is not such a mode of presentation. Once the nurse has looked at Jackie and noted enough about her to recognize her, this mode of presentation will have done its job. The nurse need not remember exactly what property of Jackie's the vet used to refer to her, when the nurse first learned of the broken leg. This particular mode of presentation drops away as irrelevant once it has "fixed the reference," to use Kripke's phrase. Third, it is the incremental truth conditions of an utterance, given the facts that determine the reference of its indexicals, demonstratives, and names, that are typically the focus of reports about what was said by the utterance. I am suggesting that the reason for this is not that this proposition is any more directly or intimately connected with the utterance than other candidates. It is less directly connected with the utterance than the pure truth conditions.[109] The reason is simply that our notion of "what is said" reflects concern with the paradigm communicative situation.

Once one abandons the principle of unique content, one comes to expect the notion of "the proposition expressed," and "what is said" to have a certain looseness. Consider the example above, about the ugly dog. Suppose I have one friend who is well known to like ugly, mean dogs. He arrives at the dog show, fits into the crowd behind me, and says "I like that dog" as a way of announcing to me that he has arrived. He wants me to turn in the direction from which the token came, because I believe that the speaker of it likes ugly, mean dogs, and have inferred from that, that my friend with the unusual taste in dogs has arrived. He is not really trying to get me to believe that he likes that particular dog; expression of that proposition is just a by-product of his utterance. The proposition he is really trying to convey corresponds to the incremental truth conditions given the facts that fix demonstratives, but not given the facts that fix indexicals: $\langle$ the speaker of x likes that dog; $u \rangle$. In such a case, is it so clear "what is said"? Or, consider the case in which someone comes up to me at a party and says, "I'm Elwood Fritchey." I learn, and am intended to learn,

---

[109] Note that one might take the fully incremental truth conditions of an utterance to be its truth-value. Truth-functional expressions would then focus on an even less direct, more incremental property of utterances than terms like "said."

that the name of the person addressing me is "Elwood Fritchey." A theory of direct reference can handle this, once it has abandoned the principle of unique content, even if we take a proposition of the form $\langle x = y; a, a \rangle$ to be "what is said." (See Barwise and Perry 1983, 167ff.) But perhaps we should go a step further and simply be a great deal more flexible about what is said. The question here is the status of an additional principle for our simple semantical theory:

(7) The proposition expressed by an utterance u of a sentence consisting of a noun phrase followed by a verb phrase is its incremental truth conditions, given the reference of the noun phrase of u.

Is this part of the semantics of "This dog has a broken leg?" Or is it really just a part of the semantics of "says"? Or is it not even that, but simply the typical result of some more complex, pragmatically driven principles about "says"? I am not sure how to answer these questions, but I am leaning towards the last answer.

If we take this line, we will find many of Donnellan's claims about the referential-attributive distinction congenial. We will see this as a distinction between cases in which the proposition expressed is to be incremental, given the facts determining the reference of the description in question, and cases in which it is not. Facts about the communicative situation of the particular utterance will dictate the answer, rather than the syntax or semantics of the particular utterance.

Truth Conditions and Incremental Content of Beliefs

I have argued in various places that we need a two-tiered theory of belief and other cognitive attitudes. (See Essays 1, 2, 4, 6; Barwise and Perry 1983.) We need to distinguish between the belief states and the propositions believed. The belief state a person is in has to do with the internal goings-on of the mind or brain. The proposition believed will depend also on various sorts of external circumstances.

Here is an example of this distinction. I think there is a certain mental state with the following typical causes and effects. It is typically caused by some combination of the following: feeling of pressure on one's thighs, buttocks and back, visual perceptions of one's body being supported by a chair, memories of sitting down, and the like. It typically causes one to be disposed to answer "Yes" to the question, "Are you sitting?" in relatively normal circumstances. If I am in this state, I believe that I am sitting. If you are in this state, you believe that you are sitting. We are in the same belief state, but we believe different propositions.

Jerry Fodor has a theory of the nature of cognitive states that we can use to think about this distinction, even if we have some doubts that it is the final truth about such issues. On his theory, there are sentences in mentalese written in various parts of our brain. So, in particular, there is a sort of belief box, in which are various tokens written. Let us assume mentalese is a lot like English. Then, in the above example, you and I both have tokens of "I am sitting" written in our belief boxes. So we are in the same belief state. But we believe different things.

Let us call my belief token b_1 and yours b_2. These two tokens have the same condition of truth:

> A belief token b of "I am sitting" is true, iff the person, in whose belief box b is written, is sitting.

The two tokens have different pure and incremental truth conditions:

> b_1's pure truth condition is $\langle x$ is written in the belief box of a person who is sitting; $b_1 \rangle$.
> b_1's incremental truth condition is $\langle x$ is sitting; John Perry$\rangle$.
> b_2's pure truth condition is $\langle x$ is written in the belief box of a person who is sitting; $b_2 \rangle$.
> b_2's incremental truth condition is $\langle x$ is sitting; you$\rangle$.

What do we believe in this case? Each of us believes that he or she is sitting. I believe $\langle x$ is sitting; John Perry$\rangle$, you believe $\langle x$ is sitting; you$\rangle$. It seems quite clear that we do not believe the pure truth condition of our belief tokens. Most people who believe themselves to be sitting do not believe, of the token in virtue of which they believe themselves to be sitting, that it is in the belief box of someone who is sitting. And, even those rare folks who do, do not have *that* belief, in virtue of that token.

The following, possibly historical, example will bring out this point. One Monday, Jerry Fodor gave a lecture in a certain room at MIT. He believed his own theory and believed that he was standing. He dubbed the belief token of his, in virtue of which he believed he was standing, X. He wrote down various things on the board about X, including

> X is a token of "I am standing."

The pure truth conditions of X are $\langle x$ is a token in the belief box of someone who is standing; $X \rangle$. Call this proposition P. Now the next day, we may imagine, Fodor happened to go into the same room and sit down, shortly after his colleague Ned Block has taught a class. In fact, Block had not used the board and it was still unerased from Fodor's last lecture. But Fodor assumed that what was written on the board was written there by Block. He assumed that Block had been doing just what Fodor did the day before, using a real-life example to illustrate the mental sentence theory. So Fodor believed that X was a token of Block's, and that Block was standing when he used it as an illustration. So Fodor believed that X was a token in the belief box of someone who was standing. Fodor now believes P, the pure truth conditions of his own token. My point is that he does not believe P in virtue of that token's being in his belief box. The belief a person has in virtue of having a token in their belief box is *not*, at least in the vast majority of cases, a belief about that very token.[110]

So, we find in the case of belief something parallel to what we found in the case of assertion. Just as what is asserted is not the pure but the incremental content of an utterance, what is believed is not the pure but the incremental content of the belief state. We are interested in what conditions a belief has to fulfill to be true, given the facts about whose belief it is, and whom the mental terms in the belief stand for.

But now consider the commonsense principles that we have, connecting beliefs, desires, and action. These will not be concerned with the proposition believed, but with the belief state, not with what a person believes, but with how they believe it. As in the case of informational and linguistic content, so too in the case of the content of the attitudes: in specific cases we are interested in incremental content, but in understanding general principles, it is pure content that is relevant.

On Being a Fregean

Now we are in a position to see the general strategy for accommodating both of the insights expressed by the quotes from Frege and Russell. Frege is right that a thought or an assertion about a thing requires a mode of presentation. Let R be the relation that, on Donnellan's theory, holds between the use of a name and the object to which it refers. If we accept Donnellan's account, the pure truth conditions of an assertion u of "Mont Blanc is more than 4000 meters high," will be $\langle x$ is such that there is a unique object that has R to the noun phrase of x, and it is more than 4000 meters high; $u\rangle$. The refocused truth conditions will be $\langle x$ is more than 4000 meters high; x is such that it is the unique object that has R to the noun phrase of $u\rangle$. The first constituent of this proposition is a mode of presentation of Mont Blanc. And some such mode of presentation is required. There is no *direct* way for a use of "Mont Blanc" to refer to Mont Blanc.

But this mode of presentation will not be a part of the proposition that the utterance expresses. Russell was right about that. It is the object referred to or thought about, and not the properties by which we refer to it or think about it, that is part of the incremental content, and it is the incremental content that is asserted or believed.

There are certain other Fregean principles that conflict with this way of accommodating things, however. Frege not only thought that modes of pre-

---

[110]This example is borrowed from Essay 14.

sentation were involved in speech and thought, he held that those modes of presentation were constituents of the propositions asserted and believed. That is, in the terminology I have been using, he thought that the proposition expressed by an utterance involving a term incorporated the mode of presentation associated with the term. And, in the case of belief, he thought that the proposition believed incorporated the modes of presentation involved in the belief. With some qualification, the accommodation I have described rejects that view. These modes of presentation find their place in the refocused truth conditions of an utterance or belief, not in the proposition expressed or believed. Frege assumed, quite naturally perhaps, that the content we would focus upon in reporting assertions and beliefs was that most intimately connected with the words used or the type of thought. But this is not how we typically report language and thought. We focus on incremental content, on what needs to be the case for the utterance or belief to be true, *given* various contextual facts. The qualification is that when we give up the principle of unique content, the whole question of the content of a statement or belief becomes a much less determinate question.

While Frege thought that modes of presentation were involved in the propositions expressed in speech and thought, it is clear that the "utterance reflexive" modes of presentation I have been discussing were not the ones he had in mind. Even if one held that such modes of presentation were constituents of the propositions statements express, it would not save all of Frege's theory. Frege held that when one reports the belief or assertion of an agent, the proposition expressed by the content part of one's report expresses the very proposition that is said to be believed or asserted by the agent. But suppose you say, "Mont Blanc is more than 4000 meters high," and I report, "You said that Mont Blanc is more than 4000 meters high." The refocused pure content of your statement, and the refocused pure content of the content part of my statement will not be the same, since the modes of presentation involved will have different utterances as constituents. This identity holds only at the level of incremental content, when modes of presentations have been left behind.

Frege's theory seems to imply that the mode of presentation, by which we think about an object, is a part of what we believe about the object. This seems incorrect. I may be thinking and talking about George Bush, in virtue of the complex role George Bush plays in the history that led to my use of "George Bush" and my acquisition of the notion I use in thinking about George Bush. I need not have any belief that George Bush plays this role, in order to talk about him and believe things about him. One may have mastery of the use of proper names, without having the concepts necessary to articulate how they work. But there is nevertheless an epistemologically central connection between the correct theory of how a class of terms work, and the relations that ordinary language users expect, between uses of those terms and the objects to which they refer. In the case of indexicals, it is plausible to suppose that competent speakers of the language pretty much understand what this relation is, even if they cannot articulate it. A person who understands a use of "I," faced with an utterance of "I am such and such," will look for the speaker of the utterance to verify the remark. Even in the case of proper names, we expect some knowledge of that relationship. Consider, for example, someone who comes across a conversation in which the name "George" is being used. He is not sure who is being referred to—is it George Bush or George Washington or George the fellow down the street? A competent language user would have some idea what counts as evidence for and against each of these hypotheses. If the straightforward approach of asking were unavailable, he would begin to look at the historical factors leading up to the use of the term in the conversation. Were the participants watching a campaign speech? Visiting a Revolutionary War battlefield? The mode of presentation of a term, though it may not be part of the content of the beliefs of someone who understands a use of the term, will still be cognitively important. If someone has mastered language, they will be *attuned* to the principles that govern relations between uses of terms and their references, even if they cannot articulate them and do not have the concepts necessary to be said to believe them. Frege's view, though incorrect, is not groundless.

A theory of reports of thought and language based on the ideas explored here, then, will not have the elegance of Frege's theory. But the modifications we have to make in his ideas are not reason to abandon his central insight. Reference is not unmediated. There is nothing particularly direct about "direct reference." [111]

[111] I am grateful to Leora Weitzman for very detailed and helpful comments on the penultimate version of this paper, and to Howard Wettstein, Syun Tutiya, David Israel, and Mark Crimmins for comments on earlier versions. The recent Stanford dissertation projects of Weitzman, Crimmins, Lisa Hall, Genoveva Marti, and Stephen Neale have influenced my thinking greatly on these matters. My work on this paper was supported in part by the Center for the Study of Language and Information at Stanford, through an award from the System Development Foundation.

14

Fodor and Psychological Explanations

with DAVID ISRAEL

Introduction: The Texts

We begin with some quotations from Fodor.

> It is crucial to the whole program of explaining behavior by reference to mental states that the propositional attitudes belonging to these [causal] chains are typically nonarbitrarily related in respect to their content (taking "content" of a propositional attitude, informally, to be whatever it is that the complement of the corresponding PA-ascribing sentence expresses). One can imagine the occurrence of causal chains of mental states which are not otherwise related (as, e.g., a thought that two is a prime number, causing a desire for tea ...).... Still if all our mental life were like this, it's hard to see what point ascriptions of contents to mental states would have.... The paradigm situation—the grist for the cognitivist's mill—is the one where the propositional attitudes interact causally and do so in virtue of their content. And the paradigm of this paradigm is the practical syllogism.... John believes that it will rain if he washes his car. John wants it to rain. So John acts in a manner intended to be a car-washing.... Our common-sense psychological generalizations relate mental states in virtue of their content (1981, 182–84).

> I dearly wish that I could leave this topic here, because it would be very convenient to be able to say, without qualification, what I strongly implied above: the opaque readings of propositional attitude ascriptions tell us how people represent the objects of their propositional attitudes (1981, 236).

What I think is exactly right is that the construal of propositional attitudes which such a psychology renders is nontransparent.... The trouble is that nontransparency isn't quite the same notion as opacity, as we shall now see (1981, 236).

Having said all this, I now propose largely to ignore it (1981, 239).

The Contents and Causal Powers of Tokens of Mentalese

Fodor takes propositional attitudes to be relations to tokens of an internal language ("mentalese") that have content. If Jerry believes that P, Jerry has a token of mentalese in his belief structure that has the content that P. These tokens have causal properties as well as content; they are related in lawlike ways in virtue of their causal properties. But the laws must (in the paradigm cases that are grist for the cognitivist's mill) make sense in terms of the contents of the tokens. It is the contents that are related in commonsense psychological principles, and it is the meshing of content and causal properties that makes it conceivable that cognitive psychology might work.

What exactly is the relation between the contents and causal properties of tokens? The first quotation above, from "Propositional Attitudes," suggests a simple answer: tokens interact as they do in virtue of their content. But Fodor begins "Methodological Solipsism" with a quotation from Hume that states a problem for this view.

To form the idea of an object and to form an idea simply is the same thing; the reference of the idea to an object being an extraneous denomination, of which in itself it bears no mark or character (Fodor 1981, 225, quoting from Book I of Hume's *Treatise*).

The fact that my idea of red is an idea of one color rather than another is an *external denomination*—a relation between the idea and a color—not something that can influence the way it interacts with other ideas. The view that emerges in "Methodological Solipsism" is not that tokens interact in virtue of their contents, but that both the causal facts and the content facts about a token are settled by its *formal* properties.[112] The formal properties are, roughly, those that a processor scanning the tokens can detect and by which its actions can be systematically determined. If both the contents and the causal powers of a token depend on its form, the two kinds of properties might mesh in the ways necessary to have the content-based principles of cognitive psychology (or commonsense psychology) backed by causal laws relating formally individuated states. One imagines a species-wide causal role for a given type of

---

[112][In his reply to this article, Jerry Fodor takes exception to this remark (1991). He takes us to be saying that the tokens have the content properties they do *because* they have the formal properties they do. But we intended something weaker than this by "settle."]

token and a species-wide interpretive function that assigns contents to types. The two mesh so that, for example, within the human species, if a belief and a desire cause a volition, then the contents of the belief, desire, and volition have some sensible, rational connection with one another.

One imagines the interpretive function fixing the reference of a certain formal type as the property of being red, once and for all—the same for each member of a cognizing species. But it seems that the reference of many of our ideas is not only external, but *circumstantial*. The interpretive function and the formal properties of a token do not fully determine the reference; particular circumstances that vary among formally identical tokens, also must be taken into account. Suppose, for example, that Jerry is looking at a cup. The cup that he is looking at will be the referent of the mentalese phrases that are analogues to "the cup in front of me" or "that cup." Tokens of the same mentalese phrases, in the head of someone else, looking at a different cup, will have different referents.[113]

How can causal and content properties of tokens mesh, if the content properties of a token depend both on its form and on such particular external circumstances, while the causal properties depend on form alone? If contents are sensitive to external circumstances, and so classify persons who are internally similar as different, and those who are internally different as similar, how can content-based principles of rationality mesh with causal laws?

If such circumstantially determined external references of phrases become part of the truth conditions of the sentences in which they occur, then those truth conditions will also be infected with circumstantiality. It seems a causally coherent psychology should not individuate states in terms of such external denominations. But the contents that are ascribed to mental states by our practices of propositional attitude reporting are often based on just such circumstantially determined external denominations. The contents that a person believes and the people who are counted as believing the same thing depend in part on external facts about reference and hence on nonformal properties of their tokens. As a result, people with formally identical tokens may believe different things; people with formally differing tokens may believe the same thing.

Fodor would have liked the following response to this worry to work:

> Transparent reports of attitudes do classify mental states in a circumstantial, nonformal way. But because this is so, we do not take transparent reports to tell us how the agent is thinking, and for this reason explanations using transparent reports are impotent. But opaque reports are explanatorily valuable, because they do tell us

---

[113]See below §3, where we argue for such analogues, and §4.2, where we sketch a semantics for mentalese in which the relation between English sentences and sentences of mentalese is taken to be identity.

how agents think; they can do this because they do not classify mental states circumstantially, but in terms of contents that mesh with formal properties.

But in the remarks quoted above from "Methodological Solipsism," he indicates that this response is not quite right. Even opaque reports rely on circumstantial classification. In effect, he postulates a level of *fully opaque non-transparent* content that works the way he had hoped the opaque classification would. But he does not provide very many details.[114]

In this paper, we sketch a theory, within a Fodorian conception of cognition, of how the formal properties and external circumstances of tokens relate to the contents of tokens, and of how commonsense explanations might work given this framework. We conclude that

- Circumstantially determined content properties can mesh with causal properties.
- Attitude reports in terms of circumstantially determined content can be explanatory, that is, can enter into adequate psychological explanations.
- It is scarcely conceivable that some content properties not be circumstantially determined.

Like Fodor, we believe cognitive psychology is possible, and that there are strong empirical arguments in favor, and only weak and avoidable arguments against, the thesis that a *component* of that psychology will be individualistic. We think of ourselves as providing a way of looking at content and content-based explanations that should be helpful to those, like Fodor and ourselves, who believe cognitive psychology can and should include such an individualistic component. There are nevertheless some points of disagreement between us and Fodor on the topics covered in this essay. We think transparent explanations can work well; Fodor does not. In our reconstruction, even fully opaque attitude reports will be somewhat circumstantial. We provide a completely non-circumstantial level of content, but claim that to understand the rationality of laws one needs to bring in the (admittedly rather modest) circumstance that the relevant tokens of mentalese belong to the same agent.

A Broader Context of Disagreement

Given the amicable goal of this essay, perhaps we should indicate some broad areas of disagreement before plunging in. Like Fodor, we conceive of individ-

---

[114]The present essay is the result of years of arguing about essays in Fodor 1981, particularly "Methodological Solipsism Considered as a Research Strategy in Cognitive Psychology." Many of the most fruitful of these arguments have involved Lisa Hall and Brian Smith, whom we thank. Special thanks to Georges Rey for a thoughtful and illuminating critique of an earlier draft. We intend the present piece as an outward and visible symbol of the inner cycles of inspiration and frustration we owe to that essay. We have not been able to pay as much attention to Fodor's later work (e.g., 1987) as would have been optimal.

ualistic cognitive psychology as requiring structured internal states that have both content and causal role. And like him, we believe that the postulation of such states is empirically reasonable and that the success and structure of our ordinary psychological concepts provides important evidence for it. We are inclined, however, to think that Fodor's talk of the language of thought and mentalese may encourage the assumption that the internal structures are more language-like than there is any reason to believe. And we worry about whether the notion of *formality* coalesces conditions from a number of different areas that have less in common than Fodor thinks that they do.[115] But for the purposes of this paper we set aside these worries.

Other areas of disagreement concern questions of how the causal and content properties of internal states relate to one another. An important issue is the source of what we shall call the interpretive function, which assigns contents to formally individuated mental states. We sympathize with the aim and intent of approaches that see content properties as ultimately reducible (in some weak sense) to causal properties, with a role for information "Wisconsin style." But we do not think that any such reduction to causal/informational concepts can succeed. Our own view is a sort of naturalistic functionalism that stresses *functions* and *purposes*—hence the results of actions measured in terms of degree of success in bringing about some specified condition—in the classification of mental states. We are inclined to think, with Dennett, that the distinction between merely attributed intentionality and real intentionality can be understood within this framework, rather than constituting a refutation of it. From this perspective, we try to practice an approach that is an amalgam of the design-oriented approach of work in artificial intelligence with H. P. Grice's conceptual creature construction (1975). This approach seeks to understand intentionality through understanding the reasons that intentionalistic theories are useful in dealing with (or designing) various systems, beginning with very subhuman systems. We think that cognitive psychology depends on naturalistic psychology and that Fodor's arguments against the possibility of the latter are not very convincing.[116]

From both our perspective and Fodor's, it is necessary to have an account of how the contents and causal powers of the structured states of individual intelligent beings can mesh in the way presupposed by common sense and by cognitive psychology. We try to provide such an account in this paper.

An Example

We shall look closely at an example that brings out the problems that concern us. Suppose Jerry wants to drink some decaffeinated coffee. He sees before him a brown cup, c; just a few seconds before, he had seen a brown cup being filled

---

[115] Our thinking on this point has been much influenced by conversations with Brian Smith.

[116] Some of these ideas are developed, or at least hinted at, in Israel and Perry 1990.

with what he believed was decaffeinated coffee. He moves his arm and hand in a complicated manner, grasping the cup, lifting it to his lips at an angle as he tilts his head a bit, and opens his mouth. Call this type of movement M for later reference. In Jerry's circumstances, this movement constitutes picking up the cup and bringing it to his lips. Gravity and his digestive system take over, and he gets what he wants. The explanation of Jerry's doings might go like this:

> Why did Jerry decide to pick up the cup and bring it to his lips?

> He wanted to drink some decaffeinated coffee, and he believed that the cup in front of him was filled with decaffeinated coffee.

This example can be used to illustrate the problems engendered by the fact that commonsense psychology classifies mental states in terms of external, circumstantial denominations. We explain Jerry's action by citing a belief and a desire. The belief and the desire make sense of the action. The action will promote the satisfaction of the desire if the belief is true. But the way the belief, desire, and action are individuated appears to depend on factors external to the formal properties of the mental tokens involved. One way to see this is by focusing on what we count as having *the same belief*. Construed transparently, the belief attributed to Jerry is individuated in terms of a certain cup c, rather than the way Jerry thinks of it. Someone would agree with Jerry—would have the same belief—who believed that c contained decaffeinated coffee, no matter how the other person thought of c. Yet only the ways of thinking, not the external reference, could conceivably be correlated with the formal properties of belief tokens.

Construed opaquely, things are a bit better. But the belief still seems to be individuated in terms of Jerry.[117] As Fodor points out, opaque attributions still allow some slack as to how the agent is thinking. Someone else, who is looking both at Jerry and at c but thinking "The cup in front of him contains decaffeinated coffee," would be said to believe the same thing that Jerry does. But then it is at least possible that Jerry could believe just what he does, opaquely construed, while being in a different state.[118] Perhaps, sitting in a Denny's, gazing in a mirror while waiting impatiently for his cup of decaf, Jerry sees a waitress fill a customer's cup from the pot with the characteristic decaf indicator—the pot has an orange neck. He thinks, "Now the cup in front of him contains decaffeinated coffee.... I wonder when the cup in front

---

[117]Here, we follow Fodor's discussion of *transparent* and *opaque* classifications, in "Methodological Solipsism." Note in particular his treatment of the "I'm sick"/"He's sick" and the "I'm ill" examples.

[118]Following Fodor and many others, we have allowed ourselves use of locutions of the form *A thinks (believes)* "....". We regard this as an alternative notation for fully opaque belief attributions, which means that there is a token of the quoted type in the agent's belief structure. See below, §4.2. It is interesting to note that this odd way of speaking is often accepted without much explanation.

of me will do so." In such a circumstance, it would be misleading to report that Jerry believes the cup in front of him contains decaffeinated coffee; but would it be incorrect, would what the reporter said be false? It seems not, for as we noted, someone else, who thinks "The cup in front of that man contains decaffeinated coffee," with reference to Jerry, would be counted as believing just what Jerry believes when Jerry thinks "The cup in front of me contains decaffeinated coffee." [119] So it seems that opaque attitude reports also do not focus exclusively on the sorts of intrinsic (formal) properties needed by a causal theory of mind. [120]

The Need for Circumstantial Content

Fodor uses the phrase "object of an attitude" to refer to the mentalese tokens that are involved in cognition according to his theory. We try to avoid this phrase, which is often used instead for what we shall call *the contents of the propositional attitudes*. We assume that the tokens have contents, and that these contents are referred to by the complements of attitude reports. So "A believes that P" means, roughly, that A has in his head a belief token, whose content is that P. We take these contents, the designata of phrases of the form "that P," to be propositions. Propositions are truth-evaluable; that is, not true or false as spoken by one person, or at one time, but simply true or false. [121] We use "believes that ... ," "desires that ... ," and "intends that ... " as canonical forms for reporting beliefs, desires, and volitions. [122]

Sentences in ordinary language may be separated into those that are *eternal* and those that are *context-sensitive*. Different utterances of an eternal sentence express the same proposition. The class of eternal sentences is arguably empty, but sentences such as "$7 + 5 = 12$" and "The first person born in the twenty-first century was, is, or will be a philosopher" are at least candidates. [123] Different utterances of context-sensitive sentences express different proposi-

---

[119] On this, compare Fodor's treatment of the "That's edible"/"This is edible" example in "Methodological Solipsism."

[120] On the view of belief reports developed in Barwise and Perry 1983, this report would be misleading but literally true. On the view developed in Essay 12, there is a reading, indeed the natural reading, on which the report would be literally false. But even on that reading, the proposition that Jerry is reported to believe is the same as that he expresses with his use of "The cup in front of me contains decaffeinated coffee"—even though the *beliefs* are different. The present authors subscribe to the latter approach. Here, however, we are dealing with the propositional attitudes themselves, not the semantics of attitude reports. It is crucial for the strategy in Essay 12 that beliefs be concrete cognitive structures. It therefore fits well with Fodor's token-oriented approach. In his dissertation, Crimmins discusses a variety of ways in which attitudes could be concrete cognitive structures that are less language-like than mentalese is often taken to be (1989).

[121] Relativity to a possible world is a different matter.

[122] For present purposes, we are simply identifying volitions and *intentions in action*.

[123] But the first seems relative to a base—it's true base 10, false base 12—while the second depends on a frame of reference for fixing dates, which seems to smuggle in some noneternality.

tions, depending on such factors of the utterance as the agent, the time, the persons the agent is addressing, the objects the agent is attending to, and other wider circumstances. The class of context-sensitive sentences includes those with indexicals, demonstratives, tense markers, and, arguably, proper names. Thus if Jerry and Zenon each say, "The cup in front of me contains coffee," they express different propositions that may be true and false independently. Context-sensitive sentences in mentalese will work the same way; if Jerry and Zenon each have "The cup in front of me contains coffee" (= S) written in their belief structure, they will believe different things. But is there any reason to suppose that there are context-sensitive sentences in mentalese? What reasons would a psychological theory that adopted Fodor's language of thought hypothesis have to include such sentences in the language postulated?

Suppose Jerry and Zenon are each thirsty, and each has a cup of coffee in front of him. They each execute movement M, and each satisfies his desire. Both the similarities and differences are easy to conceive, if we suppose that the beliefs Jerry and Zenon have are context-sensitive—in particular, if what they believe, in virtue of the occurrence of a token of S in their heads, is systematically related to the same simple fact about that token, namely in whose head it does occur. For instance, we can imagine that Jerry and Zenon have different instances of a certain type V of visual impression;[124] that because of these impressions a token of S is written in the belief structure of each; and that this, given the presence of "I drink coffee" in the desire structure of each, causes a token of "I pick up the cup in front of me and drink from it," to be written in their volitional structure, which causes each of them to execute M. Jerry and Zenon thus go through the same succession of states, and these processes are instances of the same psychological law. But Jerry and Zenon see, believe, desire, intend, and do different things. In particular, what Jerry believes could be true, while what Zenon believes is false, and vice versa. What Jerry believes (that there is a cup in front of Jerry) would not be a good reason for Zenon to execute M. It might be true that there is a cup in front of Jerry, while there is an irritable gorilla in front of Zenon. Executing M in these circumstances would not be a good idea.

We want to emphasize that it is also important to have beliefs that are less sensitive to context. Consider the case with which we began. Jerry does not just want coffee; he wants decaffeinated coffee. A moment or two ago, he saw that a certain cup contained decaffeinated coffee. Now suppose that since that time he has left the room; the cup became perceptually inaccessible to him. He needs to be able to store the relevant information about the cup, in a way that retains the same content through the change in context, as he diverts his attention from the cup and leaves the room, and throughout the [short] interval of his

---

[124]We are supposing then that they are similarly situated with respect to their respective cups, insofar as their perceptual apparatus is concerned.

absence. And he needs to retain it in a form that will allow him to reidentify the cup upon his return and make use of his knowledge. This requires a way of thinking of the cup that continues to pick out that particular cup through the changes of context. This way of thinking will probably be context-sensitive, but not as context-sensitive as the way of thinking of the cup that is associated with a contemporaneous visual perception of it. For example, he might think of it as "the cup I saw at my table a moment ago." This way of thinking does not shift its reference as Jerry moves about or shifts his attention to other objects.

A (relatively) basic physical action, like the execution of M, has different results depending on who does it, when, and in what circumstances. A system of beliefs should lead to the actions that will be successful, relative to one's desires, in the circumstances that make the beliefs true. But humans do not just depend on their perceptions at the time of action to provide them with the beliefs needed for decision and volition, but earlier perceptions, inferences, and the perceptions and inferences of others. In all of these cases in which the pragmatic effect of information is delayed or distanced, ways of preserving content through change of context are needed. It would be very misguided to take the simple and relatively automatic case of picking up a cup of coffee when thirsty as a complete guide to the role of the attitudes. Still, the need for context-sensitive representation never goes away. If he wants to drink the coffee, Jerry still has to pick up the cup in front of him.

Consider, for a different example, Jerry's making a phone call to Zenon. Here the belief, say, "Zenon's phone number is 555-5555," is relatively context-insensitive. There is the present tense marker, but phone numbers are relatively stable properties of persons, so we can ignore that. When Jerry calls Zenon, the perceptions that originally gave rise to the belief may be remote in time, and the effect of the action that fulfills the goal—the ringing of Zenon's telephone and his answering it—are remote in space. Neither the number nor Zenon needs to be thought of demonstratively or indexically to understand the transaction. But, like all human action—except perhaps pure ratiocination—the crux of the matter involves physical interactions with a physical object. The practical reasoning involved will terminate with some context-sensitive way of thinking about the telephone. The Fodorian version of half of Kant's maxim about concepts and intuitions should be "Eternal tokens of mentalese without context-sensitive tokens of mentalese are blind."

The Basic Concepts

A Fodorian Model of Cognition

We have so far been supposing a Fodorian model; we shall now sketch an extremely simple version of a mentalese account of the structure of cognitive states. We note that states are repeatable types; we shall speak of instances of such. Instances are concrete, nonrepeatable episodes. We shall assume that there are three functionally specified components of the mental states of our agent: the belief component, the appetitive component, and the volitional component. These three components are realized in three distinct, but connected, concrete structures. Conceived of abstractly, that is, functionally, each of these is like a file, into which tokens of sentences are read, in which they can be stored and manipulated in various ways, and from which they can be read. We shall further assume that mentalese is a lot like English; indeed, we shall assume that it is English.[125] With reference to the first example, we might expect to find the following in Jerry's mind:

- In the belief structure, a token of "The cup in front of me has decaffeinated coffee in it."
- In the appetitive structure, a token of "I drink some decaffeinated coffee."
- In the volitional structure, a token of "I pick up the cup and bring it to my lips."

These tokens are concrete structures, characterizable in many different ways. We have classified them by their syntactic type, given that they are tokens of English. This leaves open many difficult questions about the relations between type and token; we shall ignore these here. We can classify agents in many different ways, too, of course. We introduce three relational symbols, $thinks_B$, $thinks_D$, and $thinks_V$ for the relations that hold of an agent A, a time t, and a type T, just in case there is a token of type T in A's belief (appetitive, volitional) structure at t. We shall usually ignore the temporal relatum. We shall also treat these symbols as if they were transitive verbs. Thus $thinking_D$ "I drink some decaffeinated coffee" is an appetitive state and is also a (partial) mental state. Many different agents, at different times and locations, can be in that mental state, with or without being in the $thinks_B$ state we supposed Jerry to be in. Of course, no two instances of these states are identical; we leave open the possibility that a single agent, at a single time, can have two distinct tokens of the same type in one of its mental structures.

Following Fodor, we shall assume that there is a single central processor, which can read the tokens in the various structures and can perform various operations on them. The processor is a deterministic device. In this respect, then, the agent's psychology is lawlike. We further assume that every agent of a given kind or species has the same kind of central processor, and indeed this is partly definitive of what we mean by a kind or species of agent. Of course, different experiences will have led to quite different sentences being written in the structures of various agents of the same species.

---

[125]We hope it is clear that this assumption is for the sake of simplicity, not chauvinism.

As noted, the psychologies of our agents are lawlike. There are laws relating the various states. Here is a candidate law, implausibly simple, that we will assume to hold:

> ($\mathcal{L}$): If an agent $thinks_B$ "The cup in front of me has decaffeinated coffee in it," and $thinks_D$ "I drink some decaffeinated coffee," it will (normally or *ceteris paribus*) come to $think_V$ "I pick up the cup and bring it to my lips."

The above statement of the law conceals reference to tokens of the displayed types, but for there to be laws like $\mathcal{L}$, or like $\mathcal{L}$ except for being much more complex, the syntactic type of a mentalese token must be a property of tokens that the processor can detect. We assume that the processor can only detect local, physical properties of the tokens. It is not quite clear what this includes, but there are a number of things that are clearly not included. For example, the processor cannot detect anything about the cup or the coffee. This is not to say that the agent's sensors cannot detect such things; nor is it to say that the agent cannot. In any event the law, as stated, is quite independent of the meaningfulness of the tokens and of whatever particular contents they have.

We need to make three points about $\mathcal{L}$ and the extremely simple psychology it reflects. First, we are ignoring background beliefs and a number of interesting questions they raise. The use of the phrase "normally or *ceteris paribus*" is simply an indication that we are aware of these issues, not an attempt to treat them.[126] Second, we are making no allowance whatsoever for weighing the pros and cons of various alternative courses of action or for deliberation to resolve conflicts among appetites. Finally, we are using the volitional structure to model central motor control functions. Belief states and appetitive states lead to volitional states; these, in turn, cause bodily movements. A given volitional structure could be wired up to the wrong kind of body, one that had nothing like hands with opposable digits, or to a body with arms that were too short, etc. It could also be ill-wired to the right kind of body. We ignore all such unhappy possibilities.

A Semantics for Mentalese

We assume that a cognitive psychology assigns contents to tokens of mentalese in virtue of (i) the basic meanings associated with the types of the tokens and (ii) other facts. These other facts we gather into the following basic categories:

(A) Facts about the tokens themselves, specifically whose head they occur in (or, as we shall say, who owns them), and when; these facts determine the reference of such indexicals as "I," "me," and "now."

---

[126] Also, see below §5. We basically agree with Fodor that the laws of psychology will be *ceteris paribus* laws (1987, 4ff). But we suspect that physical laws are as dependent on *ceteris paribus* clauses as any others. See Cartwright 1986.

(B) Facts about the owners of the tokens, such as which objects they are attending to, talking to, and the like. These facts, together with facts of category (A), determine the reference of indexicals and demonstratives such as "you," "he," "her," and the like.

(C) Other facts that may be relevant, together with facts of categories (A) and (B), in determining the reference of definite descriptions and perhaps names.[127] This may include facts that are not in any clear and intuitive sense about either the token itself or its owner.

We take the meanings associated with the types to be functions from circumstances to contents, where contents may have as constituents individuals external to the mind of the agent. In these respects, our semantics follows the semantics for "schemata" in chapter 10 of Barwise and Perry 1983. But we differ with that approach in two related ways. First, we do not assign a single content to a token. Each token will have three contents: a fully opaque content, an opaque content, and a transparent content. Second, we do not take the function from context to content(s) to be the basic fact about meaning, but to result from a basic assignment of *token reflexive conditions of truth*. Thus our semantics will assign (up to) three contents to each expression: truth conditions—which we will take to be the fully opaque content—opaque, and transparent content. All are assigned circumstantially.

The following is an attempt to indicate the form of our semantic account by treating the sentence "The cup in front of me contains decaffeinated coffee" in some detail. We start with the content of the terms "me" and "the cup in front of me":

$$T = \text{"me"}$$

1. Basic condition of reference for a token t of T = *being the owner of t*.
2. Opaque content of t (condition of reference, given that Jerry owns t) = *being [identical to] Jerry*.
3. Transparent content of t (condition of reference given that Jerry owns t and any other facts) is the same as the opaque condition = *being Jerry*.

$$T = \text{"the cup in front of me"}$$

1. Basic condition of reference for a token t of T = *being the unique cup in front of the owner of t*.
2. Opaque content of t (condition of reference, given that Jerry owns t) = *being the unique cup in front of Jerry*.
3. Transparent content of t (condition of reference, given that Jerry owns t and that c is the cup in front of Jerry) = *being c*.

---

[127] Fodor's remarks on transparency, opacity, and full opacity are not too definitive with respect to names, and we steer clear of them in this essay.

T = "The cup in front of me contains decaffeinated coffee."

1. Basic condition of truth for a token t of T = *Someone x is the owner of t, something y is the unique cup in front of x, and y contains decaffeinated coffee.*
2. Opaque content of t (condition of truth, given that Jerry is the owner of t) = *Something y is the unique cup in front of Jerry, and y contains decaffeinated coffee.*
3. Transparent content of t (condition of truth, given that c is the cup in front of Jerry) = *c contains decaffeinated coffee.*

To get at the level 1 and 2 contents (fully opaque and opaque), we shall use the sentences "The cup in front of the owner of t contains decaffeinated coffee" and "The cup in front of Jerry contains decaffeinated coffee." When we do this, we will be using the descriptions *attributively*. Thus in the first sentence, t is referred to, but the owner of t and the cup are not referred to. In the second, Jerry is referred to, but the cup is not.

We use the notions of *loading* and *unloading* to get at relations between the fully opaque and the opaque, and the opaque and the transparent contents of a token of T. Loading is an operation that takes us from a proposition that contains a complex property, like being the owner of t, to a proposition that contains an object that uniquely instantiates the property, like Jerry. More precisely, we load a proposition with respect to a complex property and a set of circumstances. In going from level 1 to level 2, we are loading the proposition with respect to the property of being the unique owner of t and the circumstance that Jerry is that owner. In going from level 2 to level 3, we are loading the 2-level proposition with respect to the property of being the unique cup in front of Jerry, and the circumstance that c is that cup. Unloading is just the opposite of loading. The proposition that the cup in front of Jerry contains coffee is the result of unloading the proposition that c contains coffee with the circumstance that c is the cup in front of Jerry.[128]

We take the truth conditions of a mentalese token to be its fully opaque content. This is the only content it has that depends only on the form of the token and the interpretive function.

We said at the beginning of this essay, "Fodor takes propositional attitudes to be relations to tokens of an internal language ... that have content. If Jerry believes that S, Jerry has a token of mentalese in his belief structure that has the content that S." The picture we have arrived at requires an account that is a bit more complicated, however. First, we should note that when the context of the

---

[128] In Israel and Perry 1990, we sketch a theory of propositions, within a version of situation theory, in which these notions can be given precise, formal embodiments. Notice that the operation of unloading is *not* analogous to the allegedly impossible operation of going from a denotation (or reference) to a sense. The circumstantial fact, together with the object, determines the complex, typically relational, property.

attitude reporter and the agent differ, different sentences will be required to get at the same content. Thus to report what Jerry believes in virtue of his having a token of "I am sitting" in his belief structure, I'll have to say something like "Jerry believes that he is sitting" or "The author of 'Methodological Solipsism' believes that he is sitting." If I use a token of the same sentence, and say "Jerry believes that I am sitting," I do not convey the right message.

Second, we now have three levels of content. We shall introduce subscripts and say things like

Jerry $believes_{FO}$ ($desires_{FO}$) that ...

Jerry $believes_{O}$ ($intends_{O}$) that ...

Jerry $believes_{T}$ ($desires_{T}$) that ...

This notation is not really adequate, since there are cases in which one term in a content sentence should be taken opaquely and another transparently. For the purposes of this essay, however, this notation will suffice.

We should emphasize that $believes_{FO}$ is *not* one of our ordinary belief concepts. In the ordinary senses (opaque and transparent) of "believes," people do not usually believe the fully opaque content of their beliefs, since most people do not have beliefs about tokens of mentalese in their heads. And note further that even for people who do have such beliefs, the belief in the fully opaque content of a belief token b will not be the belief one has in virtue of having b. To see this, note that Jerry and Georges might both believe, of Jerry's belief token b, that the cup in front of the owner of it contains decaffeinated coffee. Imagine Jerry and Georges are talking about mentalese, using one of Jerry's beliefs as an example, while Jerry drinks decaffeinated coffee. This belief about Jerry's token is not the same belief that Jerry has in virtue of having the token. This may seem a bit puzzling. But suppose that Jerry uttered "The cup in front of me contains decaffeinated coffee." Call the utterance u. The belief about u, that the cup in front of the person who made it contains decaffeinated coffee, has to be distinguished from what Jerry said (the proposition he expressed) with u. What Jerry said could be true, even if he never spoke, and u never existed. This is analogous to the belief case, and perhaps will make it seem less puzzling. Our ordinary propositional attitude reports simply do not focus on fully opaque content.

So we have to be careful with $believes_{FO}$ and remember that its meaning derives from the theory, not from common usage. Saying that Jerry $believes_{FO}$ that the cup in front of the owner of b contains decaffeinated coffee is just saying that b is a token in Jerry's head, whose fully opaque content is that the cup in front of its owner contains decaffeinated coffee. Jerry does not believe this in the ordinary sense. That is, he does not $believe_{O}$ it. Georges does $believe_{O}$ it, but does not $believe_{FO}$ it. So, of Georges, but not of Jerry, it can be said that he believes that the cup in front of the owner of b contains decaf.

Rational Laws and Adequate Explanations

The basic idea of a rational law is this. Suppose a belief and a desire cause an action. Then the action should promote the satisfaction of the desire, given the truth of the belief. This is a version of Fodor's point in the initial quotation, which we have made before with respect to our example. Jerry's belief that the cup in front of him contains decaffeinated coffee and his desire to have decaffeinated coffee lead him to will to move in a way that results, if the belief is true, in his desire being satisfied. There is surely something quite appropriate about this. Suppose Jerry's belief and desire led him instead to a movement that results in splashing the coffee into his forehead. That would in some sense be inappropriate. As Fodor points out, it is perfectly conceivable that beliefs and desires, conceived as internal states, should have such inappropriate effects, but such effects of beliefs and desires are not what cognitive psychology is all about—they are not grist for the cognitivist's mill.

It will help discussion to define a relation among four propositions P, R, Q, and C, thought of as the contents of a belief, a volition, and a desire, and background conditions: (the belief that) P *rationalizes* (bringing it about that) R, relative to (the desire that) Q, given (the condition that) C. We will write this

$$Rationalizes_Q(P, R \mid C)$$

We think of this relation as one of *incremental rationality*.

> If C is given, then if P is true also, bringing it about that R will guarantee (or at least promote) bringing it about that Q.[129]

To see one source of the need for, and role of, the background condition, consider the fully opaque contents of the tokens in our basic example. Let P = the proposition that the cup in front of the owner of b contains decaffeinated coffee, Q = that the owner of d (a token of "I drink decaffeinated coffee") drinks decaffeinated coffee, and R = that the owner of v picks up the cup in front of him and brings it to his lips. Then it is not the case that bringing it about that R is true will bring it about that Q is true, if P is true—*without the further condition that b, d, and v belong to the same agent*. This is our reason for saying that without some appeal to circumstances, the rationality of laws of cognitive psychology cannot be understood.[130]

Now consider a law, like our $\mathcal{L}$, to the effect that a belief token b of type

---

[129]Since P, Q, and so on, are propositions, and since we assume that the whole clause "that S" (where S is a sentence) refers to a proposition, consistency would dictate saying "the belief S" rather than "the belief that S." But it sounds better the inconsistent way.

[130]This should not be taken to exclude the necessity of other background conditions as well, such as that the movement is taking place in the Earth's gravitational field. Some background conditions might themselves be the contents of the agent's background beliefs; the condition just noted is not likely to be one of those. See below.

B and a desire d of type D, in the same agent, will cause that agent to have a volition v of type V. Such a law is *rational* if for every b, d, and v that instantiate it,

$$Rationalizes_{Con_{FO}(d)}(Con_{FO}(b), Con_{FO}(v) \mid C)$$

where $Con_{FO}(b)$ is the fully opaque content of b, and where C is the condition that b, d, and v belong to the same agent (and conditions are normal). When beliefs and desires cause volitions in accord with such laws, we can say that they motivate in two senses. The belief and desire cause the volition, and they rationalize it.

We should say a word about *normal conditions*. In our conception of cognitive psychology, the specification of an environment, which includes specification of a range of normal conditions, will be an important part of the psychological theory for a kind or species of agent. In our conception, agents are attuned to certain environments, and the apparatus of perception and belief is used to pick up and store information about factors that vary within those limits. We see the circumstantial nature of thought as one aspect of this attunement. The way visual information is used to guide our hands, for example, involves attunement to the normal relations between the orientation of limbs and the orientation of eyes. Such attunement only goes so far, however, and that is where the function of systems of storable, manipulable, relatively context-insensitive representations come to the fore—for instance, as they are involved in belief. These points are rather tangential to our main aim in this essay, however.

The conception of a rational law explained a few paragraphs earlier makes it clear that fully opaque explanations, involving rational laws, would be fine. By subsuming behavior under causal laws, they would also subsume it under rational laws. But as we mentioned, we do not ordinarily use attitude reports to attribute fully opaque belief—what we say when we say "Jerry believes that ..." is not understood on the model "Jerry *believes*$_{FO}$ that...." We want then to consider how explanations using ordinary opaque and transparent attitude attributions could be adequate, and how they can go wrong.

The basic idea is as follows. When we explain an action in terms of a belief and a desire, we are basically explaining the occurrence of a volition of a sort for which the action is a more or less basic mode of execution.[131] The explanation will be correct only if it can be unloaded down to an instance of a rational law where the consequent volition is so executable. To see what this means, let us work through our example.

Consider this explanation of Jerry's executing movement M, thereby pick-

---

[131] The route from action to volition will be more complex when the the context of explanation includes background about other beliefs and desires of the agent that could be involved in more complex strategies of execution.

ing up c and bringing it to his lips:

> Jerry believes c contains decaffeinated coffee and desires that he drink some decaffeinated coffee.

What does this come to? Here's what:

- Jerry $believes_T$ that c contains decaffeinated coffee in virtue of $believing_O$ that the cup in front of him contains decaffeinated coffee together with the external circumstance that c is the cup in front of him. He $believes_O$ this in virtue of owning a belief b whose fully opaque content is that the cup in front of the owner of b contains decaffeinated coffee.

- Jerry $desires_O$ that he drink some decaffeinated coffee in virtue of owning a desire d whose fully opaque content is that the owner of d drink some decaffeinated coffee.

- Movement M is a basic way of executing a volition v whose fully opaque content is that the owner of v pick up the cup of coffee in front of him.

- Given the assumption that there is a rational law like $\mathcal{L}$ above, the belief and desire cited explain the action.

Now consider the case in which Jerry looks in the mirror. Here he does not actually perform any action. But we want to understand why, knowing about his belief and desire, we should not expect an action such as his reaching for the cup by executing movement M.

The type of the volition and the desire are just as before. Further, Jerry again $believes_T$ that c contains decaffeinated coffee in virtue of $believing_O$ that the cup in front of him contains decaffeinated coffee, in the circumstance in which c is the cup in front of him. He $believes_O$ this, however, in virtue of owning a token b' with the fully opaque content that the cup in front of the man whom the owner of b' is watching contains decaffeinated coffee. The belief b', the desire d, and a volition v of which the (missing) action would be an execution are not instances of a rational law. They are not instances of $\mathcal{L}$, because the fully opaque content of the belief is not right. Moreover, if there were a law linking beliefs of this type, with this fully opaque content, with desires and volitions of the types of d and v, it would not be rational. Lucky folks like Jerry would get a drink of coffee, but in most cases the agent would be knocking over things, pawing empty space, or irritating irritable gorillas.[132]

---

[132]The research reported in this paper has been made possible by a gift from the System Development Foundation.

15

Davidson's Sentences and Wittgenstein's Builders

Words stand for things of various kinds and for various kinds of things. Because words do this, the sentences made up of words mean what they do, and are capable of expressing our thoughts, our beliefs and conjectures, desires and wishes. This simple idea seems right to me, but it flies in the face of formidable authority. In a famous passage in "Reality without Reference," Donald Davidson criticizes what he calls the "building-block theory":

> [T]he essential question is whether [reference] is the, or at least one, place where there is direct contact between linguistic theory and events, actions, or objects described in nonlinguistic terms. If we could give the desired analysis or reduction of the concept of reference then all would, I suppose, be clear sailing. Having explained directly the semantic features of proper names and simple predicates, we could go on to explain the reference of complex singular terms and complex predicates, we could characterize satisfaction (as a derivative concept), and finally truth. This picture of how to do semantics is (aside from the details) and old and natural one. It is often called the building-block theory. It has often been tried. And it is hopeless. (Davidson, 1980, pp. 134–135)

The picture I find attractive and Davidson finds confused and hopeless seems to be the very one Wittgenstein saw in Augustine. At the beginning of the *Philosophical Investigations* he quotes a passage from Augustine, and finds in Augustine's words "a particular picture of the essence of human language," that goes like this:

> [T]he individual words in language name objects—sentences are combinations of such names.—In this picture of language we find the roots of the following idea: Every word has a meaning. This

271

meaning is correlated with the word. It is the object for which the word stands. (Wittgenstein, 1953, p. 2)

Davidson and Wittgenstein seem to be in considerable agreement about this picture, for similar reasons. Both Wittgenstein and Davidson insist that the interpretation of language derives from its connection with human action; Wittgenstein introduces his concept of a language game, and Davidson emphasizes the idea that semantic terms are to be explained by being connected with "human ends and activities" (Davidson, 1980, p. 137). Wittgenstein quotes with apparent approval Frege's dictum that words only have meaning as parts of sentences, one of Davidson's favorite passages.[133]

Nevertheless, there are important differences between what Wittgenstein and Davidson reject about the building block picture. Wittgenstein's main point is that we need to understand the phenomenon of words having meaning by reference to their role in the fabric of human action, as opposed, say, to their being associated with internal images. It may be, for all the considerations he raises show, that reference is the point or one of the points where linguistic theory makes contact with human intentions and actions. In fact, in this essay I'll use Wittgenstein's language game involving a builder and his assistant to argue that this is so.

Davidson's Sentence Holism

Davidson claims that the building block theory is wrong because direct contact between linguistic theory and events, actions and objects described in nonlinguistic terms must be made at the level of sentences, not at the level of individual words, and must be made via the concept of truth, rather than that of reference:

> Words have no function save as they play a role in sentences: their semantic features are abstracted from the semantic features of sentences, just as the semantic features of sentences are abstracted from their part in helping people achieve goals or realize intentions. If the name 'Kilimanajaro' refers to Kilimanajaro, then no doubt there is some relation between English- (or Swahili-) speakers, the word, and the mountain. But it is inconceivable that one should be able to explain this relation without first explaining the role of the word in sentences; and if this is so, there is no chance of explaining reference directly in nonlinguistic terms.... (Davidson, 1980, p. 135)

---

[133]Wittgenstein (1953), p. 24. Of course I don't really know how Davidson feels about various passages from Frege, but I do recall that he cites this one a lot. The closest Davidson comes to quoting the dictum in this particular paper is by citing a paper of Wallace's that takes the dictum as its title.

> When it comes to interpreting [a Tarski-style theory of truth] as a whole, it is the notion of truth, as applied to closed sentences, which must be connected with human ends and activities. (Davidson, 1980, p. 137)

The thought here comes in two parts. First, the meaning of words is to be explained by their connection with human actions and the beliefs, desires and intentions that motivate them. Second, this means that the connection must be made at the level of sentences. I'll suppose that Davidson's position would allow that the connection could be made at the level of imperatives as well as declaratives, however. Corresponding to truth-conditions for declaratives we will have compliance-conditions for imperatives.

Why sentences? Perhaps the simplest answer is because it is sentences that express thoughts. This is not just something we learn in elementary school; it is shown by the structure of propositional attitude constructions:

(1) Harold believes that Russia is in turmoil.

(2) Gretchen wants Elwood to close the door.

In (1), we characterize Harold's belief by a that-clause, and what does the descriptive work in this clause is the sentence "Russia is in turmoil." This is the sentence we use to describe Harold's belief, and it is the sentence we would expect him to use to express it. In (2), the tense-less sentence "Elwood to close the door" characterizes Gretchen's desire, and if she is in a suitable position of authority over Elwood, we would expect her to issue a request or a command using these very words.

The close connection between thoughts and sentences makes sentences a natural place to see meaning flowing from thought to language, according principles something like the following:

(A) If competent speakers assert S when they want their audiences to believe P, then utterances of S are true iff P.

(B) If competent speakers use S' to issue a command to X when they want X to do A, then such utterances are complied with iff X does A.

To elaborate on Davidson's example, suppose we have a corpus of sentences containing the word "Kilimanajaro," which are used to assert various things and request or command various things:

(3) Kilimanajaro is big.

(4) Kilimanajaro is cloudy.

(5) Kilimanajaro is a long ways away.

(6) Go climb Kilimanajaro.

(7) Look at Kilimanajaro.

(8) Point to Kilimanajaro.

Our linguist discovers the beliefs that motivate sincere speakers to utter such statements as (3), (4) and (5). She discovers the actions that will be deemed to comply with such imperatives as (6), (7), and (8). So there is a direct contact, in the linguistic theory, between these sentences and various intentions, goals and beliefs with various propositional contents (or involving the acceptance of various sentences, or whatever one wants); we list some of the facts that correspond to (3)–(8):

(F3) Sincere speakers utter (3) when they believe that Kilimanajaro is big and want their audience to believe this too.

(F6) Speakers with authority utter (6) when they want their audience to go climb Kilimanajaro

From this, we get the semantic theory, of which we list some of the postulated facts:

(S3) Utterances of (3) are true iff Kilimanajaro is big.

(S6) Utterances of (6) are complied with iff the audience of the utterance climbs Kilimanajaro.

Given the semantic facts about sentences, at least as our theorist has postulated them, a certain pattern emerges:

(P) When the word "Kilimanajaro" is found in a sentence, the truth or compliance conditions of utterances using that sentence will involve Kilimanajaro.

From this, our theorist derives the following.

(S9) "Kilimanajaro" stands for Kilimanajaro.

(S9) is not an additional fact about the language. It is a way of "summing up" a pattern that emerges in these facts.[134]

The rejected alternative is to suppose that the direct contact between language and the world is made at the level of reference. On this view, (S9) would not be derived from (S3)–(S8), but would be a fact that was part of the explanation of (S3)–(S8). But this would mean that (S9) would have to be based on some principles that link reference to nonlinguistic facts in the way that (A) and (B) link sentences to human goals and intentions. What would these principles be?

We might suppose that, say, the words are directly associated with images, so that "Kilimanajaro" was associated with an image of that mountain. This is the idea that is Wittgenstein's target, and Davidson also seems to associate

---

[134] Actually, if we take "abstraction" literally, more needs to be said; there is an important difference between claiming that the reference facts are derivative and claiming that they are abstractions.

the building-block theory with this idea.[135] Wittgenstein would argue that it wouldn't mean anything that the word was associated with an image of Kilimanajaro if the it didn't have the right role in the relevant language games, and if it did have the right role in the language games, then "Kilimanajaro" would stand for Kilimanajaro, no matter what connections there were between that word and images in ones mind.

So the argument comes to this.

(10) What makes (S9) true is that people use the word "Kilimanajaro" when they want to say something about Kilimanajaro, or when they want to request or command that something be done to, at or with Kilimanajaro.

(11) But saying something about Kilimanajaro, or commanding that something be done to, at or with Kilimanajaro, is done by uttering a sentence; it is the utterance of the sentence that has the property of being a statement about or command relating to Kilimanajaro.

(12) But that is to say that the semantic facts about "Kilimanajaro" derive from the semantic facts about the sentences of which it is a part.

I think that this argument is wrong, and that Wittgenstein's example of the builder's language game can show us why.

Wittgenstein's Builders

Early in the *Philosophical Investigations* Wittgenstein describes a simple language game:

> Let us imagine a language for which the description given by Augustine is right. The language is meant to serve for communication between a builder *A* and an assistant *B*. *A* is building with building-stones: there are blocks, pillars, slabs and beams. *B* has to pass the stones, and that in the order in which A needs them. For this purpose they use a language consisting of the words "block," "pillar," "slab," "beam." *A* calls them out;—*B* brings the stone

---

[135]Davidson's thoughts on the history of this idea are compact and can be quoted in full: "We have to go back to the early British empiricists for fairly clear examples of building-block theories (Berkeley, Hume, Mill). The ambitious attempts at behavioristic analyses of meaning by Ogden and Richards and Charles Morris are not clear cases, for these authors tended to blur the distinction between words and sentences ('Fire!', 'Slab!', 'Block!') and much of what they said applies intelligibly only to sentences as the basic atoms for analysis. Quine, in chapter II of *Word and Object*, attempts a behavioristic analysis, but although his most famous example ('Gavagai') is a single word, it is explicitly treated as a sentence. Grice, if I understand his project, wants to explain linguistic meaning ultimately by appeal to nonlinguistic intentions—but again it is the meaning of sentences, not of words, that are to be analyzed in terms of something else. The historical picture, much simplified, shows that as the problems became clearer and the methods more sophisticated, behaviorists and others who would give a radical analysis of language and communication have given up the building-block approach in favor of an approach that makes the sentence the focus of empirical interpretation." (Davidson, 1980, p. 135)

which he has learnt to bring at such-and-such a call..." (Wittgenstein, 1953, p. 3)

We can say, then, that in the builder's language the terms "block," "pillar," "slab," and "beam" stand for kinds of building stones, and that these kinds are the meanings of the words. This is what we would say looking at the language from the point of view of Augustine's picture, and, for this language game, Augustine's picture is correct.

The important point is that it is only because the words have a use in a web of activities—the orders given by the builder and the executions of those orders by the assistant—that the words have these meanings.

When the builder says "Slab," he performs a certain type of act, with certain success conditions. The success conditions are that the assistant passes a slab to him. The assistant knows the meanings of the words, if he performs the right actions when the words are given. One point Wittgenstein makes is that it is these actions are not images that may or may not appear in the assistant's mind that determine whether or not he has learned the language and knows the meanings of the words.

The point of the four words, then, seems to be to provide the builder with four different actions. Each of these types of actions will have success conditions: the assistant passes a slab, the assistant passes a block, etc. The actions are the same, except for the word the builder uses, and the success conditions are the same, except for the type of stone the assistant is to pass. Our remark that "Slab" stands for or means "slab" and so forth just seem to amount to describing the effect the utterance of each of these words has on the success conditions of the acts of which that utterance is a part.

In remark 6 Wittgenstein provides a nice metaphor for this point:

> "I set the brake up by connecting up rod and lever." — Yes, given the whole of the rest of the mechanism. Only in conjunction with that is it a brake-lever, and separated from its support it is not even a lever; it may be anything, or nothing. (Wittgenstein, 1953, p. 5)

In the case of the builder's language game, what is established is that the assistant will pass a building stone to the builder. If there were only one kind of building stone, that would be that. But since there are four kinds of stones, a question still remains once it is established that the builder needs a stone. The language, the choice given by the four words, provides a way of resolving this question. The role of the words has to be understood as the resolving of these questions. To say that "slab" stands for the slab and so forth is not incorrect, but it needs to be understood in the context of the *incremental* role the words make to the language game.

Now consider a more or less formal analysis of the builder's language game. For all we have said so far, it seems it might go like this:

(A) Analysis of Builder's Language Game

(A1) In the builders' language game, each utterance is a command of the form N where N is a noun.

(A2) A command N is executed if the assistant passes a building stone of type designated by N to the builder.

(A3) Blocks are designated by "Block," pillars by "Pillar," slabs by "Slab" and beams by "Beam."

Analysis (A) describes the builders language game as consisting of utterances of nouns. There is no mention of sentences. The nouns in BL do not occur as parts of sentences, and their meanings do not derive from the meanings of sentences, or their use from the use of sentences.

There is a direct connection here between words and extra-linguistic reality. The words are connected to the intentions and goals of the builder. The semantic facts listed in (A3) are not basic facts, and they are not based on connections between words and images. They are facts based on the role that individual words play in the articulation of a family of types of actions that are connected with the intentions and goals of the speaker.

The argument at the end of the last section is simply fallacious. To say that the semantic facts about words derive from the semantic facts about the commands of which they are a part is not to say that these facts derive from semantic facts about sentences of which they are a part. Words can play a role in the articulation of commands without being parts of sentences, and so can be connected with human goals and intentions without the mediation of sentences.

The idea that sentences are semantically basic would be brought to bear on the builders' language game as follows. The builder has the desire that the assistant pass him a slab, for example. The content of this desire is what gets communicated to the assistant. This is shown by the fact that the assistant, when he understands, then sets out to do something, and he can do either the right thing or the wrong thing. The utterance has compliance conditions, and the compliance conditions accord with the satisfaction conditions of the desire that motivated the utterance.

This seems to show that to understand the utterance, the assistant needs to understand grasp the content, *that I pass him a slab*. This is what he needs to make true in order to comply with the command, and to understand the command is to understand what one needs to do to comply with it. It seems then that the content of the builder's utterance is not just *slab*, the thing, but the proposition, *that the assistant bring a slab to the builder*. And this shows that "Slab" really isn't just a noun, standing for a kind of object, but a one word sentence, expressing a desire.

I think this argument confuses two quite different things, however. It is quite right that the content of the builder's command is the proposition that the assistant pass him a slab. But what is the contribution of the word "Slab" to the fact that the command has that interpretation? It is clearly the kind of object that is to be fetched.

Some Variations

The picture I want to suggest is that:

(i) Utterances have propositional contents, corresponding to the beliefs or desires the utterances express;

(ii) The propositional content of an utterance depends on the type of utterance and the circumstances of utterance—just as the properties of any act depend on the type of action and the circumstances in which it is done;

(iii) The job of a family of words (like the names for building stones in the builders' language) is to create a set of contrasting action types, so that performance of acts of the different types will have different propositional contents.

In the builders' language, there is a basic pattern of action and circumstance. The builder is speaking to the assistant during working hours; he is building something of stones, and the assistant is to help him by passing him the stones he needs. The four words create four action-types for the builder. Each type of action has its compliance conditions, bringing a slab, bringing a pillar, and so forth.

Only within this context, does the builder's saying, e.g., "Slab" amount to his expressing the command that the assistant is to pass a slab. Such an utterance is like connecting the rod and the lever—it amounts to what it does only in conjunction with certain circumstances. But now, given this, what is the contribution the individuals words make to the propositional content?

First, consider a case in which the builder's mumbles "Slab" and the assistant doesn't understand what command has been expressed. He knows that he is to fetch a building-stone of a certain kind, but he doesn't know which kind. When he realizes which word was spoken, he realizes which kind of stone he is to fetch. That is exactly the contribution that "Slab" makes. It is just this that we capture by saying that "Slab" stands for slab.

Next, compare this situation with the one in which there is no communication and no language involved at all. The builder works alone; when he wants a building stone he walks over to the piles of stones, picks one up, and brings it back to the building site. He goes down one of four paths to one of the four piles. Depending on which of the four piles he goes to, he gets a different kind of stone. So we have a basic pattern of action, and four different actions of this type, with four different results, that would be satisfactory for four different desires.

Now consider the sub-action of turning down the pillar path—call it "P" instead of the block, slab or beam path (call them "$B1$," "S" and "$B2$"). That sub-action determines that the overall action will be of a type that satisfies the desire to get a pillar, rather than the desire to get a slab, beam or block. That particular sub-action has a certain determinate contribution to make to the result of the whole act of which it is a part. It would be quite misguided to say that it was the turning alone which had the result that the builder got a pillar. However, given all of the other things that were set up, this is the effect of taking this sub-action rather than another.

That sub-action has that effect, because of a pre-existing fact, that this path leads to the pillars and not the slabs, beams, or blocks.

So what we have here is a pre-existing relation between a path and a kind: this path leads to pillars. And we have the path involved in one of four action-types. The result of the builder's action is due to the particular sub-action he chose, and the relation the path involved in that sub-action had to a certain kind of object.

Similarly, when our original builder says "Pillar," he performs a certain act that involves a certain object, the word "Pillar." That word has a pre-existing relationship to a certain kind of object: pillars. Its the relationship we call *standing for* or *referring*. The builder's utterance is a case of commanding that a pillar be passed, because of the type of action it was, and the pre-existing relation, reference, between the word involved in that type of action and a kind of stone.

There are of course a great many differences between the two cases. The fact that the path leads to the pillars does not depend on the habits of the builder and his assistant. The fact that the words "Pillar" means pillar does depend on the habits of the builder and his assistant. That is of course a tremendously important difference.

But the fact that the relationship depends on the habits of the builder and his assistant (and various other mental facts about them), does not mean that the relationship depends on a relationship between *sentences* involving the word "Pillar" and the truth or compliance conditions of those sentences. The two dependencies are just different issues.

One indication that this is so, is that the same fact could play such a role in determining the result of a number of different types of action. For there are many things that one could do, once one got to the end of the path, besides fetching the pillars. One could throw pillars or write graffiti on pillars or trip over pillars or learn what pillars were. In understanding how going down path P, rather than S or $B1$ or $B2$ determines that a given subtype of a pattern of action is writing graffiti on a pillar or learning what a pillar is or tripping over pillars, one appeals to the very same fact, that path P leads to pillars.

When we think of the builders' language, we think that there is a connection in the builder's and the assistant's minds between the words and the different kinds of blocks. (I am just using "minds" in the normal way, not contesting the somewhat behavior-oriented position Wittgenstein is advocating.) These connections may be the result of what the builder did to establish and teach his system to the assistant, a system he originated for the purposes of getting building stones brought to him. But one can easily imagine that the same connection could be used in new ways to create families of sub-actions for a given pattern of action. Suppose that as the builder grows frail and the assistant learns the trade, the builder has the assistant not only fetch blocks but, later in the day, place the blocks into a wall. The builder has the plans in his mind, though, and he indicates to the assistant at each step of the way what type of block should go in each place, using the four words. Now this is a different language game, in the sense that it is a different family of actions that the commands pick out. But I think it would be rather natural to suppose that once the builder has shown the assistant what the pattern of action was, he could use the very same words he had been using in the original language game and things would work fine. He would say "Block" and the assistant would put a block in the place designated, and so forth. Our analysis of this language game might look like this:

(B) Analysis of Second Language Game

(B1) In the builders' second language game each utterance u is a command of the form N where N is a noun and is accompanied by a pointing to a particular place in a wall that is being constructed.

(B2) A command u is executed if the assistant puts a building stone of the type designated by N in the place that the builder designates.

(B3) Blocks are designated by "Block," pillars by "Pillar," slabs by "Slab" and beams by "Beam."

Here clause (B3) is unchanged from (A3) of the analysis of the original language game. The difference between the two games is not in what the words stand for, but in the overall pattern of action to which each of them standing for what it does makes a differential contribution.

Issues and Answers

Davidson uses "Block" and "Slab" to illustrate the blurring of the distinction between words and sentences that Ogden and Richards and Morris indulged in.[136] And one might say, at this point, that all that I have said is beside the point, since the utterances in the builders' language game should be thought of as one-word sentences.

---

[136] See footnote 135.

I think when people say the utterances in question are "one word sentences" they have one conception of a sentence in mind, as that which conveys a complete thought. Since "Slab" conveys a complete thought, it must be a sentence, even though it does not meet some of the other conception of sentence-hood, like having both a noun phrase and a verb phrase.

Suppose someone asks you "Who will win the National League, Western Division this year?" and you reply, "San Francisco." Your reply clearly conveys the thought that San Francisco will win the pennant this year in the National League, Western Division, which is a complete thought. You can express this complete thought merely by saying the name of a city, because the other parts of the thought were, as one might put it, already in place.

Let us introduce a subclass of propositions, simple singular propositions. These may be identified with a major constituent (an n-ary relation) and a sequence of n minor constituents (individuals or nonindividuals of the appropriate sort to stand in relation R) and a polarity (1 or 0). So $\langle R, \langle a_1, \ldots, a_n \rangle, 1 \rangle$ is the proposition that $a_1, \ldots, a_n$ do stand in relation R, while $\langle R, \langle a_1, \ldots, a_n \rangle, 0 \rangle$ is the proposition that they do not stand in that relation.

Let us say that an issue is a type of simple proposition that is missing one element. The missing element I indicate with a question mark. So here are some propositions with an element missing, and the questions that would naturally express them:

$\langle Kills, \langle A, ? \rangle, 1 \rangle$	Who did A kill?
$\langle Kills, \langle ?, B \rangle, 1 \rangle$	Who killed B?
$\langle Kills, \langle A, B \rangle, ? \rangle$	Did A kill B or not?
$\langle ?, \langle A, B \rangle, 1 \rangle$	What did A do to B?

Whenever there is an issue "in the air," one can express a complete thought by supplying an answer, the missing propositional ingredient. One typically does this with a noun or a verb, rather than with a complete sentence.

I am not too concerned here with how we should treat answers to questions. My point is that there are two rather different ways of expressing complete thoughts. One can, out of the blue, utter a sentence that identifies all the necessary propositional constituents for a thought, as when I say, in the middle of a paper on the philosophy of language intended for an audience in Austria,

(10) San Francisco will win the Western Division of the National League this year

I'll call this "constructing a complete thought." It is quite a different thing to do what I'll call "completing a thought." This is what I do when the issue of who will win the Western Division of the National League this year is in the air, perhaps because someone has asked that question, and I merely say,

(11) San Francisco

Here my words are responsible for completing the thought by introducing the last needed constituent to form a proposition. It is like Wittgenstein's connecting the rod and the lever to complete the brake assembly. The point goes both ways. Surely, in the absence of the rest of the assembly, just connecting the rod and the lever doesn't amount to much of anything. But, on the other hand, in the situation in which the rest of the assembly is in position, and connecting the rod and the lever is all that remains to finish the brake assembly, that connection doesn't amount to constructing the entire assembly, only completing it.

Suppose I claim to be able to express an important law of physics in one word. You challenge me, and we put some money on it. So I tell you, "Ask me whether falling object near the surface of the earth accelerate and 32 feet per second per second." You do so, and I say, "Yes." Have I won the bet? We may or may not say that I have uttered a one word sentence, but we should not fool ourselves. I have completed a thought with a word, but not constructed one.

Now in these cases, one word can complete a thought because of the other propositional constituents have been introduced linguistically, by the words spoken by the person who asked the question. In the builder's case, however, it is not language that has introduced the other constituents. They are present in the situation not because they have been introduced, but because a number of things about the builder's interaction with his assistant have been established by custom or tradition—it is what they do every day, and they never do anything else. The job of the assistant is to bring building stones to the builder. In a more complex language game the builder might need a verb, to tell the assistant whether to get or take or make or break a stone, but a verb isn't necessary, because it is established that the pattern of action is getting a building stone.

If by language we mean words that are spoken, written or signed, then language has a very small job to do in this case. An issue is in the air:

$$\langle \text{ Bring-to-x-a-stone-of-type-y}, \langle \text{ the Builder, ?} \rangle, 1 \rangle$$

No doubt the missing component is the type of stone. Supplying it is the only job that language has in this game. It is all that is missing, it is the link between the rod and the lever in an otherwise complete brake assembly. The choice of words, by indicating the choice of stones, indicates the choice of action that will comply with the builder's wishes.

Tarski's Style

Thus far I have talked freely in ways that Davidson eschews, of such things as propositions and contents. But the claim I am criticizing was:

> When it comes to interpreting [a Tarski-style theory of truth] as
> a whole, it is the notion of truth, as applied to closed sentences,
> which must be connected with human ends and activities.

One might suspect that if we cleave to the bracketed qualification, Davidson has a case to make. But the points I have been making come out rather clearly when we consider a Tarksi-style theory.

Two initial points. First, look closely at the assertion Davidson makes about interpreting Tarski-style theories. Divide it into two parts:

(a) The notion of truth is what gets connected with human ends and activities;

(b) The notion of truth that gets connected to human ends and activities is truth *applied to closed sentences*.

These are quite different claims; one can accept the first and reject the second. It seems to me that one who follows the argument in Davidson's "Truth and Meaning" should do exactly that.

The dimly remembered picture one might have of this essay is that the Tarski-style theory recommended for analysis of natural languages was full of things that looked like this:

(12) s is true iff p

where "s" is a mention of a closed sentence in the object language and "p" is a use of a sentence in the theorist's language. The picture that Davidson's claim brings to mind is that these postulates connect the linguistic objects the theory is about to their truth-conditions via the theorist's language. This connection then spreads out via the rest of the theorists language to descriptions of the ends and activities of the humans whose linguistic objects are in question. Hence, (a) it is the notion of truth that gets connected and (b) it is a sentence, namely s, to which truth is applied.

However, this picture ignores one of the later results in "Truth and Meaning," that to be applied to languages that contains demonstratives, a Tarski-style theory needs revision (Davidson, 1967a, pp. 320ff.). This is to say that such revision is required to apply this style of theory to natural language, since demonstratives are a universal feature of natural languages.

Here is one example of what a postulate in a suitably revised Tarski-style theory might look like:

(13) "That book was stolen" is true as (potentially) spoken by p at t if and only if the book demonstrated by p at t is stolen prior to t.

Here, unlike (12), we need a lot more than a sentence to get the truth predicate applied. We need a person, a time and a demonstrated book. The person and the time become relata of the truth-relation for Davidson; what about the book?

The knowledge expressed by (13) appears to include an understanding of the conditions under which the sentence "That book was stolen" can be assigned truth-conditions. There must be a demonstrated book. That is, the linguistic knowledge expressed by (13) includes knowledge of the setting in which a certain kind of linguistic object—in this case a sentence containing a demonstrative—makes contact with truth. In a Tarski-style theory of truth, suitably revised to be serviceable for natural languages, linguistic objects, speakers, and times have truth applied to them, in such settings.

Let us grant point (a) here. Truth is the notion that is applied. What is it applied to? A person, time and sentence. But now—why a sentence? What is it in the structure of (13) that demands a sentence as the linguistic object to which (together with a person and time) the notion of truth gets applied?

The answer was clear enough with (12).

(12) s is true iff p

Nothing but a sentence would make sense on the left; what other part of speech on the left could be, without any supplementation or augmentation, connected by "is true iff" with a sentence on the right? But that rationale for preferential treatment for sentences is gone with (13). Consider:

(14) "sleeps" is true as (potentially) spoken by p at t if and only if the object under discussion by p at t sleeps.

(15) "Reagan" is true as (potentially) spoken by p at t if and only if Reagan meets the condition under discussion by p at t.

Point (a) remains inviolate in a theory that includes such things as (14) and (15). But point (b) is lost. The linguistic objects that truth is applied to are not closed sentences, but sub sentential expressions.

Given such postulates, our linguist might introduce *reference* as the relation that holds between "Reagan" and things of its syntactic ilk and the objects truth depends on when these things are spoken by persons at times discussing conditions, and *expression* as the relation that holds between "was stolen" and things of its syntactic ilk and the conditions truth depends on when spoken by persons at times discussing things. The linguist might then explain the truth of sentences as deriving from reference and expression, in virtue of the fact that reference is a way of putting things into discussion, and expression is a way of putting conditions into discussion, and a sentence is a way of creating the sort of discussion required for truth when it's not already underway. The truth of "Reagan sleeps" is thus over determined, since both "Reagan" and "sleeps" will be true. A welcome result.

As far as I can see, the points made with the free and easy terminology and ontology of sections 1–5 are perfectly compatible with things done Tarksistyle—so long as one means the revised Tarksi style that could actually be applied to a natural language.

Conclusion

We need to distinguish between two claims:

(16) The meaning of individual words derives from their role in completing thoughts;

(17) The meaning of individual words derives from their role in sentences which construct complete thoughts.

Claim (16) is the conclusion that our consideration of Wittgenstein's language game leads us to. Reference is not a simple relationship between words and things, but one that rests on the way that words give us types of action that play a role in intentional human activity. The fact that 'Kilimanajaro' refers to Kilimanajaro has to do with the way people use the word to make statements and make requests and lots of other things.

But (16) is not the same as (17). When Davidson says that "it is inconceivable that one should be able to explain [the relation between speakers, 'Kilimanajaro' and Kilimanajaro] without first explaining the role of the word in sentences..." he is wrong. It is conceivable.[137]

---

[137]Thanks to Eros Corazza, David Israel, Jerry Seligman, Anil Gupta, Dagfinn Follesdal and Elizabeth Macken for comments on various version of this essay.

16

Evading the Slingshot

The topic of this essay is "the slingshot," a short argument that purports to show that sentences[138] designate (stand for, refer to) truth values. Versions of this argument have been used by Frege,[139] Church (1956, p. 25), Quine (1976, pp. 163–164) and Davidson (1967); thus it is historically important, even if it immediately strikes one as fishy. The argument turns on two principles, which I call substitution and redistribution. In "Semantic Innocence and Uncompromising Situations" (1981), Jon Barwise and I rejected both principles, as part of our attempt to dismantle the slingshot and defend the view that sentences stand for complexes of objects and properties rather than truth values. In his book *An Essay on Facts* (1987), Ken Olson maintains that our treatment turns on the structuralist conception of facts, and that this conception leads either to a block universe of co-implicating facts, or bare particulars. I'll first review the case against the slingshot, and then consider the issues Olson raises.

Do Sentences Designate?

As a preliminary we need to consider the very idea that sentences designate anything at all. We ordinarily talk about what terms refer to, stand for, or designate, but do not use these locutions with respect to sentences. Why should we? Because we want to systematically connect the designation of complex expressions with the designations of their parts. Many complex expressions have sentences as parts; to extend our principles of designation to such expressions, we need to accord designation to sentences.

Consider (1) and (2).

(1) The total number of votes Bush received

(2) The total number of votes Dukakis received

---

[138] One should really talk about uses of sentences, since (most) sentences do not have either truth conditions or truth values—the two candidates for designata we consider—except as used on a specific occasion. But since I won't discuss issues of context sensitivity, I'll stick with "sentence," which fits with most of the literature on the slingshot.

[139] Ken Olson discusses Frege and the slingshot in Olson, 1987, pp. 65–82.

It is natural to say that (1) and (2) designate numbers. (1) and (2) designate the numbers they designate, in part because "Bush" and "Dukakis" designate the persons they designate. This suggests the principle that the object an expression designates helps to determine the object larger expressions of which it is a part designate. An account of expressions of the common form of (1) and (2) would make this dependence clear:

Des("The total of number of votes α received") = The total number of votes Des(α) received.

Des is a function from an expression to its designation. We see in the principle how the designation of the part, Des(α) on the right hand side, contributes to the determination of the designation of the whole, the left hand side. Such principles identify two roles for designating expressions: being a part that contributes and being a larger whole that receives a contribution. Sentences can play both roles. If we can identify some factor connected with sentences that is systematically determined by what their parts designate, and is systematically determines that same factor with respect to the larger sentences of which they are parts, it will not be stretching things too far to call that factor what the sentence designates.

Sentences have factors associated with them that are systematically determined by what their parts designate, and sentences contribute something to the determination of this factor for the larger expressions of which they are parts. (3) and (4)

(3) Bush won.

(4) Dukakis won.

have different *truth conditions* and different *truth values*, because there is a difference in what "Bush" and "Dukakis" designate. These dependencies are reflected in this principle:

"α won" is true iff Des(α) won.

(3) and (4) are parts of (5) and (6):

(5) It is not the case that Bush won.

(6) It is not the case that Dukakis won.

The truth conditions and truth values of (5) and (6) clearly depend on the truth conditions and truth values of (3) and (4). (5) is false because (3) is true; (6) is true because (4) is false.

In the case of (5) and (6), we could take the designation of sentences to simply be truth values. But for a wide variety of cases, truth values do not seem to work as the designata of sentences. (7) and (8) are both true, while (9) is true and (10) false, so (7) and (8) must be contributing something besides their truth values to (9) and (10):

(7) $2 + 2 = 4$

(8) Königsburg is in Russia

(9) Necessarily $2 + 2 = 4$

(10) Necessarily Konigsburg is in Russia

Here it seems that the difference in truth *conditions* between (7) and (8) accounts for the difference in truth value of (9) and (10). The conditions of the truth of (7) are met no matter what, while those of (8) are quite contingent. So we might be inclined to think that at least for a wide range of cases we should accept (A)

(A) A sentence designates its truth conditions.

I'll present the slingshot as an attempt to show that (A) leads, in spite of its motivation, to truth values as the designata of sentences: even if we want truth conditions, we end up with truth values. Since we know that truth values won't work for cases like (7)–(10), this is an unwelcome result.

Intuitively, whether the truth conditions of a sentence are met or not will come down to which properties objects have and which relations they stand in. Two sentences that will be true if just the same objects have just the same properties and stand in just the same relations will have the same truth conditions. If sentences are the same in this way, its does not seem like it should matter how those conditions get presented or built up. These considerations appear to support two further principles:

(B) Substitution of one co-designating term for another does not affect the truth conditions of a sentence.

(C) Sentences whose truth requires the same objects to have the same properties have the same truth conditions, even if they differ in syntactic structure, and so construct requirements in different ways.

(A), (B) and (C) seem to guarantee two principles of "designation-preservation" for sentences.

Substitution: (From (A) and (B)) Substitution of one co-designating term for another does not effect what a sentence designates.

Redistribution: (From (A) and (C)) Rearrangement of the parts of a sentence does not effect what it designates, as long as the truth conditions remain the same.

The slingshot starts with a sentence, and then moves, by a series of substitution and redistribution steps to a completely different sentence. Since one gets from one sentence to the other by these steps, they must designate the same thing. But the only thing the sentences have in common are their truth values, so this must be what they designate. We'll look at two versions.

Two Slingshots

The first version is inspired by Church (Church, 1956):

C1. Scott is [the author of *Ivanhoe*].
C2. Scott is [the author of 29 *Waverley* novels altogether].
C3. 29 is [the number of Waverley novels Scott wrote altogether].
C4. 29 is [the number of counties in Utah].

The steps from C1 to C2 and C3 to C4 are substitution steps. The bracketed expressions in C1 and C2 designate the same object, Scott. The bracketed expressions in C3 and C4 designate the same object, the number 29. The step from C2 to C3 is a redistribution step. Since both substitution and redistribution preserve what is designated, C1 must designate the same thing C4 does. But then it seems like what is designated must just be truth values, for what else do C1 and C4 have in common?

The argument looks like a big trick. Let's call any property, relation or object designated by a simple expression in a sentence part of that sentence's subject matter. The step from C1 to C2 changes the subject matter; some of C1's *subject matter* is lost, and some new subject matter is introduced. In C3 the subject matter is redistributed, and in C4 substitution introduces new subject matter again, while jettisoning Scott, the last vestige of the original subject matter from C1 along with the novels introduced in C2.

Olson reconstructs a version the slingshot from Gödel's discussion of Russell. This argument looks too formal to contain a trick. One needs to assume that every sentence has an equivalent of the form $k(a)$, and that for any two objects there is some true sentence of the form $p(a, b)$ about their relationship. Let S and T be any two true sentences whatsoever, and $f(a)$ and $y(b)$ be their equivalents by the first assumption and $p(a, b)$ a true sentence by the second assumption. Then, if the first sentence in this series designates a certain object the rest should designate it also:

G1. S
G2. $\phi(a)$ (First Assumption)
G3. $a = \iota x[\phi(x)\&x = a]$ (Redistribution)
G4. $a = \iota x[\pi(x, b)\&x = a]$ (Substitution, Second Assumption)
G5. $\pi(a, b)$ (Redistribution A,B)
G6. $b = \iota x[\pi(a, x)\&x = b]$ (Redistribution)
G7. $b = \iota x[\psi(x)\&x = b]$ (Substitution, First Assumption)
G8. $\psi(b)$ (Redistribution)
G9. T (First Assumption)

We need to emphasize that steps G1–G9 do not represent an *inference* from G1 to G9. We started with the assumption that G1 and G9 were both true. Each step represents a different sentence that can be seen to designate the same thing as the preceding one. The citations on the right do not refer to principles of inference, but to our principles of preservation of sentence designation. So the claim is not that G5 follows from G4, but that, given various facts about the world, including G5 itself, they designate the same thing.

In spite of its formal appearance, this argument turns on the same trick as Church's. The relation π is not part of the subject matter of G3, but is part of the subject matter of G4, while ϕ is part of the subject matter of G3 but not of G4. ϕ gets smuggled out and π smuggled in via the substitution of one description for another. The way the argument works is that the substitution moves changes the subject matter of the descriptions, while the redistribution moves push subject matter back and forth between the descriptions and the predicates. By the time we reach G8, the subject matter has changed completely.

Truth Conditions and Substitution

As Gödel notes, Russell's theory of descriptions allows him to evade the slingshot. On Russell's theory descriptions are not part of the primitive notation at all. G3 and G4 seem to put the same condition (being identical with a) on the same objects (the ones designated by the descriptions). But on Russell's theory, the descriptions do not really designate anything because they are not really there. If we look at the primitive notation, we will be under no illusions about this:

G3′. $\exists x[(\phi(x)\&x = a)\&\forall y(\phi(y)\&y = a \to y = x)\&x = a]$

G4′. $\exists x[(\pi(x,b)\&x = a)\&\forall y(\pi(y,b)\&y = a \to y = x)\&x = a]$

The Substitution Principle does not get us from G3′ to G4′ because it does not apply, since the descriptions that are substituted do not occur.

It is not necessary to adopt Russell's theory to avoid the substitution principle, however. It's only necessary to think carefully about truth conditions. If one thinks of designata of sentences as complexes of properties and objects, as Barwise and I were doing, there is an obvious distinction to be made. Consider C1 and C2. Which properties, relations and objects are involved in the truth conditions of C1? Is it Scott twice over and identity? Or Scott, identity, authorship, and the novel *Ivanhoe*? If we take C1 and C2 the first way, they can be thought of as having the same truth conditions. But if we take them the second way, they do not. A condition of C1′'s truth is that Scott wrote *Ivanhoe*, while this is not a condition of C2′'s.

The situation will be a bit clearer if we shift examples. Consider the following two sentences:

(11) The author of *Tom Sawyer* grew up in Missouri

(12) The author of *Huckleberry Finn* grew up in Missouri

Do (11) and (12) have the same truth conditions? From one point of view, we might say that they do. The same fact, that Mark Twain grew up in Missouri, makes each of them true. From another point of view, it seems that they do not. For (11) to be true, someone needs to have both written *Tom Sawyer* and to have grown up in Missouri. But this could be true, while (12) was false, and vice versa.

Barwise and I said that there were two ways of building up facts from sentences like (11) and (12), depending on whether one took the descriptions as "value-loaded" or "value-free." The value-loaded interpretations are the same, complexes of Twain, Missouri and the relation of growing up in; the value-free interpretations are different. The latter each involve authorship and a novel, rather than the author.

If we take the descriptions in Gödel's slingshot as the value-free, then the slingshot is blocked at the substitution steps. We can take the designata of descriptions to be complexes of objects and properties, and the designata of sentences to be facts or states of affairs built up out of these.

The situation is not so clear when we take the descriptions to be value-loaded. What then should be the designata of the sentences? The most natural suggestion is what we might call their *incremental truth conditions*, given the facts that determine the designation of their terms:

> Given that Mark Twain wrote *Tom Sawyer*, (11) is true iff Mark Twain grew up in Missouri.

> Given that Mark Twain wrote *Huckleberry Finn* (12) is true iff Mark Twain grew up in Missouri.

(11) and (12) agree with respect to the additional requirements they impose on the objects that fit the descriptions in them, the requirements that appear on the right hand side of the biconditionals. These incremental truth conditions can be taken as facts or states of affairs involving the described object—Mark Twain in this case—rather than the descriptive complexes. This proposal we can summarize as follows:

Expression	Designation	
	Value-free reading	*Value-loaded reading*
Description	Descriptive Condition	Object described
Sentence	Truth conditions: State of affairs involving descriptive condition	Incremental truth conditions: State of affairs involving object described

The principles we adumbrated earlier need to be modified:

(**B′**) Substitution of basic terms that co-designate do not affect the truth conditions of a sentence; substitution of descriptions does not effect the incremental truth conditions of a sentence, but may effect the truth conditions.

Substitution′: (From (A) and (B′)) Substitution of basic co-designating terms does not effect what a sentence designates. Substitution of co-designating descriptions does not effect what a sentence designates on a value-loaded reading.

Picking any reasonably coherent notion of truth conditions and sticking with it will lead to basically the same modification.

We might take the truth conditions of a statement to correspond to the models in which it comes out true. A model assigns an appropriate extension to each name and predicate in the language. G3 and G4 clearly do not pass the test of being true in the same models. They will both be true in the model that reflects the actual world (given our assumptions). In this model the object named by a will be a member of the extension of ϕ, so G3 will be true. The pair of objects named by a and b will be a member of the extension of π, so G4 will be true. But there will be plenty of models in which one of these assumptions is true but not the other, and so there will be plenty of models in which G3 is true but not G4. On the other hand, if we restrict ourselves to the models in which the assumptions $\phi(a)$ and $\pi(a, b)$ are both true both G3 and G4 will be true.

The substitution principle is also undermined by the propositions of possible worlds semantics. Consider the initial statement in Church's argument. Are we to take Ivanhoe as part of the subject matter or not? If not, we get the set of all possible worlds (or all possible worlds in which Scott exists) as the designation of C1. If we take writing Ivanhoe to be part of the subject matter, we get the set of worlds in which Scott wrote it. These are quite different sets of worlds.

The Modified Slingshot

Given these principles we can construct a modified version of the slingshot that purports to show that the lower right hand box of our diagram cannot really be the incremental truth conditions, but must be simply truth values. That is, if we give the descriptions in a sentence their value-loaded reading, we are forced to take the sentence to designate truth values rather than incremental truth conditions.

The modified slingshot purports to show that the incremental or value-loaded designata of all true sentences with descriptions are the same.

Let $\iota x[\phi(x)]$ and $\iota y[\psi(y)]$ be distinct objects and F and G be distinct properties such that it is true that $F(\iota x[\phi(x)])$ and $G(\iota y[\psi(y)])$. Give all of the sentences in the following sequence a value-loaded reading.

M1.	$F(\iota x[\phi(x)])$	Assumption
M2.	$\iota x[\phi(x)] = \iota x[\phi(x)\& F(x)]$	Redistribution
M3.	$\iota x[\phi(x)] = \iota x[x \neq \iota y[\psi(y)]\& x = \iota x[\phi(x)]]$	Substitution
M4.	$\iota y[\psi(y)] = \iota y[y \neq \iota x[\phi(x)]$ and $y = \iota y[\psi(y)]]$	Redistribution
M5.	$\iota y[\psi(y)] = \iota y[\psi(y)$ and $G(y)]$	Substitution
M6.	$G(\iota y[\psi(y)])$	Redestribution

Given our original redistribution principle and the revised substitution principle, M6 should have the same designation as M1, if both are given a value-loaded reading. To block the modified slingshot, we need to turn to the redistribution principle.

Truth Conditions and Subject Matter

In "Semantic Innocence," Barwise and I associated the faults of the redistribution steps with the problem that I have elsewhere called "losing track of subject matter" (Perry, 1989), which affects both the model theoretic and possible worlds conceptions of truth conditions.

All logical truths are logically equivalent; if we take logical equivalence as a criterion for sameness of truth conditions, they will all designate the same thing according to (A). For example (11) and (12)

(11) Mary is sitting or Mary is not sitting.

(12) Peter is picking peppers or Peter is not picking peppers.

are each true in all models for a language that contains both sentences. So, on the logical equivalence criterion, (11) and (12) have the same truth conditions.

Similarly, if we take necessary truth as our criterion of sameness of truth conditions, (11) and (12) will designate the same thing by principle (A).

Given some fairly plausible assumptions, this means that neither of these conceptions of truth conditions support the notion of truth conditions being *about* a particular object. Consider the following sequence of sentences:

P1 Peter picked a peck of pickled peppers.

P2 Peter did not pick a peck of pickled peppers.

P3 Peter picked a peck of pickled peppers or Peter did not pick a peck of pickled peppers.

P4 Mary is sitting and (Peter picked a peck of pickled peppers or Peter did not pick a peck of pickled peppers).

P5 Mary is sitting.

Intuitively the truth conditions of P1 are about Peter, since it mentions him and predicates something of him. It seems that if the truth condition of S are about Peter, those of $\sim$ S should be too, so P2 is about Peter. If the truth conditions of S and those of Q are both about an object, it seems that those of

S *or* Q will be about that object, so those of P3 are about Peter.[140] It seems that if the truth conditions of S are about an object, those of Q *and* S will be about that object, so those of P4 are about Peter. But P4 is logically and necessarily equivalent to P5, so on the conceptions in question, P4 and P5 have the same truth conditions, so those of P5 are about Peter. But this means that the concept of being *about*, on these conceptions, is essentially empty.

The fact that the model theoretic and possible worlds conceptions of truth conditions lose track of subject matter in this way raises problems in many areas, such as semantics of attitude reports.[141] In "Semantic Innocence" Barwise and I diagnosed the slingshot as another place where losing track of subject matter leads to problems. We were mainly concerned with Davidson's versions of the slingshot; he often justifies the redistribution steps by appeal to the logical equivalence of the sentences in question. We also saw the logical equivalence criterion in the background of Church's discussion although he does not appeal to it. Barwise and I criticized logical equivalence as a criterion of sameness of designation, on the basis of considerations like those adumbrated in the last few paragraphs, and on this basis, rejected redistribution steps.

Olson points out that this does not really get to the heart of the issue of redistribution steps (Olson, 1987, pp. 85ff). The argument Gödel uses does not rely on the logical equivalence criterion, but on a specific and intuitively plausible claim that two sentences have the same content. The pairs of sentences in the Gödel slingshot that are linked by redistribution steps, such as G2 and G3, do not seem to involve any dramatic changes in subject matter of the sort that the logical equivalence or necessary equivalence criteria permit. So, one can suppose that the criteria of logical or necessary equivalence are too strong for sameness of designation of sentences, while still supposing that redistribution is a correct principle. Indeed, this was presumably Frege's view at the time of the *Begriffschrift*. His carving up content principle would support the principle of redistribution, but he did not claim that all necessary truths or all logical truths had the same content.[142]

Truth Conditions and Redistribution

Consider G2 and G3. They are logically and necessarily equivalent, so by these criteria of sameness of truth conditions, they will designate the same object. But this does not seem to turn on losing track of subject matter. G3 brings in new logical apparatus, the definite description operation and the identity sign, but no new terms for objects, properties or relations (other than identity, arguably a part of the logical apparatus).

---

[140] As Olson points out (Olson, 1987, p 85), Wittgenstein's doctrines in his *Tractatus* do not agree with this, since he didn't think that tautologies had any content at all. See also Partee, 1989.

[141] See Partee, 1989 and Perry 1989.

[142] See Weitzman, 1989 for a discussion of Frege's "carving up content" principle.

Olson points out that taking sameness of fact as our criterion does not deliver such a clear answer. Can we really distinguish between the facts described by G2 and those described by G3? The question forces us to recognize two different conceptions of facts, with different criteria of identity. According to what Olson calls the "existential" conception, facts are identical if they necessarily co-exist, while on the "structuralist" conception, they are individuated by sequences of properties and objects.[143] The existential conception supports redistribution, and seems to leave us with no obvious way out of the modified slingshot.

The spirit of the structuralist conception is contrary to principle (C) and to redistribution, and certainly allows one to block the slingshot. Where $a = \iota x[\phi(x)]$, a natural structuralist representation of M1 and M2 might be as follows:

$$\langle F, a \rangle$$
$$\langle =, a, a \rangle$$

(Remember that we are dealing only with value-loaded readings). For the structuralist, we have two quite different facts designated, with different structures.

Olson is clearly sympathetic to the existential concept of facts, and to the charge that the structuralist conception improperly mixes metaphysics and syntax. He also thinks the fine-grained structuralist conception of facts will be susceptible to a sort of metaphysical slingshot inspired by Bradley.

The Metaphysical Slingshot

Olson's conclusion is not quite that that there is only one fact on the structuralist conception, but rather than any fact necessitates every other. Here is what Olson says:

> It seems to me that the structuralist approach is exposed to objections of the sort that Bradley made against Russell. For it holds that an object a has the property F if and only if there exists a fact whose constituents are a and F. Bradley's question was what manner of thing a could possibly be. Is it an ordinary thing, replete with all its properties and relations to other things? If so, how can its having F consist in its being the constituent of a fact of which F is another constituent? Its identity as a constituent depends on its properties, including F. Moreover, a is supposed to be the same in each of the facts of which it is a constituent. If the fact that a has F is determined by its constituents, and a, which is one of them, has the property G, how can this fact be compatible with a's not being G? It is true that distinct facts can necessarily

---

[143]Olson, 1987, pp. 91ff.; Olson's distinction and terminology is derived from Kit Fine's distinction between structuralist and empiricist conceptions of facts in Fine 1982.

coexist according to the structuralist. But since G can be any property of a, he now appears to be committed to what James called "the Block Universe." Each fact that exists is incompatible with any state of affairs that does not exist. For the state of affairs of a's not being G would have as a constituent a, an object which is G. The structuralist could meet this objection by taking a as a "bare particular," but I do not think that Bradley would be alone in regarding this as a form of theoretical suicide. (Olson, 1987, pp. 99-100)

This is pretty succinct. Let's see if we can spell it out a little. We'll just consider simple facts, involving an object having a property or a sequence of objects standing in a relation. I'll assume that there are both positive and negative facts; for example, there is the fact that I am sitting, and the fact that I am not standing. And I'll use *states of affairs* for fact-like things that are not facts. So my sitting and my not sitting are both states of affairs—I'll call them opposites—and one is a fact. A very basic metaphysical principle is that of two opposite states of affairs, one and only one is a fact.

Suppose that f is the fact that I am sitting, and f' is the fact that I am from Nebraska. Then, since I, as a member of f, am replete with all my properties, the first fact somehow contains the second. According to what I shall call Olson's principle, f is incompatible with the opposite of f'. Then, by the basic metaphysical principle mentioned above, f necessitates f'. And by parity of reasoning, f necessitates every other fact with me as a constituent. If we suppose that every object stands in some relation or other to every other object, and that every fact has some object as a constituent, we get the result that f necessitates every fact. So, given Olson's principle, this conception of facts seems to lead to something quite aptly called a "Block universe."

What about Olson's principle? To make it plausible, I think we need to make two assumptions about Olson's intentions. First, we need to assume that G is supposed to be an essential property of me. Only the facts essential to my existence are necessitated by facts with me as a constituent. Arguably, I would not be me, unless I had the very parents that I had. So any fact with me as a constituent, necessitates the fact that I have the parents that I do. But then, it seems, all sorts of facts about parentage are going to be necessitated, about the parents of my parents, and their parents, and so forth. We seem to have not so much a block universe as a sort of lace universe, with the fact that I am sitting necessitating an odd assemblage of facts back to facts about Adam and Eve and Cain or Abel and the like, but with lots of unnecessitated holes of random size and shape in between. But the lace universe is enough of a problem for the structuralist theory of facts.

The second assumption we need to make about Olson's intentions is that he is assuming that facts are the basic building blocks of one's ontology. On this idea, objects must derive their existence and identity from the facts in which they are involved. To then individuate facts in terms of objects, as the structuralist proposes to do, seems to be ruled out. If one is thinking of the objects "replete with their properties," prior to facts, then facts are not basic. If one is thinking of the object as bare particulars, then one surely is committing theoretical suicide, since now it is these bare particulars that are ontologically basic.

Facts and Situations

I want now to describe a view that rejects this second assumption. This is the view in *Situations and Attitudes*, although we chose in that work not to reflect the whole view in the formal apparatus. More recent versions of situation theory incorporate the entire view into the formal apparatus (Barwise, 1989). This view takes something like Olson's existentialist view about situations, but his structuralist view about facts. I then consider a problem for this view related to the metaphysical slingshot, and suggest a solution to the problem.

First let's adopt a little notation and terminology. By a scheme of individuation and classification I mean a domain of individuals together with a domain of relations. Where R is an n-ary relation and $a_1 \ldots a_n$ is an appropriate sequence of objects, I shall call $R, a_1 \ldots a_n$ an issue and an issue together with 1 or 0 a state of affairs. A scheme of individuation determines a set of issues.

Thus $R, a_1 \ldots a_n; 1$ is the state of affairs that is a fact if and only if $a_1 \ldots a_n$ stand in the relation R, while $R, a_1 \ldots a_n; 0$ is its opposite, the state of affairs that is a fact if and only if $a_1 \ldots a_n$ do not stand in the relation R. A basic metaphysical principle is that a state of affairs is a fact if and only if its opposite is not one. But what determines which states of affairs are facts? One answer might be that this is bedrock. Some just are, some are not. This is not my view, however. It seems to me that we have a notion of a reality or realities that might be individuated and classified in different ways, according to different schemes of individuation. Imagine a checkerboard, for example. We could individuate it as sixty-four squares, and classify them with the properties of being red and black, and the relations of directly under and directly to the right of. Or we could individuate it as eight rows and eight columns, and classify them in terms of the relations of being red at and being black at, being under and being to the right of. There are two different ways of getting at the same reality. I want to say that the checkerboard can be considered as a situation, which, given one scheme of individuation and classification, determines some states of affairs to be facts, and given another, determines other states of affairs and facts. Reality transcends any one scheme of individuation.

On this conception, then, facts are not basic entities from which the world is constructed, but more like the accurate measures of situations, relative to a standard of measurement. Being a fact is really a derivative property. Instead of the fundamental property of being a fact, we have the fundamental relation of being determined to be a fact by a situation.

"$s \models \sigma$" is read "situation s makes state of affairs σ factual."

Where $\sim \sigma$ is σ's opposite, two plausible principles are:

a) If $s \models \sigma$, then not: $s \models \sim \sigma$

b) If there is an s such that $s \models \sigma$, then there is no s' such that $s' \models \sim \sigma$.

a) says that no situation makes a state of affairs and its opposite factual; b) says if one situation makes a state of affairs a fact, no other situation can make its opposite a fact.

A third plausible principle (persistence) is:

c) If s is part of s' and $s \models \sigma$, then $s' \models \sigma$.

The principle that there is a world we could express this way

d) There is an s such that for all σ, $s \models \sigma$ or $s \models \sim \sigma$

The world is not the totality of facts, but something from which the objects and relations that are used to construct states of affairs—both the facts and the nonfacts—are abstracted. The additional situations I have in mind are not alternative realities to the actual world, but parts of it. We could speak, for example, of the situation in this room during the present hour.

Individuating Situations

Looking at things this way, it seems unproblematic to individuate facts in terms of their constituents. But what of situations? How do we individuate them? Unless we answer this question, can we even give an answer to the question of whether there is really more than one?

In our book *Situations and Attitudes*, Jon Barwise and I used the term "situation" both for what I am calling situations and for what I am calling states of affairs. We called the former "real situations" and the latter "abstract situations." Among abstract situations, we distinguished between factual and nonfactual. So factual abstract situations were what I am calling facts or sets of them.

One can distinguish between the internal and the external properties of situations. The internal properties are which states of affairs they determine to be factual. An example of an external property is being perceived by a person at a certain time. Another is leaving a certain issue open, being "undefined." Given principle a) above, one would know that s is not identical to s' if s determines σ to be a fact and s' determines $\sim \sigma$ to be a fact. But given principle b), this test will never apply.

However, if one thinks that situations have not just fact-determining role, but a fact-constitutive role, there will be lots of ways of individuating them. It is natural to take situations to be the constituents of facts involving perception, causation, and the like.

I want to briefly explore a certain problem related to these two roles for situations, related to the issues Olson raised. Basically the problem is that situations that are big enough to determine states of affairs to be facts are too big for most of the fact-constitutive uses for situations. Consider the fact that I am sitting (as I write this). How big does the situation have to be, that determines this to be a fact? At first glance, one would think that the situation in the room, at the present time would do it. That situation includes everything that is going on in the room at that time. Is that not enough to settle the issue of whether I am sitting or not?

At second glance, it does not really seem big enough. Let's go back to the checkerboard for an analogy. Consider the fact that row 2 is red at column 2. At first glance, it seems that just the situation at square 10 is what settles this issue. But at second glance, this does not seem right. That little patch could have been red, even if there were no rows or columns, or not the ones that there are. That patch could have been part of a board that was not suited for checkers at all, in which geometrical shapes of various colors shapes and sizes lie adjacent to it in a random way. Given the rest of the board, which guarantees the existence of the row and column and question, what goes on at that square is what settles the issue of the color of row 2 at column 2. But what goes on at square 10 does not settle it all by itself, because what goes on at square 10 does not suffice by itself to establish the existence of the column and row that are constituents of the fact.

In a way, that fact that square 10 is red, and the fact that row 2 is red at column 2, seem like the same fact. But they are not, since they have different constituents. And it is only the former fact, not the latter, that is really settled by what goes on at square 10.

The situation in the room seems similar. Just as the column and row "transcend" the square, and are not established to exist just by what goes on in the square, so I transcend the situation in my study. In some sense, things could be just as they are here, and I not exist. We do not seem to be able to find that possibility, so long as we "measure" the situation with the scheme of individuation with persons in it. But if we think in terms of "person-stages," or in terms of rooms and their properties (there is a person of such and such a type writing in this study at this time) we can find them. It seems that what is going on in this study now, the situation in this study, could be fit into various larger situations.

How large will the situation have to be, then, that settles the fact that I am now writing? It seems it will have to stretch back far enough to establish my existence. But perhaps it will have to stretch even further than that. The problem of the lace universe reasserts itself at the level of situations.

The solution to the problem, I believe, is to grant it. The situations which establish the ordinary facts we are interested in may have to be quite large. This does not show that there are no smaller situations, however, simply that the smaller ones, the ones we perceive and the like, do not establish quite as much as we thought they did.

The right way to look at it, I think, as roughly as follows. The small situations we perceive, examine, and the like do not establish the facts we are interested in by themselves. They establish them only relative to other facts. The key relation is not "determines to be factual," but "determines to be factual given certain facts." This has to do with the incrementality of situations. I want to know what the situation in this room supports about a certain filing cabinet, a certain typewriter, a certain person. I identify these individuals not by being privy to all of the fact that determine their identity, but by being in a relationship with them.

So, I suspect, the notion we need is that of *incrementally determines to be a fact*. That is, $s \models \sigma$, given σ'. I will end on this somewhat indecisive and incomplete note.[144]

---

[144]The research reported in this paper has been made possible by a gift from the System Development Foundation to the Center for the Study of Language and Information at Stanford. The paper was read at the 1990 Pacific Division Meetings of the American Philosophical Association in a symposium with Ken Olson and John Boler on Olson's book, *An Essay on Facts* (Olson, 1987). I learned a great deal from Olson and Boler's presentations, and from a point made by Mark Richard. I have also had many other rewarding conversations with Olson on the topics of this paper. The paper corresponds to a portion of the workshop on situation semantics that I gave with John Etchemendy at the San Sebastian Conference on Logic and Semantics. Etchemendy and Elizabeth Macken gave me helpful comments on the penultimate draft.

17

Broadening the Mind

The main topic of Jerry Fodor's *The Elm and the Expert* (1994), and the title of the first chapter, is "If Psychological processes are computational, how can psychological laws be intentional?" I focus on the first and second chapters; The first is devoted to setting up the question, the second to answering it.

The Problem

The topic is an old one for Fodor—as he says he has been thinking and writing about it for more than twenty years. What seems to have been constant since, say, "Methodological Solipsism," is his devotion to theses that we'll call, following his scheme in the book, (1) and (3):

(1) Psychological explanations are intentional, that is, backed by laws that classify by content.

(3) Psychological laws are implemented by computational processes.

What has changed is Fodor's view about the issue of broad and narrow content. The contents in question are those of linguistic acts and cognitive states. In the case of an assertion or a belief, contents will be or be closely related to truth-conditions: what conditions must the rest of the world fulfill, in order for the assertion or belief to be true? Content is narrow or broad, depending on how much we include in "the rest of the world," that is, what facts we take to be fixed and what we allow to vary. Take the assertion "The author of *The Elm and The Expert* likes to sail." It can be assigned two quite different contents, depending on how one thinks of the description. If we fix the fact that Fodor is the author, then in order for the assertion to be true, he has to like to sail. If we don't take that fact as fixed, then we get that in order for the assertion to be true there has to be someone who is both the author and likes to sail. The second content is *narrower* in that it fixes less and allows more to vary.

Seminal work in the philosophy of language and the philosophy of mind in the 1970's argued persuasively that the content we ascribe to linguistic acts (what is said) and beliefs (what is believed) were, by and large, and in various ways, broad.

The work of Kripke , Donnellan , Kaplan and others on the "New Theory of Reference," for example, showed that our ordinary conceptions of what is said and what is believed, in the case of assertions involving names and indexicals and the beliefs they express, are broad in the sense that they involve the individuals named or contextually indicated, rather than descriptions or conceptions of them. That is, the truth-conditions take the facts of reference involving names and indexicals as fixed, rather than things allowed to vary.

The work of Putnam , Burge and others focused on properties rather than individuals. When Elwood and Telwood use the term "water," it is not their ideas or mentalese terms for water (which are the same) that enter into what they say and believe. It is the actual kind of stuff, water or twater, that they are talking about. When Burge's patient believes that he has arthritis in his thigh, he believes something false, and the false thing he believes is a proposition about arthritis. This is broad content because it is the conventions of his particular linguistic group, even if only partly reflected in his own understanding, that determine which kind of inflammation he speaks about and thinks about with the word "arthritis."

I'll call these currents from the 70's "referentialism." Referentialism has coalesced in various ways with the informational tradition in semantics, in ways that Fodor seems to embrace but doesn't trace. By broad content, he means content that involves the properties, relations, and individuals that the ideas are *of* or the words are *about*. Which properties, relations and individuals depends not only on the nature of the ideas or words and their connections to other words and ideas, but on causal relations with their external referents.

In "Methodological Solipsism," Fodor argued that theses (1) and (3) nevertheless showed the importance of a suitably narrow level of content. Since content supervenes on computational processes, it must be narrow, i.e., not depend on circumstances outside the agent; it is determined by the agent's internal states. Other, broader, concepts of content are not the ones on which psychological laws rely.

Now Fodor has become convinced that this won't do: according to him all we have to work with is informational content, which he thinks has to be broad content. So he accepts (2), which, along with (1) and (3), create the problem for this book:

(2) Content is informational, and hence broad rather than narrow, i.e., it does depend on circumstances outside the agent, and is not wholly determined by the agent's internal states.

The problem for Fodor is reconciling (1), (2) and (3); this is what the book is about.

The problems raised by these theses are brought out by the cognitive versions of Frege cases and twin cases.

In a Frege case, there are two ways of thinking of the same thing. They have different causes and different effects in ways that lead to exceptions to putative psychological laws. Suppose, for example, Elwood knows that Cicero was a Roman orator, likes to please his teacher, and has been asked, "Was Tully a Roman orator?" A plausible principle of intentional psychology is that if someone knows that x is P, is asked whether x is P, and wants to please the person doing the asking, he will say that x is P. But Elwood won't do that.

In a twin case, there is one way of thinking of two things. People seem to fall under the same computational laws, without sharing the requisite contents. So Elwood thinks that water is good to drink, and Telwood thinks that twater is good to drink, and these states both lead them to pick up the glass in front of them, bring it to their lips and sip at it. The same computational story linking percept, belief and action applies, but not the same intentional law, for there is no broad content they both believe.

Fodor's solution is that these cases just don't occur very often. That is, in actual circumstances, or anything close enough to them to matter, sameness of computational state will mean sameness of intentional state, and difference of computational state will mean difference of intentional state. That is, there aren't often, and aren't likely to be two ways of thinking of the same thing that are unlinked as the Cicero and Tully ways were in the example, and there aren't often, and aren't likely to be, two things that we think about in the same way as Elwood and Telwood did in that example. Frege cases, Putnam cases, Burge cases and their ilk don't happen very often, and the intentional laws of psychology needn't be perfect.

I don't think this solution is correct. There is not a particularly close tie between informational content and broad content; informational content can be as narrow as one needs. Fodor is overimpressed by the referentialist tradition. It shows nothing more than that folk linguistics and folk psychology have a keen interest in relatively broad content. Absolutely nothing follows from this about the narrowness of content that cognitive science might need, nor the narrowness of content that an informational approach can provide. Whether or not there is anything that should be called absolutely narrow content, contents as narrow as are needed for any particular purpose can be provided by the framework of information. Frege cases and twin cases are not rare events; they occur everyday, pose no significant problem for those who need to describe or explain them in ordinary language. Their possibility is built into the structure of informational content.

Everyday Frege Cases

I assume, in the context of Fodor's scholarship, that by a Frege case we don't mean a case Frege actually discussed or thought about, but something that meets some abstract conception of the puzzles he introduced that interests Fodor. I think that means that a Frege case involves a single individual who has two ways of thinking about the same object or property without realizing it. This is not rare.

Suppose I am walking across campus and see someone approaching, someone whom I eventually recognize to be Fodor. Before the episode begins I have one way of thinking about Fodor, as "Jerry Fodor." I may have been thinking about Fodor's books, his ideas, his boat, etc. As I walk along, I see someone in the distance. At first I think of the person I see as "that man." Then it occurs to me that there is something vaguely familiar. Is it Paul Newman? Is it Bill Clinton? Is it David Israel? No, it's Jerry Fodor. During the interval when I am figuring out who I am looking at, I have two unlinked ways of thinking of the same person, ways we can roughly express as "Jerry Fodor" and "that man." If we construe information broadly, then when I first see Jerry I have the information that Jerry Fodor is at Stanford, for I have the information that *that man* is at Stanford, and that man is Jerry Fodor. But if, right at that point, you distracted me from my recognition process and asked, "Are there any famous philosophers on campus," I would have said, "Not unless you count the regular crew," or something like that, not "Jerry Fodor is," which is what I would certainly say a moment later.

Recognition is a familiar process that resolves a problem we cannot even state if we restrict ourselves to content individuated broadly. And yet recognition is a part of folk psychology, not particularly difficult to describe. How can this be, if we are restricted to broad content?

Or suppose that I am visiting friends in Norway and I step on their bathroom scale. It reads "90 kg" I don't know whether I have lost or gained weight. On the other hand, if it read "200 lbs," I would immediately realize I had gained a few more pounds and become depressed. The effect of the signal in kilograms—its cognitive and hence emotional significance to me—is quite different than that which a signal in pounds would have had. Note that this can be true even if I am pretty familiar with the metric system and weigh things in kilograms for all sorts of purposes, as long as the conversion of weights in the neighborhood of 200 lbs is not completely automatic. Yet the property of weighting 90 kg *is* the property of weighing 200 lbs There are two different symbols, embedded in two different systems, connected with two different ideas, of the same objective state. A Frege case. Not rare, not mysterious, and certainly no problem for a decent theory of informational content.

After we take a brief look at information, I will argue that twin cases, properly understood, are not rare either.

Informational Content, Broad and Narrow

Fodor doesn't want to provide us with a theory of content or discuss any details about content at all. It seems fair, therefore, to examine his point of view from the standpoint of the simplest, most straightforward and most metaphysically benign theory of informational content of which I am aware. This is the theory of reflexive and incremental information, developed by David Israel and myself. I'll call it "the incremental theory" for short.[145]

The incremental theory doesn't rely on anything except whatever account of laws, regularities, or constraints one uses for the rest of one's philosophy. The information an event (call it a signal) contains is what its occurrence means about what the rest of the world is like, given a set of constraints that relate the occurrence of signals of this kind to other things. As Hume pointed out, events don't mean anything at all, except relative to some laws or constraints. The basic concept of information carried by a signal σ is what needs to be true for σ to occur, given a set of constraints C. If the constraints are actual, the informational content is really information and must be true; otherwise it may be false, but still quite useful for classifying systems attuned to the false constraints. Someone may think that mushrooms nourish, even though only some kinds do. The state of mind of such a person, as they eat mushrooms, can be usefully classified by the informational content of that event given the constraint: they expect to be nourished.

Strictly speaking, from just this bare Humean concept, all we get is *reflexive* information, that is, information about the signal itself. In Hume's famous example, σ is an occurrence of bread-eating. Relative to the constraint that (eating) bread nourishes (the eater), σ carries the information that the eater in σ will be nourished. We can think of this as pretty narrow information.

Often there are other circumstances we also hold fixed, and hence get broader kinds of information. *Given* that David is the eater in σ, σ carries the information that David will be nourished—information about David, not about σ. This is called incremental information, for it is what is *added* to what is given by the signal.

My perceptual state contains the information that Fodor is on campus, given the fact that the man I see is Fodor. If we fix that fact, the information I pick up perceptually is that Fodor is on campus. If we don't fix that fact, we can still describe the content of my perceptual state in terms of information: that someone is on campus, that someone distinguished-looking is on campus, etc. The fewer facts we fix, the more narrowly we are describing the content. There are all kinds of informational contents available to characterize signals, including speech and cognitive states, and contents can be as narrow

---

[145]See Israel and Perry 1990, pp. 1–19; Israel and Perry 1991, pp. 147–160; and various papers in in this volume, especially Essay 14

as one needs. A rule of thumb is that if we are trying to explain someone's behavior by reference to the contents of their perceptual and cognitive states, we shouldn't fix facts that are not fixed by their cognitive states.

So, if you know that I have recognized the man I see as Fodor, you can say "John saw that Fodor was on campus." You can say that what I saw was just what the Stanford Daily announced, with the headline "Fodor on campus," for example. The two signals, my perception and the headline, have the same content, relative to quite different constraints and facts. We are forced to broad content, to get at commonalities of this sort.

But to deal with the process of recognition, we are forced to narrower content. I knew at the beginning that the man I was seeing was on campus. That is a content involving me and quantifying over men, and not the same content as the Daily headline had. When we say that I saw a man on campus, and after a bit recognized that it was Fodor, we are describing a transition from knowing that the man I'm seeing is on campus to knowing that Fodor is.

Understanding exactly how we manage to *describe* this sort of event involves knotty problems in the philosophy of language. But understanding the syntax and semantics of content ascriptions is not a precondition for having a good grasp of how minds handle content, any more than understanding the semantics of the language of everyday physics is a precondition for a theory of billiard ball interactions. The sort of change we are getting at is familiar to us from virtually any system we have for managing information. I have something like a file or a dossier on Fodor that includes a lot about him including his name and what he looks like. I open something like a file on the person I see, and accumulate information in it. When there is a match, I merge or link the files in some way, and the information flows between them; I learn that the person I see is a philosopher, and I learn that Fodor is on campus.

The incremental theory describes the informational content of the perception in terms of the *increment* or addition it makes to some body of information. (Note that the body of information thus incremented does *not* become part of the content. To return to our first example, the broad content of "The author of *The Elm and The Expert* likes to sail" takes as fixed the fact that Fodor authored the book. The increment it adds to what is fixed is *that Fodor likes to sail*. But the worlds in which Fodor likes to sail include those in which he liked it so much that he never got around to writing the book.)

Typically, the body of information we have in mind is that held by the perceiver. In this case, we fix only the facts that are fixed by the agent's cognitive states.

Consider a file drawer with two files about Jerry Fodor, one labeled "Jerry" and the other labeled "Fodor." These sort of duplicate files are not a rare occurrence in systems for managing information about people. (Sometimes there is a good reason to keep more than one file of the same person. A university will typically have a number of files on a given student. The file in the Bursar's Office may contain financial information not open to the student's advisors; the file in the Advising Office may contain details about academic problems of no interest to the bursar.) Then imagine a second filing drawer, just like the first, except that a rubber band has been placed around the two files to indicate that they are of the same person, as one might do after discovering that the Jerry in question was the Fodor in question.

The second file drawer contains information that the first one does not. We can't get at this information if we stick to broad content.

Consider, for example, the possibilities that meet the conditions imposed by the first drawer, assuming a referentialist account of "Jerry" and "Fodor." They are exactly the possibilities that meet the conditions imposed by the second drawer because, sad to say, there is only one Jerry Fodor. If we fix the facts about who the files are of, there is no way to get at the possibility that they are of two different people, the possibility that the rubber band in the second drawer rules out, and so no way to get at the difference. Referentialism imposes upon us an inappropriate degree of breadth for describing the informational content of the file drawers. Slavish referentialism wouldn't allow us to explain why, say, the money owed Jerry isn't sent to him, given that his address is right there in the Fodor file.

But there is nothing about *information* that limits us to such broad content. Informational content allows a graceful retreat to any number of narrower contents, that bring out the differences between the drawers. Suppose we fix the fact that the "Fodor" file is of Fodor, but do not fix the fact that the "Jerry" file is. With those things fixed, the conditions the first drawer imposes can be met even if the files are of different people, but the conditions imposed by the second drawer cannot be.

Fodor also sees informational content as limiting in another way that is puzzling. He seems to equate informational content with the information a signal contains about its *causes*, which leads him to see a conflict between informational and functional approaches. But the information contained by a signal relative to a constraint can be about the future or the past, about effect as well as cause, about behavior as well as perception. There is no particular reason that those who find their content in information cannot also be functionalists.

Suppose you believe that Fodor doesn't like to sail. This is misinformation about Fodor, since he does like to sail. Still, your being in that state carries information about you and how you will act towards Fodor, given that you have the means to recognize him. If you like him, you won't ask him to go sailing with you. A state of mind, like a state of anything, carries all sorts of information relative to different constraints and different fixed facts. Why do we characterize such states in terms of broad content, content involving Fodor, say? Because just as our cognitive capacities evolved to enable us to carry information about individuals with whom we interact, folk psychology evolved to enable us to efficiently characterize individuals who are putting those cognitive capacities to use. Describing mental states at work in terms of broad content rather than narrow is as natural as describing a wrestling match in terms of what the participants are doing to each other rather than anatomically.

Everyday Twin Cases

When we talk about broad and narrow content, we have in mind a type of signal, some constraints relative to which these signals do or would provide information both about causes and effects, and nested sets of facts, thought of as less and less restricted, that provide broader and broader content. Let f and f' be such sets of facts, where f is the more and f' the less restricted, that is $f \subset f'$. In a Frege case two signals have the same content relative to f' while having different contents relative to the more restricted set f. In a twin case, two signals have the same contents relative to some more restricted set of facts f, but different contents relative to some less restricted set f'.

In the literature, twin cases usually incorporate some kind of unlikely duplication of detail, as with Elwood and Telwood, and so of course are unlikely to occur. There is nothing essential about this massive duplication; its role is purely dialectical. The twin case is supposed to convince us of the possibility of differences in broad content in spite of sameness of internal state. To be convincing, one has to make the internal states similar in any ways one's interlocutor might deem relevant. If one's interlocutor is a holist, worships holists, was taught holism in graduate school, and the like, one needs massive duplication, so that one's interlocutor cannot trace difference of content to internal difference.

But the fact that massive duplications are rare doesn't help Fodor's case. He's not a holist, and has become a fan of broad content determined in part by external circumstances. There is nothing in his view that suggests that twin cases will be rare if by twin cases we mean differences in broad content across individuals with *relevantly* similar cognitive states.

Conclusion

At the heart of the concept of information are general principles about the way things work, in virtue of which specific signals at different times and places and connected to quite different things can carry information. The possibility of Frege cases and twin cases is built into the very structure of information. The same information can be carried by signals of quite different kinds and quite different causal roles relative to different facts and/or constraints: Frege cases. The same signals, connected to different objects, can carry different information: twin cases. If we include, among the differences that can make a difference in the incremental content of similar signals, the other signals they combine with, then systematic semantics is simply the study of twins.

18

What Are Indexicals?

The standard list of indexicals includes the personal pronouns "I," "you," "my," "he," "his," "she," "it," the demonstrative pronouns "that" and "this," the adverbs "here," "now," "today," "yesterday" and "tomorrow" and the adjectives "actual" and "present." This list is from David Kaplan (1989a), whose work on the "logic of demonstratives" is responsible for much of the increased attention given to indexicals by philosophers of language in recent years. The words and aspects of words that indicate tense are also indexicals. And many other words, like "local," seem to have an indexical element.

But what exactly is it these words have in common—what is indexicality? Two characteristics are often appealed to:

- Indexicals are "context-dependent";
- Indexicals are "token-reflexives."

Neither of these concepts is clear without further explanation. It is quite true that what an indexical designates *shifts* from context to context. But there are many kinds of shiftiness, with corresponding conceptions of context.

"Token-reflexivity" doesn't fare any better; the terms on each side of the hyphen are unclear. The term "token" is used in (at least) two ways in the literature. Sometimes it is used for the *act* of speaking, writing, or otherwise using language. At other times, it is used for an object that is produced by, or at least used in, such an act. Reichenbach, who introduces the term "token-reflexive," uses the term "token" in both ways. He first says that tokens are acts of speaking, but a few pages later he is talking about the position of a token on a page (Reichenbach, 1947).

Once we decide what it is that is said to be reflexive, we need to decide what reflexivity is. Most indexicals are not *reflexive pronouns*; "myself" and "yourself" are, but "I" and "you" are not. Contrary to what Reichenbach may seem to suggest, the content of a statement using an indexical is not usually about the token of the indexical. If I say "I am sitting," I make a statement the *subject matter* of which is me and my posture; I do not mention the token I use, and do not say the same thing as I would if I said "The producer of this very token is sitting." So in what sense are indexicals reflexive?

In this essay I try to explain the sense in which indexicals are context sensitive, the sense in which they are reflexive, and the relation between the two criteria.

Context

Presemantic and semantic uses of context

Sometimes we use context to figure out with which meaning a word is being used, or which of several words that look or sound alike is being used, or even which language is being spoken. These are *presemantic* uses of context. In the case of indexicals, however, context is used *semantically*. It remains relevant after the language, words and meaning are all known; the meaning directs us to certain aspects of context to determine what is designated.

Consider this utterance:

(1) Ich! (said by several teenagers at camp in response to the question, "Who would like some sauerkraut?").

Knowing that this happened in Berlin rather than San Francisco might help us determine that it was German teenagers expressing enthusiasm and not American teenagers expressing disgust. In this case context is relevant to figuring out which language (and hence which word with which meaning) is being used.

The vocable "ich" is a *homonym* across languages. Homonyms are words that are spelled and pronounced alike. For example, there are two words in English that are spelled and pronounced "quail"; one is a noun that stands for a small gamebird, the other a verb for faltering or recoiling in terror. It makes sense to speak of two words that are pronounced and spelled the same, because words are not merely patterns of sound or combinations of letters, but cultural objects with histories; our two words "quail" derived from different French and Latin words. The term "vocable" can be used for what the words have in common, so if we need to be precise we can say the vocable "quail" corresponds to two words in English.

Each of the German teen-agers, when they use the indexical "ich," designates herself, and so the expression "ich" designates differently for each of them. One might be tempted to consider this just more homonymy. Each has a different name for himself or herself, they just happen to all be spelled alike and sound alike; we have homonyms across idiolects of the same language. Such a temptation should surely be resisted as an explanation of the shiftiness of indexicals. For one thing, the word "ich" doesn't have different historical origins depending on which teen-ager uses it; they all learned the standard first-person in German. The homonym account would be even worse for temporal and spatial indexicals. We would have to suppose that I use a different word "tomorrow" each day, since my use of "tomorrow" shifts its designation every night at the stroke of midnight.

With both homonyms and indexicals we use context to help determine what is designated. In the case of homonyms, the context is anything about the facts surrounding the utterance that will help us to figure out which words are used. But in the case of "I" or "ich," we consult context after we know which expression we have, looking for a very specific fact—who the speaker is—to determine which object is designated in accordance with the meaning of that expression.

An *ambiguous* expression like "bank" may designate one kind of thing when you say "Where's a good bank?" while worried about finances, another when I use it, thinking about fishing. Its designation varies with different uses, because different of its meanings are relevant. Again, all sorts of contextual facts may be relevant to helping us determine this. Is the speaker holding a wad a money or a fishing pole?

It isn't always simply the meaning of a particular word that is in question, and sometimes questions of meaning, syntax and the identity of the words go together:

(2) I forgot how good beer tastes [146]

(3) I saw her duck under the table.

With (2), knowing whether our speaker has just arrived from Germany or just arrived from Saudi Arabia might help us to decide what the syntactic structure of the sentence is and whether "good" was being used as an adjective or an adverb.

Is "duck" a noun or a verb in (3)? In this case, knowing a little about the situation that this utterance is describing will help us to decide whether the person in question had lost her pet or was seeking security in an earthquake.

In each of these cases, the context, the environment of the utterance, the larger situation in which it occurs, helps us to determine what is said. But these cases differ from indexicals. In these cases it is a sort of accident, external to the utterance, that context is needed. We need the context to identify which name, syntactic structure or meaning is used because the very same shapes and sounds happen to be shared by other words, structures, or meanings. In the case of indexicals we still need context *after* we determine which words, syntactic structures and meanings are being used. The meanings *exploit* the context to perform their function. The meaning of the indexical "directs us" to certain features of the context, in order to fix the designation.

It seems then that the defining feature of indexicals is that the meanings of these words fix the designation of specific utterances of them in terms of facts

---

[146]Thanks to Ivan Sag for the examples.

about those specific utterances. The facts that meaning of a particular indexical deems relevant are the contextual facts for particular uses of it.

Indexicals are not the only expressions that use context semantically. *Anaphora* provides another example. In anaphora what one word designates depends on what another word in the same bit of discourse, to which the word in question is anaphorically related, designates. Consider

(4) Harold went into the Navy. He didn't like it.

(5) Percy went into the Army. He didn't like it.

In (4) 'he' stands for Harold and 'it' stands for the Navy; in (5), these words stand for Percy and the Army. The designata depend on what the antecedents of "he" and "it" are, and what those antecedents stand for.

So in the case of anaphora, the contextual facts have to do with the relation of the utterance to previous noun-phrases in the discourse, while with indexicality, rather different sorts of facts are relevant, having to do with the relation of the utterance to things other than words, such as the speaker, addressee, time and place of the utterance. Consider, for example "That man came to see me yesterday. He is interested in philosophy." Resolving the reference of "he" involves knowing two sorts of facts. First, one must know that the use of "he" is anaphorically related to "that man." Second, one must know at which man the utterance context of "that man" was directed.

We use the third-person pronouns "he" and "she" both anaphorically and demonstratively:

(6) A woman wrote a very interesting dissertation at UCLA. She advocated subjective semantics.

(7) (Indicating a certain woman) She advocated subjective semantics in her UCLA dissertation.

How should we treat the occurrences of "she" in (6) and (7)? No one supposes they are mere homonyms. Many philosophers are at least tempted to suppose they are occurrences of a single ambiguous word, which functions as a variable in (6) and as an indexical in (7)(Kaplan, 1989a). Many linguists find this implausible, and would prefer an account that gives a uniform treatment of pronouns, bringing the relativity to linguistic and other contextual factors into a single framework for a subject matter called "deixis" (Partee, 1989). I favor this point of view, but for the purposes of this essay I will set the issue of the precise connection of anaphoric and demonstrative uses of pronouns to one side.

Types of indexical contexts

With respect to contexts for indexicals, I need to emphasize two distinctions, which together create the four categories exhibited in Table 1:

- Does designation depend on narrow or wide context?
- Is designation "automatic" given meaning and public contextual facts, or does it depend in part on the intentions of the speaker?

I'll show which expressions fit into these categories, and then explain them:

	Narrow	Wide
Automatic	I, now*, here*	tomorrow, yea
Intentional	now, here	that, this man, there

TABLE 1 Types of indexicals

Narrow and wide context. The narrow context consists of the constitutive facts about the utterance, which I will take to be the agent, time and position. These roles are filled with every utterance. The clearest case of an indexical that relies only on the narrow context is "I," whose designation depends on the agent and nothing else.

The wider context consists of those facts, plus anything else that might be relevant, according to the workings of a particular indexical.

The sorts of factors on which an indexical can be made to depend seem, in principle, limitless. For example,

It is yea big.

means that it is as big as the space between the outstretched hands of the speaker, so this space is a contextual factor in the required sense for the indexical "yea."

Automatic versus intentional indexicals. When Rip Van Winkle says, "I fell asleep yesterday," he intended to designate (let us suppose), July 3, 1766. He in fact designated July 2, 1786, for he awoke twenty years to the day after he fell asleep. An utterance of "yesterday" designates the day before the utterance occurs, no matter what the speaker intends. Given the meaning and context, the designation is automatic. No further intention, than that of using the words with their ordinary meaning, is relevant.

The designation of an utterance of "that man," however, is not automatic. The speaker's intention is relevant. There may be several men standing across the street when I say, "That man stole my jacket." Which of them I refer to depends on my intention.

However, we need to be careful here. Suppose there are two men across the street, Harold dressed in brown and Fred in blue. I think that Harold stole my wallet and I also think wrongly that the man dressed in blue is Harold. I intend to designate Harold *by* designating the man in blue. So I point towards the man in blue as I say "that man." In this case I designate the man in blue—even if my pointing is a bit off target. My intention to point to the man in blue is relevant to the issue of whom I designate, and what I say, but my intention to refer to Harold is not. In this case, I say something I don't intend to say, that Fred, the man in blue, stole my wallet, and fail say what I intended to, that Harold did. So it is not just any referential intention that is relevant to demonstratives, but only the more basic ones, which I will call *directing intentions*, following Kaplan (1989b).

In a case like this I will typically perceive the man I refer to, and may often point to or otherwise demonstrate that person. But neither perceiving nor pointing seems necessary to referring with a demonstrative.

The indexicals "I," "now," and "here" are often given an honored place as "pure" or "essential" indexicals. Some writers emphasize the possibility of translating away other indexicals in favor of them (Castañeda, 1967), (Corazza, forthcoming). In Table 1, this honored place is represented by the cell labeled "narrow" and "automatic." However, it is not clear that "now" and "here" deserve this status, hence the asterisks. With "here" there is the question of how large an area is to count, and with "now" the question of how large a stretch of time. If I say, "I left my pen here," I would be taken to designate a relatively small area, say the office in which I was looking. If I say, "The evenings are cooler than you expect here" I might mean to include the whole San Francisco Bay area. In "Now that we walk upright, we have lots of back problems," "now" would seem to designate a large if indefinite period of time that includes the very instant of utterance, while in "Why did you wait until now to tell me?" it seems to designate a considerably smaller stretch. It seems then that these indexicals really have an intentional element.

"Here" also has a demonstrative use. One can point to a place on a map and refer to it as "here" (Kaplan, 1989a). "Now" and the present tense can be used to draw attention to and confer immediacy on the time of a past or future event, as when a history teacher says, "Now Napoleon had a dilemma..." (Smith, 1989).

Signs, Tokens and Utterances

As I said, the term "token" is used in two ways in the literature: for the *act* of speaking, writing, or otherwise using language and for an object that is produced by, or at least used in, such an act.

I use "utterance" for the first sense. Utterances are intentional acts. The term "utterance" often connotes spoken language, but as I use it an utterance may involve speech, writing, typing, gestures or any other sort of linguistic activity.

I use "token" in the second sense, in the way Reichenbach used it when he said that a certain token was to be found on a certain page of a certain copy of a book. Tokens, in this sense, are traces left by utterances. They can be perceived when the utterances cannot, and be can used as evidence for them. Modern technology allows for their reproduction. The paradigm tokens are the ink marks produced in writing or typing. When we read, tokens are epistemically basic, and the utterances that produced them hardly thought of. But the utterances are semantically basic; it is from the intentional acts of speakers and writers that the content derives.

An utterance may involve a token, but not be the act of producing it. My wife Frenchie and I were once Resident Fellows in a dormitory at Stanford, eating with the students each evening in the cafeteria. If she went to dinner before I returned, she would write on a small blackboard on the counter, "I have gone to the cafeteria," and set it on the table near the front door of our apartment. I would put it back on the counter. There was no need for her to write out the message anew each time I was late; if the blackboard had not been used for something else in the interim, she could simply move it from the counter back to the table. Frenchie used the same token to say different things on different days. Each use of the token was a separate utterance.

One can imagine the same token being reused as a token of a different type of sentence. Suppose there is a sign in a flying school, intended to warn would-be pilots: "Flying planes can be dangerous." The flying school goes bankrupt; the manager of a park near the airport buys the sign and puts it next to a sign that prohibits walking on high tightropes. In its new use the sign is a token of a type with a different syntax and a different meaning than in its original use. In principle, tokens could even be re-used for utterances in different languages; the reader can no doubt think of an example, perhaps using "ich."

In the case of spoken utterances in face to face communication, the utterance/token distinction becomes pretty subtle. One who hears the token will see the utterance which produces it. Writing brings with it the possibility of larger gaps between use and perception; letters are sent, books are put on shelves, to be read months or even years later, and so forth. The utterance/token distinction is most at home in the case of written text. It grows in importance as culture and technology develop. Modern technology allows for the storage and reproduction of both spoken and written tokens, and with such devices as email an utterance involves the production of numbers of tokens around the world.[147]

In what follows, I will speak of tokens when explaining and criticizing Reichenbach's view, but shift to utterances when I explain what I take to be correct about his concept of reflexivity.

---

[147] In (1992), Ken Olson and David Levy argue that to develop an account of documents adequate for the age of duplicating machines and computers we need to distinguish types, tokens and *templates*.

Reflexivity and Indexicality

Reichenbach Criticized

Now in what sense are indexicals *reflexive*? The most familiar use of "reflexive" in grammar is for "reflexive pronouns," such as "myself," "yourself" and "itself." A reflexive pronoun is one that designates the subject of the clause in which it occurs; it is the particle "self" that secures this result. The initial "my," "your" or "it" further constrains the reference indexically, so, for example when I say

> I gave it to her myself

the "myself" is constrained to designate both the speaker and the subject, who are thereby constrained to be the same. It is fair enough to call reflexive pronouns indexicals, but not all indexicals are reflexives, nor did Reichenbach intend to be claiming that they were when he called them "token-reflexives."

Reichenbach claimed that token-reflexive words could be defined in terms of the token-reflexive phrase "this token," and in particular, as he put it, "The word 'I'... means the same as 'the person who utters this token'...(284)." He used this idea to provide an account of a famous utterance:

> ...let us symbolize the sentence 'here I stand', uttered by Luther on the Reichstag at Worms in 1521. The utterance by Luther we denote by 'θ'. The word 'I' then can be given in the form 'the x that spoke θ'; the word 'here' will be expressed by the phrase 'the place z where θ was spoken'. We thus have, using the function 'x speaks y at z', with 'sp' for 'speak' and 'st' for 'stand'...
> $$st[(ix)(Ez)sp(x,\theta,z),(iz)(Ex)sp(x,\theta,z)]^{148}$$

Here Reichenbach associates with a statement using a "token-reflexive" a proposition that has that token *itself* as a constituent.[149] The reflexiveness seems to reside in the fact that the token *itself* is part of the subject matter of what the statement asserts.

If we take Reichenbach's claim as a literal claim of synonymy between "I" and "the person who utters this token," there are problems. For one thing, someone other than the speaker could refer to the speaker as "the person who utters this token." I might point to a note you have written and say "the utterer of this token is foolish." This criticism is a bit unfair to Reichenbach, however, for he had in mind a very special use of "this," a use that captures the way a person thinks of a token they are producing as they produce it.

---

[148]"The person such that there is a place where he speaks θ stands at the place such that there is a person who spoke θ there."

[149]My use of terms like "proposition" and "constituent" to describe Reichenbach's view is anachronistic.

Even so, there are important differences (Kaplan, 1989a). A use of "I" refers to the speaker, whereas a use of "the person who utters this token" describes the speaker. The former is what Kaplan calls a "device of direct reference" while the latter is not. Although a token of "I" will refer to the person who produces it, the token doesn't become part of the subject matter of the utterance containing the indexical. The proposition expressed by Luther's utterance was not *about* his token or utterance at all.

But on the most natural reading, a statement using "the person who utters this token" will have the token as a part of its subject matter. If Luther had uttered Reichenbach's formula (or a natural language equivalent), he would have been talking about his token rather than himself. Consider the counterfactual circumstance in which Luther is standing just where he was, but is preoccupied and doesn't say anything. What Luther in fact said, "Here I stand," is true when evaluated at that circumstance, but what he would have said with "The utterer of this token stands at the place this token is uttered" would not be evaluated as true at that circumstance.

Reichenbach Defended

Nevertheless, Reichenbach was clearly on to something. Consider these two questions:

> Given that "I am standing" means what it does in English, and that u is an utterance of "I am standing," what more has to be true for u to be true?
>
> Given that "I am standing" means what it does in English, and that u is an utterance of "I am standing," *and* that the speaker of u is Elwood Fritchey, what more has to be true for u to be true?

The answer to each of these questions could be thought of as giving the "truth-conditions" of u. But they get different answers, for they are different questions. The answer to the first is

P: There is someone who is the speaker of u and that person is standing.

This answer, I think, gets at what Reichenbach called the "meaning," and it brings out the reflexivity of the utterance, for P is a proposition about u itself. But P is *not* what is said by u, not the content of or proposition expressed by u.[150] That honor belongs to the answer to the second question:

Q: Elwood Fritchey is standing.

Q is what we standardly think of as the content of u, but it is not about u, and does not bring out the reflexivity of u.

Any time we consider the "truth conditions" of an utterance, we do so against a background of fixed assumptions. The two questions above vary in

---

[150] And, for the record, Reichenbach didn't claim that it was.

what is fixed. In the first question, only the meaning is fixed, in the second, the meaning and context are both fixed. Now the truth condition with meaning and context fixed is what usually gets the honor of being called the "content" of an utterance or "what is said" by the speaker of the utterance. Only when we fix the meaning *and* the context do we determine all things designated in the utterance, and only then do we have hold of the subject matter. Only at that point do we get the proposition that we use to consider the counterfactual circumstances in which "what is said" is true.

But the first question is reasonable, and the answer legitimate. This corresponds to what one understands, when one perceives an utterance, understands the meaning, but does not know the context. It is the truth conditions of u with only the meaning fixed.

Indexicals are reflexive, then, in the following sense. The truth-conditions of an utterance containing an indexical, considered with just the meaning and not the context fixed, will be a proposition about the utterance of the indexical. Although this proposition is not the official content of the utterance, it is a proposition that corresponds to one level of understanding of the utterance— that which a linguistically competent listener who perceives the utterance but doesn't know the essential contextual facts would have.

Given this, and what we said above about context, we can state the relation between indexicality and reflexivity as follows. Utterances containing indexicals will have reflexive truth conditions given that their meanings are fixed, but not their (semantic) contexts.

Indexicality is *not* the same as reflexivity. All utterances, including those that have no indexicals, can only be assigned reflexive truth conditions, to reflect various stages of partial understanding. What else besides the properties of the particular utterance—the pre-semantic context—could be relevant to determining which words are used, with what meanings?

Return to our example involving the German and American teen-agers. Suppose that their responses to the question "Who wants sauerkraut?" were written out and handed to a monolingual American counselor. When the counselor reads "Ich" on Hans's slip of paper, he understands the truth conditions of the response only reflexively: The speaker of *this response* wants sauerkraut iff there is a language, "ich" is a word in that language, the writer of *this response* is using that language, and given the meaning of "ich" in that language and the context of *this response*, it expresses a positive response to the question. When he learns that the language is German, the counselor moves a step closer to grasping what is said, but his understanding remains reflexive. When he learns that "ich" is the German first person pronoun he moves closer still. He now has all the facts about meaning fixed but not the contextual facts. But his understanding remains reflexive—The kid who wrote *this response* wants sauerkraut—until he learns that Hans is the kid in question. Then he grasps what was said, that Hans wants sauerkraut.

Suppose that Wilhelm, who knows when it is appropriate to use indexicals, wrote "Wilhelm, ja." Our counselor's understanding of this message will also be reflexive until he fixes the meanings of these terms.[151] Once he does that, however, he is done. Since there are no indexicals in Wilhelm's message, the subject matter and what is said about it are grasped once the meanings are fixed.

So, if an utterance has no indexicals, then once we fix the meanings of the words—using the pre-semantic context to resolve all ambiguities—we eliminate reflexivity. For such utterances, the truth-conditions given the facts of meaning will not be conditions on the utterance, but conditions on the subject matter—the things the words in the utterance designate.

But if an utterance contains indexicals, we need one further bit of knowledge, before we can arrive at a proposition that is about the subject matter, rather than about the utterance itself, namely knowledge of the contextual factors that the meanings of the indexicals exploit to determine designation.

It is natural to think of the properties of an utterance that one needs to ascertain to determine what is said as having a certain natural order. One needs to know the language, the words, the meanings, the context. We can think of the truth conditions one can assign to an utterance as becoming progressively more subject matter oriented and less reflexive as knowledge of these factors is obtained. It is with this picture in mind that we can think of indexicality as the highest form of, or perhaps the last refuge of, reflexivity. And that is because the meaning of indexicals exploits contextual features to determine what is designated, so only when these contextual features are known, does one grasp the subject matter of the utterance and what is said about that subject matter.[152]

---

[151] Here I assume that proper names are not indexicals, but correspond more closely to ambiguous words, so that when our counselor fixes the meaning of "Wilhelm" as used in this utterance he fixes the designation. This view is elaborated in (Perry, 1995b).

[152] This essay is based on two sections of (Perry, 1995a). The interested reader may consult that essay and (Perry, 1993) and (Perry, 1995b) to see the positive theory about indexicals and cognitive significance developed and elaborated. Thanks to David Israel and Elizabeth Macken, who provided helpful comments on this essay.

19

Myself and *I*

Introduction

In this essay I distinguish three kinds of *self-knowledge*. I call these three kinds *agent-relative knowledge*, *self-attached knowledge* and *knowledge of the person one happens to be*. These aspects of self-knowledge differ in how the knower or agent is represented. Most of what I say will be applicable to beliefs as well as knowledge, and to other kinds of attitudes and thoughts, such as desire, as well.[153]

Agent-relative knowledge is knowledge from the perspective of a particular agent. To have this sort of knowledge, the agent need not have an idea of self, or a notion of himself or herself. This sort of knowledge can be expressed by a simple sentence containing a demonstrative for a place or object, and without any term referring to the speaker. For example, "There is an apple" or "that is a toaster."

(Ideas of specific objects I call *notions*. Ideas of properties and relations I just call *ideas*. A judgement involves an idea being associated with a notion. A notion together with all of the ideas associated with it is a *file*.)

In self-attached knowledge, the agent has an idea of self, which is associated with a notion, which I call a *self-notion*. This is the kind of knowledge that expressed with the word "I"—what Shoemaker calls "first-person knowledge." For example, "I am a philosopher," or "I see a toaster" or "I have a headache." In the last section of this paper, I try to explain why that is an apt name—why it is that the word "I" is so intimately connected with the expression of this sort of "self-thought."

In knowledge of the person one happens to be, the agent is represented to herself in just the same way that other people are represented to her. The agent

---

[153]The first seven sections of this paper present are intended to present basically the same account that was developed in (Perry, 1990b), from which it borrows some examples and prose. I believe this essay is clearer about the structure of agent-relative knowledge and the relations between the three kinds of knowledge, and connects with the ideas developed in (Perry, 1997).

has just the same kind of idea of herself as she has of other people. This kind of knowledge can be expressed with a name or third person demonstrative. For example, "John Perry is a philosopher" or, pointing to myself in a mirror, "That man is a shabby pedagogue."

Agent-relative knowledge

Two facts about the human condition

Everything we learn about other objects we learn by employing methods that are appropriate because those objects stand in certain relations to us. And however remote from us the object we are ultimately learning about may be, our inquiry will involve detecting the properties of things in our immediate vicinity.

I may learn that Bill Clinton visited the Bay Area by reading the paper, or seeing pictures on television, or hearing the radio. I learn about Clinton by reading what is written on the paper, seeing what is portrayed on the television screen, or hearing the sounds coming from the radio. Being the radio I am listening to, or the television I am watching, or the newspaper I am reading, are all what I call *agent-relative roles*: roles that other individuals play in the lives of agents. These are agent-relative roles, because an object plays or doesn't plays such a role relative to a given agent, at a given time. For example, my computer is playing the role of *object in front of me* right now, relative to me, but not relative to you.

When I read about him, or watched him on TV, or listened to a report of what he was doing on the radio, Clinton was also playing an agent-relative role in my life, one that was derived from the role these other objects were playing, and his relation to them. For example, Clinton was the object read about, because the newspaper was the object read, and Clinton was the object the newspaper story was about.

This is the first of two very general facts I want to emphasize: any object we learn about, plays some agent-relative role, basic or derived, in our life. We learn about the object by using an epistemic method connected to the role, a way of finding out about the object or person playing that role. The way to find out about the object in front of you is too look at it, or perhaps to walk up to it and touch it. The way to find out about the object that the document in front of you is about is to read the document. Finding out about the objects around us is a way of finding out about other objects, given general facts about the way things work and specific facts about how things are related. If Clinton is the source of the image on my television, then I can find out things about him by finding out things about that image.

The second fact is that however complex our lives are, everything we do comes down to performing operations on the objects around us—objects in front of us, behind us, above us; objects we are holding; objects we can see. By doing these things, we do things to objects in less basic relations to us. By speaking into the phone I hold, I speak to the person I called, the person to whom the signals that pass through the phone I hold are ultimately directed. I know how to move my body so as to effect objects around me, and I know how effecting those objects will effect other objects related to them in certain ways.

There are then two kinds of methods connected with agent-relative roles, epistemic methods and pragmatic methods. These two kinds of methods are the key to all human intelligence and purposive activity. We know how to find out what kinds of objects occupy these roles, and we know how to perform various operations on them. Technology extends the methods, so that we can find out about things in more and more complex relations to us, and do things that will change them in predictable ways.

Our practical knowledge then, the knowledge that enables us to do things, forms a structure at whose base is information about the objects that play relatively basic agent-relative roles in our lives.

Knowledge concerning the self

Consider a simple successful transaction involving such a basic agent-relative role, and epistemic and pragmatic methods associated with it. I am hungry. I see an apple before me. I pick it up and eat it. The complex movement of arm, hand, fingers, neck and jaw was successful in getting the apple into my mouth, because of the distance and direction the apple was from *me*. What I learned from perception, then, must have been the distance and direction of the apple from *me*. Or consider a transaction with a fax machine. To press certain buttons on it, I have to move my fingers a certain distance and direction from *me*. It isn't enough to know where the buttons were relative to one another, or where the fax machine was in the building or the room. I had to know where these things were relative to *me*.

It seems then, that these basic methods already require me to have some notion of myself. For it seems I need to know who it is, for example, from whom the apple is a certain distance and direction. If it is that distance and direction from you, or President Clinton, then moving the way I did would not be a way of eating it.

However, I think this is misleading. A natural way for me to report what I saw would be to simply say:

> That's an apple

or

> There is an apple there

There is nothing in this remark that refers to me. And after all, why should there be? I didn't see myself, I saw an apple. But, one might reply, we saw above that I got the information that the apple was a certain distance and direction from me. Otherwise, how did I know that I could reach it?

When we perceive, we learn how things are around us. But that remark is a bit ambiguous. Suppose I say that when you look at an accurate clock, you learn what time it is in the time zone you are in. That's true. But is it true if said of a child, who doesn't know what time zones are? It's still true in a way. The child learns what time it is in the time zone she is in, as opposed to learning what time it is in some other time zone. But there is nothing in her thinking that reflects that she is this time zone rather than that one, so it is misleading.

Is there something defective in the child's approach to time? That depends. Given the child's life, does she need to keep track of time-zones? Does it matter to her that there are other time-zones? Perhaps it does; perhaps she talks to her grandmother in Denver, and finds the whole things very confusing. But perhaps it doesn't. Perhaps she never talks to anyone outside her time zone, and never travels. In that case, there is no point in her thinking, as she sees the clock, "It is 3 p.m., Pacific Time."

The general point is this. Sometimes all of the facts we deal with involving a certain n-ary relation involve the same object occupying one of the argument roles. In that case, we don't need to worry about that argument role; we don't need to keep track of its occupant, because it never changes. We can, so to speak, pack it into the relation. For centuries people in Europe assumed that *being a summer month* was a property of months. July was a summer month, December was not. Once they started to visit the Southern Hemisphere, they had to take account of the relativity to places. July was a summer month in the Northern Hemisphere, but not in the Southern Hemisphere. A child who is unconcerned about and even unaware of the weather anywhere but where he is, can treat the issue of whether it is raining or not as a property of a time, rather than a relation between times and places. He says, "It is raining now" rather than "It is raining here now." (In this case the argument role is no always occupied by the same place, but always occupied by a place with a fixed relation to the agent, the place he is at.) The child we thought of above says "It is *now* 7 o'clock p.m.," treating *being 7 o'clock p.m.* as a property of the present time, rather than a relation between that time and a place or time zone. Before Einstein, we could treat simultaneity as a 2-ary relation between events, rather than as a 3-ary relation between a pair of events and an inertial frame, because in our daily life we never need to worry about alternative inertial frames.

In all of these cases, I say that the judgement *concerns* the fixed, unarticulated object, even thought it is not explicitly about it. (See Perry (1986a)). The judgement concerns the object because its truth-value of the depends on the object, even when it is not explicitly represented in thought. The child's is right when he thinks "It is 7 o'clock" because it is 7 o'clock Pacific Coast Time; he is right when he judges "It is raining now," if it is raining where he is.

Let us then return to the remark that I said was ambiguous, that when we perceive we learn how things are around us. When we perceive how the world is around us and act upon it, we need to judge what distance and direction things stand relative to ourselves. But we do not need to keep track of who it is that we are judging things to be in front of or to the left of, at least as long as we are basing our actions on simple perceptual knowledge. In this case, our knowledge concerns ourselves but need not involve an explicit representation of ourselves.

Of course, humans use a wide variety of knowledge, not only the input from immediate perception. They combine this input with all sorts of facts and general principles that they know from previous experience and communication of various sorts. All of this requires a notion of themselves, and once we have one, there is an easy transition from "There is an apple" or "Apple in front" to "There is an apple in front of me." But if our cognizing were confined to discovering facts about the objects around us and acting upon them, we would only need selfless thoughts. There are systems that perceive, and use the information about their circumstances they get through perception, that do not know that it is *their* circumstances they are learning about. During our formative stages and in certain moods later on, we may be such systems.

This then is the first aspect of self-knowledge, agent-relative knowledge of things that play various roles in our lives. This kind of knowledge is self-knowledge, in that it embodies knowledge of the relations things stand in to the agent; the thoughts are true because of facts about the agent. But it does not require that the agent have an idea of self or a notion of itself.

The detach and recognize information game

The concept of agent-relative knowledge fits into what I call the "detach and recognize information game" (Perry, 1997). We live in a world where we encounter the same objects on different occasions. On each of these occasions we are in a position to learn some facts about the object. If we can accumulate this knowledge, then in later encounters we will be able to deal with the object in light of this whole file of information, rather than simply what we can pick up on that occasion.

Suppose I am talking to you at a conference. You are occupying a number of agent-relative roles in my life: the person in front of me, the person I am talking to, the person talking to me, the person I see, and so forth. I am taking in a lot of information about you and deciding what to say to you and in general how to treat you. I accumulate information—the way I am thinking about it, this means I associate ideas to the notion I have formed of you. During this whole period, this notion is *attached* to the perceptions I have of you, to roles you are playing in my life and hence to the epistemic and pragmatic methods connected with those roles. It is what I call a *buffer*.

The conference is over; you go one way, I go another. I still have a notion of you. But now it is *detached*. The notion is no longer a buffer, but what I call an *enduring notion*. It is not connected to any agent-relative roles and epistemic and pragmatic methods. I may want to ask you a question, or tell you something, or hit you or shake your hand. The ideas in my file may give me good reasons to do all of those things. And I do know how to ask questions, tell people things, hit them and shake their hands. But only when they are playing certain roles in my life. To do these, things, I need to get my notion of you attached to the appropriate roles.

Suppose then we meet again. At first I don't recognize you. I see you, form a notion, a buffer, and begin to collect information. After a while I recognize you as the person I saw before. This time the buffer doesn't endure; the information is transferred to my old notion of you, which now attached to the stream of perceptual information.

Now I am in a position to ask you a question or shake your hand. That's what recognition is: getting one's file on a person or thing attached to the roles that the person is playing in one's life, so one can bring one's information about the object to bear on one's decisions about what to say and do. Misrecognition is attaching one's file to roles that the some other object is playing; failure to recognize is not attaching one's file of an object to a role the object is playing.

In our lives, of course, we are not dependent on perception of objects to form notions of them and learn a lot about them. We can learn of people, and learn a lot about them, by talking to third parties about them, and by reading things that they have written and that have been written about them. Suppose you think W.V.O. Quine is a great philosopher; you have read many of his works and many articles about him. You understand he is going to be at a philosophy department reception; you go. You have all sorts of things you want to say to him. You have a notion of Quine, formed when you first read about him or heard your philosophy professor talk about him. You have all sorts of ideas associated with your Quine notion—that he wrote *Word and Object*, that he is sort of a modern Pythagorean, arguing that all we need to believe in is set theory; that he has a pleasant, friendly face, looking a little like David Hume might have had he gone on a successful diet and taken up vigorous walking. You have a rich mental file on Quine.

This same notion is also involved in certain desires you have. You'd like to shake Quine's hand, and tell him how much you enjoy his works, and ask him if he is serious about his Pythagoreanism.

You read that Quine will be at a reception given by the Philosophy Department. You go to the reception. You are standing in front of Quine. Let's say for a while that you don't recognize him—he looks a little older than the picture of him on your book. There are a couple of other people that you think might be Quine. But eventually, partly on the basis of your memory of how he looks, and partly on the basis of how one of the candidates seems to talk and act like a modest but great philosopher might, things sort of click and you take one of them to be Quine.

Let's focus on this period when you have seen Quine, and are noticing things about him, but haven't quite recognized him. During this period, you have two notions of the same person. One of them is the one we talked about earlier. You acquired it when you first heard of Quine. Since that time information has been accumulating around it, and desires have been forming on the basis of this information. One thing associated with that notion is the desire to shake his hand. But of course there is no simple *method* for shaking Quine's hand. You have to know where he is relative to you to do this. This sort of information, where Quine is relative to you, isn't part of your notion. Or rather nothing very specific is—you think that he is at the same reception as you are, but that's not specific enough to support handshaking.

You have a second notion of Quine, a buffer, that you formed when you entered the room, and noticed him as one of the Quine candidates. Now this notion is associated with his position relative to you. As he moves or you move you "track him," keeping his position relative to you associated with the notion, so if you conclude that it is Quine you can strike.

Now you are standing next to Quine. The next-to relation is connected with epistemic and pragmatic methods. That is, there are certain ways of finding out more information about the person next to you, and there are certain ways of effecting the person next to you. You can find out more about him by looking. You can make him move by shoving. And you can shake his hand by turning towards him, extending yours, and smiling.

At this point you want to shake Quine's hand, and Quine is the person standing next to you, and you know how to shake the hand of the person next to you. So why don't you do it? Not because you don't see him there; you are looking at him very intently, almost staring. Because you don't quite recognize him; you're not sure. The desire to shake Quine's hand is associated with one notion of him, your enduring notion of him, the method for shaking hands is connected with another, your perceptual buffer of him as the person next to you. Only when you bring these together do you turn, smile, and extend your hand.

Suppose that F is an idea. That is, F is a cognitive particular in the mind of some person that combines with notions in that person's mind to produce judgements about the objects the notions are of. We might think of notions as names and ideas as predicates in a language of thought. Or we might think of notions and ideas as different sorts of nodes in a network that can be associated by edges of some sort. All I require of an idea is that it provide a way that notions can be modified.

What makes it the case that F was an idea of some agent-relative role R? It is by being associated to the epistemic and pragmatic methods that are associated with R. I'll call these "normally R-informative ways of knowing" and "normally R-effecting ways of acting."

A notion that is associated with F, an F-notion, will serve as the *repository* of information that is normally acquired by methods for finding out about the object that plays the F role, and the *motivator* of actions that are directed at (whose success depends upon) the nature of things that play the F role.

A notion, whether buffer or enduring notion, that is associated with the idea of a role R, I call an "R-notion," for as long as the association continues. Of course, this is not an enduring trait of notions, since typically the same object will not play a given agent-relative role in our lives for very long. The apple is in front of me now, but won't be a moment from now. My apple notion is an *In-front* notion now, but won't be a moment from now. There are exceptions, of course. The role of being the planet I live on the surface of, for example, is one that has been occupied by Earth since I was born, and presumably will continue in that role until I die.

Mach and the shabby pedagogue

In 1885 Ernst Mach wrote:

> Not long ago, after a trying railway journey by night, when I was very tired, I got into an omnibus, just as another man appeared at the other end. 'What a shabby pedagogue that is, that has just entered,' thought I.

In this case, Mach had agent-relative knowledge of a certain person, which he describes as "that man." He knows how to find out whether or not a man he sees at the other end of a bus is a shabby pedagogue. He is thinking of the man he sees as a man at in front of him some distance away, for to find out more about that man he uses the methods appropriate for someone playing that role. Now in this particular case Mach wasn't motivated to do much of anything. We can suppose that he saw a bunch of lint on the man's vest. There are methods for getting the lint removed from the vest of a man a few yards in front of one, if one cares a lot about it. One can shout, "Brush that lint off your vest, you shabby pedagogue," or one can walk forward and stretch out one's hand and brush it off for him. Mach no doubt would have used those methods, had he cared that much about the lint he saw, and not gone on to make an important discovery:

> It was myself: opposite me hung a large mirror. The physiognomy of my class, accordingly, was better known to me than my own (Mach, 1914, p. 4n).

During the period when didn't know who he was looking at, Mach could be said to have known something about himself in the following sense. He knew something about a certain person, the man he was looking at, the man he referred to as "that man." And this man, that he knew something about, was in fact Ernst Mach. Let's assume Mach's belief was true. What made it true was that Mach himself was a shabby pedagogue. It was a case of Mach knowing something about Mach, and in that sense, self-knowledge.

But it wasn't what we would ordinarily call self-knowledge. Mach only had that after he recognized himself, and was ready to say, "I am a shabby pedagogue." What Mach had, before he recognized himself, was knowledge of the person he happened to be. He knew about someone whom he thought of as "that man," and that person happened to be him.

This was a failure of *perceptual* recognition; Mach failed to recognize himself as the person he was perceiving. Another kind of case of recognition and failure of recognition is what I'll call *documentary*. One fails to recognize someone that one knows as the person one is reading about (or seeing a video about or a portrait of).

Suppose that Mach, when he gets off the bus, hits his head and as a result has amnesia. "He doesn't know who he is," we would say. When he wakes up in the hospital he sees a story in the paper, "Famous Scientist is Missing." It goes on to say the Ernst Mach never returned home, and his family and colleagues at the university are upset. We can imagine Mach reading this and not recognizing himself as Mach, not knowing that he is the missing person, not remembering his name and his profession. This is a failure of documentary self-recognition. This is another case of Mach having knowledge of the person he happens to be, but not what we would ordinarily call self-knowledge.

Self-Attached Knowledge

Ordinarily all one's knowledge about oneself is integrated around a special sort of idea or notion of oneself that we express with "I." While my perception that the beer is in front of me may not require a representation of myself, the information I acquire is immediately integrated into self-attached knowledge, that I might express with "I see a beer" or "there is a beer in front of me." And when I read a piece of email, that says that John Perry's paper is overdue, I integrate this information into self-attached knowledge, "My paper is overdue," and I realize that it is me that has to get to work. I would think, "There is a beer in front of *me*, but *I* have a paper to do. So I want to turn to the question of this kind of knowledge. What did Mach lack, when he "didn't recognize himself"?

The view I advocate is simply that identity is a basic relation, and that our idea of self ("being me") is the idea of the agent-relative role, *is identical*. This is the role we each play in our own lives. That is, identity, like being in front or behind or above, is a basic relation relative to which we have epistemic and pragmatic methods. There are certain methods for picking up information about the person identical with us, and certain methods for having an effect on that person. The notion that is the repository of information gained via those methods, and the motivator of actions associated with that relation, is our self-notion. The person this notion is of, is the person we take ourselves to be.

An uncharitable summary of the view I am putting forward would be that my idea of *me* is just is the idea of *the person identical with me*, which seems clearly circular, since the defining idea seems to contain the idea of *me*, the very idea being defined. It is agent-relative knowledge that keeps the account from circularity. It is not the idea, *person identical with me* that I need, but only the role-idea, *person identical*. My idea of *me* is not a part of this idea.

But why should we think that "being identical" is one of these epistemic-pragmatic relations?

Suppose I am at a party. I bend over to pick something up, and I hear a ripping sound that is characteristic of trousers splitting. I suspect that the trousers that have just ripped are my own. But they might not be. You can hear other people's trousers splitting. Then I feel a hot flush in my face. So I am aware that someone is blushing. But who? It's a silly question. Of course it is me. It is my own blushing of which I am aware. I can be aware of the blushing of others. But I can't be aware of it in the same way that I can be aware of my own blushing. I feel myself blush, and anytime I am aware of blushing by feeling it, I know that it is I who am blushing.

This is an example of what I shall call a *reflexive method* of knowing. This is a method for finding out whether someone has some property or does not, that we can each use to find out about ourselves, but can't use to find out about others. What one finds out may be accessible to others, using different methods. But the particular method in question can only be used by the person in question to find out about himself or herself. Feeling hunger is normally a way of detecting that one's own stomach is short of food. Feeling thirst is a way of knowing that one's throat is parched or that one's body is short of water. There is a certain feeling, that children are trained to recognize, that signals that one's bladder is full. In each case, someone else can determine the same thing, using a different technique. This alternative technique may even be superior. Perhaps you can tell that I am blushing, by looking, when I am not sure. Perhaps you can be sure that my stomach is full, having noticed what I have put into it, when I am still in that charming interval between being full and feeling full. Parents are often better judges of the states of their children's bladder than the children themselves are. So the point isn't that our reflexive methods of knowing about ourselves are always infallible or superior to any other methods. It is that only we can use them.

In these examples, the fact that these methods of discovering a person's states are for the exclusive use of the person in question, is a matter of quite reliable but not quite necessary facts. We could imagine, for example, cases involving spinal columns that are connected across bodies which had the result that one person knew about the state of another person's stomach in the way that we normally know only of the states of our own stomach.

We also have reflexive methods of knowing our own mental states, and in these cases it seems quite plausible to suppose that this is a matter of necessity. There are ways that I have of knowing whether I have a headache, or a throbbing tooth, or believe that Berkeley is west of Santa Cruz, that I employ to find out about my own mental states, and others employ to find out about theirs. It is very difficult to imagine even a science fiction case in which one uses these methods to find out about someone else's mental states.

On Locke's theory of personal identity, at least according to one way of interpreting and developing it, this special way of knowing one's own mental states guarantees identity by bestowing identity. An instance of being aware of an experience, and the experience of which one is aware is known, necessarily belong to the same person, because it is in terms of this relation, that "same person" is defined.

Locke says that this method of knowing experiences and actions may be extended back in time. It seems that what he has in mind is what we might call first person memory. Compare:

(1) I remember Mach wrote *The Analysis of Sensation.*

(2) I remember Mach writing *The Analysis of Sensation.*

(3) I remember writing *The Analysis of Sensation.*

(1) might be said truly by any of us who remember that Mach wrote the book; (2) might be said by any of his family and colleagues who remember him laboring on it, but (3) could be truly said only by Mach. It seems to be getting at a way of remembering, "remembering from the inside," in Shoemaker's phrase, that we each have of remembering our own past experiences, and with which we can remember no others (Shoemaker, 1970).

But in the case of memory from the inside, it is not so clear that the link is a necessary one. In his influential paper "Persons and Their Pasts," Shoemaker develops some examples in which it seems we can remember,[154] in this way experiences we did not have.

There are also reflexive ways of acting. These are ways of bringing it about that someone has a property, that each person can use to bring it about that he or she has a property, but cannot use to bring it about that others have it. Towards the end of the movie "Spellbound" Leo. G. Carroll points his gun at

---

[154]Or at least "quasi-remember"; one quasi-remembers an experience if one fulfills all of the conditions other than being the original experiencer. See also (Shoemaker, 1984) and (Shoemaker, 1996)

Ingrid Bergman as she walks out the door of his office, having just disclosed that she knows that he framed Gregory Peck. We see this from Leo. G. Carroll's perspective. Then we see the hand holding the gun turn slowly, until the barrel of the gun is all that is visible on the screen. Then it fires. We know what Carroll has done, and to whom. He has killed someone, and the someone is him. The way Carroll held and fired the gun was a reflexive way of killing.

What is special about self-notions

So far I have emphasized the analogy between self-notions, notions that are associated with the role-idea of *being identical*, and notions that are associated with ideas of other agent-relative roles. But there is one important disanalogy. As we saw above, the other cases (or most of them), the attachment between notion and role cannot be permanent, because different objects occupy the same roles relative to us at different times. We noted one exception, the role of being the planet lived on. And of course there are indefinitely many others based on the same general idea: being the star that warms, being the part of the universe relied on most, etc. Clearly, the person with whom I am identical falls into this category of nonshifting roles, but in this case the reliability is not a contingent matter. It is logically possible that I will move to Mars, or even to a planet in the system of another sun. But it is not possible that I will ever be identical with anyone other than me. If I have picked out the right notion to be my self-notion once, it will continue to be the right one.

This is not to say people cannot be wrong, nor that they might not change their self-notion. My parents might have, as sort of a practical joke, raised me believing I was really Al Smith, former Governor of New York and Democratic Presidential candidate. They tell me that in an extreme use of the witness protection program, I was shrunken and made child-like. My memory was obliterated and then I was passed off as John Perry, the real John Perry having died in 1944 as an infant. They recommend that I go along with the story, and pretend to believe that I am really John Perry. At some point I do a bit of research, uncover the prank, and realize that Al Smith really did die in 1944, and I am John Perry, just as everyone but me and, as I thought, my parents, had always believed. At that point my Al Smith notion would cease to be my self-notion, and my John Perry notion take over that job. And I might become convinced, at some point in the future when I sink into madness or senility, that I am really Napoleon and not John Perry. One can be mistaken about who one is.

But for most of us most of the time, possessed of sober parents and a sound mind, there will never be any reason to detach our self-notion from our enduring notion of the person we are, and we and everyone who knows us takes us to be.

Back to Mach

Now let us see if this analysis provides us with a plausible candidate for what Mach lacked in the two cases we considered.

When he looks to the far end of the bus, Mach gets information about himself in a way that is not normally self-informative, but normally "person-in-front-and-looked-at" informative. So this information doesn't pass into his self-notion; it is not combined with information gotten in reflexive ways. And it doesn't motivate normally reflexive actions.

Suppose Mach looks down at his own vest and sees a big piece of lint. (Mach himself provides us with a picture of the way one's front characteristically looks to oneself.) He would have associated the idea of having a large piece of lint on one's vest with his self-notion. That's what I mean by saying that the self-notion is the repository of normally self-informative perception. Now if Mach had desired not to have large pieces of lint on himself, he would have reached out and removed in a way that works when the piece of lint is on one's own vest. If he has this desire, and the idea of having lint on one's vest is associated with his self-notion, we would expect him to take such a normally self-directed action. That's what I mean by saying that the self-notion is the motivator of normally self-directed actions.

But when Mach sees a piece of lint on the vest of the person in the mirror he does not act in this way. The information is not gotten in the normally self-informative way.[155] So it is not combined with the other information in the self-notion, and doesn't lead to the action that works to remove lint from oneself. At the beginning of the episode, Mach formed a notion for the person he saw, whom he took to be getting on the other end of the bus. This was a notion of himself, but not a self-notion. We assume Mach knew who he was, and so that he had a notion of Ernst Mach as having all of the well-known properties of Ernst Mach that was also a self-notion. Mach's beliefs change, during the episode, in that he transfers the information associated with the new notion formed when he got on the bus to his old self-notion. If, after he has made the transfer, he notices that the person in the mirror has a piece of lint on his vest, he will pick the lint of his own vest in the normally self-dependent and self-effecting way of picking lint off one's vest.

Now let us turn to the case of Mach the amnesiac, reading about himself in the paper. He plays the role in his own life of "person being read about." He forms a notion of this person; he knows he is called "Mach," is a scientist, and is missing. Even in the middle of a bout of amnesia Mach would have had at least a self-buffer, a notion tied to normally self-informative action and

---

[155]In many situations, looking into a mirror is a normally self-informative way of getting information. In Mach's case the mirror was far away and not set up for self-viewing, and he didn't seem to realize at first that he was looking into a mirror.

perception. He realizes that the table he sees in front, is in front of him, the same person who is reading the paper and can't remember who he is. He does not associate the ideas he picks up from reading the paper, of being named "Mach," being a scientist, and being missing, with his self-notion; that is, that role remains unattached to the self-notion.

Self-notions and "I"

The word "I" refers to the speaker or writer. Thus the meaning of the first person associates it with a role in the situation of discourse. One reason for having such a word is that it puts a modest cognitive load on the hearer in a variety of common speech situations. One is a face to face speech situation, in which some of the information a speaker is providing will be likely to motivate actions towards the speaker. So, for example, you and I are sitting at a table and I say, "I'd like some salt." I want you to hand the salt to me. You, being an agreeable sort, will hand the salt to anyone who wants it. In order for my request to work, I simply have to depend on you knowing English, and being able to tell that the person speaking to you is the person playing a certain perceptual role. You don't have to know anything more about me.

If, on the other hand, I were to say, "John Perry would like some salt," there is no telling what you might do. Perhaps you would say, "Good for him." My request puts a larger cognitive load on you; you need to know more in order to be expected to accede to it. You need to have recognized the person before you as a person named "John Perry." Even if I'm pretty certain that you do know who I am—perhaps we are old friends—it will still sound odd and sort of pompous to say "John Perry wants salt." The only fact relevant to your passing the salt would usually be that I am a human being who wants the salt.

On the other hand, use of the first person is inappropriate in other situations. If I call you on the phone, and you clearly don't recognize my voice, I need to tell you my name, and it's impolite to do otherwise.

The first person also puts a relatively light cognitive load on the speaker. When Mach had amnesia, he still referred to himself with "I"—or "ich" at any rate. To know that he was doing so he needed to know i) the meaning of "I" and ii) that he was the utterer of the words he was speaking. That is, he needed to realize that that the words he was going to speak, the one's he was planning to say, would be spoken by him. There is in fact a certain way of knowing whom words are spoken by, when the words are the result of one's own planning and articulating; they will be spoken by the planner and articulator, and hence, if the word is "I," will refer to that person. Thus, a person who has forgotten who they are, and so no longer has a enduring notion associated with the self-role, may nevertheless successfully and confidently refer to himself or herself.

Most of us don't get amnesia, so having a referring device that enables us to refer to ourselves without knowing very much about ourselves isn't all that important. But in philosophy, having such a device is often of great value. The point isn't that we don't know much about ourselves, but that we don't want to assume much about ourselves. Why should Descartes say "I think" rather than "Descartes thinks"? (Anscombe, 1975). When he says "I think" he does not assume that there is a person with a past like Descartes has and a name "Descartes." He can use the method of doubt to bracket all of that knowledge he has of himself.

Now what Descartes can't quite do is to refer to himself without assuming anything except what he is entitled to at the beginning of the Second Meditation. For to refer to himself with "I" (or 'je") he needs to assume that there is a language with a word in it that refers to the person who uses it. But, to be fair, to write his *Meditations*, as opposed to merely meditating them, Descartes does need to assume that, or at least play along with his inclination to believe that, there is a language.

The first person, then, does not give philosophers as secure a way of talking about themselves as their self-notions give them of thinking about themselves. I can think about myself so long as I exist and have a self-notion, even if there is no language at all, although in the case I cannot refer to myself. But first person pronouns, like "I," "ich" and "je," give philosophers a pretty secure way of referring to themselves, one that should satisfy all but the most dedicated solipsists. The most dedicated solipsists don't write very much anyway.

20

Reflexivity, Indexicality and Names

Introduction

Consider:

(1) "I am a computer scientist." (said by David Israel)
(2) "David is a computer scientist." (said by someone who is referring to David Israel with "David")

It has been persuasively argued by David Kaplan and others that the proposition expressed by statements like (1) is a *singular proposition*, true in just those worlds in which a certain person, David Israel, is a computer scientist. Call this proposition P. The truth of this proposition does not require that the utterance (1) occur, or even that Israel has ever said anything at all. Marcus, Donnellan, Kripke and others have persuasively argued for a view of proper names that, put in Kaplan's terms and applied to this example, implies that the proposition expressed by (2) is also simply P.[156]

The thesis that expressions of a certain category (names, indexicals, demonstratives, pronouns, descriptions, etc.) are *referential*[157] holds that these expressions contribute the object to which they refer, rather than a mode of presentation of that object, to the propositions expressed by statements containing them.

The thesis that indexicals and names are referential creates the challenge of explaining the difference in *cognitive significance* between statements like (1) and (2), that express the same proposition (Wettstein, 1986). The problem has two parts, which I'll call "cognitive motivation" and "cognitive impact." The

---

[156](Marcus, 1961), (Donnellan, 1970), (Kripke, 1980).

[157]David Kaplan's term is *directly referential*. Kaplan has a precise concept of "directness" in mind, but unless one is focusing on his exact words, the term "directly" is likely to suggest that there is no semantic mechanism intervening between the expression and its referent. This is pretty clearly not the case with indexicals, as Kaplan's own analysis shows; it may be more plausible for proper names. Using terminology introduces in Section 3 we can say: Kaplan's language suggests that directly referential terms *name*, but what he really says is simply that they *refer*.

problem of cognitive motivation is that in many circumstances, the beliefs and desires that might lead a competent user of English to assert (1) differ from those that might lead one to assert (2). The problem of cognitive impact is that in many circumstances the beliefs and desires a competent listener would acquire (and would be expected to acquire) from hearing (1) differ from those she would acquire from hearing (2). If (1) and (2) express exactly the same proposition, why should this be so?

Let's look at our example in some detail. First note that differences in David's beliefs might lead him to assert (1) rather than (2) or vice versa. Suppose David has amnesia. He might have figured out what his profession was, but not have remembered his name. Then he would be in a position to assert (1) but not (2). Or he might have figured out that a certain person, David Israel, was a computer scientist, without realizing that he is that person. Then he would be in a position to assert (2) but not (1).

In the normal case, in which David does not have amnesia, differences in desire could motivate him to assert (1) rather than (2), or vice versa. In normal circumstances, if Israel wants to tell someone his profession, he will use (1) and not (2). Suppose, for example, that David has made some interesting points following a paper by a guest lecturer at CSLI. After the session he chats with the speaker, who seems unsure that he can trust what David says about programming languages. It would be natural for David to say (1), and odd for him to say (2). He wants to reassure his interlocutor about the reliability of what he says about programming languages. (1) will do that; (2) might not. I'll call this example Case 1.

There are easily imaginable circumstances in which David's desires would lead him to use (2) but not (1). Suppose a government bureaucrat has the job of identifying computer scientists, who will then be sent a letter offering a well-paid job building the Information Highway. The bureaucrat himself has a clear antipathy towards computer scientists. He reads David names from a list of people who work at SRI and asks if they were then or ever had been computer scientists. When he gets to "David Israel," Israel might just say (2), figuring that the information that *he* was the person in question was simply irrelevant and would lead the bureaucrat to be rude to him. Here David would not want his interlocutor to know that he, the person being talked to, was a computer scientist but he would want him to know the individual who is designated by the token of "David Israel" on the list is a computer scientist. He thinks that he will pass on that information with (2). I'll call this Case 2.

Given that David knows that he is David Israel, his choice between (1) and (2) is based on the effect he wants his utterance to have on the beliefs of his interlocutor—what I am calling its "cognitive impact." He thinks that if he utters (1), his interlocutor will realize that the person he is talking to is a computer scientist. If he utters (2), his interlocutor might not realize that, even if he believes what David says.

In fact Israel is well-known as a computer scientist, but looks and acts more like a philosopher. A competent speaker who hears (1) may well be skeptical about what he hears, even though he readily assents to (2), or even asserts it himself, having read articles by Israel. How is this difference possible, if the propositions expressed by (1) and (2) are the same?

My thesis in this paper is that to understand the difference in cognitive significance between (1) and (2), we need to acknowledge several different kinds of *content*. The paper develops a line of argument put forward in Essays 11, 13 and 14 above. In those papers a distinction is made between *reflexive* and *incremental* content, and it is argued that the former is relevant to cognitive significance. This distinction is most intuitive in the case of indexicals. In this paper I show how the basic idea can be extended to deal with proper names, without treating them as if they were indexicals. This requires examining the difference between reflexivity and indexicality, and explaining how the concept of reflexivity can be applied to expressions that are not indexicals. But I will start with indexicals, and then move to consider names.

Indexicals

(A) captures most of what a competent English speaker knows about the word "I":

   (A) A use u of "I" designates x iff x is the speaker of u.

From this, we see that (1), will be true iff

   Q: There is an x such that i) x is the speaker of (1);
        ii) x is a computer scientist.

Q is not the proposition expressed by (1); as we saw, that is P. The truth values of P and Q will agree in the actual world, but may disagree in other possible worlds. In the worlds in which Israel is a computer scientist, but does not utter (1), P is true and Q is false. This does not mean that Q is irrelevant to the cognitive significance of (1), however. Q gives us what a competent user of English who hears (1) will know, just on the basis of those facts, about its truth conditions.

Someone who knows English and hears (1), but isn't in a position to see who said it, would still realize that Q captured the conditions under which it was true. Such a person might express this knowledge by saying "This utterance is true, iff *its* speaker is a computer scientist." The truth conditions he associates with (1) are *reflexive* in that Q is about the utterance (1) *itself*. Because he doesn't know who the speaker is, he cannot "detach" the truth conditions of (1) from (1) itself.

In contrast, someone who learns that Israel is the speaker of (1), can get at the truth conditions of (1) in a nonreflexive way: "This utterance is true iff Israel is a computer scientist." I call this the *incremental* truth conditions of (1), *given* that Israel is the speaker. "Incremental" is used here in the sense of "additional." Given that Israel is the speaker of u, what *more* has to be true for u to be true? Answer: Israel has to be a computer scientist. This is just the proposition P, the proposition expressed by both (1) and (2). The incremental truth conditions correspond to the ordinary philosophical concept of truth conditions; they are *what is said* by the speaker of the utterance. I'll also call this "official content."

The difference between Cases 1 and 2 above has to do with the *mode of presentation* that Israel wanted his hearer to associate with the belief that he was a computer scientist. In Case 1, Israel wanted the hearer to recognize that the person spoken about was also the person speaking. The plan of understanding that he has in mind goes roughly like this:

> The hearer will perceive my utterance, and, as a competent speaker of English will recognize that it is true iff the person who makes it is a computer scientist (Q). He will also see that I, the person in front of him and talking to him, is the speaker of the utterance. So he will learn that the person in front of him is a computer scientist, and will realize he can learn more about this fascinating field by asking questions of this person.

In Case 2, when Israel does not want the hearer to recognize that he is speaking to a computer scientist, he does not refer to himself with the expression "I," and so does not disclose to the hearer that the person with whom he is talking is a computer scientist.

We cannot explain all of this if we only have the official content of (1) to work with. Its official content is the singular proposition P, the same official content that (2) has. But that is not all we have to work with. We also have the reflexive content, the proposition Q. This allows us to construct an explanation of why David chose to utter (1) in Case 1 but not in Case 2.

One might object at this point as follows. The source of the original problem was the fact that according to referentialism we don't have modes of presentation of David Israel but Israel himself in the propositions expressed by (1) and (2); the difference between them is lost: they both express the same singular proposition, P. But we cannot solve this by appealing to Q, for it is also a singular proposition, containing the utterance (1) as a constituent. Just as one can have different modes of presentation of David Israel, one can have different modes of presentation of (1). In Case 1, Israel thinks of (1) in the way one thinks of an utterance one is making, while the guest lecturer thinks of (1) as an utterance made by the person one is talking to.

Suppose the room in which David utters (1) is large and cavernous and gives rise to echoes that are so clear people often fail to recognize them as echoes. A few seconds after Israel utters (1) and the guest lecturer hears him, the guest lecturer hears the echo, "I am a computer scientist." This gives the guest lecturer second mode of presentation of David's utterance. The first time he heard it, he thought of it as (roughly) "this utterance being made by the person I am talking to." The second time, when he heard the echo, he thought of it as "this strange utterance I am hearing I don't know from where."

These two hearings have quite a different cognitive impact on the guest lecturer. But the same utterance is involved both times, and hence the same reflexive content, the proposition Q with David's utterance as a constituent. The guest lecturer has two modes of presentation of (1), corresponding to the two times he heard it. Since Q is a singular proposition with (1) itself as a constituent, rather than a mode of presentation, Q can't account for the different impact the two hearings had. So Q, because it is a singular proposition, can't solve our problem.

This objection fails. The fact that P is a singular proposition gives rise to the problem of saying how the cognitive motivation and impact of (1) and (2) differ, given that they both express P. Recognizing that Q is the reflexive content of (1) but not of (2), allows us to understand how there can be a plan into which an utterance of (1) fits but an utterance of (2) does not. Q gets at the relevant difference between (1) and (2).

While Q does not get at the relevant difference in the echo case, it helps us to understand the relevance of the obvious difference between the two hearings of the same utterance. That difference is that the hearer has two different modes of presentation of the same utterance, and believes different things about it, under these different modes of presentation.

The importance of the echo case is that it brings out the fact that in our conversational plans we have to take account of the way in which the utterance will be apprehended. David's plan reflected his expectation that the lecturer would think of David's utterance as coming from the mouth of the person in front of him, not as a strange utterance coming from an unknown source.

Still, we have only solved part of our problem. In case 2, David does want his hearer to realize that the person designated by "David Israel" on his list of SRI employees is a computer scientist. He manages to bring this impact about by using his own name when he responds. How does this work?

Names

Before I develop an account of names, let me make two important distinctions about designation. The first distinction has to do with what a term contributes to the official content of statements of which it is a part. Terms *refer* if they contribute the object they designate, rather than some mode of presentation of it, to official content, so that their official contents are singular propositions about the object designated. Terms *describe* if they contribute a mode of presentation, a condition on objects, that they incorporate. In the table below, referentialism about indexicals and names is reflected by entries in the "Refers" column. Descriptions are put in the "Describes" column, since we are not assuming referentialism with respect to them.[158]

	Refers	Describes
Names	Proper names	???
Denotes	Indexicals	Descriptions

TABLE 2 Varieties of Designation

I use the words "denotes" and "names" for a different distinction. This has to do with the kind of conventions that are associated with terms of a given type. Terms *denote* if the conventions of language associate them with modes of presentation, with conditions on the object designated. This is clearly true of descriptions. For example, the rules of language do not associate any particular person with the description, "the tallest philosophy professor in America," but merely a certain condition. The person who satisfies the condition is designated by the description, but one can know the meaning of description without having any idea who that is.

Indexicals also denote, in this sense. The conventions of English do not associate particular individuals with the words "I" and "you," but conditions that individuals must satisfy to be the designata of uses of those words. So indexicals denote, as descriptions do. But indexicals do not describe. They refer. The individuals that meet the conditions, rather than the conditions themselves, are contributed to official content.

Terms *name*, on the other hand, if the conventions that secure designations for them directly associate them with objects, rather than conditions on objects. This distinction and terminology allows me to state my account of names in a way that sounds persuasively trivial: names name.

When a person or thing is assigned a name, a *permissive convention* is established: that name *may* be used to designate that person. When David Israel's parents named him "David," they established a convention that made it possible for people to designate their son with the name "David." It did not preclude people from using "David" to designate other people.

When a name is used in a conversation or text to refer to a given person,

---

[158]For this distinction see (Marti, forthcoming); see also (Recanati, 1993) for wisdom about the issues.

the speaker is exploiting a permissive convention of this sort. A single name like "David" may be associated with hundreds of thousands of people by different permissive conventions. In the abstract, the problem of knowing which conventions are being exploited when one apprehends a token containing the word "David" are considerable. And when one sees something like "David was here" scrawled on a wall one may be completely clueless as to which of the millions of Davids is being designated. But usually various factors work to make the use of proper names a practical way of talking about things. I only know a small minority of the Davids that can be designated with "David"; the ones I know overlap in various fairly predictable ways with the ones known by people I regularly meet in various contexts; principles of charity dictate that I take my interlocutors to be designating Davids that might have, or might be taken to have, the properties that are being predicated of the David in question; and I can always just ask.

The role of context in resolving the issues of which naming conventions are being exploited is quite different from its role with indexicals. In the case of indexicals, the meaning of a given expression determines that certain specific contextual relationships to the utterance and utterer—who is speaking, or to whom, or when—determine designation. Different facts are relevant for different indexicals, and the meaning of the indexical determines which. Names don't work like this. The difference between "David" and "Harold" is not that they are tied, by their meanings, to different relationships to the utterance or utterer. The role of context is simply to help us narrow down the possibilities for the permissive conventions that are being exploited.

If we have to give this phenomenon a familiar name, it would be "ambiguity." The same name has many different meanings; as with ambiguous expressions, the role of context is to help us determine which meaning is relevant in a given use, rather than to supply a specific type of fact called for by the relevant meaning. There are many differences between the phenomenon in question and what we usually call "ambiguity," however. Paradigm ambiguous expressions have only a few meanings, most of which are known to people who use the expression, or can be easily found by looking in a good dictionary. One can realistically aspire to knowing most of the meanings of many words. Many names have thousands of meanings—that is, there are thousands of individuals that they are used to designate, exploiting various permissive conventions. People who use a given name will be ignorant of the vast majority of its meanings, and it would be silly to aspire to know most of them. For help in discovering or narrowing the possibilities in particular cases one might use a phonebook, or even an encyclopedia, but not a dictionary.

So with names we have ambiguity, not indexicality. Nevertheless, we can define a useful concept of reflexive truth conditions for statements involving names.

Consider a case in which I see "David uses LISP" spray painted on a wall that I pass on my way to work in the morning. I have no idea which David is being designated. So I have no idea what proposition is expressed by the graffiti, no idea of what its official content might be. But I can say under what conditions the graffiti—call it **g**—is true:[159]

R: There is a person x and a convention C such that
    i) C is exploited by **g**;
    ii) C permits one to designate x with "David";
    iii) x uses LISP.

R is not the proposition expressed by **g**—not **g**'s official content. But it does give truth conditions for **g**. And R is reflexive; that is, it is a proposition about the very utterance of which it is the truth conditions.

Now let us suppose that **g** is actually a remark about David Israel, spray painted on the wall by a gang of teen-age admirers. In that case the content of **g** is a singular proposition about David Israel, and quite a different proposition than R. But R is a proposition we want to have available, as part of our explanation of the impact of the perception of this message has on me.

Suppose I am irritated with the graffiti, and want to find out who did it. I start with R and common sense. The people who wrote **g** were exploiting a convention that connected a particular David with their use of "David." This David uses LISP (or at least might be accused of such a thing). And the graffiti writers in my neighborhood are in a position to exploit a convention that permits them to refer to him with "David." This might allow me to figure out who the graffiti was about—I ask around the neighborhood to see if anyone knows a computer scientist named David who either uses LISP or would be shocked to be accused of such a thing. Once I track down David, I ask him who might be spray painting things on walls about his programming habits.

Now let's return to Case 2. This is the case in which David utters (2) because he doesn't want his interlocutor to know that he is talking to David Israel, although he doesn't mind if he learns that the David Israel he is asking about is a computer scientist. We imagined that the interlocutor had a list of SRI employees, and he was going down the list.

First let's ask ourselves what the bureaucrat learns when he sees the name "David Israel" on the list of people who work at SRI. The official content of the statement made by the presence of Israel's name on the list is the singular proposition that he works at SRI. It would be misleading to say that this is what the interlocutor learns, however, since we are supposing he is merely a bureaucrat who has never heard of David Israel and has no concept of him except that he gains in virtue of seeing his name on the list. He has no way

---

[159]I am sliding over the distinction between tokens and utterances here; what I perceive is a token that I take to be a trace of and evidence for an utterance. See (Perry, 1995a).

of thinking of Israel, that is, except as "the person designated by this use of 'David Israel'," which in terms of our account comes to "the person whom the conventions exploited by this use of 'David Israel' allow us to call 'David Israel'. We might then say that the bureaucrat does not fully grasp the meaning of the statement he is inspecting (which I'll call **h**). He knows the conventions associated with "works at SRI" and he knows the type of convention associated with the use of "David Israel," so he knows quite a bit. But he doesn't know everything. What he knows is that **h** is true iff:

S: There is a person x and a convention C such that
   i) C is exploited by **h**; ii) C permits one to designate x with "David";
   iii) x works at SRI.

Now the bureaucrat formulates his question: "What does David Israel do?" In asking this question, the bureaucrat exploits the convention that governs the token of "David Israel" on the list of SRI employees he is using. It is interesting that he can do this. He doesn't know the convention *as* a convention for calling a certain person by a name, but only *as* the convention that is governing a certain use of the name. As far as he knows, he has never been presented with the person designated by that token except *as* the person presented by it. It may be surprising, if one has certain philosophical predispositions, that the bureaucrat can ask a question the official content of which has David Israel as a constituent, a question which is *about* David Israel, when he knows so little about him. But it seems scarcely deniable. The bureaucrat seeks to be a conduit, taking information about Israel from person in front of him, who he assumed to have some richer level of acquaintance and interaction with Israel than he himself has, and passing it on down the line until it will be used by someone who also has a richer level of acquaintance or can gain it, say by summoning Israel to an office for an interview.

To achieve this purpose, the bureaucrat needn't know who Israel is, by any normal standards at least. What he does need to do is to make sure that the David Israel he has been asked to gather information about is the same one that the person in front of him is going to tell him about. He needs to make sure that the conventions governing his use of "David Israel" are the ones governing its use in the reply he gets. He might do that by asking, "Do you know a person named 'David Israel' who works here at SRI? Do you know more than one?" If David answers appropriately he goes on to ask, "And what does David Israel do?"

David replies with (2). The reflexive truth conditions of (2) are that

T: There is a person x and a convention C such that
   i) C is exploited by (2);
   ii) C permits one to designate x with "David";
   iii) x is a computer scientist.

David's plan is that the bureaucrat, being a competent English speaker, will grasp T. He will assume that David is being helpful, and exploiting the same naming convention that he is—the same one the question on the form he is filling out exploits. This enables him to answer the question on his form. So David is helpful. But nothing in the transaction provides the interlocutor with information that David Israel is the person that is speaking to him. So, the level of reflexive content enables us to complete our story, and see how by using (2) David can expect to satisfy the combination of beliefs and desires that he had in Case 2.

Relative Truth Conditions

We have appealed to reflexive content to solve both parts of our problem, Q for (1) and T for (2):

Q: There is an x such that:
   i) x is the speaker of (1);
   ii) x is a computer scientist.

T: There is a person x and a convention C such that:
   i) C is exploited by (2);
   ii) C permits one to designate x with "David";
   iii) x is a computer scientist.

Although Q and T are both reflexive, in the sense that they are about the very utterance whose truth conditions they are, there is an important difference between them.

Earlier we contrasted Q with P, the proposition that David is a computer scientist. I called P the *incremental* truth conditions of (1). The idea is that we fix the contextual facts: that David is the speaker of (1). Now *given* this fact, what *else* has to be true for (1) to be true? What are additional or incremental truth conditions of (1)? Simply that David is a computer scientist. However, the binary distinction, "incremental vs. reflexive" is too simple. We need more flexible concepts.

Let's step back a moment and think about the question, "What are the truth conditions of an utterance u?" I claim that the form of this question should really be "Given that utterance u has characteristics $C_1, \ldots, C_n$, what *else* has to be the case for it to be true?"

To explain what I am getting at here, let's consider some variations on Case 1:

a) The guest lecturer hears the words "I am a computer scientist," but he is not sure which of the people in front of him said them.

b) David mumbles and so the guest lecturer hears, "I am a [mumble-mumble]."

c) David's Boston accent is so bad that although the guest lecturer realized something has been asserted, he is not sure what the words were, or even what language they were in.

In these circumstances, does the speaker know the truth conditions of (1)? Not in the ordinary sense in which "the truth conditions" are used in philosophy. But in each case, there is a sense in which the guest lecturer knows the truth conditions, for in each case the speaker knows some facts about the utterance, and knows what additional conditions must be met for the utterance to be true:

a) In this case, we fix the fact that (1) was uttered by a member of the group in front of the guest lecturer and the facts about which words were spoken in what language and what they mean. This is what the guest lecturer knows. Given all of these facts, (1) is true iff *there is someone in the group who both spoke (1) and is a computer scientist*. This is not the official content of (1); it is not what David said. But it is what the guest lecturer learns; it is the cognitive impact of the utterance on him in this particular situation.

b) In this case we fix the facts that (1) was uttered by David, that it was in English, that it was of the form "I am an X," and that the words and construction mean what they do in English. This is what the guest lecturer knows. Given all of that, (1) is true iff *there is a word "K" so that David said "I am a K," and "K" stands for a certain sort of person, and David is a person of that sort*. This is not the official content of (1); it is not what David said. But given his mumbling, it is what the guest lecturer got from his utterance.

c) We fix the fact that David is the speaker, and that he is making an assertion. This is what the guest lecturer knows. Given all of that, (1) is true iff *in the language of (1) the words of (1) have a meaning that, given the contextual facts as they are, expresses a true proposition*. This is not the official content of (1); it is not what David said. But given David's terrible accent, it is what the guest lecturer got from his utterance.

a)–c) illustrate the *relative* concept of truth conditions we need for the epistemology of language. The truth conditions of an utterance u depend on what is *given*. The difference between P and Q above also illustrates this. Q and P provide answers to two different questions. Q answers the question:

> Given that an utterance u of "I am a computer scientist" is true iff the speaker is a computer scientist, what are the truth conditions of (1)— what *else* needs to be true for (1) to be true?

P answers the question:

> Given that an utterance u of "I am a computer scientist" is true iff the speaker is a computer scientist, *and* that (1) is spoken by David Israel,

what are the truth conditions of (1)—what *else* needs to be true for (1) to be true?

Both concepts of truth conditions are perfectly legitimate. And both can be used to get at the states of competent speakers who hear (1). Q gets at what is known of the truth conditions of (1) by those who hear and understand the utterance, but who don't know who is speaking. P gets at what is known of the truth conditions by those who know all of this and know that the speaker is David Israel.

There are indefinitely many relative truth conditions for an utterance, since there are indefinitely many characteristics $C_1, \ldots, C_n$ to plug into the formula "Given that utterance $\mathbf{u}$ has characteristics $C_1, \ldots, C_n$, what *else* has to be the case for it to be true?" I'll use terms of the form "content$_X$" to get at some of the more natural sets of characteristics that are useful to think about. I'll say that the content$_C$ of an utterance is its truth conditions given the facts about its meaning and its context. P is the content$_C$ of (1). Content$_M$ is the content with just the meaning fixed, so Q is the content$_M$ of (1).

Now let's look at (2). If we fix the meaning of (2), we fix the naming conventions that are being exploited. The content$_M$ of (2) is just P, the proposition that David Israel is a computer scientist. On the account of proper names we have developed, they are not treated as indexicals. Thus the content$_M$ of (2) is the same as the content$_C$ of (2). So T doesn't give us either of the main kinds of content we have identified.

What T gives us is the truth conditions of (2) given *some* but not *all* of the facts about the meaning of (2). (2) tells us what else has to be true, given the facts about the meaning of "is a computer scientist" and the fact that "David Israel" is a proper name, but not given the facts about the specific conventions being exploited by the subutterance of this name. We might call this the "content$_M$ of (1) except for 'David Israel'."

This concept of truth conditions, truth conditions with part of the meaning fixed, is very important in the epistemology of language, for it gets at what we know in a familiar and inevitable situation—when we know the meaning of some but not all of the words in an utterance. We use this level of content in planning our utterances, as when we explain the meaning of a word by using it in a sentence. We rely on our interlocutor knowing the meaning of the sentence except for the word. So their grasp of the truth conditions of what we say will be the content$_M$ of our utterance *except for* this word. If we choose our example well, he will be able to figure out the meaning of the statement as a whole. From this, together with his knowledge of what the rest of the statement means, he can figure out what contribution the word must be making, and learn its meaning.

This mechanism is at work in the simple case in which we introduce ourselves. I meet you at a party, extend my hand, and say "I am John." You learn yet another permissive convention for "John," that it can be used to designate me. You start out not knowing this convention. Assuming sincerity, and relying on what you already know, you learn the reflexive proposition, that there is a convention that allows one to call the speaker of the utterance you are hearing "John." You see that I am the speaker, and learn that I am named John. If referentialism is correct, the proposition I express is the metaphysically trivial. But who cares; that proposition is not the one my plan relies on.

On the other hand, perhaps you already know this convention. Suppose you are a new graduate student at the Stanford Philosophy Department. You have seen the name "John Perry" in the catalog, perhaps gone to the library and found an article by me; perhaps you have talked to me on the phone. So you have a notion of a certain person, and realize he can be called "John Perry." When I introduce myself at the party, you assume that the "John Perry" naming convention that I am exploiting is the one you know. What you learn in this case is a fact about the context, that the speaker is John Perry. To get at the cognitive impact of my statement on you—how it differs from my saying "I am I" or "John Perry is John Perry"—we need content$_M$. You combine this proposition with what you can see, and learn that the person before you is John Perry—the John Perry to whom you have talked on the phone and whose name you have seen in the catalog.

This allows us to see the difference between *indexicality* and *reflexivity*. In the case of nonindexicals, reflexivity disappears when meaning is fixed. Indexicality is the very special case when we have reflexivity at the level of content$_M$.

Which of these kinds of content, one might ask, is the *real* content of an utterance? The question is misconceived. An utterance has as wide a variety of contents as we may find useful to isolate, for particular purposes of description and explanation.

We can say that in at least the vast majority of cases, the common sense concept of "what is said"—what we have called "official" content—corresponds to content$_C$. This is a good reason for an account of content to recognize this concept, but not a good reason to expect it to be the only or even the most theoretically fruitful kind of content.

21

Rip Van Winkle and Other Characters [160]

If someone wants to say the same today as he expressed yesterday using the word 'today', he must replace this word with 'yesterday'.

—Frege, "The Thought"

Introduction

In "Demonstratives," David Kaplan develops an account of the meaning of indexicals and sentences that contain them based on the concepts of content, character and context. The *content* of a statement is a proposition; which proposition a statement expresses depends not only on the linguistic meaning or *character* of the sentence used, but also on the *context*: who is speaking, to whom, when, where and in what circumstances.

In his essay, Kaplan briefly sketches an analogous concept of belief: we are in a belief state with a certain character in a certain context and thereby believe a certain proposition. As Kaplan says, we believe propositions *under* characters.

Kaplan then raises the following question. Suppose you have formed a belief of the sort that you would express with a sentence containing an indexical, say, "You are a computer scientist" or "Today is a nice day." What do you need to do to *retain* such a belief, after you leave the context in which the sentence in question expresses it? What do you have to do to retain a belief that you once expressed with "You are a computer scientist," after the person you are talking to has left? What do you have to do to retain the belief you once expressed with "Today is a nice day," after that day is gone?

Frege's remark quoted above suggested a view to Kaplan: to retain a belief as one moves into a new context, one must adjust the character under which one holds the belief, to a new one that conforms to a sentence that would express

---

[160]Thanks to Pierre Jacob, Francois Recanati and Eros Corazza for comments on a much earlier version and to Elizabeth Macken for comments on the penultimate version.

355

the same proposition in the new context. There are patterns of character change that correspond to patterns of change in context of belief. To continue to think the same thing as the context of belief changes, is to think under a succession of characters that determine the same content in the succession of contexts, and conform to such a pattern. To think the thought I thought yesterday under the character of "Today is a nice day," I must now think a thought under the character of "Yesterday is a nice day."

Kaplan rejects this suggestion because of the case of Rip Van Winkle, who fell asleep for twenty years and woke up thinking he had slept for only a day. Kaplan thinks the Frege-inspired strategy would lead us to deny that when Van Winkle awoke, he had retained the belief he expressed, the day he fell asleep, with "Today is a nice day." How would he express this belief? He might try to express it with "Yesterday was a nice day," but this would fail. He would not have asserted anything about the day he fell asleep, but rather said something about the day before he spoke, a day that he slept through and of which he has no memory.

In his article "Understanding Demonstratives," Gareth Evans found this an inadequate reason to abandon the Frege-inspired strategy. He seems to think that we should simply say that Rip has failed to retain his belief:

> I see no more strangeness in the idea that a man who loses track of time cannot retain beliefs than in the idea that a man who loses track of an object cannot retain the beliefs about it with which he began. (Evans, 1981, pp. 87n–88n)

In this essay I first review Kaplan's theory of linguistic character, and then explain and motivate a concept of doxastic character. I then develop some concepts for dealing with the topic of belief retention and then, finally, discuss Rip Van Winkle. I come down on Kaplan's side with respect to the Frege-inspired strategy, narrowly construed. But I advocate something like the Frege-inspired strategy, if it is construed more broadly. On my view it is remarkably easy to retain a belief, and I think Evans is quite wrong about Rip and Kaplan. The central concept I develop, however, that of an information game, is in the spirit of much of Evans' work. I also borrow some of his terminology.

Linguistic Characters and Roles

The content of a statement is a proposition, "what is said" by the speaker in a literal sense. The context is a set of factors that determine what indexicals stand for: the speaker of the utterance, the time of utterance, the place of utterance, the circumstance or possible world in which it occurs. Characters are functions from contexts to contents. That is, a character takes a context as input (as its argument) and provides a content as output (as its value). These characters are mathematical representations of the rules that language assigns to expressions.

Character is an interpretation of linguistic meaning.

Suppose that at a specific time in 1995—call it **t**—Kaplan says to Quine, "I live west of you now." On Kaplan's theory, here is what happens:

- The character of "I" is a function from a context to the speaker of the context. In this case, Kaplan is the speaker, and so he is the content of "I" in this context.[161]

- The character of "you" is a function from a context to the person that is addressed by the speaker of the context, at the time of the context, in the circumstances of the context. So the content of "you" in this case is Quine.

- The character of "now" is a function from a context to the time of the context. In this case, the content of "now" is **t**.

- The character of "live to the west of" is a function from a context to the 3-ary relation x lives to the west of y at t. This character is not sensitive to differences in context; its content is the same at all contexts.[162]

- The character of "I live to the west of you now" is built up out of the characters of the parts. It is a function that from a context to the proposition that a lives to the west of b at t, where a is the content of "I" in the context, b is the content of "you" in the context, and t the content of "now" in the context. In this case, the content is the proposition that Kaplan lives to the west of Quine at **t**.

Kaplan doesn't assign characters exclusively to indexicals and sentences that contain them. Every expression gets a character. The characters of expressions that are not sensitive to changes of context are constant functions. The name "David Kaplan," for example, is a function that returns David Kaplan at every context. I'll call characters like this "loyal," and characters, like that of "I" and "you" that are sensitive to changes in context "flighty."

I like to interpret Kaplan's characters in terms of what I call *utterance-relative* or *linguistic* roles. This interpretation links Kaplan's ideas with an older tradition that emphasizes that indexicals are "token-reflexive.[163] Linguistic conventions assign a name like "David Kaplan," to a particular individual. But they assign an indexical like "I" or "you" to an *utterance-relative* (or *linguistic*) role: being the speaker of u, being the being the addressee of u, etc. An utterance of an indexical does not stand for or refer to the role assigned to it;

---

[161] Kaplan develops his account within possible worlds semantics, and in that setting takes the value of an expression like "I" at a context to be a rigid *intension* rather than an individual. In this case, it would be an individual concept that picked out Kaplan in each world. This complication is basically an artifact of the semantical framework, not part of the intuitive set of ideas Kaplan tries to convey. I ignore this and other complications.

[162] I am ignoring tense.

[163] See, in particular, (Reichenbach, 1947), (Burks, 1949) and (Perry, 1995a).

it stands for or refers to the object that plays that role, relative to the utterance itself.

Why are indexicals important? The answer has two parts. First, linguistic roles are closely associated with other roles that objects play in our lives. The speaker of the utterance I hear is often the person I am looking at; the place an utterance is made is usually the place the speaker occupies, and usually near the place the listener occupies. So, when I learn that an object plays a linguistic role relative to an utterance I hear, I learn about other roles that it plays.

Given this, indexicals are useful in two situations. Sometimes one wants to know more about an object that plays some linguistic role or associated role. I want to know more about the person I see before me. I ask: "Who are you?" Common sense and my facility at language assure me that the person I see before me will be the addressee of my utterance. So if I find out who the addressee is, I find out who the person before me is. I want to know the name of the city I find itself in. I ask: "What is the name of this city?" Common sense tells me that the city I am in is the city my utterance will take place in. So if I find out the name of the city in which my utterance occurs, I will find out the name of the city in which I find itself.

Sometimes I need to know what role some object is playing in my life, what its current relation to me is. I ask, "Who is David Kaplan?" You answer, pointing: "That man is David Kaplan." I wanted to know which of the people I could see was David Kaplan. Common sense told you that I would be able to identify the person you demonstrated as one of the ones I saw. I ask, "When is July 4th?" You answer, "Tomorrow." Common sense tells you that I will realize that your utterance occurs at the present time, and so that the day I am interested in is just 24 hours away.

When we hear an indexical, the first way of thinking of the referent that is afforded to us, is thinking of it as the thing that plays the utterance-relative role. So when Quine hears Kaplan's utterance **u** of "I live to the west of you now," the first way of thinking of Kaplan provided by this utterance is as the speaker of the utterance of "I." Quine's first grasp of the truth conditions of **u** is something like, "The speaker of **u** lives to the west of the addressee of **u** at the time of **u**." This phase of understanding usually slips through one's mind without stopping, perhaps without rising to consciousness, as the utterance-relative roles give way to more interesting associated roles. In normal circumstances Quine will realize that the person he sees is the speaker of the utterance he hears, that that person is David Kaplan, that Kaplan is addressing him, and that the time of utterance is, for all practical purposes, the time the utterance is heard. So Quine will think something like, "Kaplan lives west of me now."

In other cases, however, the utterance-relative role may be our only way of thinking of the objects an utterance is about, at least until we have done some detective work. I find a faded note in my old copy of Wittgenstein's

Investigations: "You are being an ass." I know that the note is true if and only if the person to whom it was addressed was being an ass at the time it was written. That may be the only grasp of the truth-conditions I can get, until I look through some papers and records and wrack my brains. Then I remember: someone passed the note to me, apparently thinking my remarks in a seminar on the private language argument were less profound that I did. Now I know that the note—or more accurately, the utterance for which the note was the token, was true if and only if *I* was being an ass.

Kaplan's system allows the possibility that we can say the same thing (utter statements with the same content) in quite different ways (using sentences with quite different characters). This happens if we use the sentences in contexts where, due to particular and perhaps peculiar circumstances, they turn out to have the same content. This happens when the same object plays two quite different utterance-relative roles. And it can happen without our knowing it.

Kaplan asks us to consider the sentences "My pants are on fire" and "His pants are on fire." The character of the first is a function that for a context with a as the speaker, returns the proposition that a's pants are on fire. The character of the second is a function that for a context with a as speaker, in a world in which a is pointing at b or otherwise calling attention to him, ("demonstrating b") returns the proposition that b's pants are on fire.

Suppose, to continue with Kaplan's example, that he says, "My pants are on fire." The content of his remark is the proposition that David Kaplan's pants are on fire. Suppose now that he sees himself in a mirror, doesn't realize that he is seeing himself, and, pointing at the man in the mirror, says "His pants are on fire." The sentence is quite different, with a quite different character, but in this particular context the content is the same, that David Kaplan's pants are on fire. Kaplan has said the same thing in two different ways without knowing it, although presumably he will recognize what is going on before long.

Now consider the difference between

(1) My pants are on fire.

(2) His pants are on fire.

(3) David Kaplan's pants are on fire on July 4, 1984 at 5 p.m.

One can think of (1) and (2) as tools. (1) is a tool for saying that oneself has burning pants. (2) is a tool for saying of someone that one can see and demonstrate, that they have burning pants. Since lots of people could, in principle at least, find themselves with burning pants, or find themselves in a position to demonstrate someone that has burning pants, these tools might be used, again and again, in different situations, to say different things about different people.

(3) doesn't contain any indexicals, just names. Even the verb can be taken as tenseless, given the way the date is filled in. As we said, Kaplan assigns all expressions a character, not just indexicals, but for nonindexicals the character

doesn't do much. It's just a way of making the theory work smoothly. So "Kaplan," for example, is assigned a character that has David Kaplan as content in all contexts. And (3) as a whole has a character that has the same proposition as content in all contexts, the proposition that Kaplan has burning pants on July 4, 1984. Thus the character of (3) is very loyal. It sticks with the same content in context after context. To put the point another way, with (3) we have a tool that allows us to express the same proposition, no matter when it is or where we are or to whom we are talking.

As a tool, (3) can seem a bit odd. Why would we need or want a tool for saying, just of one person, that he has burning pants? It seems like a very special purpose tool. We'll return to this question later.

Doxastic Characters

How can we conceive of beliefs, so that characters may be intelligibly assigned to them? One conception is that of belief as an attitude towards a sentence; the belief inherits the character of the sentence at which it is directed. I think this is a rather unsatisfactory conception. For one thing, it seems that fairly complex thoughts about things of all sorts would precede thoughts about sentences, both logically and psychologically.[164]

A more satisfactory way of conceiving of beliefs starts with the idea that they are concrete cognitive structures that arise in one's mind in certain situations; traces, as it were, of experiences of perception, learning, and inference. These structures have content; when one has a belief, there is (at least when things go right), something that one believes, a proposition P such that one believes P.

Beliefs so conceived will have two aspects that must mesh, *causal role* and *content*. The beliefs are caused by certain kinds of perceptions, and cause certain kinds of actions. But they also have a certain content; they are beliefs *that* such and such is the case, beliefs that P for some proposition P. These two aspects should mesh. A belief that P should cause action appropriate to its being the case that P, given one's desires and other beliefs.

By the *causal role* of a state I mean the various combinations of factors that bring the state about, and the various combinations of factors it brings about in

---

[164]I mention this conception mainly because many reasonably attentive readers seem to find it in "The Problem of the Essential Indexical" (Perry, 1993)(Essay 2). But it was not what I had in mind. See "Belief and Acceptance" (Perry, 1993)(Essay 3). I think this misinterpretation has three roots. I didn't properly distinguish between linguistic and cognitive roles. I underestimated the ease with which people would suppose that my view, that sentences with indexicals (or their characters), were more adequate ways of classifying belief states than were propositions, would have to rest on the view that sentences (or their characters) were what beliefs were directed at. Finally the problem referred to in the title had to do with the fact that indexicals *seemed* essential to *expressing* certain thoughts; from this some readers seem to have assumed that I thought that indexicals *were* necessary for *having* those thoughts.

turn. Consider the state of being nauseated. This state is universal and partial. To say it is universal is to say that different people at different times can be in the same state. You were nauseated last week, after a ride on the Ferris Wheel. I was nauseated yesterday, after binging on sushi and hamburgers. To say it is partial is to say that being nauseated constitutes only part of one's total state at a given time. I was nauseated and embarrassed and guilt-ridden and in a number of other states at the same time.

Each case of nausea has its own specific causes. But there are patterns. Certain combinations of factors bring about nausea, and nausea, together with other factors, has certain results. This pattern is the causal role of nausea.

On a given occasion, the causes of a specific case of nausea may be pretty similar to the causes of some other state. Perhaps the main cause of my nausea was pretty much the same thing as my feelings of guilt: massive overeating. But the effects of the two states are different. My nausea leads to me to take Alka-Seltzer; my guilt leads me to turn on the television. And in general, the patterns are not the same. Lots of things cause nausea that don't cause guilt and vice versa, and nausea, in combination with various factors, causes lots of things that guilt, in combination with those same factors, wouldn't cause.

One can think of causal roles in various strict and philosophical ways or in a sort of loose and casual way. The second will suffice for my purposes. Think of the causal role of a state as its typical causes, the things you would expect might cause an instance of that state, in more or less ordinary circumstances, and similarly with its typical effects.

We said that the causal role of a belief should mesh with its content. But Kaplan's case shows that this meshing is not simple and direct.

First, note that the causal roles of the states we imagine to occur are quite different. If we heard that someone believed that their very own pants were on fire, we would expect that something like this happened. First, they dropped an ash from a pipe into their own lap, or stood too close to a fireplace, or something like that. Then they felt some unaccustomed warmth in their nether regions. Then perhaps they smelled something like wool or cotton or rayon burning. Then they looked down where things were heating up, and saw the smoke. Those are typical causes of the state one is in when one says, "My pants are on fire." The typical effects would include strong emotions like fear, and attempts to douse oneself with water or put out the fire in some other way, and saying, "My pants are on fire."

Now consider the state Kaplan was in when he saw the man in the mirror, who just happened to be him, with his pants on fire. This state is typically caused by seeing smoke and flames erupt from the trousers of someone standing in front of one. It typically leads to concern and the attempt to help and shouting, "His pants are on fire." So the typical causes of this state are quite different from that of the first state.

Next, note that these different belief states do not line up directly with propositions believed, so there is not a simple and direct meshing between causal role and content. We can imagine a lot of people being in the "My pants are on fire" belief state; they wouldn't thereby believe the same propositions. Kaplan would believe that Kaplan's pants were on fire, Searle would believe that Searle's pants were on fire, and so forth. And we can imagine a lot of people being in the "His pants are on fire" state. They all have something in common, but its not what they believe—it's not the content. They would believe quite different propositions, depending on whom they were looking at.

At this point, it is very helpful to postulate a level of meaning for beliefs that is *analogous to* but not *derived from* that of character for sentences— characters that in fact are quite independent of language. A belief will have a certain content because (i) it has a certain character, and (ii) it occurs in a certain belief context—it is a belief held by a certain person, at a certain time, in a certain place, attending to certain objects, etc. The virtue of thinking of a belief in this way, is that it makes intelligible how this meshing between causal role and content could take place, in a systematic psychology of content, for these characters will correspond more closely to belief states than propositions do.

A wider class of roles is needed to characterize beliefs than is needed to characterize utterances. We noted that the characters that are associated with indexicals are based on *utterance-relative roles*. These roles are based on relations objects might have to a given utterance. To characterize beliefs we need what we might call *thought-relative* or *cognitive* roles. These roles are based on relations that an object can have to a given episode of thought or a particular belief, such as being the owner of the thought, (the self role), being attended to by the owner of it, being remembered by the owner of it, being held in the right hand of the owner of it, being above the owner of it, being sat on by the owner of it, and so forth.

I'll indicate doxastic characters by quoting the sentence a speaker might use to communicate the beliefs one has under the character. Of course the characters of these sentences are linguistic rather than doxastic; I supplement the indexical expressions with bracketed material to identify the underlying cognitive role involved. For example, "that man [the one I see]" and "that man [the one I remember]," "I [self]" and "now [the moment of thought]."

There is a difference between referring to someone as "you" and designating them with the phrase "the person I am addressing," even though the role of being the addressee is involved in both cases. When one refers to a person as "you," one does not *say* that one is addressing them; one exploits that fact to refer to them. One can learn how to use "you," without being able to explicitly formulate the conditions under which a use of that word refers to a person (perhaps because one has not thought about it, or has not yet attained the concepts, such as the concept of a word and the concept of reference, that would be necessary to think about it). Even so, one has *some* grasp of these conditions; one has some sort of positive doxastic attitude towards the fact that a use of "you" refers to the addressee. But one may not be properly said to *believe* that the reference of "you" is the addressee. One knows *how* to use "you" to refer to the addressee, even though one may not know *that* a use of "you" refers to the addressee. In these cases, I say that one is *attuned to* the the way "you" works.

Similarly there is a difference between being able to think of a thing or person in virtue of some role it plays in one's life, and being able to articulate that role in thought or speech and think of it *as* the thing or person playing that role in one's life. Consider a child, who is thinking about a dog that she saw an hour or so before. She has a certain memory of the dog, and it is in virtue of this memory that she is able to think of the dog. I would represent the character of her thought with "That dog [the one I remember] was very cute." This is not the same as thinking "The dog I remember was very cute." The child might lack the concepts needed to think this thought; even if she has them, it may take a bit of time and wit to figure out that the dog can be characterized as the one she remembers. Still, the child would be attuned to the fact that the dog she is thinking of is one that she remembers, in that she would know how to consult her memory for more information about the dog: to find the dog she would go back to where she had last seen it, for example.

Now let's return once again to Kaplan and his burning pants. We imagined Kaplan making two sets of observations of his own burning trousers. We imagined him using the sentences, "My pants are on fire" and "His pants are on fire," to express what he believed. But he might make the observations, and acquire the beliefs, without saying anything. Even if they don't lead to distinct utterances, the belief states are quite different. If Kaplan notices that his pants are on fire in the usual way, he will be in quite a different state than if he notices a man with burning pants in a mirror. The difference in the actions he would take in these circumstances, including the difference in sentences he would utter if he were to put what he noticed into words, *reflects* a difference in beliefs. The concept of believing under a character is intended to capture this difference. The difference in belief would be there, even if Kaplan didn't say anything. And the difference between the two cases is not the proposition that is believed, but the character under which it is believed.

There are two characters here, one corresponding to that of "My [self] pants are on fire" and one corresponding to that of "His [the man I am looking at] pants are on fire." These characters come much closer to lining up with causal roles than do the propositions believed.

Thus two things stand out at the level of character that get obliterated at the level of content. First, the difference in causal role of the two beliefs. Second, the common nature that different beliefs with different contents belonging to different people at different times might have, and in virtue of which these different situations might instantiate the same psychology of content.

Recall the distinction between flighty and loyal characters from our discussion of linguistic characters. Loyal characters yield the same content from any context; these characters are the sort that belong to sentences that don't contain indexicals. Flighty characters yield different contents in different contexts; these characters are the sort that belong to sentences that contain indexicals.

The same distinction applies to doxastic characters. "David Kaplan has burning pants at 4 p.m. on July 4, 1996" is a very loyal character; "I [self] have burning pants now [the present moment]" is a very flighty character, expressing a different proposition with each variation in time or thinker.

If we know that an utterance of sentence with a flighty character expresses a certain proposition, we may know quite a bit about the context in which the utterance occurred. If an utterance of "I am a logician" has the content that David Kaplan is a logician, then the speaker must be David Kaplan. If an utterance of "That man works for Microsoft now" has the content that Elwood Fritchey works for Microsoft on October 27, 1995, then the utterance occurred on October 27 and the speaker was someone in a position to demonstrate Elwood Fritchey. The objects that get referred to by the indexicals must be playing certain linguistic roles, and hence certain roles in the life of the speaker.

The same is true with beliefs. If I believe that David Kaplan has burning pants under the character "that man [the one I see] has burning pants," then I must be looking at David Kaplan. If anyone believes that proposition under the character "I [self] have burning pants," that person must be David Kaplan.

If my beliefs are under characters, it seems that many of the characters they are under are very loyal and not very flighty. Right now I believe that David Kaplan is a logician. I am not speaking to him, seeing him, or hearing him right now. He is playing no role in my life that would enable me to refer him by uttering "you" or by demonstrating him and uttering "he." What character do I believe these things under, and what is the point of such beliefs? What causal role, if any, do they have? Why do people have such beliefs, and why do others care whether or not they do?

Information Games

We ended each of the last two sections by wondering about loyal characters. Why do we want sentences that have loyal characters—what use do we have for such special purpose tools? And what sorts of beliefs have loyal characters, and why are they important? To consider these questions, I want to introduce the concept of an information game.

An information game involves the acquisition and later application of a belief about an individual. That is, at some time one comes to believe something about some person or object. Then, later, that belief guides one's behavior towards that object or at least an object that one takes to be the same as it. I call the object about which one acquires the belief the *source*.[165] I call the object to which one applies the belief—the object one takes to be the source—the *applicandum*. In any information game, one faces the problem of making reasonably sure that the source is the applicandum.

Suppose I meet Elwood Fritchey at a party; he tells me he is a programmer for Microsoft and I believe him. So I acquire a belief. Later I ask him if he knows why the Macintosh version of Word 6.0 works so slowly. I direct this question to him because I believe him to be a Microsoft programmer. If I didn't believe that, I wouldn't ask him. It doesn't make much sense to ask some random person this question. My belief that he is a Microsoft programmer is part of the reason I ask him; my asking him is an application of the belief.

In an information game I acquire a belief, and then later I apply the belief I acquired to a certain object: because I have the belief, and take the object to be the one the belief is about, I deal with it in a certain way. In this case, I ask a person a certain question, because I think he is in a position to know the answer.

I will describe eight information games, which I call "straight-through," "tracking," "detach-and-recognize," "updating," "recollection," "inference," "planning" and "communication." I introduce the first three by considering three scenarios for what happens in between my acquiring the belief and my applying it. First, virtually nothing comes between. I am talking to Fritchey, face to face. He says to me, "I am a programmer at Microsoft." I acquire a belief I would express with "You are a programmer at Microsoft." I say, on the basis of that belief, "Why does the Macintosh version of Word 6.0 run so slowly?" This is the straight-through information game.

I stand in a certain relationship or family of relationships to Fritchey. He is in front of me; I am looking at him; I am talking to him; he is talking to me. When someone has these relations to me, or as I shall put it, occupies these *agent-relative roles* in my life, I have ways of finding out information about him. (I'll say that there are epistemic techniques associated with the role, or for short, that it is an epistemic role.) I can look, and I can ask and listen to the answer, to mention the most obvious ways of gathering information about the person one is talking to face-to-face. There are also ways of acting, the success of which will turn on the characteristics of the person that plays this role. (I'll say that there are pragmatic techniques associated with the role, or for short that it is a pragmatic role.) The action of asking, "Why does Word 6.0 work so slowly," with the goal of finding out the answer, has a chance of being successful if the person I am talking to is a programmer at Microsoft.

In the straight-through information game, making sure that the source is the applicandum is not a big problem. The epistemic role and the pragmatic

---

[165] See (Evans, 1973) for the term "source" used in more or less this way.

role are closely associated and the time difference between acquisition and application is very short. There is not time for one object to cease to play it and another object to take its place.

In particular, I don't need to know a lot about Fritchey to successfully play the straight-through information game. I don't need to know his name, or have any way of recognizing him. I just need to be able to tell that only one object plays the role in question in my life for the few moments it takes for the game to be played.

Second case. I break off my conversation with Fritchey, after learning that he is a Microsoft programmer but before asking him about the Macintosh version of Word 6.0 . But I keep my eye on him as he and I move our various ways around the party. Other people assume the role in my life that Fritchey had: that is, I converse with them. Fritchey plays a succession of roles: object to my left, object to my right, object I am glancing at. Later we end up face to face and I ask him, "Why does Word 6.0 run so slowly."

Here the task of making sure that the applicandum is the source is more complicated. I have to *track* Fritchey, to use another apt term of Evans's (Evans, 1981). This requires that I be able to ascertain that a single object has played a succession of roles in my life. This requires more than is required for the straight-through language game, but it doesn't require that I have the ability to recognize or re-identify Fritchey if I lose track of him. track of him.

In the straight-through and tracking games, the player stays *attached* to the source, in the sense that he remains in an epistemic relation to the source from acquisition to application. In the straight-through game it is the same relation and virtually the same time. In the tracking game it is a succession of relations through an interval of time.

The third game I call the "detach-and-recognize" game. I learn that Fritchey is a programmer for Microsoft. Then I go home. I don't seem him for days or even years. At some later point I see him again. I recognize him, remember his job, and ask him, "Why does the Macintosh version of Word 6.0 run so slowly?"

After I leave the party, Fritchey is not playing an epistemic or pragmatic role in my life. He is of course still related to me. He is a certain distance and direction from me, but I am not aware of it; it is not part of my conception of him. There are various actions I could take to find out things about him, or to have an effect on him. But there is no simple technique, like looking or asking a question that I can use to find out more about him, and no simple technique like talking to him or shoving him or gesturing to him that I can use to have an effect on him.

Nevertheless, Fritchey still does play a role in my life. He is the man of whom a certain thought of mine is a memory. This role, this relation to my thought and to me, gives me a way of thinking of him. It is a very loyal character. I can carry the memory with me as I travel away from Fritchey and he from me; its being a thought of Fritchey depends on the way I acquired it, but not on my present circumstances.

As an analogy, consider the note I left in my copy of the *Investigations*. I don't remember who wrote it. The signature is hard to make out. The writing, never very legible, is faded. In spite of all this, the person who played the role, "writer of this letter," is the same as it was thirty years ago. It is a very loyal role. And the source of memories is similarly loyal.

In such a case, what is the point of continuing to believe anything about Fritchey? It doesn't have much of a point, unless there is a good chance I will encounter him again and be able to apply the belief usefully then. But of course this is something we do a lot. We acquire a belief about an object at one time, when the conditions are favorable for doing so. We apply the belief at another time, under quite different conditions. These later conditions might make it impossible to acquire the information if we did not already have it.

Doing this requires that we be able to recognize the object in question. Unless I remember a little bit about Fritchey, so I can recognize him the next time I see him, I won't be in a position to use the information I have retained. The information that we need, to make detach-and-recognize a viable information game, falls into two categories. There is the information we will use when we encounter the object again, to decide what to do. The information that Fritchey is a programmer for Microsoft is what leads me to ask about the sorry state of Word 6.0. Call this sort of information, "information for action." But there is also "information for recognition." My tidbit of information about Fritchey will sit useless in my brain, unless I remember also that he is a big man with a red beard, etc., information that will allow me to recognize him next time I meet him. Of course, these are different functions or uses for information, not different categories of information itself. In many cases, a bit of information will serve both purposes.

To be useful, then, a detached belief, like the belief that Fritchey is a programmer for Microsoft, will have to be part of a larger *file* on Fritchey. The additional elements in the file provide the facts about him that might enable me to recognize him.

Nevertheless, there is no guarantee that beliefs will be useful. Consider my belief that Fritchey was a microsoft programmer. Under what character do I continue to believe this, once I detach from Fritchey and leave the party? Simply the character:

> That man [the source of the belief] was a programmer for Microsoft then [the time the belief was required].

The belief is similar to the note I discovered in my old copy of Wittgenstein's *Investigations*. By itself, without connection to and augmentation from other sources, it is useless. This belief, by itself, includes no information about Fritchey's name, for example, so I couldn't even use it to contact him if I had a directory of Microsoft employees.

A belief that is detached and virtually useless can nevertheless be quite conscious, even vivid. The frustration that such beliefs can engender is well-known, and we have linguistic devices for expressing them. The following conversation not only makes perfectly good sense, it is all too familiar for some of us:

> "Do you know any programmers for Microsoft?"
>
> "Yes...uh, uh, what's-his-name was a programmer for Microsoft. I don't remember his name."
>
> "When did you meet him?"
>
> "I'm not sure."
>
> "Where did you meet him."
>
> "I don't remember that either. I can't remember much of anything about him, except that he was a programer for Microsoft."
>
> "Thanks."

A belief like this one, totally useless at one time, may become useful later. Recovered memories, or outside sources, may disclose more information about the person I remember. Then the apparently useless bit of information may prove quite useful.

The detach-and-recognize game provides part of the answer to our question about the point of beliefs with loyal characters. Such beliefs serve as components of larger, useful, beliefs, when the objects the beliefs are about are recognized. They are completions for pragmatically attached beliefs, broken off from earlier epistemically attached beliefs.[166]

Detached beliefs do not simply sit in our minds and gather dust while we wait to encounter the objects they are about. They are parts of various activities that do not directly affect the objects they are about, but may have profound indirect effects on them. We use such beliefs in five additional information games.

In the *recollection game*, I try to squeeze more information out of my memories. I may have formulated the explicit belief that Fritchey was a programmer for Microsoft as I talked to him; he leaves and I detach the belief, thinking of

---

[166]What we have described so far is perhaps the main variation on the detach-and-recognize information game. There is a source of my belief, or of my file of beliefs, about a certain person. But we can also have sourceless files. Sometimes we can figure out quite a bit about an object that meets a certain description, and work up a "file" about it, even though we have never encountered it or communicated with anyone that has. In this case, once we have done the reasoning, we are left in a situation analogous to having examined a source.

him as "that man [that I remember]." But associated with the belief, at least for a while, are memory images from which I can cull some more beliefs, that may aid in recognizing him—e.g., that he had a red beard and wore green suspenders over a plaid shirt and had an unusual fascination with tupperware.

I do not need to be attached to Fritchey to recollect more about him, and I also do not need to be attached to him to play the *inference* game—to draw inferences on the basis of my beliefs about him. I combine these beliefs with other beliefs I have, to flesh out my conception of Fritchey. Given his job, I infer that he is bright and likes computers. Given his dress, I assume that he is happy in Seattle and enjoys being outdoors. Given that he worked for Microsoft when I talked to him, I infer that he will probably continue to do so for some length of time.

I call a rather special kind of inference *updating*. This is an inference made not on the basis of observed or inferred movements or changes in the thing my belief is about, but on the basis of changes in my own situation, or general changes, like the passage of time. When I meet Fritchey, I think "This man [the man I see] is a programer at Microsoft now [the time of the thought]." Later I think "That man [the man I remember] was a programmer at Microsoft then [the time I remember]." The change from "now [the time of the thought]" to "then [the time of the thought]" does not represent an inference about how Fritchey has changed since I last saw him. I am just updating; changing the character in a way that preserves the content, given the new circumstance of belief.

This update is quite different from another additional thought I may have. Given the relative permanence of jobs at Microsoft, I may figure at the later time "That man [the man I remember] is a programmer at Microsoft now [the moment of thought]." This is not an update that preserves the previously believed content, but an inference—although perhaps one that is not very risky, if the time interval is short.

It is possible that I have met Fritchey before. Or perhaps I have read an article about him—let's suppose he has been involved in the Seattle Commons project and was pictured and briefly described in an article about it. I already have some concept of him. Upon reflection, I may find that this concept fits the man I thought I had just met for the first time too nicely to be coincidental, and conclude that Fritchey is the man I read about.

When I read about Fritchey in the paper, I was playing the communication information game. Someone else had met him and talked to him and taken his picture. They had been in an epistemic relation to him, and acquired information about him. The information I get is detached.

When I read about Fritchey, he plays a special sort of epistemic role in my life, one mediated by symbols. He was the man I was reading about; the man referred to by the words I saw in the paper. When I quit reading the paper, I continued to have beliefs about him—detached beliefs. For a while, my beliefs about Fritchey may have been tied to memories of the article or the paper. But often we retain beliefs about a person or things we have encountered or read about, long after the memories of the perceptions, conversations or text from which we learned about them have faded to insignificance. The role these objects play in our lives is just that of being the source of the beliefs we have about them.

The beliefs I gained about Fritchey from reading the article may be quite detached and fragmentary. Perhaps I don't remember his name; I just have a concept of a man who was a programmer at Microsoft, worked on the Commons, wore green suspenders, and had a bit of an odd name that reminded me of a British Rock Star of an earlier era. Such beliefs would seem quite useless. But there could be enough there to make a pretty plausible conjecture, going over things after meeting Fritchey at the party, that it was the same man. And then I would have a belief that, next time I met Fritchey, could lead to a question about his work on the Commons, as well as the one about Word 6.0. The fragmentary beliefs turn out to be useful after all.

So now I am sitting at home. I acquired and detached a belief about Fritchey. I have recollected and inferred. And now I intend to ask him, next time I see him, about Word 6.0 and Seattle Commons. I am not now in a position to to anything to him directly; he plays no pragmatic role in my life at the moment. But he will, and I am forming plans about what to do then—playing the planning information game.

All of these last five games, recollection, inference, updating, communication and planning, could be played while I was still attached, epistemically or pragmatically, to Fritchey. But our main interest in them is that they can be played with detached beliefs, beliefs with loyal characters, and help us see the point of having such beliefs. Beliefs with loyal characters then have a causal role that has to do with the kinds of inferences and plans they lead to, and their effects on action when combined with other attached beliefs.[167]

Misidentification

Suppose that a few days later I mistakenly take someone else to be Elwood Fritchey—Elwood's brother Alphonse, say. I see Alphonse, as tall and red-bearded as Elwood is, one day at the feed lot. "Elwood," I say, talking directly to Alphonse, "Why does the Macintosh version of Word 6.0 run so slowly?" Here I have not only lost track of Elwood, I have applied my Elwood belief to someone else.

---

[167] I am here concerned with what seems to be a rather basic part of our conceptual scheme, beliefs about individual things and people. Perhaps as an explicit disclaimer I should note that there are other important classes of beliefs to which such detached beliefs are relevant. For example, a detached belief can serve as a confirming instance or a counterexample to a generalization.

This is no reason to say that I have lost the belief. My belief, the one I acquired at the party, that Elwood is a Microsoft programmer, is part of the explanation for my question to Alphonse—it is a misapplication of that very belief. Since the belief explains the mistake, the mistake can hardly be reason for supposing the belief to have been lost. I asked Alphonse the question, *because* I believed that Elwood was a programmer at Microsoft, and I took Alphonse to be Elwood.

Suppose I say, by way of explaining my question to the puzzled looking Alphonse: "You are Elwood Fritchey, the Microsoft Programmer." This would be an indirect speech act, asking him if indeed he was Elwood. But consider the literal statement I make. Clearly it is false. The fact that I intend to be speaking to Elwood and expressing a belief about Elwood does not change the fact that the person who is playing the relevant linguistic role in my life is Alphonse.

Do I have, at this point, a belief in the singular proposition, that Alphonse Fritchey is a Microsoft Programmer or the proposition that Elwood is Alphonse? I have said these things, but do I believe them? It is not necessary to say that I do. These beliefs are not required to explain my question; it is adequately explained by my true belief about Elwood Fritchey and my false belief that I am talking to Elwood Fritchey. Those beliefs explain why I think I can say something to and about Elwood Fritchey by using a sentence that contains "you."

There are reasons for saying that I don't believe these propositions. When the mistake is discovered, I would quite naturally say, "I thought you were Elwood" or "I took you to be Elwood." It seems that not every positive doxastic attitude is comfortably described as a belief. My mistake, in taking Alphonse to be Elwood, may *lead to* false beliefs, if it remains undiscovered. But if it is simply a transitory thought, my true belief about Elwood and my false belief that this man was Elwood suffice to explain my false statement.

Thinking about days

Detach-and-recognize is a reasonable strategy for dealing with the fact that individuals come and go. They become indexically inaccessible, cease to play any epistemic or pragmatic role in our life for a while, and then re-enter it again. In the meantime, by detachment, we can retain our beliefs, update them, use them as the basis of inferences, make plans about future interactions and communicate with others.

Keeping track of the relative locations that times and immobile things have to us is easier than keeping track of people and other mobile things, at least in principle. If I keep track of my own movements in space, then I can correct for those movements and still think of all the places I have been and buildings and landmarks I have seen in terms of their relative distance and direction from me. But I don't usually do this. Right now, for example, I am working at my home. I remember walking at Palo Alto's Baylands a few hours ago. I don't think of the Baylands in terms of their relative distance and direction from me. I couldn't say right off the top of my head whether they were to my left or right, in front or behind me. If I want to think of them as "over there" I would stop and consider where I live in relation to them, and what my orientation in my house is, and figure it out from there. I might do this for example if I saw some fireworks, and wondered if they could be coming from the baylands—if the baylands were over there [where I am looking].

We do a much better job keeping track of whether each of our experiences lies in the past, present or future. This is fairly easy because there is an exact correspondence between the mode of thinking about the experience (remembering it or planning to have it or having it) and its position in time relative to the present moment. But we don't usually keep very precise track of events in terms of these cognitive roles. If I have an important appointment coming up, I will definitely be aware that it is in the future and not the past; I will probably remember the time. As the day goes on I may occasionally figure out how long it is before the event. But I don't retain my belief by constantly updating in terms of "minutes from now." I remember that the appointment is at 5; I look at the clock and see that it is 3:30, and then I think, "An hour an a half from now I see the dean" or something like that.

We can think of "now [the present time]" and "today [the present day]" as ways of thinking about days that are both pragmatically and epistemically attached. On September 1st I can find out what September 1st is like in Palo Alto by looking. On September 1st I can make September 1st a day on which I take a walk by taking a walk.[168]

On September 2nd, I can no longer make any changes in what happens on September 1st.[169] I am not pragmatically attached. I am no longer in a position to actively explore September 1st. I am not epistemically attached. I can, however, still explore my own memories, and may form new beliefs as a result of that exploration.

How about tomorrow? I am not pragmatically attached to tomorrow. I can't do anything today that will directly change what happens tomorrow. I can indirectly affect tomorrow by making changes today in myself and others that will have an effect tomorrow. I can plan a trip to a concert, or call a meeting. And I am not now perceiving tomorrow's events; I am not epistemically attached. If I am not now, and never have been, epistemically or pragmatically attached to tomorrow, how can I think about tomorrow, reason about it, make plans for it,

---

[168] See (Evans, 1981)

[169] Setting aside "Cambridge changes." I can talk about September 1st on September 2nd, thus making it, what it hadn't been before, a day talked about by me on September 2nd. But this doesn't change what September 1st was like; it doesn't change what happened on that day.

and the like?

Our system of dates provides detached ways of thinking about days that we have not yet encountered. This system exploits important metaphysical differences between days on the one hand and things and people on the other. We can systematically talk about days we have not encountered and keep track of them in our thoughts and plans, simply in virtue of their position in the sequence of days, as reflected by the calendar. This is in part because days are connected to one another in a linear, predictable, fashion, dependent only on the most general facts that circumscribe existence on earth. It is in part because of the somewhat puzzling fact that the date of a day, its position in the calendar, although seemingly a relational fact about it, seems also to be its most essential feature. We can hold a day in our modal imagination and change everything about what happens on that day. We can suppose that all sorts of things will happen on July 4, 1997; we can coherently imagine July 4, 1767 having been quite different than it is. We can even suppose that everything that will happen on July 4, 1997 could have happened instead on July 4, 1767, due to the absence of some sequence of events a couple of million years ago that delayed everything 230 years. (In this case, of course, July 4, 1767 would be called "July 4, 1997.") But we cannot consider a given day as being in a different place in the order of days than it actually is. At least it is not easy.

Can next July 4th be a *source* of my thoughts? No, for it lies in the future, and cannot be part of the cause of my beliefs. But I can have a *sourceless* detached belief about next July 4th. The combination of our system of dating, our holidays and our traditions allows me to figure out quite a bit about next July 4th, even though I have not causally interacted with it.[170]

Consider what is involved in a simple matter of arranging a meeting. We decide to meet on a certain day—say two weeks hence. The decision is recorded on a calendar. At this point I am not in a pragmatic relation to the day. I have made a plan for what will happen on the day, but I cannot make it happen. I can't attend or not attend the meeting until the day itself arrives.

The task of recognizing a day is disanalogous in many ways to recognizing an individual. When we can identify today, yesterday, or tomorrow by its date, it is because we have been keeping track, or are exploiting someone else (like the newspaper publisher), who does.

Notice here that "keeping track" does not mean following a particular day. To keep track of time is usually not to pick out a day and track it, but to be aware of which day it is. That is, to be aware of the important properties of the day that plays the "today" role—what the date is, what events are planned, etc. To lose track of what day it is, means not knowing that the day that plays

---

[170] I do not deny that we can and do have sourceless beliefs about persons and things as well as times and places.

that role has some other important attributes, like being one's anniversary or the day a philosophy paper was promised to an editor.

For the most part, apart from human activities and human institutions, like calendars and the dates on newspapers, days don't have particular features, easily ascertainable by the ordinary citizen, that set them off from other days, in roughly the same season. When Rip awakes in the hills, there is nothing about the look of things that suggests that it is a 1786 day rather than a 1766 day. It's only when he gets to town, and observes humans and human artifacts, that things begin to not fit.

So now let us review the analogies and disanalogies we have found in terms of our information games. There are clear analogues, with days, to the straight-through and tracking games. There is not a direct analogue to the detach-and-recognize game, since we cannot re-encounter a day once time has left it behind. However, the peculiar metaphysical status of days, that is reflected in our system of dates, and permits us to arrive at sourceless beliefs about them, provides an alternative route to detached thinking detached thinking, planning, information exchange, and the like.

With this all in mind, let us, finally, return to Rip Van Winkle.

Rip Van Winkle

What should we say about Rip Van Winkle?

Rip Van Winkle acquired a belief the day he fell asleep—July 3, 1766, say—a belief that that day was a fine day. He held this belief under the character "Today [the day of this thought] is nice." Then he slept for twenty years and two days, until July 5, 1786, and walked back to town.[171] What happened next?

The possibility that struck Kaplan and Evans is that Rip merely updated his belief. On July 3rd he never forms any explicit belief other than "Today [the day of this thought] is a nice day." When he awakes on July 5th, the belief is updated, due to his awareness of having slept through a night, and his lack of awareness of having slept twenty additional years, to "Yesterday [the day before the day of this thought] was a nice day." He falls out of epistemic contact with the current day when he falls asleep, but has a ready-made character in mind for when he wakes up. But then what is there left of the original belief except the false one about July 4th? But the false belief can not be the true belief, so hasn't Rip lost the belief in question? This seems to be the argument

---

[171] Actually, Diedrich Knickerbocker, the narrator, does not tell us the exact dates, just that the Declaration of Independence and the American Revolution occurred while Rip slept. I've added a day to his twenty year sleep for expository convenience; the important thing is that Rip fell asleep on July 3 and awoke on July 5 thinking it was July 4; aside from the possibility of connecting humble analytical philosophy with important literature, the extra twenty years doesn't matter much.

that threatened Kaplan and appealed to Evans.

But even in the case of such thin updating, there are backup characters for Rip to hold his belief under. When Rip believes, towards evening, as it grows dark, "Today [the day of this thought] was a nice day," he has memories of seeing the flowers and feeling the sun, and so forth. So the character, "That day [the day I remember] is or was a nice day" is available to sustain his belief, when the attempt at updating goes awry. Even if these memories fade, there is the character, "That day [the day this belief was acquired] is or was a nice day."

So my view is this. When he awakes on July 5th, Rip updates his belief according to his view of how the context has changed. His view about the change of context is mistaken, and the new character, "Yesterday [the day before the day of this thought] was nice" is not a way of believing the original content. But that is no reason to say that Rip has lost his original belief. He retains it under various other backup characters.

That's what I have to say about Rip; what about the other concrete characters that figure in our story, Frege, Kaplan and Evans?

We can't pin anything much on Frege, for we can't hold him responsible for the strategy about belief that his remark on saying inspired. We could consider whether he was right about saying, but we won't do that in this essay.

The strategy that Frege's remark suggested to Kaplan and Evans is that retaining belief consists in moving from flighty character to flighty character in ways that reflect change in context. I think I have refuted that strategy.

But my own strategy is the broad interpretation of the Frege-inspired one, generalized and freed from its association with his particular example. The detach-and-recognize strategy for handling information itself embodies a regular transition, from strong characters to loyal characters and, when recognition occurs, back to strong characters. This Frege-inspired doctrine, like most, perhaps, is inadequate when construed narrowly, plausible when given a broader interpretation.

We can't fault Kaplan for thinking that there was more to be said about Rip Van Winkle for in this he was correct. Evans was wrong, I think, about Rip and about Kaplan. But much of what I have said is similar in spirit to ideas one finds in the body of his work. I will end with a couple of remarks on interpreting Evans.

In approaching Evans, it seems to me one must try to separate his own information-oriented approach to things from the devotion to a version of Frege filtered through Davidson that crops up now and then, most especially in "Understanding Demonstratives," the essay from which the quote above was taken.

Davidson's reliance on Tarski and T-sentences in explaining his views on meaning has inspired a tradition in semantics that one might call "homogeneous meaning explanation." We explain the meaning of a sentence by using the same sentence, or one with the same meaning. The work of Kaplan belongs squarely in the tradition of "heterogeneous meaning explanation." One explains the meaning of a sentence by showing, using whatever language one might want, what sort of tool it is, how it conveys various things in various circumstances.

Imagine that you are explaining a Mercator projection map to a child. One way of explaining, perhaps, is to use another Mercator projection map. A better way is to use a globe. I think the benefits of heterogeneous over homogeneous explanation are similar.

As Davidson himself notes, the homogeneous strategy works with indexicals only when one supposes that the semanticist's explanation and the statement explained are made by the same person at the same time.[172] One interpretation of "Understanding Demonstratives," is that Evans tries, using a variety of ideas that are interesting in their own right but are not necessarily well-suited to the purpose, to extend the homogeneous treatment of indexicals beyond the special case in which it works. I think this experiment fails. And I also think that the information-oriented approach that one finds in much of Evans work, and in parts of "Understanding Demonstratives," is basically heterogeneous in its implications for semantics.[173]

---

[172]See (Perry, 1994), last section.

[173]Thanks to Pierre Jacob, Francois Recanati and Eros Corazza for comments on a much earlier version and to Elizabeth Macken for comments on the penultimate version.

References

Adams, Robert M. 1974. Theories of Actuality. *Noûs* 5:211–231.

Adams, Robert M., and Hector-Neri Castañeda. 1983. Correspondence. In *Agent, Language, and the Structure of the World: Essays Presented to Hector-Neri Castañeda with his Replies*, ed. James E. Tomberlin, 293–309. Indianapolis: Hackett Publishing Company.

Almog, Joseph, John Perry and Howard Wettstein, eds. 1989. *Themes From Kaplan*. New York: Oxford University Press.

Anscombe, G. E. M. 1975. The First Person. In *Mind and Language*, ed. Samuel Guttenplan. Oxford: Clarendon Press.

Barwise, Jon. 1981. Scenes and Other Situations. *Journal of Philosophy* 78:369–397. Also in *Stanford Working Papers in Semantics*, ed. Jon Barwise and Ivan A. Sag.

Barwise, Jon. 1985. The Situation in Logic–II: Conditionals and Conditional Information. Report No. CSLI–85–21. Stanford: CSLI Publications. Also in *The Situation in Logic*, ed. Jon Barwise.

Barwise, Jon. 1985a. The Situation in Logic–III: Situations, Sets and the Axiom of Foundation. Report No. CSLI–85–26. Stanford: CSLI Publications.

Barwise, Jon. 1985b. Situation Theory Reference Manual. Unpublished manuscript.

Barwise, Jon. 1989. *The Situation In Logic*. Stanford: CSLI Publications.

Barwise, Jon, and Robin Cooper. 1980. Generalized Quantifiers and Natural Languages. In *Stanford Working Papers in Semantics*, ed. Jon Barwise and Ivan A. Sag. Stanford Cognitive Science Group.

Barwise, Jon, and John Perry. 1980. The Situation Underground. In *Stanford Working Papers in Semantics*, ed. Jon Barwise and Ivan A. Sag. Stanford Cognitive Science Group.

Barwise, Jon, and John Perry. 1981. Semantic Innocence and Uncompromising Situations. *Midwest Studies in Philosophy* 6:387–404.

Barwise, Jon, and John Perry. 1981a. Situations and Attitudes. *Journal of Philosophy* 78:668–691.

Barwise, Jon, and John Perry. 1985. Shifting Situations and Shaken Attitudes: An Interview with Barwise and Perry. *Linguistics and Philosophy* 8:105–161. Also Report No. CSLI–84–13.

Barwise, Jon, and John Perry. 1999. *Situations and Attitudes*. The David Hume Series of Philosophy and Cognitive Science Reissues, with an introduction to the reissue edition and the authors' "Shifting Situations and Shaken Attitudes." Stanford: CSLI Publications. Original version published 1983, Cambridge, Mass.: MIT Press/Bradford Books.

Barwise, Jon, and Ivan A. Sag, eds. 1980. *Stanford Working Papers in Semantics*. Stanford Cognitive Science Group.

Blackburn, Simon. 1986. What About Me? In *Proceedings of the Aristotelian Society*, supplementary vol. 60:153–166.

Böer, Steven E., and William G. Lycan. 1985. *Knowing Who*. Cambridge, Mass.: MIT Press.

Burge, Tyler. 1973. Reference and Proper Names. *Journal of Philosophy*, 70, pp. 425–439.

Burks, A. W. 1949. Icon, Index, and Symbol. *Philosophy and Phenomenological Research* 10:673–689.

Carnap, Rudolf. 1947. *Meaning and Necessity*. Chicago: University of Chicago Press.

Cartwright, Nancy. 1986. *How the Laws of Physics Lie*. Oxford: Oxford University Press.

Castañeda, Hector-Neri. 1966. "He": A Study in the Logic of Self-Consciousness. *Ratio* 8:130–157.

Castañeda, Hector-Neri. 1967. Indicators and Quasi-Indicators. *American Philosophical Quarterly* 4:85–100.

Castañeda, Hector-Neri. 1967a. Comments and Criticism: Omniscience and Indexical Reference. *The Journal of Philosophy* 64:203–210.

Castañeda, Hector-Neri. 1968. On the Logic of Attributions of Self-Knowledge to Others. *Journal of Philosophy* 65:439–456.

Castañeda, Hector-Neri. 1968a. On the Phenomeno-Logic of the I. In *Akten des XIX Internationalen Kongresses für Philosophie*, 260–266.

Castañeda, Hector-Neri. 1977. On the Philosophical Foundations of the Theory of Communication: Reference. *Midwestern Studies in Philosophy* 2:285–351.

Castañeda, Hector-Neri. 1977a. Perception, Belief, and the Structure of Physical Objects and Consciousness. *Synthèse* 35:285–351.

Chastain, Charles. 1975. Reference and Context. In *Language, Mind, and Knowledge*, vol. 7 of *Minnesota Studies in the Philosophy of Science*, ed. Keith Gunderson. Minneapolis: University of Minnesota Press.

Chisholm, Roderick M. 1981. *The First Person*. Minneapolis: University of Minnesota Press.

Church, Alonzo. 1956. *An Introduction to Mathematical Logic*. Princeton: Princeton University Press.

Condoravdi, Cleo and Mark Gawron. 1996. The Context Dependency of Implicit Arguments. In *Quantifiers, Deduction and Context*, eds., Makoto Kanazawa, Christopher Piñón, and Henriëtte de Swart. Stanford: CSLI Publications.

Corazza, Eros. *Reference, Contexte et Attitudes*. Paris-Montreal: Vrin-Bellarmin.

Crimmins, Mark. 1989. *Talk About Beliefs*. Ph.D. diss., Department of Philosophy, Stanford University.

Crimmins, Mark. 1992. *Talk About Beliefs*. Cambridge, Mass.: Bradford Books.

Crimmins, Mark, and John Perry. 1989 (Essay 12). The Prince and the Phone Booth: Reporting Puzzling Beliefs. *Journal of Philosophy* 86, 12: 685–711. An earlier version appeared as Report No. CSLI–88–128.

Davidson, Donald. 1967. The Logical Form of Action Sentences. In Nicholas Rescher, ed., *The Logic of Decision and Action*. Pittsburgh: University of Pittsburgh Press.

Davidson, Donald. 1967a. Truth and Meaning. *Synthèse* 17.

Davidson, Donald. 1980. Reality Without Reference. In Platts (1980).

Donnellan, Keith. 1966. Reference and Definite Descriptions. *Philosophical Review* 75:281–304.

Donnellan, Keith. 1970. Proper Names and Identifying Descriptions. *Synthèse* 21:335–358. Also in *Semantics of Natural Language*, ed. Donald Davidson and Gilbert Harman.

Donnellan, Keith. 1974. Speaking of Nothing. *Philosophical Review* 83:3–31.

Dummett, Michael. 1973. *Frege*. London: Duckworth.

Evans, Gareth. 1973. The Causal Theory of Names. Aristotelian. Society, Supplementary Volume 47, pp. 187–208.

Evans, Gareth. 1981. Understanding Demonstratives. In Herman Parret and Jacques Bouveresse (ed.) *Meaning and Understanding*. Berlin and New York: Walter de Gruyter, 1981: 280–303. Reprinted in (Yourgrau, 1990), pp. 71–96.

Fine, Kit. 1982. First-Order Modal Theories III—Facts. *Synthèse* 53.

Fodor, Jerry A. 1981. *Representations*. Cambridge, Mass.: MIT Press.

Fodor, Jerry A. 1987. *Psychosemantics*. Cambridge, Mass.: MIT Press, in cooperation with the British Psychological Society.

Fodor, Jerry A. 1991. Replies. In *Meaning In Mind*, ed. Barry Loewer and Georges Rey, 255–320. Oxford: Basil Blackwell.

Fodor, Jerry A. 1994. *The Elm and the Expert*. Cambridge, Mass.: MIT-Bradford.

Frege, Gottlob. 1891/1960. Function and Concept. In *Translations from the Philosophical Writings of Gottlob Frege*, ed. Max Black and Peter Geach, trans. Max Black, 2d ed. Oxford: Basil Blackwell. Address given to the Jenaische Gesellschaft für Medicin und Naturwissenschaft, January 9, 1891.

Frege, Gottlob. 1892/1960. On Sense and Reference. In *Translations from the Philosophical Writings of Gottlob Frege*, ed. Max Black and Peter Geach, trans. Max Black, 2d ed. Oxford: Basil Blackwell. Originally appeared as "Über Sinn und Bedeutung." *Zeitschrift für Philosophie und philosophische Kritik* L (1892): 25–50.

Frege, Gottlob. 1892/1960a. On Concept and Object. In *Translations from the Philosophical Writings of Gottlob Frege*, ed. Max Black and Peter Geach, trans. Max Black, 2d ed. Oxford: Basil Blackwell. Originally appeared as "Über Begriff und Gegenstand." *Vierteljahrsschrift für wissenschaftliche Philosophie* 16 (1892): 195–205.

Frege, Gottlob. 1918/1967. The Thought: A Logical Inquiry. In *Philosophical Logic*, ed. P. F. Strawson, 17–38. Oxford: Oxford University Press. This translation, by A. M. and Marcelle Quinton, originally appeared in *Mind* 65 (1956): 289–311. The original, *Der Gedanke. Eine logische Untersuchung*, appeared in *Beiträge zur Philosophie des deutschen Idealismus* I (1918): 58–77.

Frege, Gottlob. 1923/1968. Compound Thoughts. In *Essays on Frege*, ed. E. D. Klemke, trans. R. H. Stoothoff. Urbana: University of Illinois Press. Originally appeared as "Gedankenfuge." *Beiträge zur Philosophie des deutschen Idealismus* III (1923): 36–51.

Frege, Gottlob. 1980. *Philosophical and Mathematical Correspondence*, ed. Gottfried Gabriel et al., trans. Hans Kaal, abr. from the German ed. by B. McGuinness. Chicago: University of Chicago Press.

French, Peter A., Theodore E. Uehuling, Jr., and Howard K. Wettstein, editors. 1979. *Contemporary Perspectives in the Philosophy of Language*. Minneapolis: University of Minnesota Press.

Gibson, J. J. 1979. The Optical Information for Self-Perception. In *The Ecological Approach to Visual Perception*, ed. J. J. Gibson. Boston, Mass.: Houghton Mifflin.

Gödel, Kurt. 1972. Russell's Mathematical Logic. In David Pears, ed., *Bertrand Russell: A Collection of Critical Essays*. Garden City, N.Y.: Anchor Books.

Goldman, Alvin. 1970. *A Theory of Human Action*. Englewood Cliffs: Prentice-Hall.

Grice, H. P. 1941. Personal Identity. *Mind* 50:330–350.

Grice, H. P. 1975. Method in Philosophical Psychology (From the Banal to the Bizarre). In *Proceedings and Addresses of the American Philosophical Association*, vol. XLVIII, 23–53.

Heim, Irene. 1982. The Semantics of Definite and Indefinite Noun Phrases. Ph.D. diss., Department of Linguistics, University of Massachusetts at Amherst.

Hilbert, David R. 1987. *Color and Color Perception: A Study in Anthropocentric Realism*. CSLI Lecture Notes No. 9. Stanford: CSLI Publications.

Hintikka, Jaakko. 1967. Individuals, Possible Worlds, and Epistemic Logic. *Noûs* 1:33–62.

Hume, David. 1748/1975. *An Enquiry Concerning Human Understanding*, Section V: Skeptical Solution of These Doubts. Oxford: Oxford University Press. First published in 1748.

Israel, David, and John Perry. 1990. What is Information? In *Information, Language and Cognition*, ed. P. Hanson. Vancouver: University of British Columbia Press. Also Report No. CSLI–91–145.

Israel, David, and John Perry. 1991. Information and Architecture. In *Situation Theory and Its Applications, vol. 2*, edited by Jon Barwise, Jean Mark Gawron, Gordon Plotkin and Syun Tutiya. Stanford University: Center for the Study of Language and Information, 147–160.

Israel, David, John Perry and Syun Tutiya. 1993. Executions, Motivations and Accomplishments. *The Philosophical Review* (October, 1993): 515–540.

Irving, Washington.1820."Rip Van Winkle" in *The Sketch Book*, written 1819–1820, many editions.

Kaplan, David. 1969. Quantifying In. In *Words and Objections*, ed. Donald Davidson and Jaakko Hintikka, 206–242. Dordrecht: Reidel Publishing Company. Also in *Synthèse*.

Kaplan, David. 1975. How to Russell a Frege-Church. *Journal of Philosophy* LXXII, no. 19: 716–729.

Kaplan, David. 1978. Dthat. In (French, et. al.), pp. 383–400. Reprinted in (Yourgrau, 1990): 11–33.

Kaplan, David. 1979. On the Logic of Demonstratives. *The Journal of Philosophical Logic*, 8 (1979): 81–98. Reprinted in (French, et. al.): 401–412.

Kaplan, David. 1989b. Afterthoughts. In (Almog, 1989): 565–614.

Kaplan, David. 1989a. Demonstratives. In (Almog, 1989): 481–563.

Kim, Jaegwon. 1966. On the Psycho-Physical Identity Theory. *American Philosophical Quarterly* 3:227–235.

Kretzmann, Norman. 1966. Omniscience and Immutability. *Journal of Philosophy* 63:409–421.

Kripke, Saul. 1979. A Puzzle about Belief. In *Meaning and Use*, ed. A. Margalit, 239–283. Dordrecht: Reidel.

Kripke, Saul. 1980. *Naming and Necessity*. Cambridge, Mass.: Harvard University Press.

Lewis, David K. 1973. *Counterfactuals*. Cambridge, Mass.: Harvard University Press.

Lewis, David K. 1979. Attitudes *De Dicto* and *De Se*. *Philosophical Review* 88:513–543.

Mach, Ernst. 1914. *The analysis of sensations*, translated by C.M. Williams and Sydney Waterlow, (Chicago & London: Open Court), p. 4n.

Marcus, Ruth. 1961. Modalities and Intensional Languages. *Synthèse* 1961 (303–322).

Marti, Genoveva. The Essence of Genuine Reference. *Journal of Philosophical Logic*, forthcoming.

Montague, Richard. 1974. *Formal Philosophy*. New Haven: Yale University Press.

Moore, G. E. 1959. *Philosophical Papers*. New York: Macmillan.

Moore, R. 1985. A Theory of Knowledge and Action. In *Formal Theories of the Commonsense World*, ed. J. Hobbs and R. Moore. Norwood, N.J.: Ablex.

Nagel, Thomas. 1983. The Objective Self. In Carl Ginet and Sydney Shoemaker, eds., *Knowledge and Mind*.

Neale, Stephen. 1990. *Descriptions*. Cambridge, Mass.: MIT Press/ Bradford Books.

Olson, Ken. 1987. *An Essay on Facts*. Stanford: CSLI Publications.

Partee, Barbara. 1989. Binding Implicit Variables in Quantified Contexts. *Papers of the Chicago Linguistic Society*, 25: 342–365.

Partee, Barbara H. 1989. Possible Worlds in Model-Theoretic Semantics: A Linguistic Perspective. In *Possible Worlds in Humanities, Arts and Sciences. Proceedings of Nobel Symposium 65*, ed. Sture Allén, 93–123. Berlin/New York: Walter de Gruyter.

Partee, Barbara H. 1989a. Speaker's Reply. In *Possible Worlds in Humanities, Arts and Sciences. Proceedings of Nobel Symposium 65*, ed. Sture Allén, 152–161. Berlin/New York: Walter de Gruyter.

Pendlebury, Michael. 1980. Believing. Ph.D. diss., Department of Philosophy, Indiana University.

Pendlebury, Michael. 1982. Indexical Reference and the Ontology of Belief. *South African Journal of Philosophy* 1:65–74.

Perry, John. 1977 (Essay 1). Frege on Demonstratives. *Philosophical Review* 86:474–497.

Perry, John. 1979 (Essay 2). The Problem of the Essential Indexical. *Noûs* 13:3–21.

Perry, John. 1980 (Essay 3). Belief and Acceptance. *Midwest Studies in Philosophy* 5:533–542.

Perry, John. 1980a (Essay 4). A Problem About Continued Belief. *Pacific Philosophical Quarterly* 61:317–332.

Perry, John. 1983 (Essay 5). Castañeda on *He* and *I*. In *Agent, Language, and the Structure of the World: Essays Presented to Hector-Neri Castañeda and His Replies*, ed. James E. Tomberlin, 15–41. Indianapolis: Hackett Publishing Company.

Perry, John. 1986 (Essay 6). Perception, Action, and the Structure of Believing. In *Philosophical Grounds of Rationality. Intentions, Categories, Ends*, ed. Richard E. Grandy and Richard Warner, 333–361. Oxford: Clarendon Press.

Perry, John. 1986a (Essay 10). Thought Without Representation. In *Supplementary Proceedings of the Aristotelian Society* 60:137–152.

Perry, John. 1986b (Essay 9). Circumstantial Attitudes and Benevolent Cognition. In *Language, Mind and Logic*, ed. J. Butterfield, 123–134. Cambridge: Cambridge University Press. Also Report No. CSLI–86–53.

Perry, John. 1986c (Essay 7). From Worlds to Situations. *Journal of Philosophical Logic* 15:83–107. Also Report No. CSLI–87–73.

Perry, John. 1988 (Essay 11). Cognitive Significance and New Theories of Reference. *Noûs* 22:1–18. Also Report No. CSLI–88–109.

Perry, John. 1989 (Essay 8). Possible Worlds and Subject Matter. Discussion of Barbara H. Partee's paper Possible Worlds in Model-Theoretic Semantics: A Linguistic Perspective. In *Possible Worlds in Humanities, Arts and Sciences: Proceedings of Nobel Symposium* 65, ed. Sture Allén, 124–137. Berlin/New York: Walter de Gruyter.

Perry, John. 1990 (Essay 13). Individuals in Informational and Intentional Content. In *Information, Semantics and Epistemology*, ed. , 172–189. Cambridge: Basil Blackwell.

Perry, John. 1990. Self-Notions. *Logos*, 17–31.

Perry, John. 1993. *The Problem of the Essential Indexical and Other Essays*, first edition. New York: Oxford University Press, 1993.

Perry, John. 1994 (Essay 15). *Davidson's Sentences and Wittgenstein's Builders*. APA *Proceedings*, 1994.

Perry, John. 1995a. Indexicals and Demonstratives. In Robert Hale and Crispin Wright, eds., *Companion to the Philosophy of Language*. Oxford: Blackwells.

Perry, John. 1996 (Essay 16). Evading the Slingshot. In *Philosophy and Cognitive Science*, edited by A. Clark, et al., 95–114. The Netherlands: Kluwer.

Perry, John. 1995 (Essay 20). Reflexivity, Indexicality and Names. In *Direct Reference, Indexicality and Proposition Attitudes* edited by Wolfgang Künne, Martin Anduschus, and Albert Newen. Stanford: CSLI Publications, 1997.

Perry, John. 1997 (Essay 21). Rip Van Winkle and Other Characters. In *The European Review of Analytical Philosophy* Volume 2: *Cognitive Dynamics*, 13–39.

Perry, John. 1998 (Essay 17). Broadening the Mind. Review of Jerry Fodor, *The Elm and The Expert. Philosophy and Phenomenological Research*, LVIII, No. 1, March, 1998, 223–231.

Perry, John. 1998 (Essay 19). Myself and I. In Marcelo Stamm, editor, *Philosophie in Synthetisher Absicht* (A festschrift for Dieter Heinrich), Stuttgart: Klett-Cotta, pp. 83–103.

Perry, John. 1999. *Problèmes d'Indexicalité*. French translation of Essays 1,2,3,4,9,10,11,13 and 21, "Self-notions" and "Indexicals and Demonstratives" by Jérome Dokic and Florian Preisig. Stanford: CSLI Publications. Paris: Éditions CSLI.

Perry, John, and David Israel. 1991 (Essay 14). Fodor and Psychological Explanation. In *Meaning In Mind*, ed. Barry Loewer and Georges Rey, 165–180. Oxford: Basil Blackwell. Also Report No. CSLI–91–146.

Plantinga, Alvin. 1974. *The Nature of Necessity*. Oxford: Oxford University Press.

Platts, Mark, editor. 1980. *Reference, Truth and Reality: Essays on the Philosophy of Language*. London: Routledge & Kegan Paul.

Quine, Willard Van Orman. 1953. *From a Logical Point of View*. Cambridge, Mass.: Harvard University Press.

Quine, Willard Van Orman. 1966. Quantifiers and Propositional Attitudes. In *Ways of Paradox*, ed. Willard Van Orman Quine, 183–194. New York: Random House.

Quine, Willard Van Orman. 1976. Three Grades of Modal Involvement. In W.V.O. Quine, *Ways of Paradox*, revised and enlarged edition. Cambridge: Harvard University Press.

Recanati, Francois. 1993. *Direct Reference: From Language to Thought*. Oxford: Blackwells.

Reichenbach, Hans. 1947. §50. Token-reflexive words. In *Elements of Symbolic Logic*. New York: The Free Press. Pp. 284ff.

Richard, Mark. 1983. Direct Reference and Ascriptions of Belief. *Journal of Philosophical Logic* 12:425–452.

Salmon, Nathan.1986. *Frege's Puzzle*. Cambridge, Mass.: MIT Press.

Scott, Dana. 1970. Advice on Modal Logic. In *Philosophical Problems in Logic*, ed. Karel Lambert, 143–173. Dordrecht: Reidel Publishing Company.

Shoemaker, Sydney. 1970. Persons and Their Pasts. *American Philosophical Quarterly*, October, 1970.

Shoemaker, Sydney. 1984. *Identity, Cause and Mind*. Cambridge: Cambridge University Press.

Shoemaker, Sydney. 1996. *The First-Person Perspective and Other Essays*. Cambridge: Cambridge University Press.

Smith, Quenton. 1989. The Multiple Uses of Indexicals. *Synthèse* 78:167–191.

Soames, Scott. 1987. Substitutivity. In *On Being and Saying: Essays for Richard Cartwright*, ed. Judith Jarvis Thomson, 99–132. Cambridge, Mass.: MIT Press.

Soames, Scott. 1989. Direct Reference and Propositional Attitudes. In *Themes from Kaplan*, ed. Joseph Almog, John Perry, and Howard Wettstein, 393–419. New York: Oxford University Press.

Stalnaker, Robert C. 1981. Indexical Belief. *Synthèse* 49:129–151.

Stalnaker, Robert C. 1984. *Inquiry*. Cambridge, Mass.: MIT/Bradford Books.

Stalnaker, Robert C. 1985. Propositions. In *The Philosophy of Language*, ed. A. P. Martinich, 373–380. Oxford: Oxford University Press.

Stalnaker, Robert C. 1986. Possible Worlds and Situations. *Journal of Philosophical Logic* 15.

Strawson, Peter. 1950. On Referring. *Mind* 59:320–344.

von Wright, Georg Henrik. 1972. Lichtenberg. In *The Encyclopedia of Philosophy*, ed. Paul Edwards. New York: Macmillan. Reprint ed., vol. 4.

Weitzman, Leora. 1989. *Propositional Identity and Structure in Frege*. Doctoral Dissertation, Stanford Philosophy Department.

Wettstein, Howard. 1976. Can What Is Asserted Be a Sentence? *Philosophical Review* 85:196–207.

Wettstein, Howard. 1981. Demonstrative Reference and Definite Descriptions. *Philosophical Studies* 40:241–257.

Wettstein, Howard. 1984. How to Bridge the Gap Between Meaning and Reference. *Synthèse* 58:63–84.

Wettstein, Howard. 1986. Has Semantics Rested on a Mistake? *The Journal of Philosophy* LXXXIII, no. 4: 185–209.

Wilson, George. 1978. On Definite and Indefinite Descriptions. *Philosophical Review* LXXXVII, no. 1: 48–76.

Wittgenstein, Ludwig. 1953. *Philosophical Investigations*, trans. G.E.M. Anscombe. New York: Macmillan.

Yourgrau, Palle (ed.). 1990. *Demonstratives*. Oxford: Oxford University Press.

Index